INCLUSIVE
GROWTH IN INDIA

ABOUT THE AUTHOR

Prof.S.Gurusmay, M.A. (Soc), M.A. (R.S), M.Phil., PGDHE., Ph.D is currently serving as Professor, in the Department of Sociology, Gandhigram Rural Institute, Gandhigram (near Madurai) in TamilNadu. He has contributed more than 75 research papers in reputed journals of National and International importance on themes related to Sociology of Development, Marginalized Groups, Social Defense, Rural Department, Social Welfare, Rural Sociology, Social Exclusion and Inclusive Policy etc.

He has nine books to his credit on topics such as Peasant Politics in South India, Development Sociology, Social Demography, Development Sociology, Female Infanticide, Girl Child, Human Rights and Gender Justice, Social Exclusion and Inclusion, Girl child and Inclusive Growth in India. He has produced 11 Ph.Ds. Besides teaching, research and extension activities in Gandhigram Rural Institute, he has also worked in several positions in about eight major research projects sponsored by ICSSR, SAREC, MHRD, NFCH, UGC and UNICEF. He has also served in leading National and International voluntary agencies.

He has had wide exposure and work experience with NGOs engaged in Capacity Building, IGP, MLP, PRI, RD, Social Welfare, Disaster Management and Rehabilitation of Physically Challenged at National and International levels.

He has organized a number of Seminars, Symposia and Workshops on topics like Street Children, Human Rights and Gender Justice, Social Defense in Welfare State, Inclusive Growth in Transitional Society, Child Rights and Child Abuse, Social Research Methodology, Sustainable Social Development, Social Exclusion and Marginalization. He has also served as Resource Person and Chaired Sessions in Seminars, Delivered Inaugural, Key-note, Special addresses in various seminars in university departments. Organized training programmes for NGO personnel, Refresher Courses for college and university teachers in TamilNadu and other states.

He has been instrumental for the establishment of the Centre for Study of Social Exclusion and Inclusive Policy in Gandhigram Rural Institute, Innovative Programme on Sustainable Development and served as Expert in different Committees/Boards in various Universities and Public Service Commissions in India during the past 30 years of service. He has also visited countries like Sri Lanka, Malaysia and Singapore on academic assignments.

INCLUSIVE
GROWTH IN INDIA

S. Gurusamy

MJP Publishers

Chennai New Delhi Tirunelveli

ISBN 978-81-8094-160-3 **MJP Publishers**

New No. 5 Muthu Kalathy Street,
Triplicane,
Chennai 600 005

MJP 153 MJP's imprint: 2013

PREFACE

Inclusive growth is a wider concept which incorporates various dimensions, segments, process, outcomes, disadvantage reduction, promoting equal opportunities, participation and contribution of members of society towards economic growth. The term inclusive denotes the notion of non discrimination. Accordingly inclusive growth can be characterized as broad based growth. The outcomes of growth are to benefit larger segments. Obviously it reflects pro-poor growth. Pro-poor growth is focused on the people below poverty line, where as inclusive growth is understandably more general: it desires growth to benefit all sections of society including the poor, middle income groups and even the rich. Perceived from this point of view inclusive growth should promote equal opportunities and also increased access to these opportunities i.e, growth that allows all members of society to participate in and contribute equally to economic growth. In this regard inclusive growth reduces regional, ethnic or gender disadvantages. Thus the term reflects disadvantage reducing growth.

The approach to inclusive growth is forward looking with future orientation insisting wide opportunities for participation and non discriminatory participation. It allows participation and contribution by all members of society with emphasis on economic growth, environmental sustainability, and regional integration, facilitation towards upliftment of poor and marginalized segments. The segments broadly covered in inclusive growth include dalits, minorities, gender, other backward castes, transgender, aged, physically challenges and other vulnerable segments to problems.

The approach of inclusive growth is appropriate in the Indian context as the social structure is marked by tradition bound cultural influences, religious values, stratification based inequalities resulting in social discrimination and problems like untouchability, atrocities against women, alienation of old age persons, discrimination of minorities etc, the issues and challenges emerging from social structure in contemporary Indian society are to be resolved through appropriate social intervention in order to promote economic growth with equitable and distributive social justice. To do this, the strategy is obviously inclusive growth which is expected to involve the segments hitherto remains excluded by pursuing the economic policy and social development agenda which better ensures participation of these segments towards improvement of their socio-economic standards and there by attain the vision of sustainable development.

The Department of Sociology in Gandhigram Rural Institute, (GRI) has specialized in sustainable social development by offering academic programmes from research and development activities, village outreach programmes during the past 30 years. This invariably necessitated the mission agenda of growth with social justice undertaken by Prof.S.Gurusamy, the editor of this book through his committed teaching, research, extension, advocacy, networking etc activities. The professional excellence promoted through these activities by him led to rural welfare, development of the marginalized and other segments vulnerable to problems at grass root level.

As a landmark of the committed service Prof.S.Gurusamy in the direction of promoting inclusive growth through a proposal got the funding support from University Grants Commission, (UGC), New Delhi and Indian Council of Social Science Research, (ICSSR), New Delhi for organizing the National Seminar on Inclusive Growth in Transitional Society: Issues and Challenges. The Seminar proceedings were organized in the form of Technical Sessions chaired by distinguished academia on the focused themes. There were about 75 participants in all engaged in about 10 technical sessions during the course of the Seminar. The brainstorming session organized in the Seminar and the Symposium held in the side lines of the Seminar had produced a number of recommendations dealing with policy implication and development programme planning to pursue inclusive growth among the marginalized.

I express my sincere thanks to Dr. SM. Ramasamy, Vice-Chancellor, GRI, Dr.N.Narayanasamy, Registrar, GRI for the generous help and support for the successful organization of this Seminar. I thank all the Dignitaries Dr.G.Pankajam, Dr. C.Thangamuthu, Former Coordinator of School of Economics, Madurai Kamaraj University, Madurai, Dr.Fr.Xavier Vedam, Principal, Arul Anandar College, Karumathur and Mr.Vincent Raj, Director, EVIDENCE, Madurai for their association and presentation of inaugural, key-note, valedictory, special addresses etc in the Seminar. I am grateful to all the Resource Persons and participants of the National Seminar for their effective and intellectual participation in every session and making the Seminar experiences not only a memorable but also rewarding one.

I profusely thank the Research Scholars who are working with me under my Supervision and Guidance and also other Scholars in the department as well as in the University for their Effective Logistic Support for making this Seminar a grand success. I am highly indebted to the funding agencies namely UGC and ICSSR, New Delhi for extending liberal financial support for organizing this

Seminar in GRI. I take this opportunity to express my deep sense of gratitude to my divinely mother Smt.S.Meenakshi Ammal, wife Smt.G.Mahalakshmi and son G.Muthuraja Sarathi for having generously spared me from familial commitments to concentrate on this additional official commitment for a noble cause.

I thank Smt.M.Indira who served effectively and extended all administrative support as well as organizing and typing the scripts for shaping this work in the form of book.

Last but not least I sincerely thank Mr.Pillai, Proprietor of MJP Publishers, Chennai for publishing this material in an attractive and excellent shape.

S. Gurusamy

CONTENTS

INCLUSIVE GROWTH: MAINSTREAMING TRANSGENDER

SOCIAL STRUCTURAL CONSTRAINTS IN EMPOWERMENT OF MARGINALIZED GROUPS – THE DALIT DIMENSION

SOCIAL STRUCTURAL CONSTRAINTS IN EMPOWERMENT OF MARGINALIZED GROUPS – THE ELDERLY PERSONS DIMENSION

SOCIAL STRUCTURAL CONSTRAINTS IN EMPOWERMENT OF MARGINALIZED GROUPS – THE WOMEN DIMENSION

LIST OF CONTRIBUTORS

1. **Prof. S. Gurusamy**
Professor & Seminar Director
Department of Sociology, Gandhigram Rural Institute,
Gandhigram
sellagurusamy@yahoo.co.in

2. **Prof. G. Pankajam**
Former Vice –Chancellor
Gandhigram Rural Institute
Gandhigram.

3. **Dr. C. Gobalakrishnan,** Assistant Professor,
G. Phary and **D. Deepika**
Research Scholars
Department of Sociology,
Periyar University,
Salem

4. **Dr. Manju S.Nair,** Associate Professor,
Sreejith A, Associate Professor,
Department of Economics, University of Kerala
Thiruvananthapuram.

5. **M.Kaliamoorthi,** Research Scholar,
Dr. R. Mangayarkarasu, Associate Professor,
Department of Political Science,
Madurai Kamaraj University,
Madurai.

6. **Sreegith Thankappan,** Junior Research Fellow,
Dr. Pradeep Kumar Parida, Assistant Professor,
Department of Sociology, Pondicherry University
Puducherry

7. **Dr. M. Soundarapandian,** Professor
N. Nagarajan, Research Scholar,
Department of Rural Industries and Management,
Gandhigram Rural Institute,
Gandhigram

8. **B.Rohini, M.A.** (Social Work)
rhnbalaji@gmail.com
T. Augustus Julian Lazmey, Asst. Professor,
Dept of Social Work,
The American College,
Madurai
Email: augustusjulian@gmail.com

9. **Emmanuel. D, Ph.D.** Scholar,
PSG College of Arts and Science,
Coimbatore
captain.emmanuel@gmail.com
Rev. Dr. Arul ArasuIsrael, Director,
Dept. of.Social Work.
The American College, Madurai

10. **A. IrudayaVeni Mary,** Research scholar
Dr. M. Victor Louis Anthuvan,
Loyola Institute of Business Administration,
Loyola College,
Chennai

11. **Dr. S. S. Vijayanchali,** Assistant Professor,
G. Selvarani, M.Phil Scholar,
Dept. of Home Science,
Gandhigram Rural Institute,
Gandhigram

12. **Dr. E. Arumuga Gandhi,** Assistant Professor,
Sr. Mary Louisa, Ph.D. Research Scholar,
Department of Sociology,
Christ University,
Bangalore

13. **Dr. S. Sudalaimuthu,** Reader, Department of Banking Technology,
Pondicherry University,
Pudhucherry
E-mail: sm_vcas@yahoo.com
Mr. B. Angamuthu, Research Scholar, Department of Commerce,
Bharathiar University, Coimbatore
muthuanga82@gmail.com

14. **P. Sangeetha, MSW, M.Phil,** Lecturer,
Dr. M. Kannan, Associate Professor,
Dept. of. Social Work,
Madurai Institute of Social Sciences,
Madurai

15. **K. Someegnal,** Assistant professor,
P.G.Department of Social Work,
St.Xavier's College (Autonomous).
Palayamkottai

16. **P.G. Nisha,** Research Scholar
Dr. K. Suryan, Assistant Professor,
Annamalai University,
Annamalai Nagar

17. **T. Kavitha,** Research Scholar,
Dr. K. Suriyan, Assistant Professor,
Dept. of Sociology, Annamalai University,
Annamalai Nagar

18. **Dr. Neema Gnanadev,** Assistant Professor,
Department of Rural Development,
Gandhigram Rural Institute,
Gandhigram

19. **Dr. T. Sundara Raj,** Assistant Professor,
Department of Sociology,
Periyar University,
Salem

20. **Dr. K. Suriyan,** Assistante Professor,
Department of Sociology,
Annamalai University,
Annamalai Nagar

21. **Dr. A. Balakrishnan,** Professor,
R. Vettriselvan, Research Scholar, and
S. Krishnan, Research Scholar,
Dept. of Applied Research
Gandhigram Rural Institute
Gandhigram

22. **S. Menaka & Dr. M. Hilaria Soundari**
Research Scholar Assistant Professor
Department of Applied Research,
Gandhigram Rural Institute
Gandhigram

23. **S. Raja,** Research Scholar,
Dr. S. Gurusamy, Professor,
Dept. of Sociology,
Gandhigram Rural Institute,
Gandhigram

24. **Dr. C. Kubendran,** Principal i/c,
Bharathidasan University Constituent Arts and Science College,
Nannilam

25. **K. Thamizhiniyan,** Lecturer in English Education,
Sourashtra Teacher Training Institute
Theni, ,Email: iniyaneducation@gmail.com
S. Naseema, Research Scholar
Department of Library and Information Science,
Pondicherry University,
Puduicherry

26. Dr. S. S. Vijayanchali, Assistant Professor,
Department of Home Science,
Gandhigram Rural InstituteI,
Gandhigram
Dr. E. Arumuga Gandhi, Assistant Professor,
Department of Sociology,
Christ University,
Bangalore

27. T. Augustus Julian Lazmey, Assistant Professor,
Department of Social Work
The American College,
Madurai

28. M. Jeyaseelan, Assistant Professor,
Department of Sociology,
Periyar University,
Salem

29. V. Seethalakshmi, Asst. professor (Senior)
Department of History,
Seethalakshmi Ramaswami College
Tiruchirapalli

30. Balamurugan. J, Research Scholar,
Department of Sociology,
Pondicherry University
Dr. G. Ramathirtham, Associate Professor,
Department of Sociology,
Pondicherry University

31. T. Murugesan, Research Scholar
Dr. I. Singaram, Sr. Professor,
Department of Sociology
Madurai Kamaraj University,
Madurai

32. **Dr. K. Suriyan,** Assistant Professor,
Beena M.N. Research Scholar,
Annamalai University,
AnnamalaiNagar

33. **P.M. Anu Rama,** Lecturer,
Department of Religion, Philosophy and Sociology,
The American College,
Madurai

34. **Dr. Subash Chandra Bose,** District Project Manager,
Pudhu Vazhvu Thittam,
Sivagangai

35. **H. Usha,** Associate Professor,
Department of History,
Seethalakshmi Ramaswami College,
Tiruchirappalli

36. **A. Kubendran,** Lectuer, Dept. of Sociology,
Gandhigram Rural Institute,
Gandhigram

37. **Dr.M.Mallammal,** Professor & Head,
Department of Gandhian Thought and Peace Science
Ms. M. Priyadharishini, Research Scholar
Gandhigram Rural Institute,
Gandhigram

38. **M. Suresh,** Research Scholar
Dr. R. Subburaman, Professor and Head
Department of Lifelong Learning,
Gandhigram Rural Institute,
Gandhigram

39. **Dr. V. Frank Rathnakumar,** Associate Professor of
Cooperation & Vice-Principal (D)
Mr. K.Iyappan, Research Scholar-FT, (RGNSRF),
TBML.College, Porayar

40. Sonkhogin Haokip, Assistant Professor,
Department of Political science and Development Administration,
Gandhigram Rural Insitute,
Gandhigram

41. Ranita Paul, Research Scholar,
Dr. E. Arumuga Gandhi, Assistant Professor,
Department of Sociology,
Christ University,
Bangalore

42. Dr. N.Lalitha, Professor
Department of Rural Development,
Gandhigram Rural Institute,
Gandhigram

43. Prof.S.Gurusamy, Senior Professor,
sellagurusamy@yahoo.co.in
B. Parthasarathi, Research Scholar
Sarathi979@rediffmail.com
Department of Sociology,
Gandhigram Rural Institute,
Gandhigram

44. Prof.S.Gurusamy, Senior Professor,
sellagurusamy@yahoo.co.in
S.Rajangam (RGNSRF), Research Scholar,
rajangam.phd@gmail.com
Department of Sociology,
Gandhigram Rural Institute,
Gandhigram

45. Prof.S.Gurusamy, Senior Professor,
sellagurusamy@yahoo.co.in
Mrinalini. S, Research Scholar,
snmrinalini@gamail.com
Department of Sociology,
Gandhigram Rural Institute,
Gandhigram

46. Prof.S.Gurusamy, Senior Professor,
sellagurusamy@yahoo.co.in
G.Dharani (UGC-JRF), Research Scholar
peacefuldharani@gmail.com
Department of Sociology,
Gandhigram Rural Institute,
Gandhigram

47. Prof.S.Gurusamy, Senior Professor,
sellagurusamy@yahoo.co.in
P. Dhanalakshmi, Research Scholar (RGNJRF),
kprdbhavi@gmail.com
Department of Sociology,
Gandhigram Rural Institute,
Gandhigram

1 INCLUSIVE GROWTH IN TRANSITIONAL SOCIETY: ISSUES AND CHALLENGES

Dr. S. Gurusamy

INTRODUCTION

Growth is an essential condition for inclusiveness. Inclusive growth is a broad concept which incorporates various dimensions, segments, process, outcomes, disadvantage reduction, promoting equal opportunities, participation and contribution of members of society towards economic growth. Therefore, it is important to characterize growth sequences that qualify as inclusive. Two options are possible, one focuses on the process, in the sense that the actual growth included many people who participated in the growth. In this context, inclusive growth is related to broad based -intensive growth. In addition, "inclusive" denotes the notion of nondiscrimination, a feature that is less clear with the other terminologies. Accordingly inclusive growth can be characterized as broad-based growth that includes nondiscriminatory participation. The second option focuses on outcomes of the growth process. Inclusive growth benefits larger segments. This option is closely related to the concept of pro-poor growth. Pro-poor growth refers to increased income for the poor, while its relative definition refers to growth that leads to disproportionate increases in income among the poor. While inclusive growth extends beyond people below the poverty line, this makes the concept very wide. Interpreted in terms of outcome, inclusive growth is not quite the same as pro-poor growth. There is the question of whether inclusiveness is related to absolute or relative interpretation of pro-poor growth. If it was related to the absolute explanation of pro-poor growth, inclusive growth would only reduce poverty, however this cannot happen.

Pro-poor growth is focused on the people below poverty line, whereas inclusive growth is understandably more general: it desires growth to benefit all sections of society, including the poor, middle income groups, and even the rich. Therefore, one could make out that inclusive growth should benefit everyone. Ali and Zhuang (2007) and Zhuang and Ali (2009) define inclusive growth as growth that promotes equal opportunities and also increases access to these opportunities (i.e., growth that allows all members of society to participate in and contribute equally to economic growth, regardless of individual circumstances. The UNDP formally define inclusive growth, but rather emphasizes inclusive growth as growth with low and declining inequality, economic and political participation of the poor in the growth process, and benefit sharing from that process. The UNDP's concept of inclusive growth encompasses process and outcome, income and non-income, and participation and decision making. This concept would require a very broad set of indicators and the question would surely arise about how to weight and aggregate the concepts that are included in this domain of inclusive growth.

Inclusive growth may be defined as mainly benefiting groups that are otherwise disadvantaged; such growth is more appropriately defined as "disadvantage-reducing" growth. In this regard, one could think particularly about growth that reduces regional, ethnic, or gender disadvantages, and this might be one useful way to differentiate an outcome-focus of inclusive growth from pro-poor growth. Thus, in terms of outcome, inclusive growth could be termed "disadvantage-reducing" growth. An approach that considers both process and outcome aspects is particularly useful for defining inclusive growth. If one considers outcomes, inclusive growth should not focus solely on poverty reduction because interpreting it in terms of disadvantage-reducing growth is potentially more interesting. Thus, a conceptual approach to inclusive growth could be nondiscriminatory growth that provides equal nondiscriminatory access to growth, plus disadvantage-reducing growth i.e., reducing disparities of disadvantaged segments. Inclusive growth can easily be extended to non-income dimensions of well-being.

Approach to Inclusive Growth

Inclusive growth is wholly forward-looking, focused on what future growth can achieve in terms of being more inclusive. It strongly emphasizes the process aspect of growth. This is particularly true of the first strategic focus, which emphasizes wide opportunities for participation. The second strategic focus is very close to the ideas of nondiscriminatory participation and disadvantage-reducing growth, combining both process and outcome. In this sense, it goes a bit further than the proposal by the Eminent Persons Group, which focused largely on disadvantage-reducing growth. Major areas of operations reveal that the operational part is focused mainly on the process aspect of inclusive growth and strongly emphasizes improvements in infrastructure, market access, education, and financial intermediation. Safety nets, redistribution, and disadvantage reduction are limited to some basic social protection—safety nets to prevent extreme deprivation, measures to promote gender equity, and initiatives that promote human capacities. The strategy of inclusive growth basically proposes a largely process oriented approach to inclusive growth, emphasizing growth that enhances opportunities and equalizes access to these opportunities. The highest level uses the Millennium

Development Goals (MDGs), Gross Domestic Product (GDP) and outcomes to monitor outcomes, business environment, governance, regional integration, and trade. Inclusive growth is interpreted as pro-poor improvements in social opportunities and analyses to what extent social opportunities e.g., access to health or education is distributed based upon income and how this distribution changes over a period of time. Inclusive growth occurs when improvements are shifted towards the poor income-groups.

Hence a simple approach to inclusive growth is necessary. On the basis of these interpretations, it is proposed to define an "inclusiveness" which,

- Allows participation and contribution by all members of society, with particular emphasis on the ability of the poor and disadvantaged to participate in growth (the "nondiscriminatory" aspect of growth); and Associates with declining inequality in non-income dimensions of well-being that are particularly important for promoting economic opportunities, including education, health, nutrition, and social integration (the "disadvantage-reducing" aspect of inclusive growth).
- More formally, an inclusive growth process requires. positive per capita income growth rates; Primary income growth rates for predefined, disadvantaged groups, e.g., ethnic minorities, backward regions, the income poor, rural areas, women at least as high as growth rates for per capita incomes, indicating that such groups have been able to participate in the growth process at least proportionately; and
- Expansions of non-income dimensions of well-being that exceed that average rate for pre-defined disadvantaged groups. Non-income dimensions include schooling achievements; improvements in survival rates (e.g., inverse mortality rates for children under the ages of 1 and 5 years); improvements in nutritional status; and access to transport, communications, and household services (e.g., clean water, electricity, refuse removal); this would ensure that an income growth episode was disadvantage reducing. Inclusive economic growth, environmentally sustainable growth, and regional integration policy dialogue, loans, equity investments, guarantees, grants, technical assistance.

Segments and Application of Inclusive Growth

1. A major weakness in the economy is that the growth is not perceived as being sufficiently inclusive for many groups, especially Scheduled Castes (SCs), Scheduled Tribes (STs), and minorities. Gender inequality also remains a pervasive problem and some of the structural changes taking place have an adverse effect on women.

2. The central vision of this is to build our strength to accelerate a development process which ensures broad-based improvement in the quality of life of the people, especially the poor, SCs/STs, Other Backward Castes (OBCs), Minorities and Women.

3. Economic growth across regions has not been balanced, with some of the most backward areas yet to experience any significant growth. The delivery of essential social services at the grass roots level is also poor and this is a major causative factor in unequal growth. Much higher levels of human development can be achieved even with the given structure of the economy, if the delivery system is improved. However the target is not just faster growth but also inclusive growth, that is, a growth process which yields broad-based benefits and ensures equality of opportunity for all. This broad vision includes several inter-related components: rapid growth that reduces poverty and creates employment opportunities, access to essential services in health and education especially for the poor, equality of opportunity, empowerment through education and skill development, employment opportunities underpinned by the Employment Guarantee Schemes, environmental sustainability, recognition of women's agency and good governance.

INCLUSIVE GROWTH: DIMENSIONS

Rapid growth and poverty reduction The perpetuation of poverty on the scale at which it still exists is not appreciable. A decisive reduction in Poverty and an expansion in economic opportunities for all sections of population should therefore be a crucial element of the vision. Rapid growth of the economy is an essential requirement to achieve this outcome since it is an instrument for achieving a steady growth in employment and income for large number of people. The governments at the Centre and the States have launched a large number of initiatives at substantial public expense to achieve the objectives of growth with poverty alleviation and inclusiveness. It is desirable if a significant portion of the labour force is to shift out of agriculture, where it is currently engaged in low productivity employment, into a non-agricultural activity that can provide higher income per head. This must be accompanied by efforts to improve the income-earning opportunities of those who remain in agriculture by raising land productivity. This process would also lead to higher farm income and a rise in real wages of agricultural labour whose bargaining power will improve as surplus labour is shifted out of this sector. The ability to sustain a labour-intensive growth process depends crucially upon the expansion of skill capabilities in the labour force.

Social justice and empowerment The vision of inclusiveness must go beyond the traditional objective of poverty alleviation to encompass equality of opportunity, as well as economic and social mobility for all sections of society, with affirmative action for SCs, STs, OBCs, Minorities and Women. There must be equality of opportunity to all with freedom and dignity, without social or political barriers. This must be accompanied by an improvement in the opportunities for economic and social development. In particular, individuals belonging to disadvantaged groups should be provided special opportunities to develop their skills and participate in the growth process. India's democratic polity, with the establishment of the third layer of democracy at the Panchayat Raj Institution (PRI) level, provides opportunities for empowerment and participation of all groups with reservations for SCs, STs, and women. These institutions should be made more effective through greater delegation of power and responsibility to the local level.

Environmental sustainability Environment protection is to focus the centre stage of policy formulation. What is perceived as development may actually lead to a deteriorating quality of life. This seems to be happening all around, in the poor and generally worsening quality of air in cities and even villages; in the increasingly polluted waters of our lakes and rivers, which are not fit for even bathing, let alone drinking; in the loss of biodiversity, and in the shrinking habitats of wild animals. This degradation of natural resources reduces the well-being of people, and the poor and women suffer more, as they depend much more on natural common property resources for fuel and water, and also have fewer resources to take inclusive growth.

Gender equity For the first time in the history of Indian planning there is an attempt to move beyond empowerment and recognize women as agents of sustained socio-economic growth and change. This approach needs to be continued till gender equity is achieved.

Education and skill development Education and skill development meet the needs of a growing economy and to promote social equality by empowering those currently excluded because of unequal access to education and skills to participate fully in the growth process.

Health and nutrition Good health is both an end in itself and also Contributes to economic growth. Meeting the health needs of the population requires a comprehensive and sustained approach. Our health services should be affordable and of reasonable quality to strengthen all aspects of the health care system—preventive, promotive, curative, palliative and rehabilitative. This will be accompanied by emphasis on access to clean drinking water, sanitation, diet, hygiene and feeding practices, which will significantly affect the health status of the people.

Women and child rights Inclusive growth envisages respecting the differential needs of all women and children and providing them with equal access to opportunities. This can only happen when women are recognized as agents of socio-economic growth with autonomy of decision-making and the rights of children are respected. Gender equity, this includes economic empowerment; social empowerment; political empowerment; strengthening mechanisms for effective implementation of women-related legislations; and augmenting delivery mechanisms for mainstreaming gender. For children, it adopts a rights framework based on the principles of protection, well-being, development and participation.

Livelihood security and rural development Accelerating agriculture development with emphasis on watershed development in dry land areas and a special focus on small farmers will increase employment and help reduce poverty in rural areas and place emphasis on several other initiatives which will increase economic well-being and opportunities in rural areas.

Science and technology Science and Technology are important stimulators of economic growth and development in the contemporary world. The contemporary status is critical and major positive steps in this area will intensify the country's attempts towards achieving sustained and rapid growth in the future. In order to enlarge the pool of scientific manpower in the country and to attract and foster talent in creative and innovative research programme.

INCLUSIVE GRWOTH IN TRANSITIONAL SOCIETY

Indian social structure is marked by tradition bound cultural influences in life patterns, cumulatively shaped the social organization. Social life is characterized by religious values and conformities which perpetuated the traditional influences. That apart, the structure is also prone to the stratification based inequalities emerging from caste, gender, regional imbalances etc, which have resulted in social discrimination and problems like untouchability, atrocities against women, dowry, female infanticide/foeticide, alienation of old age persons etc. In addition, the disparities also emerged between haves and have not's, upper and lower segments of population, minorities, divisions among occupational groups, communalism, fundamentalism, fanaticism etc, have further segregated the people. Economy in view of uncertainties and market influences, lack of industrialization, indigent condition in agriculture, industry, service sector the poor segments remained the worst victims, obviously resulted in unemployment, migration, indebtedness, child labour etc. Educational attainment of individual over a period of time, though shown improvement, illiteracy ignorance and unawareness of people have affected their social participation in main stream society. As a result civil society consciousness is lacking among citizens.

Politics and governance have its share of immoral and unethical practices which have affected responsive and good governance in contemporary society due to corruption, favoritism etc. The victims of these socio, cultural, educational, political, religious dimensions are the dalits, women, old age persons, children in difficult circumstances and others termed as marginalized groups. The issues and challenges emerging from the social structure in the contemporary transitional society are to be resolved through appropriate social intervention which is expected to promote economic growth with equitable and distribute social justice. To do this the strategy is obviously inclusive growth which is expected to involve the segments hither to remained excluded and a development agenda which better ensures participation of these segments shall definitely improve the socio economic standards of not only these segments but also accelerate the nation building activities.

ISSUES

Some of the major issues involved in the process of inclusive growth are listed below:

Participatory planning, pro–poor approach, non-discrimination, economic growth, distributive social justice, livelihood security, environmental ustainability, poverty alleviation, literacy/awareness/knowledge, information knowledge society, structural transformation, change in mindset, reformation, rationality/ objectivity/equity, information science/technology, production with quality–productivity, population/population control/quality population, vocationalisation/ professionalization, local/global linkages, infra structure for inclusive growth, modernization/urbanization, industrialization, occupational change/social change, value change/structural change, secularization, empowerment of marginalization groups for inclusive growth.

CHALLENGES:

Social and economic disparity and problems–poverty, unemployment, untouchability, dowry, lethargy, lack of understating of good governance, accountable administration, corruption, gross root democracy, lack of people's participation, inadequate growth in contemporary society, full employment, unity, integration, division, secularity, structural transformation/structural adjustment safety net, health–public-sanitation environmental sustainability, human development /social development/civil society.

CONCLUSION:

Inclusive growth in transitional society is affected by socio-economic disparities and discriminatory social practices. The hiatus between the advantaged and disadvantaged seem to prevail in view of perpetuation of traditional influences and social structural features of inequalities. Consequently the victims of inequalities are unable to participate and contribute in developmental process as equal partners. The outcome of this scenario is exclusion, marginalization and alienation of people affected by these socio-economic inequalities. Inclusive growth is focused on facilitating economic and political participation of the poor in the growth process and thereby decline inequalities. The programmes of poverty alleviation, gender equity, and social justice, and civil society consciousness, empowerment of the marginalized group, education, employment and social participation shall accelerate disadvantage reduction among the affected people. This obviously necessitates a drastic change in our strategy of planned and directed social change with a focus on economic growth with equitable and distributive social justice. The agenda for this inclusive growth is socio-economic and political empowerment of the disadvantaged facilitated by structural transformation, proper enforcement of the policy of protective discrimination, good governance, capacity building at grassroots level, human rights conscious civil society where in equality of opportunity and increased access to resource sharing for all for each and each for all becomes a social reality. Millennium Development Goals (MDGs), providing Urban Amenities in Rural Areas (PURA) increased Gross Domestic Product (GDP), larger use of Science and Technology, faithful implementation of National Missions, pro-active role of Commissions etc., show the directions to achieve the goal of inclusive growth in transitional society and successfully solve the issues encountered in the process and challenges are converted as opportunities.

2 INCLUSIVE GROWTH FOR SUSTAINABLE DEVELOPMENT

Prof. G. Pankajam

"Earth provides enough to satisfy every man's need, but not everyman's greed"

- Mahatma Gandhi

"Inclusive growth means much more than poverty reduction. Issues of equity, both inter- generational and between rich and poor, regional inequities and the needs of minorities need to be factored in," said Montek Singh Ahluwalia, Deputy Chairman. Basically inclusive growth means, broad based, shared and pro-poor growth. It decreases the rapid growth rate of poverty in a country and increases the involvement of people into the growth process of the country. Inclusive growth by its very definition implies an equitable allocation of resources. Three pillars of sustainability are economic growth, human development, social and environmental protection. These three include all the components of human life and well being. Of course our immediate concern when we think of sustainable and inclusive growth is economic growth and poverty alleviation for sustainable development by enhancing the living conditions of population as a whole with emphasis on raising the standard of living of the poor. "Our Common Future" a land mark report produced by the World Commission in 1987, on "Environment and Development defines sustainability as "Sustainable development is development that meets the needs of the present, without compromising the ability of future generations to meet their own needs" This suggests that while we attempt on sustainable development we have to think of the future too. There is growing concern and anxiety about biodiversity, protection of plants and animals and community based activity.

Growth in the Indian economy was quite low in the first 30 years after Independence from 1950 to 1980 due to increase in population and other reasons including non-judicial use of resources that led to degradation of nature. Forests are being destroyed and the constructions are taking their place. Though there were some fluctuations, in the next two decades gradual and sustained improvement produced an average rate of growth of 5.7% per annum for the 20 years. Building on that base, the economy have achieved take-off into a higher growth plane, with real GDP growth averaging 8.1% per annum in the three years 2003-04 to 2005-06, and the target growth rate of 8.5% over the 11th Five Year Plan period, 2007-12. The theme of the eleventh Five-Year Plan. 2007 to 2012 was 'towards faster and more inclusive growth', which clearly reflected a sustainable balance between growth and inclusion. To ensure an inclusive growth is a challenge for India today. It sets a direct relationship between macro and micro determinant of the economy and its growth. The micro dimension includes the structural transformation of the society and macro dimension includes the country's Gross National Product (GNP) and Gross Domestic Product(GDP). By creating an environment of equality in opportunity in all dimension of livelihood by creating employment, market, consumption, production, and poor to access good standard of living. For the last two decades the world is focusing on long-term, sustainable, and inclusive growth in order to provide development opportunities for all sections of the society. Inclusive growth has created a platform to inclusive marketing. There is a huge consumer base in the rural market which is unexplored. This is because there is a huge competition in regular market.

Now India is ready for a new era of growth with a young workforce, an abundance of entrepreneurial skill, drive and vigour, a highly competitive international services sector, and massive untapped consumer demand in tis rural populations. Growth should be considered to be pro-poor where poor people also benefit in the areas of income, consumption, expenditure, nutrition, literacy, and other indicators of welfare. We are worried about problem of unemployment because unemployment does mean not having the money; it's also about the lack of skills, relevant work experience and poor health. A new social contract is needed which demands responsibility and guarantees individuals' access to the support and resources they need to make choices about their lives. There should be a paradigm shift; we need a model which better integrates our social and economic goals. Economic growth alone is not enough It must translate into individuals, achievements and social inclusion.

ATTRIBUTES OF INCLUSIVENESS

There are four important attributes of 'inclusiveness' in the context of a developing society. The economy of an inclusive society would provide many opportunities for better livelihood to its people, facilitating increase incomes. It would also provide various means for the people, to enhance their capabilities to utilize those available opportunities. Access is the third of the attributes of an inclusive society, which actually brings opportunity and capability of individuals together. If an individual has access to social needs like education and health services, appreciate self -values in society better; a sense of his or her true place in the larger community, and its obligations. The fourth dimension of an inclusive society is security, which ought to be provided by the government to its citizens in a rapidly growing economy safety in terms of predictability and stability of livelihood to its people. In the Indian context, this dimension of security in sustainable inclusive growth must be considered as paramount importance, as majority of our population is still primarily dependent on agriculture-based livelihood activities.

GROWTH IN AGRICULTURE AND CONSTRUCTION INDUSTRY

Sustainable Agriculture is being defined as environmentally friendly methods of farming that allow the production of crops and livestock without damage to the farm, soil, water supplies, biodiversity and other natural resources that preserve ecosystem. Growth in agriculture generates the highest benefits for the poorest households and the unskilled workers. Construction industry is the next best source of poverty reduction due to its unskilled workder intensity. Deforestation, deterioration of critical water sources is likely to affect water supply. The quality of land resources has been redueced by erosion, pollution, and land conversion. These resulted in decrease in agriculture activities leading to poor food production as well as less employment in agro based industries. Prosperity in India can come from rural area by building their capacities and capabilities to manufacture, value added products and remain sustained with agricultural production and agro based industries. The great resources of diversity, earth resources, knowledge and skills that rural India possess could thus be greatly enhanced.

INFRASTRUCTURE AND ENERGY

Enabling inclusive growth requires improving access for the poor, allowing them to participate in the mainstream development eco-system through economic opportunities. Information and Communication Technology (ICT) has important role to play in economic growth of any country. Any inefficient transport network and unreliable power supply are the most significant infrastructure constraints on overall growth. India has a huge problem with power generation. Rural India does not have easily accessible electricity. Power generations from renewable resources are the most effective methods of energy production. Localized energy can help India's growth. Pressures on India's infrastructure could be attributed to rapid growth of population, expansion of trade, priority for higher growth of manufacturing, the rapid urbanization, modernization, and competiton in the global market due to globalization, the revival and diversification of agriculture. These pressures created Serious bottlenecks in the mobility of people and goods across the country, access to power, drinking water and sanitation for the vast majority of India's population.

PUBLIC EXPENDITURE ON EDUCATION

Literacy plays a vital role in poverty reduction as it enhances equality, employability by providing the means for people to create or enhance their capabilities in order to exploit available opportunities. Hence it becomes important to provide quality education to all. There are three components that are to be emphasized; provide basic skills that the individual needs to function within his socio-economic environment such as literacy, numeracy and, in today's times, some basic IT capabilities that are relevant to the market. Productivity will increase only when the individual is able to fit into a team with the larger collective objective.

PUBLIC EXPENDITURE ON HEALTHCARE

When we are aiming at"Health for All" India's public expenditure on health care, at 0.9 percent of the GDP, is very low even while comparing with the standards of other developing countries in the world. Only 35 percent of the population has access to medicines now. In India people are now living longer than a century ago and the Indian population is slowly ageing. The ageing factor plays a vital role not only in healthcate planning and healthcare delivery, dependency ratio also increases. We should also strive together to strengthen the capacity of health care systems to deliver basic health services and to reduce environment-related health risks by providing health awareness and medical expertise to people.

SECURITY / SAFETY

It becomes an important component to provide adequate security and safety measures to people to protect themselves against either a temporary or permanent loss in agriculture due to un foreseen circumstances. As there is growth in science and technology, industries and machineries also become obsolete and new ones emerge. Predictability and stability of their livelihoods can be quite brutal as majority of our population is still dependent on agriuclutre. Weak protection to the investors and a high degree of social conflicts, natural disasters and calamities can damage physical infrastructure, directly affecting human lives and health of livelihoods, particularly the poor and vulnerable. Ensuring the security of their livelihoods is important for sustainable development. With increasing purchasing power, wasteful consumption linked to market driven consumerism is stressing the resource base of developing countries. It is therefore, important to counter this through education and public awareness.

ACCESS

There is no guarantee for the basic daily nutrition needs, access to improved sanitation, medical facility, potable drinking water, and school and so on. How to eradicate poverty and how to close the income gaps between the developing Asia and the developed countries if we do not adopt aright development strategy and good opportunities to achieve dynamic growth and development strategy and good opportunities to achieve dynamic growth and equitable income distribution in their process of development and access to education and jobs. Investment in the human resources is the important component for broad-based growth. This requires equitable access to basic social services, social safety and social protection against shocks. The major priority reforms in education have to be spelt out and implemented. It should ensure that such programs are accessible to the needs of the vulnerable groups, children of sexes, women, the elderly, and the disabled. Education is critical for promoting sustainable development and improving the capacity of the people to address environment and development issues. This type of individual alone will be self regulated, self dependent and could contribute better to a sustainable society.

HOW TO BRING INCLUSIVE AND SUSTAINABLE GROWTH?

As Gandhiji said"We cannot have ecological movement designed to prevent violence against nature, unless the principles of non-violence beome central to the ethics of human culture," Accoirding to him the industrialization and urbanization have created multiple problems and miseries for the modern man. Industrizlization, modernization and urbanization have led to lop-sided development. Rapid depletion of natural resources is a danger for natural environment. The displacement of human lobour is an essential characteristic of a machine. Machinery leads to mass production, not production by masses. Mass production necessarily leads to over production, problem of storage and transportation. We have to create provision for all these to avoid lop sided development in the society. "Mechanization is good when the hands are too few for the work intended to be accomplished. It is an evil when there are more hands than required for the work" said Gandhiji.He was in favour of technology and development of cottage and small scale industries at village level because these industries are localized, energy saver, and job intensive and less polluting. Gandhiji suggested building up a local economy where everybody in the area would be employed and self-sufficient. They could sustain themselves and their family with dignity with their earning. He was for bottom up approach in growth for inclusive and sustainable growth by using appropriate technology in industries.

Appropriate technology is the kind of technology that fits small-scale, grassroots, community centered economics with people as the centre. It is the contribution of the British economist Dr. Fritz Schumacher, author of the book "Small is Beautiful-Economics as if people mattered", which is still the foundation for a sustainable future. Appropriate technology fits in to the infinite variety of life on Earth, rather than forcing life to fit the technology fits in to the infinite variety of life on Earth, rather than forcing life to fit the technology. A developing country needs to have an appropriate strategy that guides their technology/ industrial borrowing from the developed countries. For example Khadi is the symbol of unity of Indian humanity, of its economic freedom and equality. Moreover, khadi also means decentralization of production and equable distribution. It is eco friendly and produced locally by masses and consumed locally by masses.

CONCLUSION

Simple living and high thinking will lead to inclusive and sustainable growth and development. Using India's natural human resoureces to sustain the economy without the excessive or massive pollution of the environment is very important. Globalization has resulted in increased competition and the drive to make more at a cheaper cost has increased our reliance on machinery leading to pollution, energy crisis, unemployment and other social evils in the society. Use of appropriate technology is an alternative to all these evils and an attempt to address the problems of resource in India and provide a sustainable growth model based on self reliance. It would be an answer to Energy crises across the world increasing food prices and inflation by going in for renewable energy sources.

Corruption, bureaucracy and resources to name a few are major stumbling blocks for the future and growth of inda. Localizing production and maintenance of resources such as energy can promote inclusive growth, alleviate poverty and help in creating local self and decentralized good governance-the bottom-up approach in which each individual is an active participant in making his or her own government. The poor villages are being exploited by the city dwellers. The villages produce the food and go hungry. They produce milk and their children have no milk to drink. They live in poverty, ignorance and with less medical facilities. Nehruji, the first Prime Minister of India, who was for modernization of India, if alive today, would have written to Mahatma Gandhi that " I revise my outlook on your (BapuJis) Constructive Programme. I am seeing the havoc that modern technology and civilization are causing to our earth. Today we speak of Sustainable Development and in doing research on this Endeavour I found that the fundamental edict of this initiative is much in conformity with your concept of village Swaraj. Forgive me {Nehru} for taking your idea, as you state- I am convinced people will have to live in villages" Village Swaraj and Sustainable Development Mahatma Gandhi's Ideas as Seen through the Eyes of Pandit Jawaharlal Nehru Today–Dr. Rukmin Maharaj . As Muhammad Yunus says, "The poor themselves can create a poverty- free world–all we have to do is to free them from the chains that we have put around them".

We should therefore, restrict our requirements and reduce our needs to move towards an inclusive growth which will be pro poor, eco friendly and sustainable.

It does not mean that we should not be modern; we should not be progressive; we have to follow what is appropriate for our country, what will make a large growing population live with dignity, without taking a begging bowel even for our basic requirements. To achieve this let us all follow what Gandhiji wanted "Be the change you want to see in the world".

DIMENSIONS OF INCLUSIVE GROWTH

3 POVERTY AND NUTRITIONAL STATUS OF THE RURAL WOMEN

Dr. C. Gobalakrishnan, G.Phary and D. Deepika

INTRODUCTION

No doubt, women are the source of continuity of life, nurturing the future. Young children first start to learn through contact with their mothers. As they grow older, education at home is fundamentally important in planting ethics and stimulating change in attitudes. Thus as world's caretaker of the home, women play a significant role in providing effective health care to their families. What about the health status of women? Health care of women is of paramount important for the promotion of health care of the children and the family. Enabling women to make informed choices in areas like education, employment and health is one of the parameters of women's empowerment which has been clearly mentioned in the National Policy for Empowerment of Women in 2001. Inspite of existence of such policies and programmes, patriarchal traditions still persists, which subordinate women to the tunes of age old customs and practices. In most Indian families, a daughter is viewed as a liability, and she is conditioned to believe that she is inferior to men. Sons are idolized and celebrated. This type of gender disparities is also evident in the breast-feeding and food consumption. Girls are breast-fed less frequently and for shorter durations in infancy. Similarly in childhood and adulthood, males are fed first and better. In India, until the late '80s, the female mortality rate was higher than the male mortality rate.

According to Sen (2001), "the mortality disadvantage of women works mainly through a widespread neglect of health, nutrition and other interests of women that influence survival". We have enough evidences to show that, in India, malnutrition among girls and women is higher than boys and men of same age group and the lower nutritional status is due to inadequate dietary intake by females in quantity as well as quality (Chaterjee, 1989). In a study on women and cooking energy, Batliwala (1983) argues that since women's average daily energy expenditure on various activities is higher than men, the dietary low intake affect women's nutritional status. The reduced access to food is often due to the gender inequalities that prevail in the intra-household relations (Agarwal, 1984; Harris, 1995). The present paper aims to find the economic disparities among gender with the help of nutritional status of the women.

MATERIALS AND METHODS

The present study is based on the recent data from the Third National Family Health Survey-3, 2005-06 (NFHS-3). The Third National Family Health Survey (NFHS-3), coordinated by the International Institute for Population Sciences (IIPS) under the aegis of the Government of India, was conducted in 2005-06. The NFHS-3 sample covers 99 percent of India's population living in all 29 states. Fieldwork for NFHS-3 was conducted in two phases from November 2005 to August 2006. Eighteen research organizations, including six Population Research Centers, collected the data and conducted data entry and editing operations. The NFHS-III collected information from a nationally representative sample of 109,041 households, 124,385 women age between 15-49 years, and 74,369 men age between 15-54 years.

RESULTS

a. *Socio-economic Characteristics of the Sample Population*?Among the total population, thirty-five per cent is under the age of 15, and only 5 percent in the age of 65 and above. Fourteen percent of heads of households are women. More than two-thirds of the population (69 %) lives in rural areas. Based on the religion of the household head, 82 percent of households are Hindu, 13 percent are Muslim, 3 percent are Christian, 2 percent are Sikh and other religions together account for less than 1 percent of households. One-fifths of household heads (19 %) belong to the scheduled castes, 8 percent to the scheduled tribes, and 40 percent to the other backward classes (OBC). About one-third do not belong to any of these three groups. Twenty-seven percent of households have a below poverty line (BPL) card. More than four-fifths of children below age 18 (83 %) live with both their parents, and 4 percent live with neither parent. A slightly higher proportion of urban children live with both parents (87 %) than rural children (81 %).

Among the total population, thirty-five per cent is under the age of 15, and only 5 percent in the age of 65 and above. Fourteen percent of heads of households are women. More than two-thirds of the population (69 %) lives in rural areas. Based on the religion of the household head, 82 percent of households are Hindu, 13 percent are Muslim, 3 percent are Christian, 2 percent are Sikh and other religions together account for less than 1 percent of households. One-fifths of household heads (19 %) belong to the scheduled castes, 8 percent to the scheduled tribes, and 40 percent to the other backward classes (OBC). About one-third do not belong to any of these three groups. Twenty-seven percent of households have a below poverty line (BPL) card. More than four-fifths of children below age 18 (83 %) live with both their parents, and 4 percent live with neither parent. A slightly higher proportion of urban children live with both parents (87 %) than rural children (81 %).

The 2011 Indian census found a sex ratio of 914 women per 1,000 men for the population age 0-6 years. Approximately five years after the census, NFHS-III finds the sex ratio of the population age 0-6 years (girls per 1,000 boys) to be 918 for India as a whole. There is little gender-disparity in age appropriate education at the primary school level; however, a higher proportion of boys (57 %) than girls (46 %) age 11–17 are in secondary school. Just over half (55 %) of women age 15-49 are literate, compared with 78 percent of men in the same age group. NFHS-III shows that even among those in the age group 15–19, only 74 percent of women and 89 percent of men are literate. Nationally, 35 percent of women and 18 percent of men are not regularly exposed to newspapers/ magazines, television, radio, or cinema. Forty-three percent of women age 15–49 are employed, compared with 87 percent of men in the same age group.

b. *Marriage and Fertility* More than half of women are married before the legal minimum age of 18. Among women age 20-49, the median age at first marriage is 17.2 years. By contrast, men in the same age group get married six years later, at a median age of 23.4 years. Urban women marry more than two years later than rural women; the median age at marriage among urban women age 20-49 is 18.8 years, compared with 16.4 years among their rural counterparts. The median age at first marriage in India is almost two years higher for women age 20-24 than for women age 40-49. Fertility continues to decline in India. The current total fertility rate (TFR) of 2.7 is down slightly from 2.9 children per woman at the time of NFHS-2, but is still well above the replacement level of just over two children per woman. In urban areas, the TFR has reached replacement levels (2.1), but in rural areas the TFR is 3.0. Unplanned pregnancies are relatively common. Among births in the five years before the survey, 10 percent were mistimed (wanted later) and 11 percent were not wanted at all. Among births to women age 30-49, more than one four births (29 percent) were not wanted at all. If all women were to have only the number of children they wanted, the total fertility rate would be 1.9 instead of 2.7. In India, the median interval between births is 31 months. Eleven percent of births take place within 18 months of the last birth, and 28 percent occur within 24 months.

Teenage pregnancy is common. Overall, one in six women age 15–19 has begun childbearing: 12 percent have become mothers and 4 percent were pregnant with their first child at the time of the survey. Among women age 20-49, half had a birth before they were 20 years old, and more than one in four before they were 18 years old. Early childbearing is most common in rural areas and among women with no education. The perinatal mortality rate, which includes stillbirths and very early infant deaths (in the first week of life), is estimated at 49 deaths per 1,000 pregnancies that lasted 7 months or more for the 2001-05 period. The perinatal mortality rate for pregnancies within 15 months after a previous pregnancy is 71, compared with only 30 to 31 when the birth interval is 27 months or more. Perinatal mortality is also very high for very young mothers (67) and for first pregnancies (66). According to socio-economic characteristics, perinatal mortality is highest for rural mothers, mothers with no education and less than 5 years of education, and mothers in the lowest wealth quintile.

c. *Maternal Health Care* Although 76 percent of women who had a live birth in the five years preceding the survey received antenatal care, only 44 percent started antenatal care during the first trimester of pregnancy, as recommended. Another 22 percent had their first visit during the fourth or fifth month of pregnancy. Just over half of mothers (52 percent) had three or more antenatal care visits. Urban women were much more likely to have three or more antenatal visits than rural women. Many women do not receive high quality antenatal care. Only 36 percent received information about pregnancy complications. Sixty-five percent received (or bought) iron and folic acid (IFA) supplements for their most recent birth, and only 23 percent took IFA for at least 90 days, as recommended. Thirty-nine percent of births in the five years preceding the survey took place in health facilities; more than half took place in the woman's own home; and 9 percent took place in parents' homes. However, in more than 9 in 10 home deliveries, the mother reported that a clean blade was used to cut the umbilical cord. Overall, less than 1 in 10 (9 percent) births in the five years preceding the survey were delivered by caesarean section. Among the 34 percent of births that were weighed at birth, over one in five (22 percent) were of low birth weight (less than 2.5 kg).

Postnatal check-ups soon after delivery help safeguard the health of mother and baby, particularly for births occurring outside of health care facilities Almost 6 in 10 women (58 percent) did not receive any postnatal check-up after their most recent birth. About one-quarter of women (27 percent) received a health check-up in the first four hours after delivery, and 37 percent received a health check-up within the critical first two days after delivery. Although the likelihood of a timely postnatal checkup is closely associated with having an institutional delivery, it is notable that 15-24 percent of births even in institutions did not receive a postnatal check-up. Among births delivered at home, only 9–12 percent of births received a postnatal checkup within two days of delivery.

d. *Child Nutrition and Health* While breastfeeding is nearly universal in India, very few children are put to the breast immediately after birth. Only one-quarter of last-born children who were ever breastfed started breastfeeding within half an hour of birth, as is recommended, and almost half (45 percent) did not start breastfeeding within one day of birth. Most mothers (57 percent) gave their last-born child something to drink other than breast milk in the three days after delivery. Only 69 percent of children fewer than two months of age are exclusively breastfed. Exclusive breastfeeding drops to 51 percent at 2-3 months of age and 28 percent at 4–5 months of age. Children are considered fully immunized if they receive one BCG injection to protect against tuberculosis, three doses each of DPT (diphtheria, pertussis, tetanus) and polio vaccines, and one measles vaccine. In India, only 44 percent of children age 12–23 months is fully vaccinated, and 5 percent have not received any vaccinations. Immunization coverage has improved substantially since NFHS-1, when only 36 percent of children were fully vaccinated and 30 percent had not been vaccinated at all. There is very little change, however, in full immunization coverage between NFHS-2 (42 percent) and NFHS-3 (44 percent).

e. *Women's Nutrition* NFHS-3 collected information on the height and weight of women age 15249. The height and weight measurements provide an estimate of the body mass index (BMI), a measure of nutritional status. The BMI is defined as weight in kilograms divided by height in meters squared (kg/m2). A cut-off point of 18.5 is used to define thinness or acute under-nutrition, and a BMI of 25 or above indicates overweight or obesity. More than one-third (36 percent) of women age 15–49 in India have a BMI below 18.5 indicating chronic nutritional deficiency, including 16 percent who are moderately to severely thin. The proportion of ever-married women who are thin (33 percent) has decreased slightly from 36 percent in NFHS-2. Women who are undernourished themselves are also much more likely than other women to have children who are undernourished. Obesity, the other side of poor nutrition, is a substantial problem among several groups of women in India, particularly urban women, well-educated women, women from households with a high standard of living, and among Sikhs. Fifteen percent of ever-married women are overweight or obese, up from 11 percent in NFHS-2. Anemia is a major health problem for adults as well as children, affecting 55 percent of women and 24 percent of men. he prevalence of anemia for ever-married women has increased from 52 percent in NFHS-2 to 56 percent in NFHS-3. Pregnant women are much more likely than non-pregnant women to be moderately to severely anemic. Only 37 percent of currently married women participate (make the decision alone or jointly with their husband) in making all four decisions like their health care, on making large household purchases, making purchases for daily household needs, and on visiting their family or relatives.

DISCUSSION

Food and nutrition are essential for good health. Policy makers recognized that the optimal nutrition and health as prerequisites for human development. Article

47 of the Constitution of India states, that the State shall regard raising the level of nutrition and standard of living of its people and improve the public health is among its primary duties". However, the above results indicated that the women have less median age at first marriage than men. Similarly, the prevalence of nutritional deficiency and the prevalence of anemia are more common among women than men. Malnourished women are more likely to give birth to low birth-weight babies, and if the underweight baby is a female who survives, she in turn is likely to continue throughout her childhood, adolescence and adult life. This lack of nourishment has detrimental effects on her reproductive and lactating capacities and overall development. Poor health has repercussions not only for women but also their families. Women in poor health are more likely to give birth to low weight infants. They also are less likely to be able to provide food and adequate care for their children. Likewise, a woman's health affects the household economic well-being, as a woman in poor health will be less productive in the labor force. A recent study (Dharmalingam et al. 2009) indicated that the impact of Nutritional Status of mother is more pervasive than the impact of other factors on birth weight. The prevalence of micronutrient deficiencies - a study carried out by NNMB (2003) revealed that the overall prevalence of anemia was observed to be highest among lactating women (78%) followed by pregnant Women (75%) and adolescent girls (70%).

The above said data clearly shows that the nutritional status of the Indian women are comparatively low level and it seeks more concentration by the government and non-governmental organization to improve it, nearly 60% of Indian women are anemic, this is not a good feature of a developed nation. To conclude, it is clear that for women besides mental strong/health, physical health is also very important to enhance themselves and really reach the beak of empowerment. For this, nutritional status of women should be improved and gender disparity should be totally uprooted. The dream of 2020 is our nation's navme also present in the list of developed country is only possible by improving the health status of our Indian women. Therefore, the existence health and nutrition education has to be strengthened through department of health, providing awareness about the balanced diet and nutritional food and furnish the subsidized nutritional food products like cereals, pulses, milk etc., through the public distribution system, conducting regular checkup in rural as well as in urban areas to ensure the nutritional status of the women. This thing helps for the inclusion of the women in the healthy society.

REFERENCES

Agarwal, Bina. *A Field of One's Own: Gender and Land Rights in South Asia*. New York: Cambridge University Press. 1994.

Batliawala, Srilatha. "Women in Poverty: The Energy, Health and Nutrition Syndrome" In *Tyranny of the Household: Investigative Essays on Women's Work*, Ed. Devaki Jain, Nirmala Banerjee, New Delhi: Shakti Books. 1985.

Chaterjee, Meera. "Socio-economic and Socio-cultural influences on Women's Nutritional status and Roles", In *Women and Nutrition in India*, Ed. C. Gopalan, Suminder Kaur. Nutrition Foundation of India, Special Publication, Series 5. 1989.

Dharmalingam A, Navanethan K, Krishna Kumar CS 2009. Nutritional Status of Mothers and Low Birth Weight in India. *Maternal and Child Health Journal* – online publication, 7, February, 2009.

Harris, Barbara. "The Intra family Distribution of Hunger in South Asia", In *The Political Economy of Hunger, Selected Essays*, Ed. Jean Dreze, Amarya Sen, Athar Hussain, New Delhi: Oxford University Press. 1995.

National Family Health Survey-3. 2005-06. Mumbai: International Institute for Population Sciences.

National Nutrition Monitoring Bureau 2003. Prevalenceof Micronutrient Deficiencies. *NNMB Report No.22.*Hyderabad: National Institute of Nutrition.

Sen, Amartya K. "Gender and Cooperative Conflicts", In *Persistent Inequalities: Women and World Development*, Ed. Irene Tinker. New York: Oxford University Press. 1990.

WHO. *Women of South-East Asia - A Health Profile*. Regional Publications, SEARO No. 34, New Delhi. 2000.

4 FINANCIAL INCLUSION: A CRITICAL ASSESSMENT AS A TOOL FOR INDIA'S INCLUSIVE GROWTH

Dr. Manju S.Nair, A. Sreejith

INTRODUCTION

India adopted different strategies and policies from the initiation of the first five year plan for its economic and social development. The main objective of these programmes was *growth with social justice*. With the initiation of the Eleventh Five Year Plan, India's growth and development strategy is "inclusive growth". Now India's target is not just faster growth but also inclusive growth i.e. a growth process which yields broad based benefits and ensures equity of opportunity for all. It implies participation in the process of growth and sharing of benefits from growth. Inclusive growth stresses the importance of growth for the reduction of poverty and inequality. Therefore it focuses on creation of more productive employment opportunities and ensures equal access by all sections of society, rather than on direct income redistribution. The objective of inclusive growth calls for significant new initiatives in many sectors. It needs special attention on both economic and social aspects of the economy. The Eleventh Five Year Plan proposes different policies for the attainment of inclusive growth. The policies pertaining to the agriculture sector is the key for the attainment of inclusive growth. The main constraint for the agriculture growth is the lack of access to formal sector credit. Based on this background, the objective of this paper is a critical review of the polices of inclusive growth in India and examines the role of financial inclusion for inclusive growth.

Towards Inclusive Growth: The Eleventh Plan (2007–2012)

The central vision of the *Eleventh Plan (2007-2012)* is to build strategies to trigger a development process which ensures broad based improvement in the quality of life of the people, especially the poor, SCs/STs, Other Backward Classes (OBCs), minorities and women. The National Development Council (NDC) in approving the Approach to the Eleventh Five Year Plan endorsed a target of 9 per cent GDP growth for the country as a whole. If this is achieved, it would mean that per capita GDP would grow at about 7.6 per cent per year to double in less than 10 years. However, the target is not just faster growth but also inclusive growth i.e. a growth process which yields broad based benefits and ensures equity of opportunity for all. The broad vision of the Eleventh Plan includes several inter-related components; rapid growth that reduces poverty and creates employment opportunities, access to essential services in health and education especially for the poor, equality of opportunity, empowerment through education and skill development, employment opportunities underpinned by the National Rural Employment Guarantee Act, environmental sustainability, recognition of women's agency and good governance.

Policies and Strategies for Faster and more Inclusive Growth

The transition towards faster and more inclusive growth calls for significant new initiatives in many sectors. The Approach Paper has identified areas where new policy initiatives are needed to achieve the 9 per cent growth target and its desired sectoral composition. The following section briefly discusses some of the major strategies of the Eleventh Plan.

a. *Policies towards Agriculture* The objective of doubling the growth rate of agriculture GDP to 4 per cent per annum is critical to ensure the inclusiveness of growth. This sector still provides livelihood to nearly 60 per cent of our people and remains vital for food security. This however, poses major policy challenges in the immediate future. To increase the growth rate in agriculture and at the same time maintain prices and profitability, the Approach Paper provides policies should focus on corresponding increase in demand for agricultural output matched with the supply side response based on productivity improvements is required. The demand side requires renewed focus on the Minimum Support Prices (MSP) policy and the need for a supportive tariff policy to deal with import price variability. The strategies to raise agricultural output supply gave particular attention to water management problems in the dry land rainfed areas Therefore, it is necessary to adopt region specific strategies focusing on the scope for increasing yields with known technologies and the scope for viable diversification, keeping in mind marketing constraints. It is necessary to improve the functioning of the agricultural development administration, especially the extension system, which is the key to bridging the knowledge gap.

b. *Investment Requirements* One set of issues concerns the aggregate resource requirements. An average growth rate of 9 per cent over the 11th Plan period will require an increase in domestic investment rates from 27.8 per cent in the 10th plan to 35.1 per cent in the 11th Plan. Therefore Approach Paper draws attention to the need for improves the investment climate. It is particularly important to take steps to encourage entrepreneurship and expansion among small and medium enterprises. State governments have a major role to play in this context by improving the investment climate. Many state governments are taking steps in this direction but much more can be done. As far the Centre is concerned, it must ensure that there is financial inclusion for micro, small and medium enterprises (MSMEs) and that the financial system functions in a way which supports the investment needs of MSMEs.

c. *Policies for Industrial Growth* The 11th Plan aim at raising the rate of growth of the industrial sector to 10 per cent and manufacturing growth to 12 per cent per annum. The most critical short-term barriers to growth of the manufacturing sector are absence of world-class infrastructure (power in particular), shortage of skilled manpower, inspector raj, and lack of labour flexibility. Therefore, the 11th Plan should place special emphasis on infrastructure and skill formation. The National Manufacturing Competitive Council has proposed a strategy for manufacturing which should be operationalized in the 11th Plan.

d. *Policies for Developing Infrastructure* The biggest constraint on rapid growth in the years ahead will be the lack of physical infrastructure and its poor quality compared with our competitors in other developing countries. Both the Centre and the States have responsibility in this area as different types of infrastructure fall under different jurisdictions. The Approached Paper proposed to increase the public investment in this area. However, the total resources require to correct the infrastructure deficit exceed the capacity of the public sector. The strategy for infrastructure must therefore encourage Public Private Partnerships (PPP) wherever possible. He development of rural infrastructure is crucial for ensuring inclusiveness and for giving a new deal to rural areas. The Bharat Nirman Programme has made a good start in the 10th Plan and will continue into the 11th Plan. Homestead sites must be provided to all by 2012. The implementation of the NREG Programme and the Backward Regions Grand Fund provides two additional sources of funding infrastructure development in the most backward districts of our country. In order to cope with poor infrastructural problems that have emerged as a result of rapid urban growth, the Jawaharlal Nehru National Urban Renewal Mission (JNNURM) was launched on 3rd December 2005. The 11th Plan will have to make substantial provision of funds under the JNNURM.

e. *Policies Promoting Access to Health and Education* Along with sectoral policies aimed at improving livelihood support and increasing employment, a strategy of inclusiveness also calls for new emphasis on education health and other basic facilities. Inadequate access to these essential services directly limits the welfare of large sections of our population and also denies them the opportunity to share fully in the benefits of growth. Achieving the 11th Plan targets for health and education requires a greatly expanded role for the State in these areas. This is because access to essential public services such as health, education, clean drinking water and sanitation is not an automatic outcome of raising incomes. It calls for deliberate public intervention to ensure delivery of these services. It is in this context that the National Rural Health Mission has been launched in order to improve the access and availability of quality health care, sanitation and nutrition. Development of children is at the centre of the 11th Plan. Therefore, the 11th Plan must universalise the Integrated Child Development Programme (ICDS).

f. Special Focus on Weaker Sections The 11th Plan gave special attention to the needs and requirements of the SCs, STs and minorities and other excluded groups to bring them at par with the rest of society. The Central and the State governments' implementation of the special plan for SCs and STs got special attention in the 11th Plan and the 15 point programme for the welfare of minorities circulated to all state governments must be implemented with serious concerted effort.

The key element of the strategy for inclusive growth must be an all out effort to provide the mass of our people the access to basic facilities such as health, education, clean drinking water etc. While in the short-run these essential public services impact directly on welfare, in the long-run they determine the economic opportunities for the future. It is important to recognize that access to these basic services is not necessarily assured simply by a rise in per capita income. Therefore, Governments at different levels have to ensure the provision of these services and this must be an essential part of our strategy for inclusive growth. However, based on these different strategies for inclusive growth, one major policy question is "Will the aim of Inclusive Growth is achieved?" The crux of the problem is the poor performance of the agriculture sector. The objective of doubling the growth rate of agriculture GDP to 4 per cent per annum is critical to ensure the inclusiveness of growth. A first step in making economic growth more inclusive is to identify the groups that have been excluded from the past growth and examine why they could not participate in the growth process in the first instance, we need to look at the composition of growth, in terms of sectors and activities. Here a major reason for the iniquitous and non-inclusive growth is seen in the slow growth of agriculture. While the overall economy has grown at over 7 per cent, average growth of agriculture sector has been only around 1.5 per cent and agriculture still employs 55 per cent workers and it is the major sources of livelihood for almost 60 per cent of population. Industry and service sectors which have experienced much faster growth rate at around 9 and 10 per cent have not been able to draw many people away from agriculture in their employment and provide them the opportunity for raising their levels of living. As a result of the slow growth of agriculture, the larger masses of rural population have remained insulated from the benefits of the high aggregate growth of the economy. Their exclusion has been further reinforced by the fact that urban centered and high technology based subsectors in industry and services have been the main engine of recent growth. This deceleration in the agriculture sector is the root cause of the problem of rural distress that has surfaced in many parts of the country and reached crisis levels in some. The literature pointed out that there are many reasons for this decelerartion in agriculture, viz. inadequate productivity growth, low prices of agricultural output etc. One of the major reasons for the agricultural deceleration is the lack of accessibility of adequate formal sector credit at reasonable rates, to push many farmers into crippling debt (GOI, 2006). Therefore, the 11th Plan put forward the need for the accessibility of formal sector credit for the agricultural and micro, small and medium enterprises (MSMEs). Thus, financial inclusion is a prerequisite for achieving the 11th Plan objective of inclusive growth.

Role of Financial Inclusion for Inclusive Growth

There are both supply side and demand side factors driving inclusive growth. Banks largely are expected to mitigate the supply side processes that prevent poor and disadvantaged social groups from gaining access to the financial system. Apart from the supply side factors, demand side factors such as lower income and /or asset holdings also have a significant bearing on financial inclusion. Financial inclusion is one of the methods through which Inclusive Growth can be achieved in India where large sections are unable or incompetent to participate in the financial system. An inclusive financial system mobilizes more resources for productive purposes leading to higher economic growth, better opportunities and reduction of poverty. On the other hand financial market imperfections, such as information asymmetries and transactions costs adversely affect the poor, the micro and small enterprises resulting in lack of opportunities, persistent inequality and slower growth. Also financial inclusion is inevitable in creating economic opportunities to the poor, sustaining it, overcome the risk associated with it and continue to participate so that they become successful economic agents to the growth process of the economy. Keeping this in mind Government, RBI banks and other financial institutions are making policy interventions to accommodate the vulnerable in to the financial system.

Financial Inclusion: Definition

Defining financial inclusion/exclusion is crucial from the viewpoint of developing proper policies for curbing the exclusion. A good review of existing studies suggests that there is no universally accepted definition of financial inclusion. Over the years, several definitions of financial inclusion/exclusion have evolved. Since measuring inclusion is perceived to be difficult, financial inclusion has generally been defined in terms of exclusion from the financial system. Broadly, financial exclusion is construed as the inability to access necessary financial services in an appropriate form due to problems associated with access, conditions, prices, marketing or self-exclusion in response to discouraging experiences or perceptions of individuals/entities. In Indian context, the Rengarajan Committee on Financial Inclusion defines financial inclusion as the "process of ensuring access to financial services and timely and adequate credit where needed by vulnerable groups such as weaker sections and low income groups at an affordable cost" (GoI, 2006). The literature pointed out that there are both demand and supply side reasons for financial exclusion. Most of the financially excluded people are socially and economically vulnerable sections of the population.

Extent of financial Inclusion in India

As per NSSO data (2003), 45.9 million farmer households in the country (51.4 per cent), do not access credit, either from institutional and non-institutional sources. Overall 73 per cent of farm households do not have access to formal credit sources. Exclusion is most acute in Central, Eastern and North-Eastern regions – having a concentration of 64 % of all financially excluded farmer households in the country. Marginal farmer households constitute 66 % of total farm households. Only 45 % of these households are indebted to either formal or non formal sources of finance. Among non-cultivator households nearly 80 % do not access credit from any source.

Policies for Financial Inclusion in India

The process of financial inclusion in India can be broadly classified into three phases. During the First Phase (1969–1990), the focus was on channeling of credit to the neglected sectors of the economy. Special emphasis was also laid on weaker sections of the society. Second Phase (1990–2005) focused mainly on strengthening the financial institutions as part of financial sector reforms. Financial inclusion in this phase was encouraged mainly by the introduction of Self-Help Group (SHG)-bank linkage programme in the early 1990s and Kisan Credit Cards (KCCs) for providing credit to farmers. The SHG-Bank linkage programme was launched by NABARD in 1992. During the Third Phase (2005 onwards), the financial inclusion was explicitly made as a policy objective and thrust was on providing safe facility of savings deposit through "no-frills accounts".

No Frills Accounts

The RBI concerns the issue of financial inclusion for the first time in its Annual Policy Statement for the year 2005-06. RBI noted the banking practices that tent to be exclude rather than attracts the vast sections of population and urged banks to review their existing practices to align them with the objective of financial inclusion. In the Mid Term Review of the Policy (2005-06), the RBI exhorted the banks, with a view to achieving greater financial inclusion, to make available a *basic banking* "no-frills account" either with nil or very minimum balances as well as charges that would make such accounts accessible to vats sections of population. The nature and number of transactions in such accounts would be restricted and made known to customers in advance in a transparent manner. All banks have been urged to give wide publicity to the facility of such no frills account. A number of banks have since come out with schemes for such no frills account facility. Number of no-frills accounts opened by scheduled commercial banks in India is shown in table 1. Based on this no-frills account, Palackad district in Kerala state achieved 100 per cent financial inclusion for the first time in India and subsequently almost all the states in the country achieved 100 per cent financial inclusion in the country based on no frills account.

Table 1 Number of No-Frills Accounts Opened by Scheduled Commercial Banks (Cumulative) in India

Bank Group	2007	2008	2009
Public Sector Banks	5865419	13909935	29859178
Private Sector Banks	860997	1845869	3124101
Foreign Banks	5919	3115	41482
Total	**6732335**	**15788191**	**33024761**

Sources: RBI, Report on Currency and Finance 2009-2010

Kisan Credit Card Scheme (KCCS)

Kisan credit card is a key product for enhancing growth in agriculture credit system. The kisan credit card scheme was introduced in 1998-1999 with the objective of providing timely and adequate credit support to farmers for their production needs in a flexible and cost effective manner. The scheme has been implemented by commercial banks, RRBs and cooperative banks through out the country. All the commercial banks used kisan credit card scheme to bring the rural and semi-urban under privileged into total financial inclusion scenario. Loans disbursed under KCCS are now covered under Rashtriya Krishi Beema Yojana of the General Insurance Corporation. KCC holders are being provided personal accident insurance cover of Rs.50,000 for accidental death and Rs. 25,000 for permanent disability.

Simplification of Know Your Customer (KYC) norms

In order to ensure that persons belonging to low income group, both in urban and rural areas do not encounter difficulties in opening bank accounts, the Know Your Customer (KYC) procedures for opening accounts has been simplified for those persons with balances not exceeding Rs 50000 and credits in the accounts not exceeding Rs 100000 in a year.

General Purpose Credit Card (GCC)

Banks have been asked to consider introduction of a General purpose Credit Card (GCC) facility up to Rs. 25000 at their rural and semi urban branches. The credit facility is in the nature of revolving credit entitling the holder to withdraw upto the limit sanctioned. Based on assessment of household cash flows, the limits are sanctioned without insistence on security and purpose. Interest rates on the facility is completely regulated.

The BC/BF Model

The Business Correspondent/Business Facilitator (BC/BF) model that the RBI had initiated in 2006 offers a significant opportunity to scale-up and deepen financial access by creating an extensive network of village-level touch points. Business Facilitators are primarily involved in creating awareness, processing and opening accounts where as Business Correspondents in addition mobilize deposits and distribute credits on behalf of the banks. In order to make the BC/BF model effective certain measures are required from the current level of operations. These include, putting in place an extensive network of village-level touch points, providing basic infrastructure, initial finance to cover pre-operative costs, training and building the capacity of BCs for high quality origination, high quality technology for smooth, easy and efficient operations, long-term working capital loans for ensuring sustainability and providing additional credit line for BCs to originate loans. (In January 2006, banks were permitted to utilise the services of non-governmental organisations (NGOs/SHGs), micro-finance institutions and other civil society organisations as intermediaries in providing financial and banking services through the use of business facilitator and business correspondent models.

One Time Settlement Scheme (OTS)

Another policy of the RBI for financial inclusion is the One Time Settlement Scheme (OTS). Banks have been asked to offer a One Time Settlement Scheme (OTS) to all borrowers where the principal amount is less than RS. 25000. As there are large number of such very small NPAs with banks offer of such an OTS is expected to restore borrowing relationship with the formal system and thereby obviate the need to go back to the informal system. Bank, however need to give wide publicity to the scheme at their rural and semi urban branches.

Agent Banking – India Post

Post Offices in India can play an important role in providing banking services to rural areas in view of the low-bank penetration, credit needs of workers, and wide occupational, income and educational variations found in villages. India Post has the largest postal network in the world with 155,000 post offices, 139,000 of which are in rural areas, holds 220 million savings accounts and 11 million insurance policies providing rural outreach that is so vital for financial inclusion. Post offices in India have provided savings since 1882, life insurance since 1884 and money remittance scheme, thus involved in financial inclusion process long back. The Expert Committee appointed by the Government on 'Harnessing the Indian Post Network for Financial Inclusion' suggested some major steps in this direction. These include delivery of lightweight, low cost bank accounts by post offices to all Indian citizens and especially to the financially excluded population. India Post should look for ways to leverage its low cost platform by providing India Post branded accounts to other strategic partners, such as MFIs, mutual fund and insurance companies, and telecom operators.

Mobile Banking

In India, mobile banking is considered the next big step in banking expansion particularly in the rural sector. Mobile banking provides a banking interface at low transaction cost using technology. Cost of an ATM transaction is five times that of a M-banking transactions and transaction at a bank branch is almost 15 times more expensive. Banks can tap financial inclusion effectively through M-banking as mobile penetration is increasing in rural areas. For the rapid expansion of mobile banking in the country a pro-active participation of big technology players and communication companies with the banking system is important.

Role of MFI and SHGs for Financial Inclusion

The post liberalization period saw banks shying away from lending to rural areas as it was based on a belief that small and poor borrowers are not bankable and lending to such a target group were not in the interest of banks especially in a competitive environment (Kelkar, 2008). Although, it is ironic that this became the starting point for the MFI which held a contrary view and saw the poor as bankable and having a business potential.

Self Help Group (SHG)–Bank Linkage Programme

One of the most important programmes for promoting financial inclusion through micro-finance is the SHG-Bank Linkage programme (started in 1992, by NABARD) which aims at improving access of the weaker and other sections of the society from formal financial institutions. The ability of people to pool their micro-savings, provide collective social collateral for banks to lend against and add to the SHGs' funds and the collective allocation of Funds to meet emergent credit needs of the SHG members, charge rates which reflect risks and management cost of funds, are the unique feature of this movement which has enabled banks to assist in meeting the credit needs of very poor people without sacrificing their funds and has helped rural women especially to empower themselves both economically and financially. Over the last 15 years, the Micro-Finance initiative of NABARD has assumed the shape of a micro finance movement in the country by linking around 30 lakh SHGs with the formal banking system by March 2007. Studies conducted by various experts show that the programme has indeed helped in the social and economic empowerment of rural folk, especially women, causing significant up-scaling of social capital while at the same time delivering crucial financial services.

Joint Liability Groups (JLGs)

Absence of ability to provide adequate collateral security work as a major hurdle for landless/tenant in securing loans. The inability of this section of farmers to provide collateral often excludes them from the purview of formal credit cover. Keeping this in view, a pilot project on financing Joint Liability Groups (JLGs) was initiated for developing effective credit products for such clients, which reduce risk and transaction costs for the banks and also introduce a greater degree of flexibility for the credit user to determine their credit needs and priorities. Joint Liability Groups (JLGs), established under the project, comprise a group of 5-10 member clients who are together informally recognized by the bank as group. The group members offer an undertaking to the bank that enables them to jointly receive such amounts as deemed eligible by the bank for pursuing any activity, individually or jointly, as found suitable by the group.

Role of Information Communication Technology (ICT) for Financial Inclusion

The banking system has grown enormously in the last several years keeping pace with and in some cases leading the country's remarkable economic growth. Simultaneously, the banking system has improved its strength, efficiency and resilience. There have also been significant improvements in the payments and settlements system and electronic payments and RTGS is now much more in use. IT has played a major role in these achievements. Today banks have centralised operations, more and more banks and branches are moving to CBS , network based computing, new delivery channels such as networked ATMs, internet banking, smart card based products, mobile access etc and are using IT for customer relationship management, customer transaction pattern analysis credit profiling and risk management. To be able to ensure that the challenges of banking the unbanked are met effectively and converted into growing and sustainable business for banks, there is no alternative to adoption of ICT solutions on a very large scale and range. ICT solutions are required to capture customer details, facilitate unique identification, ensure reliable and uninterrupted connectivity to remote areas and across multiple channels of delivery, offer multiple financial products (banking, insurance, capital market) through same delivery channel while ensuring consumer protection, develop comprehensive and reliable credit information system so essential for efficient credit delivery and credit pricing, develop appropriate products tailored to local needs and segments, provide customer education and counseling , enable use of multi media and multi-language for dissemination of information and advice. Now we turn to the specific initiatives of RBI in regard to ICT for Financial Inclusion. The very first initiative was emphasizing the use of IT solutions while adopting the agency or BC model for financial inclusion. Three working groups set up by RBI to consider support to RRBs and UCBs in computerizing their operations and adopt IT solutions for financial inclusion have recommended that the IDRBT could offer interest free loans to UCBs and RRBs for adoption of IT. Based on comments and response RBI will be firming up these schemes. The NFS is able to offer nationwide networking of ATMs and can facilitate banking transactions including remittances through ATMs linked to the NFS. Effective from April 1, 2009 a customer will be able to use any ATM (including other bank ATMs) to operate his /her account at no cost.

CONCLUSION

The policies adopted for inclusive growth includes policies towards agriculture, investment, industrial growth, access to formal sector credit, health and education etc. But the attainment of inclusive growth still remains a mirage as a large number of rural population remain insulated from the benefit of high aggregate growth of the economy. Financial exclusion of the economically and socially vulnerable sections of the people questions the attainment of inclusive growth. Financial inclusion, though well recognised as a means for inclusive growth, is constrained by several factors in India. The banks are faced with high operating cost in extending the financial services to the remote areas. High maintenance cost of these accounts as well as small ticket size of the transactions is also adding to the problem. Further, reaching out to the illiterate people or people who can handle only the regional languages is also difficult without developing a sustainable communication mode. The success of inclusive growth polices depends upon the synergisation of proper planning and targeted implementation of these policies by the different stakeholders operating in the economy.

REFERENCES

Chavan, Pallavi (2007), 'Access to Bank Credit, Implications for Dalit Rural Households', *Economic and Political Weekly*, Vol. 42, No. 31 pp. 3219-3224.

Chakrabarty, K.C (2009): Banking: Key Driver for Inclusive Growth. Paper presented at the Mint's Clarity Through Debate series on August 10th, 2009 at Chennai.

GoI (2006), "Towards Faster and More Inclusive Growth: An approach Paper to the Eleventh Five Year Plan", Planning Commission, Government of India, June 14.

GoI (2008), "Report of the Committee on Financial Inclusion", January 4.

Kelkar, Vijay (2008): Financial Inclusion for Inclusive Growth. Paper presented at N.P. Sen

Memorial Lecture, Administrative Staff College of India, Hyderabad, India .

Sarath Chandran, B.P. and Manju, T.K.(2010): Financial Inclusion Strategies for Inclusive

Growth in India, paper available at: http://mpra.ub.uni-muenchen.de/33569/

Thorat, Usha (2007), "Financial Inclusion- The Indian Experience", paper presented in the Financial Inclusion Conference 2007, Whitehall Place, London on 19th June.

Thorat, Usha (2008): "Inclusive Growth-the Role of Banks in Emerging Economics", Independence Commemoration Lecture, 2008 at the Central Bank of Sri Lanka, Colombo, 28th February.

5 INCLUSIVE GROWTH AND POVERTY ALLEVIATION

Dr. R. Mangayarkarasu, M.Kaliamoorthi

Inclusive growth focuses on economic growth which is absolutely necessary for poverty alleviation. Inclusive growth is in line with the absolute definition of pro poor growth. Rapid and sustained poverty reduction requires inclusive growth that allows poor people to contribute to and benefit from economic growth. Using the absolute definition the aim is to increase the rate of growth to achieve the greatest pace of poverty reduction. The Eleventh Five Year Plan, which covers the period 2007–08 to 2011–12, aims at faster and more inclusive growth. Empowerment of disadvantaged and hitherto marginalized groups is an essential component of inclusive growth. The strategy of faster with and inclusive growth includes several inter-related components. Five interrelated elements of inclusive growth are:

- Poverty reduction and increase in quantity and quality of employment
- Agricultural development
- Social sector development
- Reduction in regional disparities
- Protecting the environment

Even though five interrelated elements are cardinal for achieving inclusive growth, both poverty alleviation and employment generation are concentrated in this study for the purpose of in depth analysis.

Active government policies such as provision of gainful employment for the working poor under the Mahatma Gandhi National Rural Employment Guarantee Act (MGNREG Act) have played a critical role in strengthening the ability of our economy to face global challenges. The employment growth along with equity and distributive justice can be a powerful instrument for achieving the national agenda of 'inclusive growth'. The employment is a primary means through which citizenship is made real for the people to overcome the insecurities of old age and ill- health and ensure a better future for their children.

OBJECTIVES OF THE STUDY

The paper under study is based on the under noted objectives

- To analyze the reasons for the incidence of poverty.
- To highlight the methodology and policies adopted by the government authorities to ensure inclusive growth and poverty alleviation.
- To suggest ways and means to the policy makers to improve the quality of inclusiveness.

MULIDIMENSIONAL ASPECTS OF INCLUSIVENESS

Inclusiveness is a multidimensional concept and progress needs to be assessed in multidimensional aspects. Most policies aimed at inclusiveness have an impact only over a relatively long term. Even when policies are moving in the right direction, the results may be evident much later. The extent of reduction in the percentage of population below the poverty line is clearly a very important indicator of progress. The Eleventh plan explicitly recognized the multi-dimensional nature of inclusiveness by enumerating 27 targets of which GDP growth was only one among them. While setting the context for the Eleventh Five year plan, Planning Commission noted that 'rapid GDP growth was regarded necessary for two reasons; First to generate the income and employment opportunities that were needed for improving the living standards for the bulk of the population, and second to generate the resources needed for financing social sector programs aimed at reducing poverty and enabling inclusiveness. The social sector programs will have to ensure that the poor get access to services in a consistent manner that will allow them to achieve capabilities that can raise their income levels well above the poverty line.

POVERTY REDUCTION TO ENABLE INCLUSIVE GROWTH

The Indian economy is the 12th largest in the world and average annual growth rates have exceeded eight percent between 2004 and 2010 .Despite the sharp decline in the proportion of Indians living in poverty, more than one in three continue to live below the poverty line .India is ranked 119 among 169 countries in the 2010 Human Development Index .The Eleventh Five Year Plan and the Approach Paper to the Twelfth Five Year Plan stress on inclusive growth as means to reduce poverty.

INCOME AND POVERTY:

- Average GDP growth rate of 9% in the Eleven Plan period

- Agriculture GDP growth rate of 4% per year on an average
- Create 58 millions new work opportunities
- Reduce educated unemployment to below 5%
- Raise real wage rate of unskilled workers by 20%;
- Reduce the headcount ratio of consumption poverty by 10 percentage points

MEASURES ADOPTED FOR INCLUSIVE GROWTH IN THE ELEVENTH PLAN:

The important measures of inclusive development articulated in the Eleventh Plan are described below.

AGRICULTURE:

- Rastriya Krishi Vikas Yojana
- National Food Security Mission

RURAL DEVELOPMENT:

- National Rural Employment Guarantee Act
- Pradhan Mantri Gram Sadak Yojana
- Rajiv Gandhi Grameen Vidyutikaran Yojana
- Bharat Nirman : Irrigation, Rural Housing, Rural Road Connectivity, Rural Water Supply, Rural Electrification, Rural Telecommunication.

POVERTY - LIVELIHOOD SECURITY AND RURAL DEVELOPMENT:

A decisive reduction in poverty and an expansion in economic opportunities for all sections of the population is a major component of inclusiveness. The Eleventh Five Year Plan has envisaged reduction of the poverty ratio (i.e., the percentage of poor in total population) by 10 percentage points in the five year period. In order to achieve this goal, a number of initiatives have been taken in recent years for creation of social and economic infrastructure in rural areas to fulfill basic needs of the rural poor. Rapid growth of the economy is an essential requirement to reduce poverty since growth is an instrument for achieving a steady expansion in employment and incomes for large number of people. The growth should also be better balanced to rapidly create jobs in the industrial and services sectors, because it is necessary to shift a significant portion of the labor force from agriculture in which people are engaged in low productivity employment, into non agriculture activity, which is capable of providing higher real incomes per head.

POVERTY ISSUES

The poverty ratio or the head-count ratio, which expresses the percentage of people living below the poverty line, though has declined, the average level of poverty as per the latest official estimate of 27.5% in 2004-05 is considered high. The incidence of poverty among certain marginalized groups, e.g. the Scheduled Tribes, is higher than the national average. Besides, as a result of the population growth, the decline in the number of poor people has been only marginal. Two issues appear central to the poverty scenario in the country. First, the incidence of poverty is concentrated in specific areas and with varying levels of poverty and its intensity among the different state and Union Territories. Among the 35 States and Union Territories, three states, namely, Bihar, Madhya Pradesh and Uttar Pradesh account for 40% of all the poor population in the country. These are also among the slowest growing State with a per capita SDP growth of 2 to 3% per annum between 1993-94 and 2004-05. Generally, the acceleration in growth during this period was less in the poorer States. Two-third of all the poor live in just six states. These are: Bihar, Madhya Pradesh, Maharashtra, Orissa, Uttar Pradesh and West Bengal. Second, the interstate disparity in the level of poverty is widening, partly as a result of the faster decline in the poverty ratio in some state as compared to others. However, the average rate of decline in poverty ratio is such that at the above rate of decline in poverty, it will take twenty years from 2004-05 to bring poverty in the country down to 5 percent, which is the level of poverty in Punjab in 2004-05. In fact, the disparity in the state level poverty is so large and consequential that some parts of rural India have a higher poverty rate than even the most deprived countries of Africa while at the other end few States are fast approaching the prosperity levels of some middle-income Latin American countries. This underlines the importance of the several measures taken in the Eleventh Plan to make the growth more inclusive.

SAXENA COMMITTEE REPORT–REVIEW OF METHODOLOGY

An Expert Group headed by Dr N.C. Saxena was constituted by the Ministry of Rural Development to recommend a suitable methodology for identification of BPL families in rural areas. The Expert Group submitted its report in August 2009 and recommended doing away with score–based ranking of rural household followed for the BPL census 2002. The Committee has recommended automatic exclusion of some privileged sections and automatic inclusion of certain deprived and vulnerable sections of society, and a survey for the remaining population to rank them on a scale of 10.

AUTOMATIC EXCLUSION

- Household that fulfill any of the following conditions will not be surveyed for BPL census:
- Families who own double the land of the district average of agricultural household if partially or wholly irrigated (three times if completely un irrigated).
- Families that have three or four wheeled motorized vehicles, such as, jeeps
- Families that have at least one mechanized farm equipment, such as, tractors power tillers, threshers, and harvesters.
- Families that have any person who is drawing a salary of over 10,000 per month in a non-government / private organization or is employed in government on a regular basis with pension or equivalent benefits.
- Income tax payers.

AUTOMATIC INCLUSION

The following would be compulsorily included in the BPL list:

- Designated primitive tribal groups.
- Designated most discriminated against SC groups, called Maha Dalit groups.
- Single women-headed households.
- Households with a disabled person as breadwinner.
- Household headed by a minor.
- Destitute households which are dependent predominantly on subsidies and concessions for survival.
- Homeless households.
- Households that have a bonded laborer as member.

Survey of the remaining rural households is to he conducted and scores given depending upon the different socio-economic parameters recommended by the committee. The Ministry of Rural Development is in the process of conducting the pilot studies and Participatory Rural Appraisal (PRA) exercises to fine tune the methodology.

CAUSES OF FAILURE TO ERADICATE POVERTY

Production – oriented approach of planning without altering the mode of production resulted in the appropriation of gains by the owners of instrument of production. Thus most of the programmes designed to alleviate the poverty were unable to deliver the results. In fact the strategy of government was itself faulty. It suffered from following limitations.

- The income generation of poverty alleviation programmes does not recognize the importance of increased flow of social inputs through family welfare, nutrition, social security and minimum needs programmes.
- The programmes did not ensured that the poor get adequate food all the year round for the family with the increased income, because this depends on price, supply ease and time distribution of income.
- The programmes failed to build the "group power" for developing land and water resources, for preventing perpetuation of exploitative practices and from channelizing purchasing power in favor low income households.
- The present approach did not recognize the existence of "secondary poverty". It is the wasteful expenditure by poor people on activities such as drinking, gambling, etc which leaves little with the poor to buy other needs and decreases his physical efficiency.
- The failure of government to make necessary change in anti-poor laws and policies.
- Lack of political will to bring about institutional changes.

The problem of poverty eradication is one of providing employment and raising the productivity of low level employment. The following measures can help to enlarge employment and in the process lead to removal of poverty:

- Redistribution of land acquired after the imposition of a ceiling of 10-12 acres among the small and marginal farmers.
- Provision of security of tenure of sharecroppers and temporary tenants.
- The need to industrialize the rural India with labour intensive techniques.
- To develop towns with a population range of 10,000 to 20,000 as growth centers using local labour and available raw materials. For instance, implementation of PURA (Providing Urban amenities in Rural Areas).
- To create opportunities of self-employment by extending credit to low income groups both in rural and urban areas.

- To encourage production of items of mass consumption, especially wage goods, in small scale and cottage industries.
- Overcrowded agriculture sector is one of the reasons for the failure of poverty alleviation schemes
- Bulk of the employment in India is concentrated in agricultural sector. In rural areas, Agriculture constitutes up to 68 percent of the total rural employment.One of the important policy implications to promote rural non-farm activities is to provide skill and training to women workers in rural areas.
- Lack or regular employment in poorer states :
- Poorer states such as Bihar, Chhattisgarh, Jharkhand, Orissa and Uttar Pradesh have high proportion of workers engaged in casual work .In contrast developed states such as Maharashtra, Tamil Nadu Punjab and Delhi have high proportion of regular employment.

SUGGESTIONS TO IMPROVE THE QUALITY OF INCLUSIVNESS

The employment is a primary means through which citizenship is made real for the people to overcome the insecurities of old age and ill-health and ensure a better future for their children. Major strategies and targets include Employment growth to be targeted at least at 2.5 percent per annum compatible with the 9 percent growth in the economy. The undernoted suggestions may be considered by the policy makers and the planners to improve the quality of inclusiveness.

- Expansion of the outreach of Rashtriya swasthya Bima Yojana (R S B Y) Scheme to all poor households.
- Re-skilling the retrenched workers for redeployment
- Collection and compilation of employment/unemployment data on annual basis regularly
- Developing information base and E-monitoring on real time basis
- Enhancement of regular employment for less advantaged groups and in poorer states
- Focus on self employed and casual workers for improving their livelihood
- Enhance the scope of employment in the organized sector
- Comprehensive coverage of unorganized sector workers under social security schemes

- Promote diversification of rural work force to off-farm and non-farm activities
- Target regions with concentration of vulnerable social groups such as SC, ST, minorities, and women, illiterate and less skilled for active labour market policies.
- Creating large number of skill development institutions
- Up-gradation of all training providing institutions and strengthening delivery through Public Private Partnership (PPP) model
- Eliciting practical suggestions for further improving the quantitative as well as qualitative aspects of employment generation in India.
- Productive employment generation is an important concern for the national agenda of " inclusive growth".
- Raising the wage levels of casual workers both in agriculture and non-agriculture needs adequate policy attention
- Strict implementation of Minimum Wages Act of 1948 and targeted employment generation programs are important policy considerations
- Standardization of minimum wages across the states through centrally fixed and periodically revised statutory National Minimum Wage may be an important policy consideration to ensure Inclusive growth.
- Apart from casual labourers, there are sections of the society such as small and marginal farmers, small manufacturers, traders, hawkers, street vendors, forest produce gatherers and, rickshaw pullers. From the purpose of 'distributive justice', these categories of working poor deserve priority and focused attention.
- The government should ensure good governance with transparency and effective enforcement of the poverty alleviation programs.
- Special programs for livelihood support for the poor and vulnerable aims at increasing the income earning capabilities.
- There is a pertinent need to generate employment for disadvantaged groups such as SCs,STs and OBCs to achieve regular jobs in private sector, of course based on some baseline merit.

CONCLUSION

Most of the schemes for the amelioration of the poor get distorted during the process of implementation. It is, therefore, essential that programs of rural development are not put under the charge of panchayats, instead, special development councils should be set up in which majority representation should be given to the small and marginal farmers, the artisans and landless labourers. Unless the structure of development councils is revolutionized, it would not be possible to implement the policies designed for poverty alleviation. Year after year, Budgets which make huge allocations for the poor, and programmes initiated with honest intentions of assisting the poor, often lead to perverse outcomes. Institutional weaknesses, and implementation failures are the major contributive factors for the failure of poverty alleviation schemes .The failure of our social expenditure to reach the targeted poor is the collective failure of our entire economy, our polity and our society .Unless India ensures that its poverty alleviation schemes reach the targeted poor beneficiaries under B P L status ,our National Agenda of 'Inclusive Growth' will be one another verbal gymnastics which will entertain the educated elite in their leisure time through electronic media.

REFERENCES

1. C.A.K Yesudian-Poverty alleviation programmes in India; A social audit-October 2007.
2. Inclusive Growth, Poverty and Economic Development in India -Prof.S.Mahendra dev-Chairman, Commission for Agricultural Costs and Prices, Government of India.
3. Conceptualising social exclusion in the context of India 's poorest regions; Arjan de Haan, with statistical analysis by Amaresh Dubey-March 2004.

6 SCHEDULED TRIBES AND THEIR ACCESSIBILITY TO EDUCATION: A PATHWAY TO INCLUSIVE GROWTH

Dr. Pradeep Kumar Parida, Sreegith Thankappan

PART-I

Social Exclusion is one way of viewing a society. It gives a view about the social arrangement of that particular society. In the social arrangement some groups are marginalized, isolated and deprived. Social Exclusion is a social process that excludes, discriminate, isolate and deprive some groups on the basis of caste, ethnicity and religion. These excluded groups include former untouchables or Dalits, Adivasis and some religious minorities. Although these social groups experienced exclusion and isolation that caused deprivation and poverty, there are differences in sources and process of deprivation. The source of poverty among these groups is rooted not only in the economic structure but in the process of social exclusion as well. The exclusion in political participation and in governance affected the capacity of the excluded group to use the political institutions and the State apparatus to their advantage. Social exclusion, in fact, has a variety of possible meaning and of foci. Perhaps the best definition which gives us a sense of the meaning of social exclusion was expressed by the child poverty action group (Walker, Alan and Walker, Carol: 1997). Social exclusion refers 'to the dynamic process of being shut out, fully or partially, from any of the social, economic, political and cultural systems which determine the social integration of the person in society'[1].

Our vision of strong and developed India has to be measured not only in terms of raising income but also to what extent the excluded groups also have equal share in the increased income. Similarly, the strength of the political parties needs to be measured not only in terms of number of seats in legislature alone but by the share of excluded groups and the success of governance will have to be measured by counting the participation of the excluded groups in decision making and administration. Inclusive growth is become a target. The idea of social inclusion

1. David, Byrue. (2009). Social Exclusion, New Delhi: Rawat Publication, p.2.

is now the central legitimating concept of social policy in everywhere in the world in general and India in particular. The approach of growth with equity has been followed in India since Independence. Inclusive growth is a broader concept covering economic, social, and cultural aspects of development. To certain extend 'inclusive growth' as synonymous with 'equitable development'. In other words one can say growth with equity is a fundamental for social inclusion. The present paper has three parts. The first part of the paper deals with the scheduled tribes of India and their present educational status. The second part of the paper aims to analyze the different programmes in the eleventh five plans and the importance of social capital formation for ensuring inclusive growth among the STs and the third part of the paper explain the role of education in social capital formation and the suggestion and recommendation for mainstreaming the STs of India.

THE SCHEDULED TRIBES OF INDIA

India holds a unique position in the tribal map of the world. The largest concentration of tribal communities in the world, next to Africa is in India (Verrier, Elwin 1963:5). These scheduled tribes constitute 573 groups and sub groups and are distributed in different proportions in most of the states and union territories of this sub-continent. The scheduled tribal population of India is 84,326,240 as per 2001 census constituting only 8.2 percent of the total population of the country. Out of the total 573 tribal communities 75 tribal communities were categorized in to Primitive Tribal Groups (PTGs) on the basis of pre-agricultural level of technology, low literacy, and diminishing number of population. There is a wide variation in their social system, economic organization and political structure. A majority of scheduled tribes of India are economically, socially and educationally backward. Many of them are primitive and geographically isolated. These tribal communities in India live in around 15 percent of area of the country most of which are hills and dales, forests and plateaus and therefore, under developed and inaccessible. In order to probe tribal problems thoroughly and deeply, it is necessary to take a broad view of the socio-economic background of different tribes of India. They are still in a state of impoverishment and identify themselves as a distinct section of the society. It is worthwhile to trace their socio-economic and cultural commonalities in the perspective of their backwardness, underdevelopment and isolation. STs constitute 8.2% of the total population of the country with 91.7% of them living in rural areas and 8.3% in urban areas. The sex ratio of ST population in 2001 was 978, which was much higher than the national average of 933. The proportion of ST population to the total population had also increased from 6.9% in 1971 to 8.2% in 2001. The proportion of STs to the total population in States/UT was highest in Mizoram (94.5%) and Lakshadweep (94.5%) followed by Nagaland (89.1%) and Meghalaya (85.9%). Within major States, Chhattisgarh (31.8%) had the highest percentage followed by Jharkhand (26.3%) and Orissa (22.1%). Of the total ST population in the country, Madhya

Pradesh accounted for the highest proportion of ST population (14.5%) followed by Maharashtra (10.2%), Orissa (9.7%), Gujarat (8.9%), Rajasthan (8.4%), Jharkhand (8.4%) and Chhattisgarh (7.8%). In fact, 68% of the country's ST population lives in these seven States only (Eleventh Five Year Plan: 110).

Definitions of Tribe

In the Indian Constitution, Article 342 lays down that "The President may, by public notification specify the tribes or tribal communities or part of or groups within the tribes or tribal communities or part which shall, for the purposes of this constitution, be deemed to be scheduled Tribes..." Scheduled tribes have been identified as one of the most depressed, oppressed, marginalized groups of Indian society.

"A tribe is a collection of families bearing a common name, speaking a common dialect, occupying or professing to occupy a common territory and is not usually endogamous, though originally it might have been so"

- Imperial Gazetteer of India[2]

"A tribe is an independent political division of a population with a common culture"

- Lucy Mair[3]

"A tribe is a group united by a common name in which the members take a pride by a common language, by a common territory, and by a feeling that all who do not share this name are outsiders, 'enemies' in fact"

- G.W.B. Huntingford[4]

Constitutional Safeguards for the STs of India

The constitution of India guarantees protection from social justice and all forms of exploitation. It guarantees equality before law (Art.14), and enjoins upon the State not to discriminate against any citizen on grounds of caste (Art.15 (1)). Untouchability is abolished and its practice in any form is forbidden (Art.17). The Constitution mandates that no citizen shall, on grounds only caste or race is subjected to any disability and restriction (Art.15 (2)). It empowers the State to make provisions for reservation in educational institutions (Art.15 (4) and (5). The Constitution of India has made several provisions to safeguard the interest of the STs in Articles 15(4), 16(4), 46, 243ZC, 244, the first and second provisions to 275(1), Article 334, 335 ,338A, 339(1), and the Fifth and Sixth Schedules.

2. Kumar, A. (2002). Tribal Development in India, New Delhi: Sarup & Sons, p.8.
3. ibid
4. ibid

Besides these, several laws have been enacted by the Central Government like the Protection of Civil Rights Act, 1955; the Scheduled Castes and Scheduled Tribes (Prevention of Atrocities) Act, 1989; the Provisions of Panchayats (Extension to Scheduled Areas) Act, 1996; the Scheduled Tribes and Other Traditional Forest Dwellers (Recognition of Forest Rights) Act, 2006 as well as by the State Governments (relating to the prevention of alienation and restoration of tribal land, money lending, reservations and so on). The Center has been given the authority of giving directions to the State Governments (cf. Article 339(2), Para 3 of the Fifth Schedule) in the interest of the tribal people. Further a National Tribal Policy is on the Central anvil.

Present Educational Status of STs

Education is the most effective instrument for the social empowerment of the scheduled tribes of India. It is a mean for renewing the knowledge and shaping the potentialities for the better tomorrow. Educational status of the STs can be assessed by looking in to the present literacy rate of the group. Between 1961 and 2001, the literacy rate of STs increased 5.32 times, while that of total population increased 2.69 times. However, the gap between the literacy rates of STs and the general population continued during the three decades between 1971 and 2001 almost the same level of 17.70% and above but with marginal variations. This evidence strongly tells that they are still excluded from the educational system. Table -1 show the literacy rate of general population and ST population during 1961-2001.

Table 1 Literacy Rate of General Population and ST Population during 1961-2001

Year	General			ST		
	Male	**Female**	**Total**	**Male**	**Female**	**Total**
1961	34.44	12.95	24.02	13.83	3.16	8.53
1971	39.45	18.70	29.45	17.63	4.85	11.30
1981	46.89	24.82	36.23	24.52	8.04	16.35
1991	64.1	39.3	52.2	40.65	18.19	29.60
2001	75.3	53.7	64.8	59.17	34.76	47.10

Source: Government of India, Eleventh Five-Year plan, 2007–12, Vol-II, New Delhi, Planning Commission

The drop out rate is a critical indicator reflecting lack of educational development and inability of a given social group to complete a specific level of education. Among the STs, dropout rates are still very high – 42.3% in Classes I to V; 65.9% in Classes I to VIII; and 79.0% in Classes I to X in 2004-05. Table-2 show the dropout rates of STs during 2004–05.

Table 2 Dropout Rates, 2004-05-ST (Provisional)

Year	Sex	Classes I to V			Classes I to VIII			Classes to X		
		All	ST	Gap	All	ST	Gap	All	ST	Gap
2004–05	Boys	31.8	42.6	(–) 10.7	50.4	65.0	(–) 14.6	60.4	77.8	(–) 17.4
	Girls	25.4	42.0	(–) 16.6	51.3	67.1	(–) 15.8	63.9	80.7	(–) 16.8
	Total	29.0	42.3	(–) 13.3	50.8	65.9	(–) 15.1	61.9	79.0	(–) 17.1

Source: Government of India, Eleventh Five-Year plan, 2007–12, Vol-II, New Delhi, Planning Commission

Gross Enrolment Ratio (GER) is the another indicator to assess the access to education in the country/region/class it is the ratio of students enrolled at each level of education, as a proportion of the population of the relevant age group. If we look in to the Enrolment Ratio of STs in to the higher education, we can understand the exact position of these groups in this sphere. In case of higher education the relevant age group is 18-24 years. Table -3 provides an analysis about the disparity in enrolment to higher education between the poor and the non-poor in India.

Table 3 Gross Enrolment Ratio for Poor and Non-Poor in India: 1991–2000

Poor

Social Group	Gross Enrolment Ratio		
	Rural	Urban	Total
ST	1.11	4.78	1.55
SC	1.35	3.86	1.89
OBC	1.13	5.16	2.30
Others	1.66	7.00	3.58
All	1.30	5.51	2.43

Non-Poor

Social Group	Gross Enrolment Ratio		
	Rural	**Urban**	**Total**
ST	7.81	23.19	9.7
SC	4.38	15.71	6.68
OBC	5.10	19.98	8.69
Others	10.74	34.01	19.73
All	7.12	27.15	12.81

Entire Population

Social Group	Gross Enrolment Ratio		
	Rural	**Urban**	**Total**
ST	5.12	15.87	6.43
SC	3.38	11.55	5.08
OBC	4.10	15.53	7.00
Others	9.00	29.28	16.74
All	5.58	21.75	10.10

Source: NSS, 1999–2000

From the Table-3 it is found that wide variation exists in access to higher education between the poor and non-poor according to the NSS data for 1999–2000. GER for the poor was 2.43 per cent which was almost six times lower compared with 12.81 per cent for non-poor. In rural and urban areas the GER for the poor was 1.30 per cent and 5.51 per cent respectively where as the GER for the non-poor in the rural and urban areas were 7.12 per cent and 27.15 per cent respectively. The above figures showed that the educational performance and participation of the STs are not satisfactory. The present educational statuses of STs are not only inadequate, but also inefficient to fulfill the aspirations of inclusive growth. Ensuring 'access' to education is a matter of great concern here. Education is the lever of social change. It is a fact that children who are exposed to early literacy activities can more likely to adopt to formal literacy classes at different levels. At the same time the educational accessibility opens so many social connections to the individual. When tribal people are socially included they fell valued and supported. Lack of access to education always had a negative impact on the inclusive development of the STs of India. STs educational accessibility to different levels of education as well as continuation of education in high schools in the rural and remote areas has always suffered do to lack of institutional facilities, non-viability and absence of teachers in the schools, negative attitude of the parents, poor socio-economic condition and so on. The real and genuine inclusive growth will happens only when these groups overcomes all the hurdles in the developmental process. Ducational accessibility is definitely a pathway for inclusive development and it offers a variety of 'accesses' to the beneficiaries.

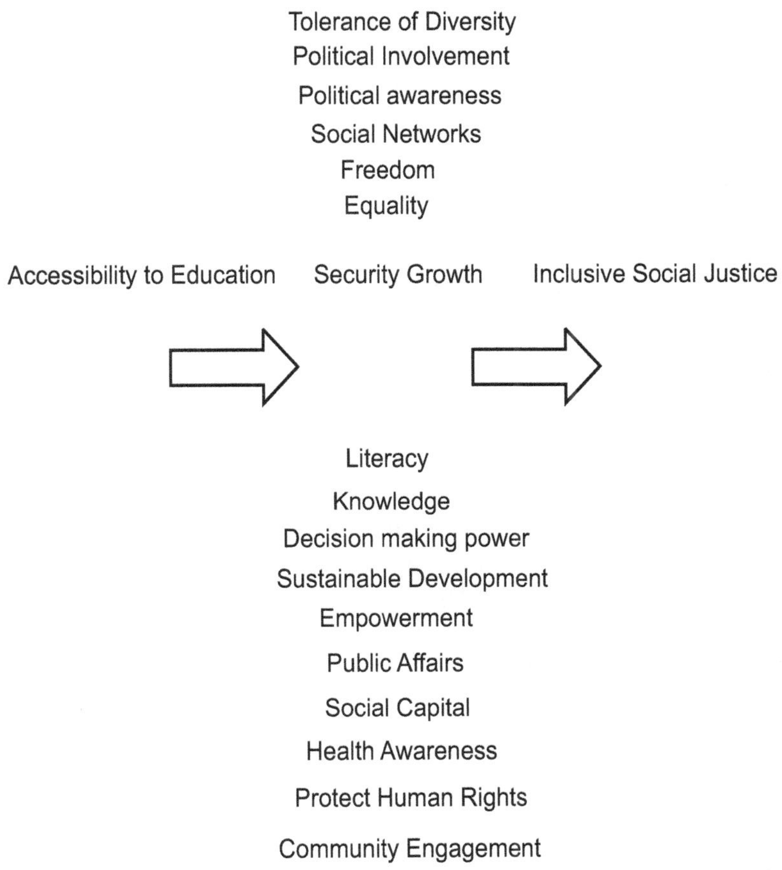

PART-II

Welfare and Development Programmes for the STs

Programmes for educational development, economic and social empowerment of socially disadvantaged groups and marginalized sections of society are implemented through State Governments, UT Administrations and NGOs. Public private Partnership approach is also one of the strategies for attaining the objective of development of the targeted groups. For the welfare and development of the STs, an outlay of Rs 3,205 core has been provided in the Annual Plan for 2009-10, which is 33.82 per cent higher than the outlay of Rs 2,121 core for 2008-09. The 2009-10 outlay has a Rs 900.50 core component provided as Special Central Assistance (SCA) to the Tribal -Sub Plan (TSP), which includes Rs 100 core for development of forest villages. An Additional Central Assistance (ACA) of Rs

500 core was also provided during 2009-10 for a special initiative of providing residential education to tribal children in Schedule V and Naxal-affected areas. The SCA to the TSP is a 100 per cent grant extended to States as additional funding for family-oriented income-generating schemes, creation of incidental infrastructure, extending financial assistance to self-help groups for community-based activities, and development of forest villages. Grants-in-aid under Article 275 (1) are also being provided to States with an objective to promote the welfare of the STs and improve administration to bring them on par with the rest of the States, and to take up such special welfare and development programmes which are otherwise not included in the Plan programmes. Under the Scheme of Post-Matric Scholarships, 100 per cent financial assistance is provided to ST students whose family income is less than or equal to Rs 1.08 lakh per annum to pursue post-matric level education including professional, graduate and postgraduate courses in recognized institutions. The Scheme of Top Class Education for STs provides financial assistance for quality education to 625 ST students per annum to pursue studies at degree and post degree level in any of the 125 identified institutes. The family income of the beneficiary ST students from all sources should not exceed Rs2.00 lakh per annum. Financial assistance is also provided to 15 eligible ST students for pursuing higher studies abroad in specified fields at Masters and Ph.D level under the National Overseas Scholarship Scheme. There is great emphasis on the education of ST girls, especially in the low literacy areas and schemes for strengthening the Education among ST girls in Low Literacy Districts to bridge the gap in literacy levels between the general female population and tribal women is being implemented (Economic Survey, 2009-10:290)

Eleventh Five Year Plan and Inclusive Growth

Inclusive growth demands that all social groups have equal access to the services provided by the State and equal opportunity for upward economic and social mobility. The Eleventh Plan Approach Paper 'Towards Faster and More Inclusive Growth' emphasizes reducing disparities across regions and communities by ensuring access to basic physical infrastructure as well as health and education services to all. The plan strategy clearly stated that 'A key element of the strategy for inclusive growth must be an all out effort to provide the mass of our people the access to basic facilities such as health, education, clean drinking water etc that they need'. In the short run these essential public services impact directly on welfare. In the longer run they determine economic opportunities for the future....better levels of health and education are necessary pre conditions for sustained long term growth. Inclusive growth means inclusion of the marginalized groups due to caste, class, and 'vicious circles of poverty' that has kept the poor enslaved. Towards 'faster and more inclusive growth is a huge task and requires enormous energy, resourcevs, ideas and visions. In a globalizing world, India is simultaneously facing challenges as well as opportunities at local and global levels. In this context ensuring inclusive growth among the marginalized groups assumes enormous significance if it is mobilized in a proper way towards development.

The Eleventh Five Year Plan gave immense importance on the educational development of the STs of the country. The plan recommended that the following measures to accelerate the educational progress among the tribal population.

- In the deficit areas, the requisite number of primary schools needs to be established. Specific norms for middle schools and high schools for tribal areas will be evolved and deficiencies made up. All schools should have proper school buildings, hostels, water, toilet facilities (particularly for the girls' schools).
- Residential high schools for ST boys and girls will be set up at suitable places. At the Gram Panchayat level, ensuring girls' hostels will be attached to the existing primary/elementary schools that do not have hostels, wherever it is feasible to do so.
- Textbooks in tribal language, especially at the primary level, will be produced to enable better comprehension by ST students in classes up to III. Side by side, adequate attention will be paid to the regional language so that children do not fell handicapped in higher classes.
- Efforts will be made to set up Industrial Training Institutes (ITIs) in the TSP areas. Other training centers will include community polytechnics, and undertaking rural/community development activities in their proximity, through application of science and technology.
- Timely distribution of fellowships, scholarships, textbooks, uniforms and school bag to students
- The ICDS/Anganwadi schemes for tribal areas will be evaluated and shortcomings eliminated.
- A larger number of special coaching classes will be organized and the concerned institutions will be suitably aided to enable ST students to compete in entry-level competitive examinations for professional courses.
- Adult education will be paid adequate attention.
- Steps will be taken to promote tribal languages, culture and heritage through adaptation of pedagogical methods, community participation in school management and so on.
- There is a need to constitute a special committee composed of eminent sociologists, anthropologists, educationists, administrators, representatives

of ST communities, and so on, to comprehensively assess the problems of ST education and make recommendations for implementation.

Introducing the Concept of Social Capital into Inclusive Growth

Social capital describes circumstances in which individuals can use membership in groups and networks to secure benefits. The term social capital is believed to be have been used in 1916 by L.J Hanifan, a state supervisor of rural schools in West Virginia USA saw regular contact between neighbours as an accumulation of social capital. In the 1950's the concept was applied within Canadian urban sociology in connection with studies of club memberships. About a decade later, the term was used by a sociologist, Jane Jacobs, in connection with neigbourhood as a resource for individuals and groups. Thus the first applications of the term social capital were mostly sociological in scope, linked to neighbourhood networking and education, often unequally distributed among groups. In social science Bourdieu and Coleman discussed the term social capital in a different fashion.

Definitions of Social Capital

Social Capital as "the aggregate of actual or potential resources which are linked to the possession of membership in a group" –Bourdieu[5] "Social Capital is defined by its function. It is not a single entity, but a variety of different entities having two characteristics in common: they all consist of some aspect of social structure, and they facilitate certain actions of individuals whom are within the structure. Like other forms of capital, social capital is productive, making possible the achievement of certain ends that would not be attainable in its absence" – Coleman[6] "Social Capital refers to features of social organization, such as trust norms and networks that can improve the efficiency of society by facilitating coordinated actions" - Putnam [7]

Bonding, Bridging and Linking Social Capital

Different combinations of network characteristics affect the overall capacity of social capital. In the social capital theory and research, distinctions have been made on the basis of different combinations of network characteristics, between 'bonding', 'bridging', and 'linking' social capital. Putnam (2002:22) has defined "bonding social capital consists of 'inward looking networks' that tend to reinforce exclusive identities and homogeneous groups while bridging social capital as open networks that are 'outward looking networks' and encompass people across diverse social cleavages". In other words bonding social capital is generated when

5. Christian, Kroll. (2008). Social Capital and the Happiness of Nations, New York: Peter Lang, p.61
6. ibid
7. ibid p.60

we reinforce our associational activities with already known or related people. Thus, it refers to the trust and reciprocity in dense or closed networks. Bonding networks can provide members of a local community with crucial resources especially through material aid, service, work, and emotional support that family and close friends can supply. Bridging social capital is generated when we connect with people who are outside the circle of our natural or instinctive acquaintances. Such people are in sufficiently different circumstances from us. The differences might be of class, ethnicity, religion, education or income. Bridging social capital involves overlapping networks which may give access to resources and opportunities which exist in one network to a member belonging to another. Heterogeneity of network members is said to enhance the bridging capabilities of social capital. Xavier Briggs has stated that the bonding social capital is good for 'getting by' and the bridging social capital for 'getting ahead'. Linking social capital is a relatively newer concept and involves social relations with those in authority, which may be used to garner resources or power. The interaction between the individual and the authorities can build valuable benefits and returns for each other. Participation in the governmental and non-governmental organizations are different mean for linking social capital. The mobilization of the bonding, bridging and linking elements of social capital formation is very much needed in inclusive growth. If the individual has close valuable relations with in the community and out side the community, the theories of social capital believed that he can expect more support and benefits from these relations. It is fact that the diverse friendships and relations attained through education is a possible way to activate the three process involved in the capital formation.

Benefits of Social Capital

Social capital is a fundamental element in the alleviation of vulnerability and the expansion of opportunities. Larger social capital leads to greater risk sharing among the villagers and act as an informal safety net. Social capital is a resource embedded in the social relationship of an individual. The diffusion of more relationships may facilitate greater linkages among the individuals. The co operation and mutual support demands in social capital is an important factor inclusive development. Social capital has a number of benefits for the individual as well as society at large. It has, therefore, been called a resource comprising beneficial social connections and relationships. The individual is helpless socially if left to himself, but if comes into contact with his neighborhood, nearby villagers and different public and private institutions, he can see the invisible hands of social capital which may immediately satisfy his societal needs. Norms of reciprocity create a willingness to help others, generating good will, fellowship and sympathy among individuals of a social unit. Individual rich in social capital can cope better with traumas and even fight illness better. According to Putnam in high social capital areas public spaces are cleaner, people are friendlier and streets are safer. As such, social capital is a great source to be harnessed and used in development. Social capital is very much useful in economic development. In Indonesia, local industrialization caused social capital to increase and tide over the economic depression during the late 1990s. Social capital acts as a buffer against economic disadvantages by mitigating the effect of deficiency of economic sources (Gupta, K.R., 2008:9).

PART-III

Education and Social Capital

Education is a powerful generator of social capital. According to recent research on the United States, Italy, and United Kingdom more educated individuals tend to join more voluntary associations, show greater interest in politics, and take part in more political activities. They are also more likely to express trust in others (social trust) and in institutions (institutional trust) and more inclined to 'civic cooperation'-or at least to profess that they do not condone 'uncivil' behavior Education is clearly not the only factor that predisposes people towards joining, engaging, and trusting, but it is a powerful predictor, at the individual level, even when controlling for other variables, such as wealth, income, age and gender (Andy Green & John Preston, 2001:247). Education has a very powerful effect on trust and associational membership as well as many other forms of social and political participation (Putnam, 1995:667). Wong, R.S. (1998:22) found that social capital as social networks outside the educational system playing an important role in the educational attainment of children. The study pointed out that the parent's involvement in political activities had several effects on children's education. Parents belonged to the privileged/skilled choosers possess and mobilize their social capital for the benefit of their children (Gewirtz et al, 1995). Study among the black women in Britain showed that social capital as a source of positive outcomes in education. The social networks among the black women functions as a safety net against their marginalization in the educational system (Mirza, H.S. & Reay, D. (2000). The current literature supported that education can play a great role in mobilizing the social relationships and there by re generating the social capital of an individual. If so why don't the STs of India? The accessibility to education widens their relationships as well as increases their participation in the community. The active participation in the society in turn enhances their social capital. Education can play a vital role here. It is a powerful and potent instrument of empowerment. It provides a ground and a plenty of opportunities to the deprived learner to actualize his/her potentiality. Education empowers the deprived STs by imparting appropriate and relevant information which are essentials for their development. Only the right knowledge can give the ability and power to these deprived classes to make right choice and decision in their life. In the absence of education, the marginalized groups are handicapped to discriminate between good and evil, or between right and wrong. They are one of the groups who are relatively isolated from the surrounding society. Most of them are residing in the outskirts of the villages and few of them are residing in the interior part of the forest. The geographical isolation and withdrawal tendencies further add more deprivation in to their life. It is through education the tribal's can expose themselves to the outside world, widening their horizon and providing with information about several matters relevant to the present society.

Capability Approach, Education and Social Capital

Amartya Sen is one of the key thinkers and commentators of the late twentieth and early twenty first centuries. Influential as a Nobel Prize winning economist and a political philosopher, Sen is a key contributor to identifying, detailing, and campaigning against forms of global inequality. A major theme of his work is how to evaluate human well-being. His ideas on evaluation, equality, freedom and rights stand at the center of the capability approach (Melanie Walker & Elaine Unterhalter, 2007:1). Sen defines a capability as "a person's ability to do valuable acts or reach valuable states of being", [it] represents the alternative combinations of things a person is able to do or to be" (Sen, 1993:30). Thus capabilities are opportunities of freedom to achieve what an individual reflectively consider valuables. A core idea in the capability approach is the distinction between capabilities and functioning. Functioning are achieved outcomes. Capabilities are the potential to achieve these functioning's. The capabilities to be well-nourished and protected. It enables the individual to participate in social interactions without shame. Sen classifies the capabilities into five namely political freedom, economic facilities, social opportunities, transparency guarantees and protective security as being fundamental. Education is central to the capability approach. Sen (1992:44), for example, identifies education as one of "a relatively small number of centrally important beings and doings that are crucial to well-being". Nussbaum (1997, 2002, 2004 & 2006) in her work on higher education in the United States and India and on schooling in Indian has discussed the importance of education for women's empowerment and importance of public education as crucial to democratic societies. She identifies three key capabilities associated with education: first, critical thinking or "examined life"; second the ideal of the world citizen; and third, the development of narrative imagination. The works of Amartya Sen and Martha Nussbam pointed out that education is itself a basic capability that affects the development and expansion of other capabilities.

According to Amartya Sen's Capability Approach the capabilities are ends while income, infrastructure and rights are considered to be resources in capability approach. Without access to these resources the so-called capabilities cannot be acquired. The educationist and researchers are of the opinion that education is a powerful tool for development. Educational attainment is positively correlated with income generation. Having the opportunity for education and the development of an education capability expands human freedoms. Education, argues Sen (1999), fulfills an instrumental social role in the critical literacy, for example, fosters public debate and dialogue about social and political arrangements. It has an instrumental process role by expanding the people one comes into contact with, broadening our horizons. Finally, it has an empowering and distributive role in facilitating the ability of the disadvantaged, marginalized, and excluded to organize politically. It has redistributive effects between social groups, households, and within families. Overall, education contributes to interpersonal effects where people are able to use the benefits of education to help others and hence contribute to the social good and democratic freedoms. In short, education is a potential capability for achieving many of the functioning's of the society.

Suggestions and Recommendations for Inclusive Growth

The objective of inclusiveness will be achieved through the following ways

1. Reduction of regional imbalances.
2. Establishment of new schools in the tribal areas.
3. Support to institutions located in border, hilly, remote, small towns and educationally backward areas.
4. Support to institutions with larger student population of STs
5. Supporting to the ST students with special scholarships, fellowships, hostel facilities, remedial coaching and other measures.
6. Setting up of an equal opportunity offer in all universities to bring all ST students under one umbrella for effective implementation of inclusive growth.
7. Teachers in the rural areas should be appointed for conducting awareness campaigns among the tribal communities.
8. Along with the Government, NGOs, and Voluntary organization should frame genuine programmes and policies for the educational development of the tribal people.
9. Incentives should be given for attending the Gram Shaba and PTA meeting for ensuring their participation.
10. Incentives should be given to each tribal student and their parents after completing each level of education

CONCLUSION

Indian society is a stratified society. Because of this stratification the growth among the different groups of the society are uneven particularly among the STs of India. STs of India are economically, socially, and educationally backward when compared to the mainstream society. The over all backwardness in turn isolates, marginalize, and discriminate them from the entire social participation. The literacy rate of the STs is very low compared to the general population. The high rate dropout and low rate of enrollment in to the school education add more to the educational backwardness of STs. Education is a powerful generator of social capital. For the marginalized STs of India, there is a need to mobilize their social capital through education. Education itself is a capability that can assure inclusive growth. The development of social capital may leads to stronger trust in the mainstream society and various institutions of the society. Only through this trust STs can enter in to the process of inclusive growth. In Order to bring them within the ambit of inclusive growth the government, NGOs, and voluntary organizations must frame genuine policies and provide means to improve their social position, especially through education. Accessibility to education widens their social participation and interaction. It also provides so many other valuable accesses to them. Only through these accesses they can ensure inclusive growth. Once they are educationally better off they are a part of inclusive growth otherwise they are the excluded among the excluded.

ABBREVIATIONS:

STs - Scheduled Tribes

PTGs - Primitive Tribal Groups

GER - Gross Enrolment Ratio

UT - Union Territory

NGOs – Non Governmental Organizations

SCA – Special Central Assistance

TSP – Tribal Sub Plan

ACA – Additional Central Assistance

ICDS – Integrated Child Development Scheme

NSS- National Sample Survey

REFERENCES

A.K,Lal. (2003). Social Exclusion: Essays in Honour of Dr. Bindeshwar Pathak, Vol-1, New Delhi: Concept Publishing company.

Baviskar, B.S., & Mathew, George. (2009). Inclusion and Exclusion in Local Governance: Field studies from Rural India, New Delhi: Sage Publications.

Charles, Karelis. (2007). The Persistence of Poverty: Why Economics of the well-off can't help the Poor, New Delhi: Oxford University Press.

Christian, Kroll. (2008). Social Capital and the Happiness of Nations, New York: Peter Lang.

Dash, L. N. (2010). Education and Inclusive Development in India, New Delhi: Regal Publications.

Gerwirtz, S., Ball, S.J., & Bowe, R. (1995). Market Choice and Equity in Education, Buckingham: Open University Press.

Ghanshyam, Shah. (1997). Social Transformation in India, New Delhi: Rawat Publications.

Government of India. (2008). Eleventh Five Year Plan 2007-12, Vol-II, New Delhi: Planning Commision.

Government of India. (2010). Economic Survey 2009-10, Ministry of Finance, New Delhi: Oxford University Press.

K.R. Gupta. (2008). Social Capital: An Overview, In: K.R, Gupta., Haase, Gunnar Lind., & Prasenjit Maiti, Svendsen (Eds) Social Capital, Vol-1, New Delhi: Atlantic Publishers & Distributers Pvt Ltd.

Kumar, A. (2002). Tribal Development in India, New Delhi: Sarup & Sons.[8]

Mahendra Dev, S. (2007). Inclusive Growth in India: Agriculture, Poverty and Human Development, New Delhi: Oxford University Press.

Margaret, Ledwith. (2006). Community Development: A Critical Approach, New Delhi: Rawat Publications.

Melanie,Walker., & Elaine, Unterhalter. (2007). Amartya Sen's Capability Approach and Social Justice in Education, New York: Palgrave Macmillan.

Mirza, H.S., & Reay, D. (2000). Redefining Citizenship: black women educators and the 'third space', In: M. Arnot & J.A. Dillabough (Eds) Challenging Democracy: International Perspectives on Gender, London: Routledge Falmer.

8

Nussbaum, Martha C., & Sen, Amartya (Eds). (1993). The Ouality of life: Studies in Development Economics, Oxford: Oxford University Press.

Samal, Kishor C. (2007). Poverty, Social Capital and Natural Resource Management, New Delhi: Rawat Publications.

Sheppard, Michael. (2008). Social Work and Social Exclusion: The idea of practice, Ashgate: USA: Ashgate.

Sukhadeo, Thoral. , & Narender, Kumar. (2008). B.R. AMBEDKAR: Perspective on Social Exclusion and Inclusive Policies, New Delhi: Oxford University Press.

Walker, Alan and Walker, Carol. (1997). Britain Divided: The growth of social exclusion in the 1980s and 1990s, London: Child Poverty Action Group.

Putnam, R. (1995). Turning in, turning out: The Strange disappearance of Social Capital in America, Political Science and Politics, 28, pp.664-683.

(2000). Bowling Alone: The Collapse and Revival of American Community, New York: Simon & Schuster.

Remakantan, N., & Retna, Raj. (2008). Decentralization and Social Inclusion of Scheduled Castes in Kerala, Trissur: Kerala Institute of Local Administration.

Sen, Amartya. (1992). Inequality Re-examined, Oxford: Oxford University Press.

(1993).Capability as Well Being, In: Nussbaum & Sen: The Ouality of life: Studies in Development Economics, Oxford: Oxford University Press.

Verrier, Elwin. (1963). New Deal for Tribal India, New Delhi: Government of India, p.5.

Wong, R.S. (1998). Multidimensional Influences of Family Environment in Education: the case of socialist Czechoslovakia, Sociology of Education, 71, pp.1-22.

Yagati, Chinna Rao.,& Sudhakara, Karakoti. (2010). Exclusion and Discrimination: Concepts, Perspectives and Challenges, New Delhi: Kanishka Publishers.

7 EMPOWERMENT OF SCHEDULED CASTE AND SCHEDULED TRIBES THROUGH MGNREGA: ISSUES AND STRATEGIES

Dr. M. Soundarapandian, N. Nagarajan

INTRODUCTION

The Mahatma Gandhi National Rural Employment Guarantee Act (MGNREGA) Guarantees 100 days of employment in a financial year to any rural household where adult members are willing to do unskilled manual work. The act has come in to force in 200 selected districts of the country w.e.f. 2nd February 2006. Now all the districts of the country have been brought in the ambit of the act from April, 2008. MGNREGA is a demand driven scheme. Therefore, separate earmarking of employment/resources for SCs/STs has not been provided. However the report of physical achievements during 2009 to reveal that out of total employment generation of 191.16 crore person days in the year employment generated for SCs and STs was 57.41 crore person days (30 %) and 41.48 crore person days (22 %) respectively. Thus, 52 % of the total person days of employment generated were for the SC/STs household. Providing full equality of opportunity to the people, particularly for SCs and STs is an essential component of any development intervention. The mandate of ministry of rural development is to alleviate poverty in the rural area with the objective to provide avenues of employment to mart disadvantaged section of the society including SC/STs. The Ministry of RD is implementing various schemes/programmes through special employment generation programmes. The ministry has made specific provisions in the guidelines of the programmes being implemented to ensure adequate flow of resources to SC and STs. The assistance for the poor household of SC/STs communities under the major programmes is as under.

OBJECTIVES

- To analysis the empowerment of SCs/STs employees under MGNREGS
- To study the strategies and problem faced by SCs/STs category in MGNREGS.

METHODOLOGY

The information's and data were also collected from secondary sources such as census reports, national sample survey reports, and government office reports and also from websites.

Table 7.1 Performance of NREGA – State wise Participation

State/UT	% HHs in NREGA to total working HH*	% of rural population of poverty BPL**	% of SC poverty in India **	% of Street poverty in India **	% of SC/Street person-days in NREGA ***				% of HH completed 100 days***	
					2006-07	2007-08	2008-09	2009-10	2008-09	2009-10
India	24.8	41.8	53.8	61.3	61.8	57.0	42.1	38.0	7.4	5.7
Andhra Pradesh	39.5	32.3	41.8	60.3	42.8	40.7	39.0	39.9	5.7	5.7
Assam	34.4	36.4	45.3	28.8	55.0	51.7	17.8	18.1	4.8	0.6
Bihar	22.4	55.7	77.6	59.3	50.3	47.4	35.1	30.8	0.6	0.9
Chhattisgarh	51.6	55.1	48.6	65.5	57.6	56.8	48.9	46.4	5.6	3.4
Gujarat	8.7	39.1	49.3	57.1	71.3	70.3	55.2	41.5	2.6	3.5
Haryana	3.5	24.8	47.5	0	60.0	56.8	50.6	49.1	1.6	4.6
Himachal Pradesh	33.0	25	39.5	35.4	52.8	45.1	36.9	37.1	5.4	2.7
Jammu & Kashmir	7.7	14.1	14.7	26.5	28.6	30.7	21.5	17.6	1.7	3.0
Jharkhand	30.6	51.6	61	60.6	63.8	62.8	55.0	54.7	3.0	6.2
Karnataka	9.0	37.5	57.4	50.5	53.4	50.3	34.6	26.3	2.4	11.3
Kerala	9.5	20.2	30.8	56.9	32.5	32.8	24.3	23.3	0.6	1.8
Madhya Pradesh	50.8	53.6	62.6	80	64.5	67.0	51.3	50.4	8.0	13.3
Maharashtra	5.0	47.4	66.1	73.2	57.1	55.1	50.0	31.9	3.1	7.2
Orissa	12.3	60.8	67.9	84.4	73.0	66.1	56.0	56.6	1.8	3.6
Punjab	3.1	22.1	38.4	30.7	69.4	75.2	78.2	72.2	0.4	0.8
Rajasthan	70.6	35.8	48.5	59.3	80.4	65.3	38.1	39.3	20.7	18.5
Tamil nadu	34.4	37.5	51.2	47.3	58.5	58.8	46.8	33.8	8.6	3.4
Uttar Pradesh	14.7	42.7	56.6	42	59.5	54.5	20.8	23.9	8.7	2.9
Uttaranchal	13.5	35.1	46.2	32.4	28.1	33.2	19.0	20.6	1.4	1.4
West Bengal	19.2	38.2	37.1	54.3	54.7	50.6	48.3	43.6	0.2	0.5

Source : * Census of Population – Projected : ** Report on Incidence of Poverty by Tendulkar Committee :
*** Official website of MoRD.

The available statistics on the state-wise performance of NREGA throw some more light on the performance of NREGA. A striking feature of these two tables is the occurrence of wide inter-state variations in the performance of NREGA. The participation of working households in NREGA is the highest in Rajasthan (70.6 per cent), followed by Madhya Pradesh (50.8 per cent). Andhra Pradesh (39.5 per cent) and Tamil Nadu and Assam (34.4 per cent). The lowest participation is in Punjab and Haryana, where 3.1 per cent and 3.5 per cent of the working households participate in NREGA, respectively. Although this gap between the highest and the lowest participation appears to be due to the gap in the incidence of rural poverty in the states, our study shows that the correlation coefficient (0.31) between the incidence of poverty and the participation rates is not significant. Perhaps some other factors such as the commitment of the state government, and social mobilization of workers for demanding work, etc., are also responsible for the variations in the performance of NREGA. Another important feature is that the

Participate of the SC and ST population in NREGA is quite high in all the states, including the states where the overall participation in NREGA is low. This indicates that NREGA tends to cover the poor as beneficiaries. The decline in their participation in 2008 – 09 and 2009 – 10 is largely because of the inclusion of non-SC-/ST dominated districts under NREGA during these years.

Table: 2 Performance of NREGA – State wise – Wages and Incomes

State/UT	NREGA income per HH (Rs.)				Daily wage rate (Rs.)				No. of days per HH			
	2006-07	2007-08	2008-09	2009-10	2006-07	2007-08	2008-09	2009-10	2006-07	2007-08	2008-09	2009-10
India	1920	2983	3899	4401	45	70	81	90	43	42	46	47
Andhra Pradesh	3014	3809	3372	5310	86	83	84	90	35	46	40	59
Assam	5561	3312	1802	1844	67	72	75	88	83	46	24	21
Bihar	5114	1838	1777	2258	80	80	85	94	64	23	21	24
Chhattisgarh	3696	4446	2492	2564	62	68	71	77	60	65	35	33
Gujarat	3113	2532	1839	2697	56	63	68	87	56	40	27	31
Haryana	5313	6664	4634	5168	97	115	136	152	55	58	34	34
Himachal Pradesh	3108	2908	3951	5008	74	79	90	128	42	37	44	39
Jammu & Kashmir	2082	0	2702	2690	69	70	71	73	30	0	38	37
Jharkhand	0	3873	3696	3804	0	82	88	95	45	47	42	40
Karnataka	3149	2896	2812	4643	67	72	72	88	47	40	39	53
Kerala	3141	4618	2770	3767	121	118	115	130	26	39	24	29

Source : * Census of Population – Projected : ** Report on Incidence of Poverty by Tendulkar Committee :
*** Official website of MoRD.

State/UT	NREGA income per HH (Rs.)				Daily wage rate (Rs.)				No. of days per HH			
	2006-07	2007-08	2008-09	2009-10	2006-07	2007-08	2008-09	2009-10	2006-07	2007-08	2008-09	2009-10
Madhya Pradesh	4403	4655	2322	2904	60	63	65	88	74	74	36	33
Maharashtra	4563	3528	4315	4328	104	84	86	114	44	42	50	38
Orissa	3225	2948	3312	3633	53	76	92	104	61	39	36	35
Punjab	4700	3808	2152	2636	94	100	108	126	50	38	20	21
Rajasthan	4420	5107	4866	4335	51	61	81	85	87	84	60	51
Tamil Nadu	2560	4889	1839	2380	80	78	63	68	32	63	29	35
Uttar Pradesh	1967	3428	2527	2935	56	90	97	101	35	38	26	29
Uttaranchal	2610	3225	1967	2247	73	73	85	107	36	44	23	21
West Bengal	1190	1978	884	1490	70	79	68	93	17	25	13	16

Source : * Census of Population – Projected : ** Report on Incidence of Poverty by Tendulkar Committee :
*** Official website of MoRD.

The average number of days of work per household under NREGA also shows wide variations. The lowest number is in West Bengal (16 days) and in Uttaranchal, Punjab and Assam (21 days), while the highest number is in Andhra Pradesh (59 days), Karnataka (53 days) and in Rajasthan (51 days). Once again, poverty is not an important factor here, as some poorer states like Bihar (24 days), Madhya Pradesh (33 days) and Orissa (35 days) have low average number of days of NREGA work per household. An important point to be noted here is that the percentage of NREGA households completing 100 days of work is still very low in all the states. This percentage is a more 5.7 at the all-India level (in 2009 – 10 up to February 2010), and it varies from 18.5 in Rajasthan, to 13.3 in Madhya Pradesh and 11.3 in Karnataka to 0.5 in West Bengal, 1.4 in Uttaranchal and 2.7 in Himachal Pradesh. However, in 13 out of the total of 20 states, the percentage has shown an increase between 2008 – 09 and 2009 – 10 (up to February 2010). If the level of participation by working households, the average number of days of NREGA work, and the percentage of households completing 100 days in assessed, one can say that the potential of NREGA is still far from fully tapped.

CRITICAL ISSUES

1. NREGA Wage Rate and Market Wage Rate

NREGA workers are entitled to the legal minimum wages, and are paid, if not the legal wage rate, a much higher wage rate than the local wage rates when NREGA is implemented on a large scale. This is likely to raise local wage rates, which, in turn, is likely to create a number of complications, as delineated below.

(i) Impact on Agriculture

It is argued that when NREGA pushes up the agricultural wage rate prevailing in the local economy, it will raise the cost of cultivation which, in turn, will further reduce the viability of agriculture that is already low in many areas. The farmers, who use hired labour on a large scale, are likely to incur losses in the process. This argument, however, is not all applicable universally. In many cases, agricultural workers, who form the poorest rung of the rural economy, are exploited because of their poor bargaining strength. Studies have clearly shown that inter-state variations in agricultural wage rates cannot be explained satisfactorily by labour productivity in agriculture alone and that the bargaining strength of workers is an important factor for explaining the variations. Again, it is to be noted that NREGA is only enforcing the legal minimum wages, that is, the wage rate that is due to workers. An increase in the local wage rate as a result of NREGA should, therefore, be seen as a positive development in many parts of the country. Again, there will be many regions wherein NREGA assets such as wells, farm ponds, de-silted dams and tanks, and other water harvesting structures, all with a short gestation period, are likely to increase the area under irrigation I the short run. This will, in turn, increase the area under irrigated crops, and promote multiple cropping and improved cropping as well as the increased use of agricultural productivity and labour productivity, both of which will enable farmers to pay higher wages to workers, that is, well-planned NREGA assets with a short gestation period will enable farmers to pay higher wages.

The argument, however, will be valid in the regions where NREGA works will not promote agricultural growth in the short run ad where low agricultural wages are largely due to very low productivity in agriculture. Such regions would be dry land farming areas, which have been badly degraded over the years due to poor investments and poor care by farmers. In such regions, however, workers do need higher wages and incomes. NREGA products can, therefore, be planned in such a way that the works are undertaken during the lean season, by developing a calendar for NREGA works as has been done in some parts of Andhra Pradesh. It must be kept in mind; however, the NREGA works are directed systematically towards raising productivity in agriculture so as to push up the wage rate gradually. Also, the guarantee of 100 days of work must be enforced strictly in such regions.

(ii) Danger of De-skilling of Artisans and Other Skilled Workers

It is quite possible for NREGA to attract skilled workers who are employed in skilled work but are earning low wages/incomes. NREGA can thus lead to de-skilling of workers employed in traditional crafts like weaving, embroidery and other handicrafts related to the traditional heritage of the country. NREGA can also attract workers from other areas of skilled employment in manufacturing, services and trade. This would mean a loss of skilled workers, who, as it is, are in short supply in the economy. The payment of minimum wage rates is also likely to attract those workers engaged in animal husbandry and dairying who earn low incomes. In short, the changes in the relative wage structure brought about through NREGA are likely to impact the allocation of workers across different activities, thereby creating the danger of de-skilling in the process. It is clear that one cannot prevent these skilled workers from entering NREGA, as they earn higher incomes in it. Under such situations, it is important to promote these skills and activities. One approach could be to identify such centre's/clusters where skilled artisans are located and to set up special projects for them to raise their productivity and earnings by organizing programmes for skill up-gradation and improving their access to credit, infrastructure and links with the market. Funds and technical support for designing and implementing such projects can come from other rural development programmes. In the case of other sectors like animal husbandry, it would be useful to plan NREGA works to support to activities by raising their productivity and earnings. For example, projects involving grassland development on common lands for animal husbandry, and rejuvenation of water bodies for fishery would augment the livelihoods of people and facilitate diversification of agriculture into animal husbandry, dairying, foresting sericulture, horticulture, etc. The above recommendations once again underscore the importance of preparing a sound perspective plan, and implementing sound planning techniques and systematic action plans under NREGA.

MGNREGA STRATEGIES

A useful strategy in this context would be that of promoting labour-intensive sectors in the economy so that the overall employment elasticity of growth improves. It is important to note that there are several strong links between NREGA and the full employment growth path in our economy. Firstly, NREGAS can strengthen the sectors in which the poor are predominantly located. These sectors are agriculture and allied activities like animal husbandry and dairying, forestry, fishery, sericulture, etc., which suffer from low productivity as well as uncertainty arising from fluctuating production and incomes. NREGS can be used in a way that it helps stabilize these sectors by reducing fluctuations and promotes their growth by raising labour productivity. Some of the activities in this context would be expansion in irrigation in small and big irrigation schemes, and construction of water harvesting structures including farm ponds as well as revival of traditional structures like ponds and tanks, land development forestation and grassland development, among other things. Secondly, the construction of socio-economic infrastructure under NREGA can also promote labour-intensive development. The absence of adequate socio-economic infrastructure is a major cause of low level of development in most rural areas. Implementation of measures such as the construction of these basic infrastructure facilities such as approach roads, that is, feeder roads and milk roads that improve connectivity; water harvesting for ensuring water supply; drainage, sanitation and arrangements for disposal of solid and liquid waste; internal roads including paving of internal roads; housing for the poor; and buildings for providing basic educational and health services can promote employment-intensive development. These facilities can promote crowding in of private investments, augment health and educational facilities to enhance labour productivity and enhance local infrastructural facilities to improve quality of life of people.

CONCLUSION

India has formulated and implemented a number of centrally sponsored schemes for rural development and protecting the welfare of the poor. But MGNREGA is unique in terms of its concept and implementation to enhance the livelihood security of the rural poor and thereby eradicating poverty. In fact, it integrates the government and the people under the rural development mission. This is the first scheme, a clear example of decentralized planning since independence in India, to empower the will society and local panchayat in addressing the welfare of the poor. The MGNREGS has served the purpose in providing employment to the rural poor families and enhanced their livelihood by supplementing additional family income

REFERENCE

1. Annual Report (2009-10.) " Scheduled Caste sub-plan and Tribal sup-plan" Ministry of Rural development government of india; chapter – 10,

2. www. NREGA.nic.in

3. RTBI – Indian Institute of Technology, Madurai; Evaluation of NREGA in Tamil Nadu; May-2009

4. The National Rural Employment Guarantee Act 2005; aperatinal guidelines; ministry of Rural development Dept. of Rural development Govt of India New Delhi.

8 SILENT LOSS - CRISIS OF HEALTH CARE: A BIRD'S EYE VIEW

B.Rohini, M.A., T. Augustus Julian Lazmey

Health is considered to be the right more over to conceive the wealth for every individual. Health is a major issue that dominates the life cycle of every individual. April 7th World Health Day aims to reduce the health problems by antimicrobial resistance which is witnessed as no action today, no cure tomorrow. According to World Health Organization, the health is not merely the absence of disease but health is considered to be the state of physical wellbeing, psychological wellbeing, social wellbeing and spiritual well being. Health determinants are more dangerous. Urgent and consolidated efforts are needed to avoid regressing to the pre-antibiotic era. Lack of research; no commitment; weak surveillance; poor drug quality; irrational drug use; no infection control are the six point policy package introduced by the World Health Organization to combat the spread of the anti microbial resistance. Anti microbial agents are medicines used to treat infections caused by micro organisms like bacteria, fungi, parasites and viruses. Antimicrobial resistance is facilitated by the inappropriate use of medicines, lack of government commitments to address these issues and poor surveillance for the control of drug resistance.

Public health is the science and art of preventing diseases, prolonging life and promoting health through the organized efforts of society, organizations, public and private communities and individuals. The health is evaluated by the epidemiology; biostatistics and health services on the basis of environment, behavioral, occupational and social fields which emancipate social distribution and social determinants that affect health. The health care deals with preventive aspect rather than curative aspect of health and deals with health issues on population level rather than individual level. Although health care has its roots in antiquity, it is considered to be a modern concept. From the beginning of human civilization, people attempted to regulate behaviors related to health. The focus of the public health intervention is to prevent disease rather than to treat a disease through surveillance of cases and the promotion of health behaviors. The government placed responsibility on leaders to develop policies and programs to gain some understanding on the causes of diseases and thus ensure social stability, prosperity and maintain order. Efforts on research focused on how the built environment and socioeconomic status affect health. Success of community health programs relay on the transfer of information from health professionals to the general public, using one- to-one or one-to-many communication. There is a vast discrepancy in access to health care. In the developing countries public health infrastructures are still forming. There is not enough trained health workers to provide even a basic level of medical care and disease prevention. A large majority of disease and mortality in the developing countries results from poverty and contributes to extreme poverty.

The health care systems are designed to meet the health care needs of the population. Health care planning is often to be evolutionary rather than revolutionary. In India, the hospitals are run by governments, charitable trusts and by private organizations. The government hospitals in rural areas are called the Primary Health Centre with preventive mode. Major hospitals are located in districts or major cities with increasing degrees of specialization and technical sophistication. Only the patients who require special attention either for diagnosis or treatment could reach the Secondary for advisory level or the Tertiary for specialized treatment, where the cost of service becomes increasingly higher. The medical cost at any level in the country is usually borne by the government. Health care at all levels should be available to all patients without any bias. Such a health care system is said to be universal. The Primary Health Centers are non existent in most places, due to poor pay and scarcity of resources. Due to delivery system failure 40% of the Sub Centers are not functioning. Patients generally prefer private health clinics. In these days some of the major corporate hospitals are attracting patients who are affordable by providing quality treatment to their satisfaction. Health has become a commodity which is accessible for the person who can afford it. Privatization has fragmented the health care sectors on the basis of profit rather than service oriented. The life expectancy 63.9 years for male and 66.9 years for female is much to be improved to the life expectancy of around 80 years in industrialized countries and 72 years in China. The sex ratio with only 940 women for 1000 men makes an adverse impact in the society. Register General of India and Census Commissioner C.Chandramauli said that child sex ratio (0-6) in 2001 was 927 females per 1000 males born, which declined to 914 females per 1000 males. The child sex ratio at India level 914 is the lowest since Independence. 55% of the Indian children under the age of two do not receive routine nutrition. India has the highest number of children dying under the age of five due to diarrhea-cough-cold. The non governmental organization Save Children says that among 25 developing countries, India has the highest number of children who do not receive even the most basic of health care service. The area where there is no treatment facility available for the identified disease is known as Health Care Dessert. About 1.2 million children under the age of one die every year in India of largely treatable and even preventable disease. In closer views some parts of Delhi are identified as Health Care Dessert because part of people is not exposed to medical treatment. The lack of awareness and affordability is the root cause for nil health care availability among the people.

The major health challenges of the 21st century are, control of preventive disease; food security-leads to malnutrition; no proper healthy policy that suits and reach the real need; poverty-which leads to out of pocket expenses to maintain health which results in indebtedness; shortage of PHC-low investment in Heath Expenditure which leads to low technology and low care; corruption in implementing programs; health inequalities due to different layers of marginalization; mobility to health care centre become a major factor in rural areas. Proper care is upset due to lack of transport which leads to early death. This determines that the health is a social factor and not a biological factor alone. India pledged along with World Health Organization member nations, HEALTH FOR ALL by 2000 at Alma Ata in 1978 and in the same year signed the International Covenant for Economic; Social and Cultural Rights, in which the state is obliged to achieve the highest attainable standard of health. However the health scenario in India is abysmal. Government aided schemes and programs are run by the Central Government for the health and welfare of the citizens. The people of the country are one of its most valuable resources. The programs are aimed at increasing the standard of health of the people and decreasing the incidence of disease and death due to illness. According to the Indian Constitution, the subject of 'Health' comes under the purview of State Governments. This means that the State Governments are responsible for maintaining and bettering the health of the people who lives under its jurisdiction. The Ministry of Health and Family Welfare comprises the Department of Health and Family Welfare; the Department of AYUSH; the Department of Health Research; the Department of AIDS Control. The various schemes and policies are launched by the government on the basis of health for the benefit of the citizens of India. In spite of all discrepancy government launched and initiated various health related programs to uplift the health scenario of every individual with public concern.

The government of state and central is a public sector and it plans, evaluates and implements the vivid program to uplift the life stages of its valuable human resources mainly considering the marginalized and the vulnerable section of the society. The schemes are entangled in half pathway due to scanty resource person in implementing and the rattling corruption in service sectors. This emancipates a wider gap between the providers and the receivers. This can be effectively bridged out by sensitizing the issues to the masses with the support of the civil society to empower every individual to recognize their responsibilities and bring a change in their attitude and perception to come out of their hidden zones to cherish with the welfare activities. If the people are restrained by any determinants from being a beneficiary then they have to demand their needs with more care and concern in an assertive way as the Health is a Right to be demanded rather than a wealth or a commodity to be purchased. The decline in the investment and expenditure in the health sector and the user fees for public health services adversely affected the poor and the vulnerable society. The time has come to reclaim public health and a make a paradigm shift to enlighten the health scenario as a right based issues to be demanded.

REFERENCES

file:///C:/Documents%20and%20Settings/BALAJI/My%20Documents/World%20Health%20Day%202011%20-%20Health%20%20National%20Portal%20of%20India.htm

http://articles.economictimes.indiatimes.com/2011-03-31 news/29365989_1_ratio-males-girl-child

http://censusindia.gov.in/Census_Data_2001/India_at_glance/fsex.aspx

http://india.gov.in/day/world_health_day/health_day.phpfile:///C:/Documents%20and%20Settings/BALAJI/My%20Documents/Downloads/Emergency%20Care%20in%20India%20%20Long%20Way%20to%20Go%20-%20Express%20Healthcare.htm

ISSUES IN INCLUSIVENESS IN CONTEMPORARY SOCIETY

9 CHALLENGES FACED BY A CONTEMPORARY SOCIETY: THE ROLE OF NGOS IN ENCOUNTERING THE ISSUES

Emmanuel. Rev.Dr.Arul ArasuIsrael

INTRODUCTION

This paper attempts to enumeratethe issues and challenges faced by the contemporary Indian society and the role of NGO's with these issues. The first part provides a brief bird's eye view of the issues present in the contemporary society. Secondly, this paper deals with the role of NGO's in resolving this crisis. Finally an attempt is made to suggest measures to strengthen NGO's after identifying the problems faced by the NGO's. The day by day rise of non-profit organizations as well as non-governmental organizations in the contemporary society has been mentioned by a number of observers (Example: Schneider-1988; Salamon-1993). These organizations seem to play a main role in every segment of political, economic and social development activities. This in turn has given ample opportunity for these organizations to make their presence felt in the contemporary society as they have a greater scope for contributing to the sustainable growth of the society.

ISSUES IN A CONTEMPORARY SOCIETY

India has been listed under the category of developing countries by the United Nations Organization. Even though India attained its independence almost six decades ago, it has been striving hard to attain heights through spreading awareness, providing education to all, taking strides in scientific innovations, evolving new ideologies in technologies, excelling in sports and so on. The life expectancy of the Indian people has increased to a larger extent due to the focus of the medical sciences in eradicating a number of diseases and in controlling epidemics.Despite these developments, still the Indian Society suffers from a number of social problems that stunt its growth and keep it listed under `developing countries'. As a result, since every issue is a cog in the machine disturbing it's functioning, it has become a dire necessity to enumerate the various issues and explore avenues to gradually free the Indian Society of these issues.

POVERTY

Half of the world, that is, nearly three billion people lives with less than two dollars a day. According to the United Nations Development Program (2010) data, 37.2% of people living in India are under the poverty line. Although the Indian economy is developing, it has notbeen consistent in addressing this issue sufficiency with a view to eradicating it. A recent report by the Oxford Poverty and Human Initiative states that eight states in India are poorer than twenty six African Nations. Many studies have shown or proved that the children from the backward area or poverty affected area are lagging behind compared to the other enriched or developed areas. So the performance level in most of the areas is found to be below the expectancy level.

GENDER DISCRIMINATION

Both men and women are equally important for the development and well-beingof individual man, the family the microcosm as well as the society, the macrocosm. Women in the society play a very important role of a mother, sister and wife in the life of man. However in many cases in the contemporary society, the situation is not favorable to women. Women are treated as the fairer sex, but also the weaker sex by the society. In India most of the women are dependent upon their father or husband. Due to this, the men folk take undue advantage of it and they succumb as victims to this exploitation. Even though women sacrifice most of their ambitions and interest for the sake of the wellbeing of the family, they are not given due recognition within the family and the society. This is ridiculous considering the self sacrifice of the members of this gender.

CORRUPTION

Corruption is nothing but a payment for services (either through goods or cash) for which the recipient is in no way eligible and has no right at all under law. The same is called as bribery or kickback in colloquial terms. Corruption is more prevalent among the government officials working in the District Collectorates, police authorities, judicial sector and also politicians. Due to this there is lack of insistence in standards and quality in Government projects like construction work, etc. The substandard work is always a threat to everyone within the society. There are mainly two forms of corruption in the developing world. They are honest corruption and dishonest corruption. In honest corruption, the bribe receiver will give back the bribe if the work could not be completed. In dishonest corruption, the bribe once taken is taken. It will not be given back. Honest corruption is mostly found in countries like Thailand. Dishonest corruption takes place in countries like India.

ILLITERACY

Illiteracy is emerging as the biggest problem in the contemporary society. People do not have the awareness that their opportunities have been denied by the creamy layer of society. Reading,writing and arithmetic skills are very important for an individual if he or she wants to have an upswing in life. It has become very imperative that one strives very hard and takes all efforts to become literate. There is a saying that "You can only take a horse to the river, but you cannot make it drink". In tune with this, it is the basic duty of the society to uphold every person his or her right to literacy and extend it accordingly. But it is in the hands of the recipients whether they grab the opportunity or not. Even though the government tries to give free education to the children, many families force their children to go for work in their childhood itself in order to supplement the income of to a very less income of the family.

GLOBAL WARMING

Global warming is another main issue which is of great concern as a result of air pollution. Many researchers including scientists agree that the temperature of the planet is going up. The main cause of the global warming is due to the emissions of Carbon-di-oxide and methane gas into the atmosphere. These substances emanate high density of heat as they evolve around the atmosphereincreasing global temperature. Global warming is the major hazard causing damages to the ozone layer. Due to its disaster many species are gradually becoming extinct today. As the temperature increases, the water level in the planet also increases due to the melting of ice in the artic and the Antarctic regions. This rise in the water level reduces the land mass slowly submerging it.

WAR

War is a prolonged conflict that is well planned and organized that is carried out between two or more countries. A war fought between countries is full of aggression, social disruption, etc. In the contemporary society usually a war is fought with weapons which bring in irrevocable damage to life and properties. When a war is been fought between countries, it brings collapse of the economy as large quantity of money is spent on warfare. Again it involves loss of human lives resulting in dislocation of families in particular and societies at large. As a result of social, economic as well as cultural damage, the outcome would be that of chaos and crisis. Winning or losing is only a secondary, were as losing lives, property, wealth, peace, economical break down of a country has to be taken into consideration before entering into a war.There is a quote which says "If the third world war is been fought, then the fourth world war will be fought in stones and sticks"

ROLE OF NGOS

Alleviating poverty

Although the poor yearn for their right and dream of a life devoid of poverty, they are left helpless as it is something beyond their reach. There are many factors within the social strata that suppress them by way of marginalization forcing them to succumb to their prevailing condition of poverty. They are victims of environmental degradation, diseases due to unhygienic conditions, climatic stress, etc. In theendeavor to uplift to poor, it has become essential for the NGO's to intervene and play a vital role in creating awareness among the masses. Only through this awareness it is possible to as the saying goes `not to offer food, but to teach a person to fish'. The marginalized should come forward willing to oppose any violation to their rights. Only then the efforts by the NGO's would be fruitful. At this juncture, the NGOs play a vital role, in giving a helping hand to those living under the poverty line. The NGOs provide many social and economic services to the needy were the governments fail to do so. Micro financing comes under the economical service provided by the NGOs.. The NGOs also help the poverty affected people by tapping out the government resources which are available to them wherever possible.

Empowering women

There is a saying "educate a man, you empower an individual, were as you educate a woman you empower a family". Since women's empowerment is a key factor for many socio economic in this contemporary society, the NGOs give more importance in bringing in more innovative ideas to empower the women folk. Such schemes include providing education, forming self-help groups, micro finance, vocational training, etc. The NGOs also teach the poor women how to save money and spend at times of unemployment. They also help the women who possess skills in getting a job according to their strengths by also not stressing them a lot. It is not that easy to establish rapport with the women folk in the rural or backward areas. So the NGOs take necessary steps in order to encounter them and to the needful help.

Corruption eradication

The NGOs in the contemporary society create awareness among the public in regards to the corruption as it damages the economy of the society to a greater extent. The NGO being a single institution cannot fight against corruption in the society. But the NGOs can spread awareness to the public and make them participate in the social action campaigns. The NGOs have the ability to make the individuals think, arise and fight for the rights (especially in regards to corruption). As the corruption is an evil in contemporary societies like India, the individuals are triggered of stimulated in a larger scale to tackle the issue. But still the NGOs, groups and individuals are not able to pass a bill against corruption against in the Indian parliament. The politicians will be very careful in eating the people's money as many are been caught by the government officials. To an extent the abolition of corruption has taken its swing but then not fully.

Providing education

The main purpose of social work is to empower people so that they themselves can live on their own. So the NGOs provide education in various settings. They are formal, non-formal and informal education. Formal education is a well-organized model with a well-structured curriculum given by the association of the educational institutions which are affiliated with the government organizations. In non-formal education system, the pattern is almost the same like the previous one, but the eye to eye contact between the teacher and the student will be very less. It is something said to be like distance education pattern. In informal education the main goal is to enrich the knowledge, but it does not follow any curriculum. Here no degree or diploma is given. This type of education does not expect any requirements but helps to develop the skills and be self-sufficient in getting on to a job.

Awareness for global warming

There is a tremendous growth of NGOs working for creating awareness in the contemporary society. Many scholars agree that the NGOs make more differences in the environmental issues. Some Non-GovernmentalOrganizations work for creating awareness and some NGOs for activism. Usually NGOs working for the environmental issues spread awareness on planting trees, stop using plastics, proper disposal of wastes, disposals, etc. Only few organizations in the modern society raise their voices against the government and people by conducting rallies, etc. Even in facing this tough issue the NGOs require the community participation and involvement in full phase.

PROBLEMS FACED BY THE NGOS IN THE CONTEMPORARY SOCIETY

Internal problems faced by the NGOs:

Lack of commitment from staff

Without a commitment and the thirst to serve the needy, a social worker cannot survive in NGOs as he needs to humble himself before the community and serve the mankind. In this 21st century the motive of the individuals is to earn money and settle in life. Most of the people do not even have time to think about the people who are dying without the lack of services. People of this generation don't even what to see the people who are in hunger and cry. So a social worker with a humbleness, commitment, thirst, dedication to serve the needy are in a very few number.

Lack of Training facilities

As many NGOs do not have large budgets, they will be concentrating more on the development activities in their target area. For a social worker the theoretical knowledge is alone not enough to serve the community. He also needs a very good exposure and a practical knowledge. This can be given only by means of training the individual. As social work profession is not been paid like other profession, (doctors, engineers, lawyers) well motivated quality workers are not interested to come for this profession. Only training gives more ideology in regards to deal with the community. As there are lacks of funds in many NGOs in a contemporary society, training is not given more importance. So quality work is missing among many NGOs.

Misappropriation of funds

In some NGOs the workers are been paid with a less salary which is not sufficient for them to run their family. As their family is in a tough situation, some tend to misappropriate the funds which are yet to be spent for needy. When a worker with a stone heart works only for the sake of his family members and not for the needy, there arises problem inside the organization and everything collapses. The money which is yet to be spent for the community when it goes into some employee's pocket, automatically there is a downfall in the development to the community.

EXTERNAL PROBLEM FACED BY THE NGOS:

Fund raising

Fund raising or marketing are considered to be more stressful work in regards to the NGOs. As some NGOs are not fulfilling their visions and missions, the donors are not interested to contribute their valuable donations to help the needy. And also people think that the donations are been spent more on the administrative section, they are not interested to contribute. The economic crisis or the inflation rate has got an upswing, and many individuals have lost their job because of the effect. So in this contemporary society people hesitate to donate to the NGOs. So whatever strategy the social workers follow in regards to fund rising, it goes vain.

Community Participation

In a contemporary society urbanization and modernization plays a vital role in it. As there is a positive change seen in the society, also a negative change within the individuals occurs. When people lived in the rural areas, they were very close and attached. But now after coming to the cities people fail to have a rapport within their neighborhood. In result of it the individuals do not even talk properly out of their family and the family set up which was prevailing in the rural areas has perished. And also people started thinking people who are involved in service will take care of the needs of the needy. So their participation is very less. Some community people involve in service for their religious aspect, some for the name and fame. Now days they don't even care about it. So the NGOs here find it difficult to organize people for the useful work in the community.

Lack of Trust

Trust is a very important which bridges the community and the NGOs who are working for them. Even in a contemporary society there is a lack of trust. In an initial phase the community people see the NGOs as a religion spreading institutions. And when they get their funds from overseas they confirm it. Sometimes the community people get into miss -guidance from other people. Even if the NGOs do a wonderful work in the community, the people are not interested to get their service and mingle with them. So the NGOs in long run get fed up with the people and close down their projects and move on to an another area. Even to establish rapport and build trust it takes long time for the organizations.

CONCLUSION

In a contemporary society the role of NGOs is tremendous and they are known for their services provided to the needy sections of society. To meet the issues in the contemporary society, a demand is placed on the NGOs to increase their capacity so as to meet the challenges internally and externally. This paper talks about the issues prevailing in a contemporary society and the role of NGOs in tackling those issues.In today's fast moving world, people in the society always look forward to a sudden change. It is not possible because it is a slow process. Better understanding of the roles and the problems faced by the NGOs or support organizations will give way to effective intervention for the betterment of the contemporary society. If the NGOs continue striving for the development of the contemporary society, then one need not have even an iota of doubt that this community that has benefitted will stand by these NGO's in future. This ensures sustainable development in the contemporary society.

REFERANCES:

- Dudley Poston.L. Jr. and Leon Bouvier.F (2010), Population and Society: An Introduction to Demography, Cambridge University Press, New York, U.S.A.
- PartapAgarwal.C(1917), Caste, Religion and Power: An Indian Case Study, Veda Vrata the RaisinaPrintery, New Delhi, India.
- Tandon R.K. (1998) Status of Women in Contemporary World, Commonwealth Publishers, New Delhi, India.
- Peter Roland deSowya (2000), Contemporary India-Transitions, Sage publications, New Delhi, India.
- Devasia.V.V, Ajith Kumar (2009), Social Work Concerns and Challenges in the 21st century, A.P.H.Publishing Corporation, New Delhi , India.
- Ruth Moore (1975), Man in the environment, Tata McGraw-Hill Publishing Company Ltd., New Delhi, India.
- SeemanthiniNiranjana, (2001) Gender and Space, Sage Publications India Pvt. Ltd., New Delhi, India.
- DevidasMulley.M. (1987), Rural Development-Administration, Problems and Prospects, Chugh Publications, Allahabad, India.
- Dr.Agnihotri.V.K. (2002), Socio-Economic Profile of Rural India, Concept Publication Company, New Delhi, India.
- Dr. VivekRajan Bhattacharya (1971), Challenge of Village India, Metropolitan Book Co. Pvt. Ltd., New Delhi, India.
- Bhatnagar. C.P. (1971), The Crisis of Indian Society, National Publishing House, New Delhi, India.

- Webliography
- http://www.turkishweekly.net/article/159/organizational-problems-of-non-governmental-organizations-ngos-.html
- http://www.egyankosh.ac.in bitstream/123456789/36324/1/Unit-10.pdf
- http://www.socialsciences-ejournal.org/5.9.%20K.%20Prabhakar.pdf
- http://en.wikipedia.org/wiki/Non-governmental_organization
- http://en.wikipedia.org/wiki/Poverty_in_India
- http://www.nios.ac.in/secpsycour/unit-19.pdf40

10 SOCIAL ENTREPRENEURSHIP AND INCLUSIVE GROWTH

A. IrudayaVeni Mary, Dr. M. Victor Louis Anthuvan,

Social entrepreneurship is a fast growing field that plays an important role in the wellbeing of the poor, vulnerable and marginalized people. Social entrepreneurship is a venture that has been set up to find innovative solutions to social and economic problems prevailing in the society. This venture can be either profit or non-profit seeking. One could find social entrepreneurs in the field of children welfare, women empowerment, rural development, educational development, health care, agricultural development, environment protection etc., and Social entrepreneurship can bring an egalitarian society. Social entrepreneurs are one genus of entrepreneurs who are passionate and concern towards their society's wellbeing. Their focus is not on the profit but on social and economic upliftment of the marginalized.The purpose of this paper is to highlight, how social entrepreneurship is one of the strategies through which inclusive growth can be achieved.

INTRODUCTION

Inclusive growth is one of the most required criteria to reduce India's major social and economic problems and build an egalitarian society. One of the major problems faced by the Indians is poverty. Tendulkar committee reported that the number of poor in India was 27.5% in the year 2004-05.Changing the method of calculating poverty the committee submitted the revised report in the year 2009 in which it was said that there were37.2% of the people living below poverty line. But ArjunSengupta, the head of National Commission for Enterprise in the Unorganised Sector reportedin the year 2007 that 77% of the Indians lived on less than 20 a day.

THE CAUSES OF POVERTY

The causes of poverty were categorized as social causes, economic causes, political causes, disturbances by nature and physical causes. The economic causes include unemployment, underemployment, slow growth in agriculture, etc.,The opening of our market to foreign countries and much importance given to heavy industries also lead tothe disappearance of small scale and cottage industries in many places. This has forced the rural youth to migrateto urban areas. Indians spend a lot for religious rituals and ceremonies. They even go to the extent of borrowing money for interest and finally end up in indebtedness. Indeed, this indebtedness made them lose their assets and land.Disturbances caused by nature are flood, cyclone, epidemic, drought, earthquake, tsunami etc.,The natural causes reduce the income of the people. In fact many a time people had lost their assets and suffered. Unavoidably the physical causes also lead to poverty. The physical causes are sudden death of an earning member in the family, affected by major disease and illness, etc. Illiteracy is alsoone of the major factors those cause poverty.

Major steps taken by the Government of India to reduce poverty

The Government of India has taken various steps to eradicate poverty through poverty alleviation programmes in the five year plans. In the first five year plan, an important evolution that is the land reform policy led to the abolition of intermediary institutions and systems of Zamindari, which were highly exploitative. In the second five year plan, the industrial policy resolution, paved way for industrial development which raised the employment opportunity and income. Before planning for the fifth five year plan, an empirical study proved that the poverty was very severe among the wage labourers, Scheduled castes and Scheduled tribes, and among the people living in the backward regions. This situation stimulated the policy makers to introduce development strategies those address the problems of the disadvantaged people in the fifth five year plan. Three main approaches such as creating income-generation asset base for the rural poor, generating wage employment opportunity and area development programmes. Also, industrial development programmes such as Rural Industrialization Programme (RIP) and Rural Artisans Programme (RAP) were introduced to provide employment opportunity on a large scale. Since these programmes reduced poverty rate, these strategies were continued in the sixth and seventh five year plans also. Nearly 20 percent of poverty rate has been reduced during these three plans. In the eighth plan, it was observed that not only economic deprivation causes poverty but also the other causes like lack of freedom to choose, state of health, education and demographic characteristics. Because of these reasons, strategies were introduced to ensure development with social justice. The primary focus was on ensuring health care, education and a special plan for SC and ST people. Large numbers of programmes were introduced for the disadvantaged people such as women, children, aged, disabled and Scheduled caste and Scheduled tribes people. In the tenth plan, the states allocated huge resources to ensure people's participation in the implementation process of poverty alleviation programmes, used food stocks to run food for work and schemes for drought affected states and serve cooked mid-day meals for primary school children. During the tenth five year plan, National rural employment act was introduced to eradicate rural poverty. (KaushikRanjanBandyopadhyay,2007). As an evidence, for the achievement made by these five year plans; in the year 1973/74 the poverty rate was 54.9%, in 1977/78 the poverty rate was reduced to 51.3%, and in 1983 it was further reduced to 44.5%. Nearly 6 percent of poverty rate was reduced in the year 1987/88, another 3 percent was reduced in 1993/94. Ten percent of the poverty rate was reduced in the year 99/2000.(James W. Fox 2002).

Although India has reduced the poverty rate but still it has a long way to go.India is the second fastest growing country (according to ranking list given by International Monetary Fund in the year 2011).It is crucial at this moment for India to focus on sustainable development and bring an egalitarian society by reducing the gap between haves and have-nots.But if one sees the rank given by Human Development Index in the year 2011, India is in the 134th position among the 187 countries.This ranking is based on the measurement of life expectancy, literacy and standards of living. Although India is growing very fast, the human development index ranking and percentage of the people live below poverty line clearly indicate that the growth is not equally enjoyed by all citizens. With this in mind, the planning commission adopted inclusive growth asstrategy in the 11th year plan (2007-2012). Further, the government can involve privatization strategy to some level to bring down the poverty rate. One strategy can be involving social entrepreneurs. Thesocial entrepreneurs are one genus of entrepreneurs who are skilled in blending the social and economic objectives. There are two types of social entrepreneurs - the non-profit social entrepreneursand for-profit social entrepreneurs. The non-profit social entrepreneurs combine social objective of solving a problem by using the entrepreneurial skills. They depend on funds and grants from other donors and through their income generation activity at micro level to meet and sustain their mission.Thefor-profit social entrepreneurs combine the social objectives and their business objectives. They fully depend on the income derived from their business to meet and sustain their social mission. On the whole, the work of these social entrepreneurs aim towards inclusive growth at the micro level by solving the social problems they come across. However, the models adopted by the social entrepreneurs are replicable.

INCLUSIVE GROWTH

Focusing on inclusive growth in the country will enable India to achieve sustainable development and an egalitarian society. According to SubirGokarn (2007), the inclusive growth includes four attributes. They are - opportunity, capability, access and security. Opportunity would mean that the economy must enable the people to generate more income, provide varied ways to earn their living and increase their income over a time. Capability relates to education and skill creation by which the economy can provide the means for people to create and enhance their capabilities to make use of the existing resources. Access is the ability to bring the opportunity and capability together. The economy must make sure that the citizens get easily access to opportunity and capability.Security is ensured when the economy provides the resource for the people to protect themselves from temporary or permanent loss of livelihood. Terry McKinley(2010) identified two dimensions of inclusive growth.They are

1. Achieving sustainable growth that will create and expand economic opportunities and
2. Ensuring broader access to theseopportunities so that members of society can participate in growth.

He further says that inclusive growth can be interpreted both narrowly and broadly. In the narrow aspect, "inclusive growth implies a focus on economic growth, within which expanding human capabilities is regarded as instrumental to improve economic outcomes. For the broader aspect he quoted the sayings of Rauniyar and Kanbur(2010), that inclusive growth empathizes the non-income measures of well-being and valuing human capabilities, such as good health and literacy, primarily as human development outcomes. Overall, apart fromeconomic growth, the inclusive growth ensures social justice and equality among people.

SOCIAL ENTREPRENEURSHIP

The social entrepreneurs are the citizens who are concerned with the wellbeing and betterment of the poor and the marginalized people. The social entrepreneurs are the people driven by passion and genuine concern towards the betterment of the society. The social entrepreneurs are people who come up with innovative ideas to bring a solution for a social problem. They work with perseverance until they achieve their mission. Various authors have defined social entrepreneurship and social entrepreneurs in different words. A few are given below:

According to David Bornstein and Susan Davis (2010) "Social entrepreneurship is a process by which citizens build or transform institutions to advance solutions to social problems, such as poverty, illness, illiteracy, environmental destruction, human rights abuses and corruption, in order to make life better of many."Leadbetter(1997), defines "social entrepreneurship is the use of entrepreneurial behavior for social ends rather than for profits objectives, or alternatively, that the profits generated from market activities are used for the benefit of a specific disadvantaged group." Bill Drayton the founder of Ashoka Foundation which encourages and supports social entrepreneurs both financially and intellectually defines social entrepreneurs as, "Social entrepreneurs are individuals with innovative solutions to society's most pressing social problems. They are ambitious and persistent, tackling major social issues and offering new ideas for wide-scale change. Rather than leaving societal needs to the government or business sectors, social entrepreneurs find what is not working and solve the problem by changing the system, spreading the solution, and persuading entire societies to take new leaps. Social entrepreneurs often seem to be possessed by their ideas, committing their lives to changing the direction of their field. They are both visionaries and ultimate realists, concerned with the practical implementation of their vision above all else".

The authors HeikoSpitzeck and Frank Janssen, (2010) say that the social entrepreneurs develop products and services addressing the social needs and discover new sources of profitability. The social entrepreneurs do not only adapt to a given environment – they envision and create it. The definition itself tells the importance of social entrepreneurs for social development. There are three key elements in which the social entrepreneurs are committed to it; they are people, profit and planet. The social entrepreneurs always put others needs at the top of their mission. They aim towards a sustainable change in the society. Social entrepreneurs are the people, who bring sustainable change, invest and earn money for others and through which they strengthen the weak. The social entrepreneurs show intangible outcomes to funders as well as to their commercial activity (Robert Ashton 2010).

ROLE OF SOCIAL ENTREPRENEURSHIP IN INCLUSIVE GROWTH

Social entrepreneurs are one of the contributors for inclusive growth at the micro level. Social entrepreneurs are the people who identify social problem through proper investigation, experiment by continuous innovation to bring an apt solution to the problem. The social entrepreneurs serve the society in two different methods. According to Boschee (1995), there are two types of social purposes enterprises. They are Affirmative Business and Direct-service Business. The affirmative business focuses on creating economic wealth and jobs for the people who are physically, mentally challenged, economically, and educationally deprived people who are found on the margins of the society. The social enterprises act as change agents who bring these marginalized people into the main stream of economy. The direct-service businesses bring development through community based trainings and care. The community based training are like vocational training, life skills and job training. The care services are like child/adult care, training for the disabled, garden and home maintenance (Sherri Leronda Wallace, 1999).

NON-PROFIT SOCIAL ENTREPRENEURS

One could find social entrepreneurs in the fields of education, community development, women and child welfare, health, environment protection, caring the differently abled, rural electrification, microfinance, income generation activity, information and Technology, etc.,around the world. Let us see a few examples of Indian social entrepreneur both in the perspective of non-profit and for-profit social entrepreneurs. First, let us learnthe various contributions of non-profit social entrepreneurs for the social development which may lead to inclusive growth in India at the micro level.JerooBillimoria, who had innovated and founded childline-1098, to help the children in distress caused by the situations like injuries, abuse, abandonment, assault, suffering in major illnesses etc.. JavedAbidi, is the social entrepreneur who fights for safeguarding the rights of the differently abled person. He is the director of National Centre for the promotion of employment for the disabled People (NCPED) in Delhi, and the founder of disability Rights Group. He trains the differently abled persons to campaign and advocate for their rights.He played a very significant role in policy changes those benefit the differently abled people. His major achievements are,he influenced the Government to bring 3% reservation for the differently abled people in Civil Services, played an important role in bringing inclusive education policy for children and youth with disabilities, policy to ensure disabled friendly atmosphere in the educational systems by the year 2020. Also, he played a major role for including the differently abled people in the 2001 census andhe drafted the chapter on disability which has been reproduced in the XIth Five Year Plan (2007 – 2012), etc.,

Another social entrepreneur, Anshu Gupta, founded Goonj in 1998. Goonj is the organisation which recycles the urban waste for the rural poor and for the people who were affected by disaster. They recycle the waste cloth and make new products out of it. The products are balls, different bags and purses, sanitary napkins etc.They also make mats out of audio tape films. They make note books, art books and Braille papers for the visually impaired personsfrom one sided used chart papers.These recycled products can be sold by which they create huge employment for the people. If the clothes collected, are in good condition and usable, they wash it, iron it and give it neatly to the people who were affected in disaster. RangaswamyElango, is a scientist worked at the Council for Scientific Industrial Research. When Elango visited his village named Kuthambakkam, he found the hardships of poverty, caste riots, illiteracy and illicit arrack trade. After being exposed to these he left his job in 1994 and contested independently in the panchayat election in 1996 and won in the election. As panchayat president he created his village Kuthambakkam as a model village. He eradicated the illicit arrack trade by providing an alternative job opportunity for the men who were involved in illicit arrack trade. He rehabilitated 200 families affected by illicit arrack trade by providing them employment in constructing infrastructures such as houses, drains and roads. He converted 216 huts in to low-cost compressed mud-block housing with the combination of Government fund and collaborative work of the villagers. He improved the infrastructure of the village by constructing roads and putting street lights. He facilitated the village with rain water harvesting system and water supply. He formed Self-help groups. He increased the literacy level by improving the infrastructures in the schools. Now the village has an Indira Gandhi Open University (IGNOU). He had setup small scale rural industries to provide permanent employment. He had set up an information center and computer education centerin collaboration with TNF (USA). He continues to innovate more and more facilities to further develop the village.

FOR-PROFIT SOCIAL ENTREPRENEURS

Now let us see the contribution offew social entrepreneurs involved in for-profit social entrepreneurshipwith special reference to reducing rural povertyand provision of decent employment opportunity based on the people's capability. DesiCrew Solutions is the Rural BPO which aims to promote inclusive growth in India. This BPO is founded by Saloni Malhotra in the year 2007. DesiCrew BPO in Tamil Nadu, is situated in the village called Kollumangudi in Mayavaram and also another BPO in Karnataka. DesiCrewrecruits staffs whohave passed twelfth standard, graduation in art and engineering andin Diploma.It trains and orients the recruited personsin soft skills, english, email etiquettes, corporate culture and shift time with a stipend.Once the people are employed, they are paid Rs. 4900/- at the entry level together with employee benefit schemes such as Savings, ESI, PF, Medical allowances and maternity benefits. Every six months there is an appraisal in the company.Based on their performance there will be an increment in the salary. The higher the experience the higher will be the salary. The social impact of the DesiCrew solutions on the rural areais explained here.

- It has provided employment opportunity for rural people especially for women. Overall, DesiCrew has given employmentfor 310 people out of them 200 are women, which comprises 75 percent.
- It has prevented the underemployment of rural educated people.
- It has stopped migration of rural youth to cities in search of employment. The confidence level of women has been increased as they are able to support their family financially. Since the young girls come for work, their age at marriage had gone up. The employed youth are able to support their younger siblings.
- The untapped potential of women has been utilized efficiently. Apart from the company, the very existence of the BPO had motivated other small business around the company.

ROPE is a social entrepreneurship organisation, which involves in the manufacturing of house hold articles using ecofriendly materials. They recruit skilled artisans; through them they provide training for the unskilled people and then employ them. ROPE has given employment opportunity for more than thousand people, among them a majority that is 60% of them are unskilled workers who were trained and given employment. This organisation also provides employee benefit schemes such as PF, ESI, Medical allowance and Maternity benefit. Due to the inadequate transport problems, ROPE functions at the village level. It covers thirty villages in four districts.

LEARNINGS FROM THE CASE STUDIES

Overall, if one analyzes the contributions of social entrepreneurs for the development of the poor, vulnerable and marginalized people, both in other countries and in India are tremendous. The work ofsocial entrepreneurs has brought millions of poor to the main stream of economy through micro credit and self-help group strategy anddeveloped agricultural production.On the whole, the social entrepreneurs play an important role in policy change, empower and enable the poor and the needy. If one actually analyse the performance of thesocial entrepreneurs with the perspective of inclusive growth,it matches with the indicators of inclusive growth. The social entrepreneurship organisations have provided employment opportunity for the people at their door steps to earn a decent income for which they train them to develop their capability to do the job. With regard to access, the organisations have provided job opportunities in the village itself. As far as the security part is concerned, the employees are given job security for the presentand are provided employee benefit schemes for the future. We could find many more social entrepreneurs both in the sector ofnon-profit and for-profit social entrepreneurship. These types of entrepreneurs enable the citizens to come out of their poverty by providing them decent employment, to live in a better society through their community development programmes, welfare programmes, advocacy to bring a policy change.

SUGGESTIONS AND CONCLUSION

One may think that the social entrepreneurs work at the micro level that is just one small part of the country, how can they bring inclusive growth in the country? There are two possibilities; the first one is, the social entrepreneurs are spread all over the country. When all of their work put together they have uplifted millions of people. They have brought justice and have brought the poor and the needy to the equal position to that of others. This they have achieved through their advocacy and lobbying work to safeguard the rights of marginalized and vulnerable, by creating awareness among them about their rights to life, healthetc.., bringing them together to campaign to secure their rights, to earn their livelihood through self-help groups, creating an opportunity to earn their livelihood through income generation programmes. Secondly, the social entrepreneurs' models are already tested. Therefore, it can be applied in all over the country by the government with the collaboration and guidance of the social entrepreneurs. This will ensure justice and equality. As these social entrepreneurs work persistently towards social change through effective use of their innovative idea and entrepreneurial skill for the betterment of the society, it is important to include them in the policy planning. It was proved by Evelyne de Leeuw (1999) that social entrepreneurs play key role for policy change. Social entrepreneurs are the people who possess the quality of listening and observing the real needs of the real people. Since these social entrepreneurs have already adopted an innovative model, implemented the model and achieved success in the upliftment of the societythey are the right people at the time of policy planning.

It is government's duty to nurture more and more social entrepreneurs by making the registration procedure easier, providing income tax exemption to an extent for the for-profit social entrepreneurs. When the non-profit social entrepreneur's campaign for the cause of social development the government should listen and grant government schemesavailable easily. Most importantly, the agricultural sector in India has been weakened over the years. In 1950 the contribution of agricultural sector to the GDP was 52.2 percent (RenukaMahadevan 2003) but in year 2008 contribution is drastically being decreased to 17.2 percent (Business Maps of India2012). In such situation, the government should identify people with innovative ideas in the agricultural sector, train them with the entrepreneurial skill and encourage and motivate them to venture into social entrepreneurship. To conclude, planningand working collaboratively with social entrepreneurs and nurturing more social entrepreneurs in various fields may be one of the strategies that can be adopted by the government to achieve inclusive growth in India.

REFERENCE:

Books:

David Bornstein (2005). How to Change the World – Social Entrepreneurs amd the Power of New Ideas.Penguin Books of India, New Delhi, Panchseel Park.

David Bornstein and Susan Davis (2010). Social entrepreneurship: what everyone needs to know.OXFORD University Press, USA.

K B S Kumar (2007).Social Entrepreneur - The change maker.The Icfai University Press, Hyderabad, India.

Robert Ashton (2010). How to be a Social Entrepreneur Make Money & Change the World.Capstone Publishing Ltd. (A Wiley Company), West Sussex,

United Kingdom.Email.Id. robert@robertashton.co.uk/ e-newsletters @ www.robertashton.co.uk.

WEBSITES:

Business Maps of India (2012).India GDP Composition Sector Wise.From http://business.mapsofindia.com/india-gdp/sectorwise./.On 11.2.2012 at 12.8 noon.

Career Launcher (2009).Disability Rights.Career Launcher India Ltd. From http://www.careerlauncher.com/csr/disabilityRights.html, india, on 29.02.2012 at 3.00 pm

Eco WALK the Talk (2010). Anshu Gupta's GOONJ: Recycling urban waste for the rural poor.From http://www.ecowalkthetalk.com/blog/2010/08/04/anshu-guptas-goonj-recycling-urban-waste-for-rural-poor/.on 29.02.2012, at 3.15 pm.

Evelyne de Leeuw (1999). Healthy Cities: urban social entrepreneurship for health. Health Promotion International, Vol.14, No.3. Oxford University Press, Great Britain. From http://heapro.oxfordjournals.org/content/14/3/261.full.pdf+html on 09.03.2011 at 7.37pm

J. Gregory Dees (1998). The Meaning of .Social Entrepreneurship.From http://www.caseatduke.org/documents/dees_sedef.pdf on 17th August, 2011 at 7.11 pm.

James W. Fox (2002). Poverty in India Since 1974 Country Case Study. NATHAN Associates Inc..From http://www.ekh.lu.se/ekhcgu/teaching/401d4/poverty%20in%20india.pdf on 9.03.2012, at 4.23pm.

Jayathi Gosh (2011).India's official poverty line doesn't measure up. The guardian. From http://www.guardian.co.uk/global-development/poverty-matters/2011/oct/04/india-measuring-poverty-line.On 8.3.2012 at 3.02pm.

KaushikRanjanBandyopadhyay(2007). Poverty Alleviation and Pro-Poor Growth in India. Asian Institute of Transport Development, New Delhi. From http://www.dise.in/Downloads/Use%20of%20Dise%20Data/Kaushik%20Ranjan%20Bandyopadhyay.pdf, on 9.03.2012, at 4.40pm

Planning Commission(2006).Towards Faster and More Inclusive Growth An Approach to the 11th Five Year Plan 2007-2012.Government of India.From http://planningcommission.nic.in/plans/planrel/app11_16jan.pdf on 15.02.2012 at 5.00 pm.

Planning Commission (2008).Eleventh Five Year Plan (2007–2012) Agriculture, Rural Development, Industry, Services and Physical Infrastructure Volume III. Government of India.

From http://planningcommission.nic.in/plans/planrel fiveyr/11th/11_ 3/11th_vol3.pdf.On 15.02.2012 at 5.10 pm.

RenukaMahadevan (2003).Productivity Growth in Indian Agriculture: The Role of Globalization and Economic Reform. Asia-Pacific Development Journal Vol. 10, No. 2, December 2003.Fromhttp://www.unescap.org/pdd/publications/apdj_10_2/mahadevan.pdf.On 11.2.2012 at 12 noon.

Sherri Leronda Wallace (1999). Social Entrepreneurship: The Role of Social Purpose enterprises in Facilitating Community economic development.Journal of Developmental Entrepreneurship.Vol.4, No. 2.Fall/Winter. 1999. From http://search.proquest.com/business/docview/208425218/fulltextPDF/1321E8943581C02F077/1?accountid=39490, on 10th August,2011 at 2.50 pm.

SubirGokarn (2007).Inclusive growth in India: Dream or reality? From http://www.rediff.com/cms/print.jsp?docpath=//money/2007/dec/31guest.htm , on 5.3.2012 at 10am.

Terry McKinley (2010). Inclusive Growth Criteria and Indicators: An Inclusive Growth Index for Diagnosis of Country Progress. Asian Development Bank. From http://www.adb.org/Documents/Papers/ADB-Working-Paper-Series/ADB-WP14-inclusive-growth-criteria.pdf on 01.03.2012 at 11.30 pm.

The South Asian (2002).Elango'sKuthambakkam: A Model Village.From http://www.thesouthasian.org/archives/2002/elangos_kuthambakkam_a_model_v.html, on 29.02.2012, at 3.30 pm.

Wikipedia (2011).List of countries by GDP (PPP).From http://en.wikipedia.org/wiki/List_of_countries_by_GDP_(PPP), on 8.3.2012 at 4.19pm.

Wikipedia (2011).List of countries by Human Development Index.From http://en.wikipedia.org/wiki/List_of_countries_by_Human_Development_Index, on 8.03.2012 at 4.28pm.

Major Social Problems of India.From http://nos.org/331courseE/L-29%20MAJOTR%20SOCIAL%20PROBLEMS%20OF%20INDIA.pdf . On 15.02.2012 at 4.30 am

11 PLIGHT OF MENTALLY RETARDED CHILDREN

Dr. S. S. Vijayanchali, G. Selvarani

INTRODUCTION

A disability is a condition or function judged to be significantly impaired relative to the usual standard of an individual or group. The term is used to refer to individual functioning, including physical impairment, sensory impairment, cognitive impairment, intellectual impairment, mental illness, and various types of chronic disease. Mental handicap is a condition characterised by subnormal intellectual ability and arrested or delayed development. The terms 'mental retardation', 'mental deficiency', 'mental handicap' and 'mental sub-normality' refer to the same condition. Persons with less than average mental ability or intelligence are called 'mentally retarded'. It is a development disability that is marked by lower than-normal intelligence for daily living skills. Normally it presents at birth or develops early in life. Child with mental handicap finds it difficult to learn, to use past experience for solution of current problems to remember, understand and adjust to various situations. Mental handicap may or may not be accompanied by concurrent physical disability epilepsy or speech defects. Mental handicap is not curable by use of medicines. If the causative factor is iodine deficiency, metabolic disorder or blood group incompatibility, prompt action may help, but facilities for timely detection and intervention are either inadequate or non-existent even in the metropolitan cities.

There are several causes which result in mental handicap. Hereditary factors can't be ruled out in some causes. Cerebral palsy that is paralysed brain function may result in mental handicap. Some persons with cerebral palsy are intellectually normal, but have problems only with coordination of their body movements. Other causes include lack of iodine in the diet of the mother, the brain infections before and after birth, inadequate antenatal care, birth injuries, low birth weight, and inadequate nutrition in the first two years of life, injuries and untreated in childhood and poisoning from lead, and pesticides. Mental retardation can occur in any family and cuts across the lines of racial, ethnic, educational, social and economic backgrounds. A child with mental retardation is born every 5 minutes in the United States. Based on the 2001 census, an estimated of 6.2 to 7.5 million people have mental retardation in India that is about 3 per cent of our total population, or one American out of 35. Mental Retardation would be defined as disabilities of the mind and body due to brain damage. A developmental disability characterized by significantly sub average general intellectual functioning with concurrent deficits in adaptive behavior. Mental Retardation is a state of developmental deficit beginning in childhood that results in significant limitation of intellect (or) cognition and poor adoption to the demands of everyday life. Table 1 shows the classification of mentally retarded children based on the IQ level.

TABLE: 1 Intelligence Quotient (IQ) of Mentally Retarded Children

Class	Intelligence Quotient (IQ)
Profound Mental Retardation	Below 20
Severe Mental Retardation	20 - 34
Moderate Mental Retardation	35 - 49
Mild Mental Retardation	50 - 69

NUTRIENTS AND MENTAL HEALTH

Low energy intake often feels apathetic sad or hopeless. Developing fetuses and young infants are particularly susceptible to brain damage from malnutrition. Proteins are made up of amino acids linked together in various sequences and amounts protein intake and intake of individual amino acids can affect brain functioning and mental health. Dietary intake of fats may also play role in regulating mood and brain function. Some studies suggest that reducing fat and cholesterol in the diet may deplete brain serotonin levels, causing mood changes, anger and aggressive behaviour.

Thiamine deficiency can develop "Wernicke - Korsakoft syndrome" which is characterized by confusion, mental changes, abnormal eye movements and unsteadiness that progress to serve memory loss. Vitamin B -12 is needed to maintain the outer coating, called the myelin sheath on nerve cells. Inadequate, myelin results in nerve damage and impaired brain function. Vitamin B – 6 deficiencies characterized by mental changes such as fatigue, nervousness, irritability, depression, insomnia, dizziness and nerve changes. Vitamin B – 6 is needed by the body to produce most of the brains neurotransmitters. Acute magnesium deficiency can progress to apathy, delirium, convulsions, coma and death. Zinc is very important to brain functions, and its involved in maintaining cell membranes and protecting cells from damage. Zinc deficiency can cause neurological impairment, influencing appetite, taste, smell and vision and it has also been associated with apathy, irritability, jitteriness and fatigue. Selenium is needed for the synthesis of some hormones and helps protect cell membranes from damage, selenium deficiency is very rare and its toxicity has occurred in regions of the world with high selenium soil content, selenium toxicity causes nervous system changes, fatigue and irritability.

NEED FOR THE STUDY

A healthy society begins with a healthy child, and when a child has some developmental disorder, it affects the entire family and in turns the society. India has a very large number of disabled persons. A comprehensive country wide survey of persons with disability revealed that approximately over 90 million people are suffering from one or other kind of disability. It has been estimated that ten percent of world's population i.e. about 500 million people are either physically or mentally handicapped all over the world. The developing and the under developed countries have the lion's share of world's handicapped population and 350 million handicapped are out of reach and out of help. The risk of impairment and disability is greater for the poor. The birth of an impaired child, or the occurrence of disabilities are more prevalent in rural than urban. In about one-third of all cases, the cause of mental retardation is not known. The remaining two-thirds of cases are thought to be caused by one of six factors: heredity, prenatal problems, prenatal problems, childhood illnesses, economic status and cultural deprivation and environmental factors. The rate of disability is increasing especially in mentally retarded. They are neglected by the society and their own family members. They are viewing in the sympathetic and not in empathy. If the quality of life of a person with disabilities can be improved, by way of rehabilitation, he or she can be totally integrated into the society. Hence, it is the felt need that to prevent the children from the disabilities particularly mental retardation in future the causes for it have to be identified thereby the problem of mental handicap would be solved. Therefore, the present study is one such modest attempt conducted among children who suffers of mental retardation in children.

OBJECTIVES OF THE STUDY

- To know the demographic profile of the Mentally Retarded children;
- To assess the nutritional status (height, weight, MUAC, weight for age, height for age, weight for height and nutritional requirement)and
- To study the associated health problems of the mentally retarded children.

SETTING OF THE STUDY

The study was conducted in Dindigul District. Nilakkottai was the area purposively chosen for the study since a school for Mentally Retarded children was situated. A total of 80 children with different level IQ in the age group of 6 – 12 years comprising both male and female children were selected for the study by using purposive random sampling method. Body size and growth were assessed through the measurements like height, weight and MUAC. Anthropometric index of weight for age, height for age and weight for height were calculated as an indicator of growth status of the children. Height an individual is measured by using weighing scale. To collect the demographic profile of the mentally retarded children a structured interview schedule was prepared and used.

SUMMARY OF THE STUDY

Who are Vulnerable to Mental Retardation

It is found that mental retardation is found more among males than females. The sex-wise distribution of mentally retarded children accommodated in the school reveals that of the total (119) two-thirds (66.4%) of them are constituted by males whereas females' proportion in the total is 33.6 per cent. The same also reveals in the sample of the present study that of the total (40) children included in the present study males constituted 67.5 per cent. Most (85%) of the children are in the age group of 5-15 and the mean age for them is 9.6. It is observed that mental retardation is mostly prevalent among Hindus (95%) and of them more than three-fourths (77.5%) belongs to Backward Castes while the rest constituted by Scheduled Castes (22.5%). It evidences that the prevalence of mental retardation is found more among Backward Castes in the study area. The educational status of mentally retarded children's parent reveals that of the total a large majority of their parents are literates (65%) followed by illiterates (30%) and altogether constituted 95 per cent in the total. It proves that gave birth of children with mental retardation is more among educationally poor in the society. As far as parental occupation of such children is concerned three-fourths (75%) of them are daily wagers followed by farmers (10%), weavers (12.5%), and teachers (2.5%). What the study illustrates that poor income group is more vulnerable to gave birth of child with mental retardation. The classification of the parental monthly income shows that of the total 55 per cent of them earns Rs. 1,000 – 2,000/- per month whereas another 22.5 per cent earns Rs. 2000 – 3,000/- while the remaining 22.5 per cent belongs to various income categories. Rs. 1,975/- stands for the average monthly income to the mentally retarded children's parents.

The study brings out the fact that the occurrence of mental retardation is more in small families and the mentally retarded children's household includes an average of four members. More than half (52.5%) of the mentally retarded children are first born followed by second (32.5%), third (12.5%) and fourth (2.5%) birth ordered and the mean birth order for them is one (1). Hence, it is obvious that the first born child is more prone to born with mental retardation.

Causes for Mental Retardation

While probing the causes for mental retardation it is proved through the present study that early marriage of women made them to give birth of child with mental retardation. It is found that while mother's mean age at the time of marriage is 20.5 years 25.5 stands for father's age. Half of the total parents (50%) gave birth within two years from their marriage while after three years by another 30 per cent of the parents. It is found that the mentally retarded children in the study area are born after an average of two years from their parental marriage and the mother's mean age during gave birth of child with mental retardation is 22.3. A large majority (82.5%) of the mentally retarded children are born at hospital of which 80 per cent of them born normally. It is proved that early birth and low birth weight causes mental retardation in children. Their average weight at birth is 2.4 kg and the mean foetus period for them is 9 months. More than three-fourths (77.5%) of the parents noticed their child's disability while they are at an average of 2.2 years old. It is to be mentioned that the children accommodated in the school for mentally retarded are found with several deficiencies along with mental retardation. The pattern reveals mental retardation alone (27.5), mental retardation with hearing impairment (20%), mental retardation with speech impairment (25%), mental retardation with both speech and hearing impairment (25%), and mental retardation with stunting (2.5%). The Figure 1 evidences this.

Pattern of Mental Retardation found among Children

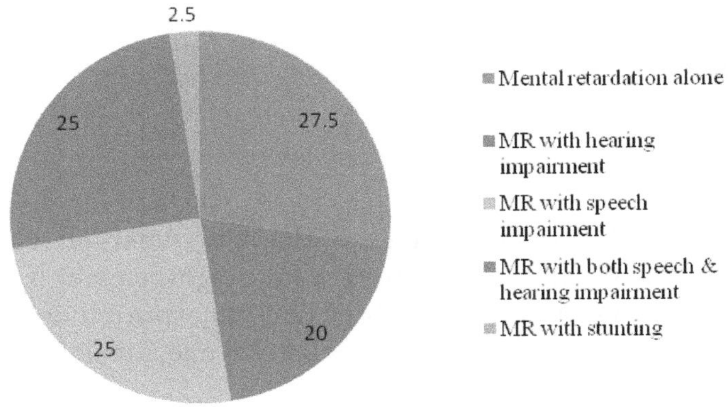

It is important to note that a large majority (80%) of the mentally retarded children is not affected by any diseases after birth; three-fourths (72.5%) of their ancestors are not affected by any disability; and almost all (95%) their family members are also free from mental retardation, according to the parents. While probing the parental health status during pregnancy a large majority (82.5%) of the children's parents are not affected by any disease. It indicates the fact that even though the parents are free in term of disease or disability they gave birth to mentally retarded child which proves the disability-mental retardation is determined during pregnancy. It is also to be mentioned that 85 per cent of the total mentally retarded children's parents are not relatives prior to their marriage.

TABLE: 2 Mentally Retarded children by their IQ Level

Intelligence Quotient (IQ)	Number	Percentage
Mild (< 40 %)	8	10
Moderate (40 – 60 %)	50	63
Severe (60 – 80 %)	22	27
Total	80	100

Table 2 shows the Mentally Retarded children by their IQ level. Children were with Mild Retardation (< 40 %) IQ were 10 %, Moderate (40 – 60 %) and Severe (60 – 80 %) retardation constituted 63 % and 27 % respectively.

TABLE: 3 Mean values of Mentally Retarded Children by their Anthropometric Factors

Anthropometric factors	Mean & SD of male	Mean & SD of female	T - test
Mid Upper Arm Circumference (MUAC)	15.5 ± 2.48	16.1 ± 2.2	1.015
Weight for age	67.0 ± 13.9	62.0 ± 13.3	1.491
Height for age	85.5 ± 7.5	84.8 ± 8.01	0.360
Weight for height	90.0 ± 13.6	86.9 ± 17.1	1.074

Table 3 shows the Mean values of Mentally Retarded children by their Anthropometric factors like MUAC, weight for height, weight for age and height for age. It indicates that Mentally Retarded children were malnourished according to weight for height, weight for age and height for age. Mean values of MUAC was with in the normal range.

TABLE: 4 Associated Health Problems of Mentally Retarded Children

Associated Health Problems	Male		Female		Total	
	NO	%	NO	%	NO	%
Cerebral palsy	9	8	2	4	11	12
Down syndrome	5	4	1	2	6	6
Cretinism	1	1	-	-	1	1
Micro cephalous	3	3	1	2	4	5
None	39	34	18	42	58	76
Total	57	50	23	50	80	100

Table 4 shows the associated health problems of Mentally Retarded children. Majority 12 percent were affected by Cerebral Palsy (CP). Down syndrome, Micro cephalous and Cretinism constituted 6 percent, 5 percent and 1 percent respectively.

TABLE: 5 Mean Intake of Nutrients in the Mentally Retarded Children

Nutrients	6 -9 years		10 - 12 years			
			Male		Female	
	RDA	Mean & SD	RDA	Mean & SD	RDA	Mean & SD
Energy (kcal)	1950	1478.9 ±237.9	2190	2690.2±595.4	1970	2121.8±511.8
Protein (g)	41	45.9±1.0	54	76.4±22.3	57	71.19± 15.3
Fat (g)	25	27.9±7.82	22	63.34±23.8	22	42.4± 23.5
Betacarotene(μg)	2400	496.2±164.3	2400	827.3±336.4	2400	694.8± 210.8
Thiamine (mg)	1.0	0.4463±0.16	1.1	0.9400±0.34	1.0	0.63± 0.32
Riboflavin (mg)	1.2	0.4661±0.135	1.3	0.97±0.588	1.2	0.857±0.588
Calcium (mg)	400	438.9±110.5	600	655.7±157.8	600	544.2±133.9
Iron (mg)	26	13.4±2.8	34	17.6±2.3	19	15.9±2.4

The mean intake of energy, beta carotene, thiamin, riboflavin and iron of the mentally retarded children in the age group of 6-9 years were comparatively lesser than the RDA allowances. On the other hand the mean intake of protein, calcium and fat were higher than the RDA allowances. The mean energy, protein, fat and calcium is higher than the RDA allowances in the case of male children of the 10-12 years of age and the other nutrients like beta carotene, thiamin, riboflavin and iron were taken in a lesser quantity. The female children in the age group of 10-12 years were having higher mean intake in energy, protein and fat but their mean intake of beta carotene, thiamine, riboflavin, calcium and iron is comparatively less than the RDA.

IMPORTANT FINDINGS

- Majority (63 %) of the mentally retarded children were moderately (40 – 60 %) IQ level.
- Majority of the mentally retarded children were malnourished according to weight for age, height for age and weight for height. Mean values of MUAC was within the normal range.
- One fourth of the mentally retarded children were with in the associated health problems like cerebral palsy, Down syndrome, Cretinism and Micro cephalous.
- Dietary pattern of the mentally retarded children shows that half of the children were consumption was less than Recommended Dietary Allowances (RDA).

Majority of the children were malnourished by weight for age, height for age and for their weight for height. The quality of their food intake is poor. This study reveals that there is an urgent need to generate awareness and to import training to the caregivers of the children with mental retardation to improve their knowledge, Attitude and Practice (KAP) level on nutrition and health which can help to improve the health of the mentally retarded children.

CONCLUSION

While concluding the present study on mental retardation it is important to be highlighted that educationally weaker and economically poor people's children are vulnerable to mental retardation. Mostly mental retardation is prevalent in small families and the first born child is prone to mental retardation. Early marriage and early pregnancy, early birth and low birth weight causes mental retardation in the child. Majority of them found with moderate IQ level and malnourished according to weight for age, height for age and weight for height. Many of them were with the associated health problems like cerebral palsy, Down syndrome, Cretinism and Micro cephalous. Half of their food consumption was less than Recommended Dietary Allowances (RDA).

REFERENCES:

1. Arumuga Gandhi, E "Socio-Economic Roots of Mental Retardation" Journal of Community Guidance and Research, Vol.28 No.1, Jan-March, 2011 (ISSN: 0970-1346): 107-115

2. Compilation of Reading in Special Education by Spastics Society of Tamil Nadu.

3. Frazer, W.I. Mac Gillivray, R.C. and Green, A.M. Caring for People with Mental Handicaps. Oxford: Butterworth Heinmann, 1991.

4. Halander, E et al. Training the Community for People with Disabilities. Geneva: WHO, 1989.

5. Madhavan, T and Kalyan, M. Mental Retardation: A Manual for Multi-Rehabilitation Workers. Secondrabad: National Institute for the Mentally Handicapped, 1988.

6. Puri, M and Sen, A.K. Mentally Retarded Children in India. New Delhi: Mittal Publications, 1989.

7. Study notes on Paper I (Mental Retardation: Nature and Needs). D.S.E. (M.R.), Secondrabad: National Institute for the Mentally Handicapped.

8. Sen, A. Mental Handicap among Rural Children. New Delhi: Sage Publications, 1992.

12 VOLUNTARY EFFORTS AND EMPOWERMENT MEANS FOR AN EXCLUDED COMMUNITY: A STUDY OF HIV/AIDS AFFECTD

Dr. E. Arumuga Gandhi, Sr. Mary Louisa

INTRODUCTION

There are hundreds of social problems, big and small, like the problems of poverty and dependency, crime and delinquency, sickness and physical handicap, unemployment and discontent, ignorance and superstition, war, population pressure and success of other social ills that blight and mar the prosperity and progress of society. The nature of social problems in India is not very different from that in other civilized countries of the world, though there are certain problems peculiar to the country because of differences in culture, social set up and certain other historical and political reasons. For example, unemployment, gambling, crime etc. are indeed social problems, but the causes giving rise to them may differ due to differences in political, economic, social and cultural setting in different countries. Child labour, prostitution, poverty, caste system, population explosion, pollution and deterioration of environment are some of the problems particularly in urban centres. They need to be solved for the well-being of the society. But solving is not an easy task as every problem is multidimensional and complex with its intrinsic characters. HIV/AIDS is such a complex social problem mostly in urban areas. Individuals with HIV disease face numerous barriers to obtaining care, including financial, transportation, language and cultural barriers. HIV infected individuals often need to access diverse and multiple points of service and hence, access to care is critically important. In addition, since the disease has currently no known cure, access to clinical trials and other avenues for experimental treatment and high cost treatment is essential. Many HIV/AIDS service providers struggle to serve under the pressures of resource constraints and health care policy changes, particularly changes in medical aid. HIV/AIDS services and providers' networks have emerged around communities of HIV infected individuals and often represent the most knowledgeable and appropriate providers for individuals with HIV. Therefore, reform efforts need to support providers by assisting them in increasing their capacity and ability to compete within a changing health care system.

AIDS IN INDIA

India is among the worst affected nations in the world in terms of the HIV/AIDS epidemic. At the last count by the National AIDS Control Organization (NACO), reported that there were over five million positive people in the country. The Indian epidemic, in fact, is believed to be one of the fastest growing HIV/AIDS epidemics in the world. What is unique about HIV/AIDS in India is its combination of the medical nature of the disease (incurable), the main route of transmission (unprotected sex), the social exclusion spin–offs (stigma, discrimination), and the fact that the epidemic's spread in the country is fuelled by poverty, illiteracy and lack of education, unemployment, migration and the relative powerlessness of women vis-à-vis men. This is compounded by several prejudices about sex and sexuality that make sex a taboo in our society but allows sexual experimentation to slip through the cracks as long as it remains silent and without visible repercussions. What HIV/AIDS is doing is to challenge Indian society to turn itself inside out, to focus on those sizeable sections of the population who were hitherto inconsequential, i.e., women, young people and those minorities who were hitherto invisible, untouchable and unmentionable like prostitutes, men who have sex with men, *hijras* (transvestites) and pull all people disabled by the incurable affliction of HIV out of the margins and bring them to the centre. It has to be realised that the protection of these groups in terms of their human rights to health security, dignity, freedom of choice, and equality with other citizens is inseparable from the security of the rest of the society. What will tilt the scales in their favour and in the process set off eddies of change with repercussions for mainstream society is if these affected groups also develop a strong sense of agency and commitment to the cause.

At present our society is plagued by social problems such as drug abuse, alcoholism, corruptions, AIDS, child abuse, terrorism, poverty, unemployment, homicide etc. Our Indian society has some specific social issues like caste related violence and discrimination, similarly religious discrimination and violence, naxalism, child labour and so on. However, the reaction of the general public to all these problems is varied. Different people react differently and the degree and intensity of the problems varies from one region to another that is in rural and urban areas. The impact of these reactions on the victims at times is so great that it inflicts severe losses in different ways on the victims. And the victims are often deprived of many things in life. Many of their needs are not taken care of; they feel isolated; they suffer under feelings of being segregated from their community. In short, one could say that they become the socially excluded.

HIV/AIDS AFFECTED: AN EXCLUDED COMMUNITY

Health and long life have been a quest of mankind throughout the ages. It has been an unsuccessful quest until our day in history. Men sought, but did not find, the "fountain of youth". And in much of the world still, millions are chronically diseased. Specially the marginalized, who are also mostly the ones vulnerable to health hazards,. Each year marks the development of some new health discovery and life saving drug or invention to make us more safe and free from some disease like the polio vaccine which has greatly reduced the threat of this killer and crippler of children and young adults. But every now and then new diseases also crop up in different parts of the world. Though infectious diseases once seemed to be on the wane, a new worldwide epidemic can break out at any moment. Therefore, good health which is a matter of outstanding importance is a big challenge. Each of us is custodian of his/her own health to a very great extent. When struck by a disease our health care becomes a big problem. But when the diseases are communicable, it also becomes a public problem. Communicable diseases are a threat to the welfare of the community. When one individual becomes a victim of disease, others in his family or neighbourhood group may become victims as well. Diseases of this nature are not subject to individual control, but must be regulated by society through preventive measures, such as quarantine. The cost of health services is a matter of public, as well as private concern. Each society has gone to great lengths to protect individuals from diseases and other health dangers through sanitation, control of communicable and contagious diseases, pure food and drug laws, and regulation of the common safety through traffic laws and safety regulations in industry and mining. Studying health and health care issues around the world offers insights on illness and how political and economic forces shape health care in nations. Disparities in health are glaringly apparent between high income and low-income nations when we examine factors such as the prevalence of life-threatening diseases, rates of life expectancy and infant mortality, and access to health services. Beyond all these when a disease becomes an epidemic, steps have to be taken for prevention and rehabilitation. But this is not the state of affairs in many afflicted societies. When the affliction is severe the victims in their disabled states are left alone, deserted by friends, families and abandoned by the societies.

In the present times one of the major health threats which disables and discriminates the victims is AIDS. It is presumed to have originated in Central Africa in the late nineteenth century or early twentieth century. But now it is a pandemic and a major killer disease. Much more than the deaths caused by AIDS the social implications are also very severe. AIDS has cut life expectancy by five years in Nigeria, eighteen years in Kenya, and thirty-three years in Zimbabwe. AIDS results in higher mortality rates in childhood and young adulthood, stages in the life course when mortality is otherwise low. Although AIDS almost inevitably ends in death, no one actually dies of AIDS immediately. As discussed earlier rather AIDS reduces the body's ability to fight diseases, making a person vulnerable to many diseases such pneumonia – that results in death. The biggest medical hurdle in the treatment of AIDS is that there is no permanent cure for AIDS. There are some drugs which can prolong the life of AIDS infected and improve their quality of life. But they are far too expensive for the economically marginalised or even middle class people in many countries. Such burning issues are not the priorities even for international organizations that protect human rights.

OBJECTIVES OF THE STUDY

The present study on HIV/AIDS affected – an excluded community was carried out with the following objectives:

1. To understand the socio-economic background of the HIV/AIDS affected;
2. To know the history of their illness;
3. To bring out the care provided for the HIV/AIDS affected;
4. Their perception towards supporting facilities made available to them in urban area in which they are living ; and
5. To suggest ways and means to include them in the social stream of life.

RESEARCH DESIGN

There are many NGOs functioning in and around Bangalore. The present study was done in one of them using both primary and secondary sources of data. The primary data was collected directly from the HIV/AIDS affected. The interview schedule administered to them consisted of questions to elicit information regarding personal data, family particulars, socio-economic status, marital details and circumstances leading to HIV infection and their perception towards the strategies and services from which they benefit, the number of years they are suffering from HIV /AIDS, family support and the training given to them. All were approached personally to avoid the interference of others and to collect systematic and unambiguous data. Descriptive methods of data analysis like percentage, proportion and averages for some selected variables have been used for analysing and interpreting the data collected from the respondents and hence generalisations achieved. There was no necessity to form study hypotheses and to test them accordingly since sample size was too small.

SUMMARY OF THE STUDY

Socio-Economic Status of HIV/AIDS Affected

The study shows that of the total (50) HIV/AIDS affected people included in the study 60 percent of them are males and the rest 40 percent are females. The distribution of the HIV/AIDS affected by their age- group reveals that 44 percent of the total infected is in the age group of 30 to 40, followed by the age-groups 21-30 (26%) and 41-50 (20%) and the rest belong to various other age-groups. The mean age for them is 34. Therefore, it is concluded that most of the respondents who are affected by HIV/AIDS are in their middle age. The educational status of the HIV/AIDS affected shows that a large majority of them pursued Upper Primary (34%), S.S.L.C. (28%) or PUC (18%) education. Only one of them was a graduate. Illiterates' proportion in the total is found to be 16 percent. What the study evidences that almost all the HIV/AIDS affected are having lower educational status and their poor educational level is found to be one amongst the reasons for the HIV/AIDS affliction. The distribution of the HIV/AIDS affected by their religion reveals that of the total large majority of them (88%) are Hindus followed by Christians (10%). The Muslims constituted only 2 percent of the total. Therefore, the conclusion is that the majority of the HIV/AIDS affected people belong to Hinduism. The distribution by their caste groups indicates that of the total 30 percent of them belong to Other Backward Classes followed by Scheduled Castes (14%) and Backward Classes. However, a significant proportion in the total denied to respond. What is inferred from the analysis of the HIV/AIDS affected people's birth order is that the eldest children seem to be the most vulnerable with 36 percent followed by second (26%), third (18%) and fourth (16%) birth order. The mean birth order for them is 2.

The distribution by their occupation reveals that of the total, both employed and unemployed constituted 30 percent, each respectively and together constituted three-fifths (60%) of the total, while another 22 percent were daily wagers. Dependants constituted 18 percent in total. Hence it is concluded that most of the HIV/AIDS affected are the source of income for their families' livelihood. Their distribution by the number of children they have shows that of the total about three-fifths (58%) have two children, while another 14 percent have three children. The respondents having only one child constituted 16 percent in the total. It is found that all the HIV/AIDS affected people having an average of two children. Of the total a large majority of (84%) of the HIV/AIDS affected have 1-3 dependent members while the rest belong to different categories. It is found that all the HIV/AIDS affected have at least an average of two members as dependents. The grouping of the HIV/AIDS affected by the type of family to which they belong shows that nuclear family (62%) is predominant among them. Only 16 percent live in joint families whereas the rest 22 percent are from extended families.

Hence, it is concluded that the respondents who live in nuclear families became the victims of the HIV/AIDS. The grouping of the HIV/AIDS affected by the source of earning shows that of the total in nearly three-fifths (58%) of the families, the respondent himself/ herself is the only source for the earning, whereas in another 40 percent of the respondents' families others also earn. Therefore, what is evident is that most of the HIV/AIDS affected people are the only source of earning for the livelihood of the entire family. The grouping of the HIV/AIDS affected by their family annual income shows that, of the total, nearly three-fifths (58%) of them earn less than Rs.25,000/- per annum while another 22 percent up to Rs. 50,000/-. Up to Rs. 100,000/- is earned by only 10 percent in the total respondents' family. The mean for their family's annual income is Rs. 24,000/-.

HISTORY OF ILLNESS

While probing the respondents by the number of years that they are suffering from HIV/AIDS it is revealed that about two-thirds (66%) of the total have been suffering from HIV/AIDS for more than a year, while the rest (44%) for about one year. The respondents' distribution by the means of knowing the HIV/AIDS infection shows that of the total nearly two-thirds (64%) of them came to know about the infection while they were suffering from some illness while 26 percent in the total accidentally became aware of that. The rest 10 percent came to know through different circumstances like having an infected spouse. Hence, it is understood that most of the respondents - HIV/AIDS affected came to know about the infection through various illnesses. The respondents' distribution by any of their family members being affected by HIV/AIDS prior to them shows that of the total more than half (52%) of the respondents' family members were not found with HIV/AIDS while another 42 percent in the total accepted the same. Therefore, it is evident that a significant proportion of the respondents' family members were also with HIV/AIDS. The respondents' distribution by that whether any of their family members are affected of HIV/AIDS shows that, of the total more than three-fifths (62%) of them responded that their family members are not affected with HIV/AIDS because of them, while another 30 percent agreed to it. The rest (8%) of the total didn't respond to the question. The respondents' distribution by the reaction of family members when they came to know about the infection of HIV/AIDS in respondents reveals fear (28%), shame (18%), blame (14%), and guilt feeling (10%). Another 14 percent expressed mixed emotions of the above said. However, the rest 16 percent of the total denied responding. It is to be mentioned that all the HIV/AIDS affected are migrants from the adjacent areas of Bangalore, Andhra Pradesh and Tamil Nadu. Hence, all of them obviously stated that if they were at their hometown they would not been victims of such a disease and according to majority of them migration to Bangalore was the main reason for their present condition.

TABLE: 1 Mean for some selected Indicators

Indicator	Mean (N = 50)
Age	34
Birth Order	2
No. of Dependents	2
Household Size	4
Annual Income (in Rs.)	24,000/-
No. of years suffering of AIDS	1.3

CARE RECEIVED AT BANGALORE

While probing that from where they receiving adequate care to combat the present conditions it is found that Snehadaan – a Non-Governmental Organisation – functioning in Bangalore extended its fullest support exclusively for them at a care centre. All the HIV/AIDS affected invariably felt that they are getting adequate medical care and also that doctors are available whenever they feel ill. Medical care is of utmost importance for the HIV/AIDS affected and the centre is giving them full care. All of them agreed that they were given nutritious food at the Centre. Hence, it is no wonder that all of them feel physically much better than before they came to the centre. All the HIV/AIDS affected said that they receive counselling; Counsellor were available to them always and that they benefit from the Counselling. All of them agreed that they have got more information about their condition after coming to the centre. And the information and awareness helped them a lot. Since the inpatients stay only for 15 days there was a variation in their response about the periodicity of the awareness programmes. While eliciting their response towards vocational training and job opportunities, 96 percent said that they don't receive any training. However a small number of them (10%) said that they have the opportunity to work at the centre presently for a salary of Rs. 2000/- for two people, more than 3000 rupees for one person. More than three-fourths (78%) of them were confident that the centre would help them find jobs when they leave the centre. Their distribution by the means of source for approaching the centre reveals community care centre (62%), friends (22%) and from other sources (16%) like government and private hospitals and parish priests. This is a positive indicator that the community care centres are active too in helping the HIV/AIDS affected.

Perception on Care Facilities availed to them

The nature of counselling given to the HIV/AIDS affected reveals that nearly half (46 %) of the total undergo individual counselling, while another 46 percent of the total receive both individual and group counselling depending on the need. Only 4percent of the total receive group counselling. It indicates that most of the respondents-HIV/AIDS affected are given individual counselling at the centre. The HIV/AIDS affected peoples' preference towards the kind of counselling shows that of the total 58 percent felt that both types of counselling is useful, whereas another 26 percent preferred individual counselling and the others (16%) preferred group counselling. This evidences that all the HIV/AIDS affected want counselling. Half of (50%) the total HIV/AIDS affected said that awareness programmes were conducted weekly while another 30 percent said monthly. Only 12 percent said fortnightly. Since the inpatients stay only for 15 days there was a variation in their response about the periodicity of the awareness programmes. However, all the respondents - HIV/AIDS affected are the beneficiaries of the programme organised by the Centre. Their perception about spiritual programme organised by the Centre shows that of the total, two-thirds (66%) of them felt an increase in their own faith after attending the programmes. While anther 30 percent in the total denied the same. Two of the total refused to respond. However, it is clear that most of the HIV/AIDS affected have been imparted spiritual help to face their future through such programmes. The HIV/AIDS affected peoples' perception on the availability of job/employment after leaving from the centre reveals that of the total more than three-fourths (78%) opined "yes" simply because of the thought that they have 'it' in Bangalore!' whereas another 20 percent said "No". It indicates that a majority of the HIV/AIDS affected are in positive perception towards the availability of jobs for them after getting discharged from the centre. Their perception about the centres support for their children shows that three-fifths (60%) of the total denied that the centre extends its support for their children another 36 percent in the total accepted centre's support for their children. What it evidences is that depending on the requirement the centre extends its support to the children of the HIV/AIDS affected.

The HIV/AIDS affected peoples' distribution by the problem faced with other inmates shows that of the total a large majority (84%) of them never faced any problems with their inmates while the rest 16 percent had problems such as language, place, socio economic background etc. with other inmates. Hence, it is clear from the table that except very few, almost all of the HIV/AIDS affected faced no problems with their inmates. It is found that almost all the HIV/AIDS affected (98%) were accepted with friendliness and understanding when they came to the centre. While probing the HIV/AIDS affected people's perception towards the availability of accommodations a large majority of the respondents (86%) said that they had no difficulty in getting an accommodation at the centre.

All unanimously agreed that they all availed of accommodation is at free of cost. It is indeed a big support for the affected who are from economically marginalized communities.

PERCEPTION ABOUT FUTURE

It was indeed very good to hear that 96% of the HIV/AIDS affected felt confident that they would be able to face the challenges/hurdles and other problems when they leave the centre; 94% of them were satisfied with the services of the centre and all of them said they would recommend the Centre to others. This is a very positive response and hence a big compliment for the NGO which unlike the Government Organizations which don't perform has provided good services to the HIV/AIDS affected. All of them said that they have been assured of follow up medical checkups. All the HIV/AIDS affected unanimously agreed that the staff members are kind and understanding to them and also that the staffs are committed.

CONCLUSION

Even after three decades of HIV/AIDS no cure has been found. Though the life expectancy of the victims and the quality of life of the victims can be improved dramatically with the life saving drugs, there are many deaths occurring. The main reason is the stigma and discrimination associated with the disease which is decreasing only very slowly. Many of the affected don't come forward to take treatment. If they get adequate care and nutrition HIV/AIDS can be considered as any other chronic medical conditions like diabetes and the entire profile of the epidemic would be different. The voluntary efforts from NGOs have contributed positively towards this. Therefore, it would be concluded that urbanism is a blend of both curses and blessings. It depends on the individual, the path he/she prefers as mean of his/her life. Only then urbanism would be a "real blessed way of life" to the individual as well as the whole community living in urban centres.

REFERENCES:

Barooah Vani K. "Social Exclusion and Job Reservation in India," Economic and Political Weekly, Vol. XLV, No. 52, 2010.

Bhat, Vighnesh N. Some Conceptual Issues Concerniy Health and Human. New Delhi: Seriab Publication, 2010.

Cavalli, Tommaso et all. HIV/AIDS Care and Treatment. Delhi: AIT BS Publishers and Distributors, 2008.

Chhabra, Rami. "National AIDS Control Programme," Economic and Political Weekly, Vol. XLII, No. 2, 2007.

Claeson and Wilson. HIV/AIDS in South Asia. Jaipur: Rawat Publicaiton, 2010.

Feigal Ellen G, Alexandra Levine M, and Biggar Roberts J. AIDS Related Concerns and their Treatment. New York: Marcel Dekker, 2000.

Kates, Jennifer. Encyclopedia of AIDS: A Social, Political Cultural Scientific Record of HIV Epidemic. Chicago Fitzroy Dearborn publishers, 1985.

Lewis, David and Wallace, Tina. Development NGOs and Challenge of Change. Jaipur: Rawat Publication, 2003.

Nayak, Bimal Kanta. Social Workers and HIV/AIDS Intervention –A Reflection, Health Action. Secunderabad: Jeevan Institute of Printing, 2010.

Pawar S.N, Ambekar J.B, and Shrikanbt D.N. NGOs and Development: The Indian Scenario. Jaipur: Rawat Publications, 2004.

Ramamurthy, V. AIDS and the Human Survival, Community Development and AIDS Prevention. New Delhi: Author Press, 2000.

Ramasubban, Radhika and Rishyasringa, Bhanwar. AIDS and Civil Society. Jaipur: Rawat Publications, 2010.

Shruivastava, Harsh and Venkateswaran, Shankar. The Business of Social Responsibility. Bangalore: Books for Change, 2000.

Singh, Avtar. "Combating AIDS: A Development," Yojana, Vol. 48, 2004.

Sinha, Sunitha. AIDS Awarness. New Delhi: Anmol Publications, 1995.

Usdin, Shereen. The No Nonsense: A Guide to HIV/AIDS. New Delhi: Rawat Publications, 2005.

Varmain, Sudhir. Gender, HIV and Social Work. Jaipur: Rawat Publication, 2010.

13 ACCEPTANCE LEVEL OF SELF-SERVICE TECHNOLOGY-ENABLED FINANCIAL INFORMATION MEDIUMS AMONG THE WOMEN CUSTOMERS

Dr. S. Sudalaimuthu, Mr. B. Angamuthu

INTRODUCTION OF THE STUDY

INTRODUCTION

An Self-service Technology-enabled (SSTe) financial information mediums allows customers to access their accounts at any time (24 hours a day X 365) through the credit card banking, internet banking, Automated Teller Machines (ATMs), Mobile banking (m-banking) etc throughout the world. Further, SSTe financial service is a financial inclusion medium because it is providing efficient banking services with reasonable cost to the all sections of peoples without discrimination. This is followed by financial inclusion helps to extensive usages of information technology solutions. In the year 1946, credit card concept developed by John C. Biggins at the Flatbush National Bank of Brooklyn, New York. But, 1960 Bank of America developed the present credit card operating system viz. Visa international and Master card. This is followed by, 1967 introduced cash dispenser by Barclays bank, UK. The growth of card banking in India is moving upward trend for every year. In the end of March' 2011, India has card based value of financial information is Rs. 114207 Crores. The following table provides development of card based financial information in the Indian context from 2005-06 to 2010-11.

Table: 1 Performance of Card-based Financial Information Value of Payment of Transactions (In Rs. Crores)

Card type	2005-06	2006-07	2007-08	2008-09	2009-10	2010-11
Credit	33,886	41,361	57,985	65,356	61,824	75,516
Debit	5897	8,172	12,521	18,547	26,418	35,705

Source: RBI, Annual Report 2009-10 & 2010-11

1.2 INFORMATION TECHNOLOGY AND SSTE FINANCIAL INFORMATION MEDIUMS (ATMS & M-BANKING, INTERNET BANKING) IN INDIA

Now-a-days the acceleration technology has produced an extraordinary effect upon our economy through the expanding the scope and utility of financial services. The first ATM was installed by HSBC bank in the year of 1987. After reforms in the year of 1990_S, banking sector especially public, private and foreign sector which led to brought in SSTe financial services to their customers. But, in the year of 2010 statistics suggest that there were 60, 153 ATMs available in the scheduled commercial banks with the branches of 69160. Thereafter, in the year 2008, the RBI issued m-banking guidelines to the banks. Now, 19 public sector, 12 private sector and 4 foreign sector banks are providing m-banking based financial services and those banks are achieved in the end of March'2011overall performance of m-banking is 8278529 transactions and its value of Rs. 7154270120. Now, India has 23 million internet banking users. The cost per transaction of internet banking is Rs.10 which is less than the branch banking (Rs.66) and ATM (Rs.22).

1.3 ISSUES RAISED FOR THE STUDY

The success of SSTe financial services to the customers depends upon their acceptance level because acceptance means continuous usage of SSTe mediums. But, changing technological environment, increasing women customer education, modern life style of the women customers, cost of living, and requirement of financial services by the women customers is influenced their acceptance. So, the study regarding acceptance level of SSTe mediums among the women customers is needed for certain period of distance. For that reason, this study is to made with following issues

a) What is the acceptance level of SSTe financial information mediums?

b) Which type of factors is related to the women customer acceptance of SSTe financial information mediums?

1.4 OBJECTIVE OF THE STUDY

The primary aim of the study is to assess and analyze the acceptance level of Self-Service Technology-enabled (SSTe) financial information mediums among the women customers and comparison of their acceptance of SSTe financial information mediums among the various groups.

1.5 HYPOTHESES

Ho_1: There is no significant relationship between personal factors of the women customers and their acceptance level of SSTe financial information mediums.

Ho_2: There is no significant difference between personal factors of the women customers and their acceptance of SSTe financial information mediums.

1. RESEARCH METHODOLOGY

Empirical study was adopted. This study was conducted to assess and analysis the acceptance of SSTe financial information mediums among the women customers in Coimbatore District of Tamilnadu. This empirical study conducted by using the following methodology.

2.1 Data and source

Both primary and secondary data related to SSTe financial information mediums are used but the analyses were made mainly using primary data collected through interview schedule from women customers. In addition, secondary data collected from various books, journals and websites etc.

2.2 Sample

The valid customers include for the study were 100, those are taken from public and private sector bank branches those branches are functioning throughout the Coimbatore District. Purposive sampling method is adopted for selecting the sample.

2.3 Interview schedule

Primary data collection instrument have two different parts. The first part covers personal factors of the women customers like, banking sector, age group, educational status, occupational status and family income. The second part covers; SSTe financial information mediums acceptance related statements and those statements are twenty five in numbers. Acceptance related data collected through the five-point Likert-scaling technique from strongly agree to strongly dis agree. The statements regarding acceptance of SSTe financial information mediums becomes both positive and negative in nature. The positive statements scored for strongly agree '5' to strongly disagree '1'and vice-versa for negative statements. This is followed by acceptance level of the each and every customer is to find out through the techniques used by Sudalaimuthu.S (2011).

2.4 Period of the study

This study collects primary data during the year 2011 from July to November.

2.5 Area of the study

Area of the study refers to Coimbatore district. Coimbatore is a second largest Distict in Tamilnadu next to the Chennai according to the branches of commercial banks. In Coimbatore district there are 533 branches as per the statistics on 2009.

2.6 Framework of Analysis

Following tools are used while analyzing the collected data through the interview schedule. They are percentage analysis, cross Tabulation, chi-Square analysis, one-way ANOVA and independent sample t-test.

2.7 Limitation of the study

The main limitation of the study is focus on all self-service technology-enabled financial information mediums not for only one medium.

3. ANALYSIS AND INTERPRETATION

This part involves collect the inference through the application of statistical tools based on the information collected from customers.

3.1 Personal factor of the customers

Desired personal factors help the researcher to find out which groups of customers have high acceptance of m-banking. The select profile of the customers is given in the table below.

Table 2 Personal factors of the Customers

Characterstics	Attributes	No. of Customers	%
Banking Sector	Public	52	52
	Private	48	48
Age Group (In Years)	Below 25	50	50
	26-50	35	35
	Above 50	15	15
Educational Status	No formal education (I-VII)	47	47
	Upto school level (VIII-XII)	35	35
	Higher education	18	18

Characterstics	Attributes	No. of Customers	%
Occupational status	Government employee	28	28
	Private Employee	32	32
	Home-maker	16	16
	Students	24	24
Family Income (In Rs. Per Month)	Below 10000	33	33
	10001-20000	35	35
	Above 20000	32	32
Source: Primary data			

The table-2 shows that 52% of the customers belong to public sector banks. About half (50%) of the customers are in the young age group (below 25 years). Majority (47%) of the customers have education is I-VII, nearly 1/3rd of the customers are working in private sector and 33% of the customers' family earned their monthly income is below Rs.10,000.

3.2 Acceptance level of SSTe financial information mediums

This study, customers are grouped into three categories as low, medium and high acceptance of SSTe financial information mediums based on their obtained score. Customers whose score is < 78 are considered to have low acceptance. Those whose scores lies from >= 78 to >=112 medium acceptance. The customers who have scores > = 112 belong to high acceptance category. According to the above technique, assessment of acceptance level of the customers is shown in the table - 3 below:

Table: 3 Acceptance level SSTe financial information mediums

Acceptance	No. of Customers	Percent
Low	16	16
Medium	70	70
High	14	14
Total	100	100
Source: Primary data		

It is observed from the table 3 for acceptance level among the customers, sixteen (16%) customers are at low acceptance level, 70 (70%) customers come under medium level of acceptance and the remaining fourteen (14%) customers belong to high level acceptance of SSTe financial information mediums.

It is concluded from the above table that 7/10th of the customers have medium level of acceptance of SSTe financial information mediums.

3.3 Banking sector and Acceptance level

Assessment of acceptance level among the customers based on their banking sector is given in the table below and the discussion is based on the medium and high level acceptance.

Table: 4 Banking Sector and Acceptance level

Banking sector	Acceptance level			Total
	Low	Medium	High	
Public	9 (17.31)	37 (71.15)	6 (11.54)	52 (100)
Private	7 (14.58)	33 (68.75)	8 (16.67)	48 (100)
Total	16	70	14	100

Source: Primary data (The values in brackets are percentages)

It could be observed from the table 4 that more the 7/10th of the public sector bank customers and more than 2/3rd of the private bank customers (68.82%) have medium level of acceptance of SSTe financial information mediums. On the other hand, more number of private sector bank customers has higher acceptance than the public sector bank customers.

3.4 Age group and Acceptance level

Assessment of acceptance level among the customers based on their age group is given in the table below and the discussion is made based on the medium and high level acceptance.

Table: 5 Age group and Acceptance level

Age group (In Years)	Acceptance level			Total
	Low	Medium	High	
Below 25	8 (16)	36 (72)	6 (12)	50 (100)
26-50	6 (17.14)	24 (68.57)	5 (14.29)	35 (100)
Above 50	2 (13.33)	10 (66.67)	3 (20)	15 (100)
Total	16	70	14	100

Source: Primary data (The values in brackets are percentages)

It is obvious from the table 5 that majority of the customers are in all the age groups and they have medium acceptance of SSTe financial information mediums. On the other hand, the highest number of customers who belong to the age group of above 50 years; the extent of their acceptance is higher than the other age groups.

3.5 Educational qualification and Acceptance level

Assessment of acceptance level among the customers based on their educational qualification is given in the table below and the discussion is made based on the medium and high level acceptance.

Table: 6 Educational qualification and Acceptance level

Educational qualification	Acceptance level			Total
	Low	Medium	High	
No formal education (I-VII)	11 23.40)	30 (63.83)	6 (12.77)	47 (100)
School level education (VIII-XII)	4 (11.43)	25 (71.43)	6 (17.14)	35 (100)
Higher Education	1 (5.56)	15 (83.33)	2 (11.11)	18 (100)
Total	16	70	14	100

Source: Field data (The values in brackets are percentages)

It is noticeable from the table 6 that majority of the customers have medium acceptance of SSTe financial information mediums among the all educational qualifications. On the other hand, more number of the customers are held by high level of acceptance who possess school education compared to others.

3.6 Occupation and Acceptance level

Assessment of acceptance level among the customers based on their occupation is given in the table below and the discussion is made based on the medium and high level acceptance.

Table: 7 Occupation and Acceptance level

Occupation	Acceptance level			Total
	Low	Medium	High	
Government employee	2 (7.14)	24 (85.71)	2 (7.14)	28
Private Employee	5 (15.63)	22 (68.75)	5 (15.63)	32
Home-maker	4 (25)	10 (62.5)	2 (12.5)	16
Students	5 (20.83)	14 (58.33)	5 (20.83)	24
Total	16	70	14	100

Source: Primary data (The values in brackets are percentages)

It is noticeable from the table 7 that majority of the customers have medium acceptance of SSTe financial information mediums among all the occupational status but more number of student customers have high acceptance of m-banking than others.

3.7 Family Income (Rs. per month) and Acceptance level

Assessment of acceptance level among the customers based on their family income is given in the table below and the discussion is made based on the medium and high level acceptance.

Table: 8 Family Income and Acceptance level

Family income (In Rs. Per month)	Acceptance level			Total
	Low	Medium	High	
Below 10000	6 (18.18)	24 (72.73)	3 (9.09)	33 (100)
10001-20000	4 (11.43)	23 (65.71)	8 (22.86)	35 (100)
Above 20000	6 (18.75)	23 (71.88)	3 (9.38)	32 (100)
Total	16	70	14	100

Source:Primary data (The values in brackets are percentages)

It is noticeable from the table 8 that highest percent of the customers have medium acceptance of m-banking among the all income groups. On the other hand, the highest number of customers who belong to the family income is between Rs. 10001-20000; the extent of their acceptance is higher than the other income groups.

3.8 Relationship of the Personal factors and Acceptance level of SSTe Financial Information Mediums

Pearson chi-square ($\chi 2$) statistic should be used to find out the relationship between two variables like, personal factors of the customers and their acceptance level with the testing of following hypothesis. Ho: There is no significant relationship of the customers' acceptance level of SSTe financial information mediums among the various groups of banking sector, sex, age group, educational qualification, occupational status and family income.

Table: 9 Relationship of personal factors of the customers and Acceptance level of SSTe financial information mediums

Factor	χ^2	df	Asymp.Sig	Result
Banking sector	0.605	2	0.739	NS
Age group (In years)	0.688	4	0.953	NS
Educational qualification	4.423	4	0.352	NS
Occupational status	5.953	6	0.425	NS
Family income (Rs. Per month)	3.868	4	0.424	NS

Inferred from the table 9, the asymptotic significant value of χ^2 comes out between the banking sector, age group, educational qualification, occupational status, family income of the customers and their acceptance level is .739,.953, .352, .425, .424 respectively which is greater than 5% level of significant value 0.05. So, the null hypotheses are accepted and it can be reported that there is no significant relationship of the customers' acceptance level of SSTe financial information mediums among the various groups of banking sector, age group, educational qualification, occupational status and family income.

3.9 Comparison of the Customers Acceptance of SSTe financial information mediums

Here, t-test and One-Way Analysis of Variance (f-statistics) test are applied to find the difference of acceptance within the groups of various personal factors (Banking sector, Age group, Educational qualification, Occupation, and family income) of the customers based on their average acceptance of SSTe financial information mediums. In order to each personal factor of the customers treated as independent variable and overall acceptance as dependent variable. The difference of acceptance establish through the testing of hypothesis with suitable measurement of data. This is followed by comparison of acceptance of SSTe financial information mediums among the various groups through the mean acceptance.

Ho: There is no significant difference between personal factors (banking sector, age group, educational status, occupational status and family income) of the customers and their acceptance of SSTe financial information mediums.

Table: 10 Comparison of Customers Acceptance of SSTe Financial Information Mediums

Character	Variable	N	Mean	SD	t/f-Statistic	df	Sig. value	Result
Banking Sector	Public	52	93.48	16.44	-1.147	98	0.254	NS
	Private	48	97.35	17.33				
Age Group (In Years)	Below 25	50	94.60	16.42	0.355	99	0.702	NS
	26-50	35	94.94	18.21				
	Above 50	15	98.73	15.97				
Educational status	No formal education (I-VII)	47	93.09	18.86	0.873	99	0.423	NS
	Upto school level (VIII-XII)	35	98.03	16.01				
	Higher Education	18	96.00	12.60				
Occupational status	Government employee	28	99.00	10.72	0.901	99	0.444	NS
	Private Employee	32	94.22	16.71				
	Home-maker	16	90.63	21.80				
	Students	24	95.71	19.35				
Family income (Rs. Per Month)	Below 10000	33	93.67	15.16	0.949	99	0.391	NS
	10001-20000	35	98.51	17.55				
	Above 20000	32	93.59	17.88				

It is evident from the table 10 that all the significant value of t/f – statistic between personal factors of the customers and their acceptance level of SSTe financial information mediums comes out to be is .254, .702, .423, .444, .391 which is greater than five percent level of significant value (0.05). Therefore, the null hypothesis is accepted and it can be concluded that there is no significant difference between banking sector, age group, educational and occupational status, family income of the women customers and their acceptance of SSTe financial information mediums. In addition the above table provides comparison of the each group of the customer acceptance through the mean value.

4. CONCLUSION

The above completed research work concludes that 7/10th of the women customers are having their acceptance level of SSTe financial information mediums as the medium. This is followed by more number of private sector bank customers has higher acceptance than the public sector bank customers. Banking sector, age group, educational qualification, occupational status, family income of the women customers is not related with their acceptance of SSTe financial information mediums. Finally, acceptance of SSTe financial information mediums is not differing among the various groups of customers.

REFERENCES

- Berger, A.N., Kashyap, A.K et.al (1995): "The Transformation of the US Banking Industry: What a Long, Strange Trip It's Been", *Brookings papers on Economic Activity*, 2, pp. 55-218.
- Bhattacharya, S. and Chiesa, G. (1995): "Proprietary Information, Financial Intermediation and Research Incentives", *Journal of Financial Intermediation*, Vol.4, pp. 328-357.
- Gurusamy (2007): *"Merchant Banking and Financial services"*, Second Edition, Vijay Nicole imprints Private Ltd. Chennai.
- Kumbhar V. M (2011): "Customers' Satisfaction in ATM Service: An Empirical Evidences from Public And Private Sector Banks In India", *Management Research and Practice*", Vol. 3, Issue 2, pp. 24-35.
- Milind Sathye (2003) "Efficiency of banks in a developing economy: The case of India", *European Journal of Operational Research*, Vol. 148, pp 662–671.
- Sudalaimuthu. S (2011): *"Right to Information Act – Its Progress, Public Awareness, Responsibility of Public Authorities and Functioning of Information Commissions – A Study with special Reference to Tamil Nadu"*, Major Research Project Report submitted to the Indian Council for Social Science Research, New Delhi, November.
- Sundaram. N, Tomar A.K et.all (2010): "Financial Inclusion – A Serious issue of Rural India", *Journal of Business Management*, Vol. 2, No. 2, pp. 301-307.
- Misra S.K., Puri V.K. (2002): *"Economic Environment of Business"*, Himalaya Publishing House, Mumbai.
- Vijayaragavan Iyengar (2007): *"Introduction to banking"*, Excel Books, First edition, New Delhi.
- RBI (2009-2010): *"Trend and Progress Report"* and various websites.

14 ENTREPRENEURSHIP: PATHWAY FOR SOCIAL INCLUSION OF WOMEN

P. Sangeetha, Dr.M.Kannan

INTRODUCTION

Social inclusion refers to a policy designed to ensure that all people are able to participate in society regardless of their background or specific characteristics, which may include: race, language, culture, gender, disability, social status, age, and other factors. Compared to the general population, groups with such special characteristics are much more likely to face low education, unemployment, homelessness -- and resulting poverty and social exclusion. The goal of social inclusion is to give all people an equal chance for participation in society. In order to achieve this goal, the barriers to participation in all aspects of life, such as education, employment, leisure, and citizenship must be addressed. The barriers may be material, such as physical inaccessibility; but very often the barriers are intangible, for example, discrimination, which serves to exclude.

"What we need is an entrepreneurial

Society in which innovation and

Entrepreneurship is normal, steady

And continual."

Peter F. Drucker

Entrepreneurship is a core component to build socially inclusive and well developed economy in global competitive world. As women are considered as weaker sex in our country they are deprived of their rights and loose their identities in larger extent. Hence, entrepreneurship is a key element to uplift the status of women in society.

ENTREPRENEURSHIP:

It's a process through which individuals identify opportunities, allocate resources, and create value. This creation of value is often through the identification of unmet needs or through the identification of opportunities for change. Matching the basic qualities required for entrepreneurs and the basic characters of women reveal that, much potential is available among the women on their entrepreneurial ability. There are a number of mental, social and cultural barriers that women have to overcome for becoming successful entrepreneurs. Given the social context of rural India, they need a lot more time and nurturing before they develop the confidence to become full- fledged entrepreneurs, independently handling all aspects of their enterprise, including marketing,. Even if women display a number of entrepreneurial competencies, they may still not develop into entrepreneurs, because even competent women are not comfortable to take up work that would invite comments and derision from the community. A few examples of technologies being used by these women for income generation are smokeless household stoves, biomass based dryers, and energy efficient domestic lighting. Entrepreneurship education can help promote an entrepreneurial and innovative culture by changing mindsets and providing the necessary skills.

CONTRIBUTION OF GOVERNMENT:

The Ministry of Women and Child Development seeks to promote economic empowerment of women through policies and programmes cutting across sectors, mainstreaming gender concerns, creating awareness about their rights and facilitating institutional and legislative support for enabling them to develop to their full potential. . The important programmes in different areas are,

SKILL UP GRADATION:

A. Support to Training & Employment Programme for Women (STEP):

A Central Sector Scheme launched in 1986-87, seeks to upgrade skill of poor and asset less women and provide employment on sustainable basis by mobilizing them in viable cooperative groups, strengthening marketing linkages, support services and access to credit. The scheme also provides for enabling support services in the form of health check-ups, legal and health literacy, elementary education, gender sensitization and mobile crèches. The ten traditional sectors identified for project funding under STEP comprise of agriculture, animal husbandry, dairying, fisheries, handlooms, handicrafts, khadi and village industries, sericulture, waste land development and social forestry. The scope and coverage of the scheme is being broadened with introduction of locally appropriate sectors being identified and incorporated into the scheme.

B. Rajiv Gandhi Scheme for Empowerment of Adolescent Girls (RGSEAG) – 'Sabla'

A centrally-sponsored scheme was approved by the Government. The scheme is being implemented in 200 districts across the country on a pilot basis. ***Sabla*** is being implemented through the State Governments/UTs with 100 per cent financial assistance from the Central Government for all inputs other than nutrition provision for which 50 % Central assistance to States is provided. Anganwadi Centre is the focal point for the delivery of the services.

OBJECTIVES:

- Life Skill Education and accessing public services,
- Vocational training for girls aged 16 and above under National Skill Development Program (NSDP)

C. Central Social Welfare Board (CSWB)

In order to address the socio-economic needs of the women and children of selected eight most backward districts in the North Eastern region in the economic arena, Central Social Welfare Board has formulated the Integrated Scheme for Women Empowerment (ISWE). The scheme is being implemented on pilot basis since 2008 and has the objective of meeting the felt needs of the area by mobilizing community action, converging available services and resources of the area, income generation through feasible and sustainable activities for women and to provide services for health awareness, career counseling vocational training, preventing child trafficking and other social evils.

ECONOMIC IMPROVEMENT:

A. National Mission for Empowerment of Women

The extent of empowerment of women from a holistic and macro-point of view is largely determined by 3 factors viz. economic, social and political identity. These factors are deeply intertwined and linked with many cross cutting linkages. The objectives of the Mission are to:

1. Ensure economic empowerment of women,
2. Ensure that violence against women is eliminated progressively,
3. Ensure empowerment of women with emphasis on health and education,

4. Oversee gender mainstreaming of programmes, policies, institutional arrangements and processes of participating Ministries, institutions and organizations, and Economic Empowerment of Women is to be achieved through convergence of the schemes and programmes having focus on formation and promotion of SHGs so as to enable women to have access to micro credit and micro finance. Programmes like National Rural Livelihood Mission. The Mission would see that access to credit by women SHGs under schemes of NABARD, Rashtriya Mahila Kosh, etc,

B. Rashtriya Mahila Kosh - (National Credit Fund for Women)

The main objective behind the setting up of the Rashtriya Mahila Kosh (RMK) under the Department of Women and Child Development (now Ministry) was to provide micro-credit to poor women for various livelihood support and income generating activities at concessional terms in a client-friendly procedure to bring about their socio-economic development.

SUPPORT SERVICES:

A. the Scheme of Working Women Hostel envisages provision of safe and affordable hostel accommodation to working women, single working women, women working at places away from their home-towns and for women being trained for employment.

B.Rajiv Gandhi National Crèche Scheme-With a view to encourage women to join/ continue with gainful employment, Rajiv Gandhi National Crèche Scheme for children of working mothers (RGNCS) was introduced in 2006. The scheme seeks to provide day care facilities to children in the age group 0-6 years from families with a monthly income of less than Rs. 12,000/-. In addition to being a safe space for the children, the crèche provide services like supplementary nutrition, pre- school education, emergency health care etc.

C. Indira Gandhi Matritva Sahyog Yojana (IGMSY) – Conditional Maternity Benefit (CMB) scheme is a Conditional Cash Transfer scheme for pregnant and lactating women to contribute to better enabling environment by providing cash incentives for improved health and nutrition to pregnant and nursing mothers. . It would address short term income support objectives with long term objective of behavior and attitudinal change. The scheme attempts to partly compensate for wage loss to pregnant & lactating women both prior to and after delivery of the child. Practitioners also need to systematically take into account the specific needs related to gender. They should adopt a gender-aware approach to enterprise support including a strategic vision with specific objectives and targets. Partnerships with specialised organisations and the implementation of quality standards can improve the consideration of gender-specific needs. It is therefore important to stimulate networking and information exchange between business support organisations targeting women, research facilities and other relevant actors in the field of female entrepreneurship. Moreover, there is a need to foster more and lasting local networks between potential and established female entrepreneurs. Networks serve several purposes, such as mentoring, provision of role models, technical assistance, training and lobbying, and have a considerable impact on the entrepreneurial activity of women. In addition, the positive influence of role models presented through the media should be further explored. The industrial polices and five-year plans of the government have encouraged entrepreneurs to increase the tempo of industrialization. The government now provides various incentives and concessions, which include capital subsidy, technical know-how, marketing facilities, providing industrial sheds and other infrastructure facilities. After the establishment of Industrial Financial Corporation of India (IFCI) by the Central Government, Several state governments have started their own financial corporations to help entrepreneurs in raising finance and providing technical facility. Further, institutions like

- Industrial Development Bank of India (IDBI),
- Small Industrial Development Bank India (SIDBI),
- Small Industries Development Organization (SIDO),
- National Small Industries Corporations (NSIC),
- Small Industries Service Institutes (SISIs),
- State Small Industries Development Corporations (SSIDC),
- District Industries Centres (DICs)

Thus entrepreneurship is seen as a potential solution to many of the barriers to social inclusion of women and the provision of education is seen as a method for empowering women in our country. Entrepreneurship and entrepreneurial skills are core components to building socially inclusive and highly participatory economies in an increasingly global and competitive world. Awareness of the importance of entrepreneurship education in spurring economic growth and achieving the Millennium Development Goals, it also urges action.

INCLUSIVE GROWTH: MAINSTREAMING TRANSGENDER

15 A STUDY ON SOCIAL STATUS OF TRANSGENDER IN CONTEMPORARY SOCIETY

K.Someegnal

Transgender is the state of one's "gender identity (self-identification as woman, man, neither or both) not matching ones "assigned sex" (identification by others as male, female or intersex based on physical/genetic sex). The term *transgender* (TG) was popularized in the 1970s (but implied in the 1960s) describing people who wanted to live cross-gender without sex reassignment surgery. In the 1980s the term was expanded to an umbrella term, and became popular as a means of uniting all those whose gender identity did not mesh with their gender assigned at birth. In the 1990s, the term took on a political dimension as an alliance covering all who have at some point not conformed to gender norms, and the term became used to question the validity of those norms or pursue equal rights and anti-discrimination legislation, leading to its widespread usage in the media, academic world and law. The term continues to evolve. In recent years transgender has emerged as a subject of increasing social and cultural interest. Alongside a 'cultural turn' to transgender - signified by a rising focus on transgender within the media and popular culture - shifting attitudes towards transgender people are evident in the law. These social, cultural and legislative developments reflect the ways in which transgender is acquiring visibility in contemporary society, and mark transgender as an important and timely area of social and cultural inquiry. This includes welfare schemes initiated by the Government and acceptance of transgender people into the mainstream society. For example the government of Tamil Nadu (a state in South India) established a transgender welfare board in April 2008. Social welfare minister will serve as the president of the board. This effort is touted to be the first in India and even in the world. The government has also started issuing separate food ration cards for transgender people.In additional effort to improve the education of transgender people, Tamil Nadu government also issued an order on May 2008 to create a third gender for admissions to government colleges.The Government has also decided to conduct a census on the transgender population in order to issue identity cards.

In media also the projection of transgender is positive way. Karpaga, a transgender person born in Erode, Tamil Nadu performs a lead role in a new Tamil movie "Paal", thus becoming the first in India ever to achieve such a milestone. Kalki Subramaniam, a transgender person born in Pollachi, Tamil Nadu performs a lead role in a new Tamil movie "Narthagi. Sahodari Foundation is an organization working for the transgender rights. Founded by activist and actress Kalki Subramaniam in 2007, Sahodari Foundation is a well known organization in India for its creative and alternative advocacy methods. Also there is a telephone helpline called "Manasu" ("mind" in English) (0091-44-25990505) was set up by Tamil Nadu AIDS Initiative-Voluntary Health Services (TAI-VHS) for members of the transgender community, their families and the public. It functions between 10 a.m. and 6 p.m. and was launched by V. K. Subburaj, Principal Secretary of Health Department of Tamil Nadu. Subburaj launched the services in March 2009 and said it will be helpful in finding employment for transgender people. But the mainstream society in India does not always accept Transgender who are often, objects of ridicule, mockery and exploitation. The social and cultural practice of exploitation with discrimination coupled with poverty, illiteracy and limited opportunities of employment have forced the community onto a path of high-risk behaviour including sex work. So the researcher find it is an important issue to be addressed and made an attempt to know why transgender are still excluded even there are humpty number of reasons and policies to include them socially in the mainstream society.

THEORETICAL FRAME WORK & REVIEW

Sex is Physical and Natural. One may born Woman or Man. There is no choice given before birth. Although man or woman is born that, he or she has attraction nature of the opposite sex. Masculine and Feminine qualities are in everyone. Dominance of one sexuality defines one's Identity. But one may have orientation towards the other side. This is due to the circumstances in which one grows up and experiences one get from the life. Nothing wrong in having orientations. But problems comes, when such orientation lead to efforts in becoming the opposite sex. If Man wants to become Woman he has to change physically. This leads to moral crisis. In liberal societies this change of sex is accepted and tolerated. But in conservative societies it is prohibited. Therefore, this issue had to be approached with utmost care and sensitivity. The person who struggle to become different sex other than what is give naturally has to respected and empathized. So, on this aspect, the Suppressed people of this nature to be considered. They must be identified as a normal human being to the society. Mostly Transgender-Aravanis or Tirunangais in TamilNadu live at the margins of society with very low economic status. Only few Employment opportunities available for TGs. Many get their income from performing at ceremonies, begging or from prostitution. Violence against Transgender especially sex workers, is brutal and occurs in public places, police stations, prisons and at their homes. Now TGs unite themselves as Associations and work for their araisement. Everyday there are news related on Transgenders.So, the life of Transgender in the Democratic, Secular society is to be visualized to the public. They are one of our neighbours in our society. They are our neighbours. So, it is necessary to understand them. For this purpose we are going to study and so the regarding topic is selected.

METHODOLOGY

For this study the suitable methodology is Case study because Case study is an ideal methodology when a holistic, in-depth investigation is needed. Case studies have been used in varied investigations, particularly in sociological studies. Case studies are multi-perspectival analyses. This means that the researcher considers not just the voice and perspective of the actors, but also of the relevant groups of actors and the interaction between them. This one aspect is a salient point in the characteristic that case studies possess. They give a voice to the powerless and voiceless. When sociological investigations present many studies of the homeless and powerless, they do so from the viewpoint of the "elite". So the researcher found it is the suitable method to analyse the Social status of the Transgender. The samples were the age group of 20 and above 40 years drawn from different areas with the help of Voluntary organisation by convenient sampling.

RESULTS AND DISCUSSION:

Data collected through the case study were analyzed the result and discussions are as follows.

SOCIAL STATUS OF TGS

A Proverb Says "Suppressing a people is teaching them Courage" Like that, the discriminated TGs are also raised. They fight for their rights from government and the society. The Government does not express any special view on TGS until they get down in the road for their rights. But the scene has been changed. They fight for their Identity and Life.

PROBLEM OF TGS

Human Being is a social animal. The society is the platform for each individual. The rights and recognization in the society is the thing each individual expects. So as TGs expect these things. These problems are also identified and focused in the Documentary films Appal, the Third gender, Beyond the frame, AtchuPizhai, And Thirunangai. Problems suchs as gender identity, SRS operation, Employment, Govt support etc., are all visualized.

GENDER IDENTITY

Human Being is Identified as a male or female as per their gender. The TGs required their identity as TGs. They do not want to bear the identity that their sense is not in it. Mostly Female or Male identity is easy than recognization of Male to Female. This Gender Identity problem is the cause for all other problems of the TGs. So they appeal govt. should take steps to recognize their Third Identity.

LEGAL SRS OPERATION

In foreign countries if a person wants to change his/her gender identity they under go some tests and formalities. Then they could change their sex by SRS, Sex Reassignment Surgery. They can also change their names. Even a high-restricted Islamic country Malaysia is providing these facilities. This operation is not legal in India. So these operations are done illegally by Doctors or by TGs themselves. The cost of operation is also very high. Without proper equipments, they cause problems after the operations. Now our TamilNadu government is allowing doctors doing the operations in Government Hospitals. Without these legal permissions, they could not change names in the government Gazette.

LEGAL MARITAL RIGHT

Some TGs live as wife to male. Though they feel as husband and wife, law will not accept their marriage. They marry in temples as per Hindu Culture. Anyhow, they could not register their marriage. They feel marriage is a social and psychological support. They put their husband's name with their name e.g.PriyaBabu. In Gujarat, transsexual marriage between one tarunlatha who underwent a sex change operation and became a man with the name Tarunkumar. The validity of the said marriage Challenged on the ground that it was a lesbian relationship, which comes with purview of section 377of IPC 1860 dealing with unwanted offences.

CHILD ADOPTION

Though TGs get married, they could not give birth to a child. So they adopt children. This adoption is also not legalized by the govt. Anyhow they adopt children and live for them.

PROPERTY RIGHT

TGs get out their homes in their childhood or teenage. They were born as males. Indian penal code has given property of right from their parents. But most of the TGs families refused to give property of share to them. They treat them aggressively. The policy forces are also some times not favour to these TGs.

EDUCATIONAL RIGHT

Mostly TGs get out their homes in their teen ages. They discontinued their education. When they want to continue their education after they become TGs they have no proper certificate. If they have certificates, their name and sex in the certificate is opposite to the situation now. They could not even join in the Open University courses says Asha Bharathi. Now the Govt. Has ordered to arrest the discriminations in educational Institutions in the name genders.

RATION CARD

Every citizen must be cared by the state. Then only it will be a Welfare State. The TGS must also be cared by the govt by providing proper rights. Ration card is one of the citizen rights for providing him the civil supply gods for basical needs. It is also a permanent residential ID proof. This refused to TGs once. Some TGs are not having permanent residence. So they could not get their cards. But now they got these cards.

VOTER'S ID

It was a great plea of the TGs to Issue voting power. It was able in June 2003 only. Nearly 1 lakh of TGs voted in education. But it is a result of great struggle and climb on the Court. Former Election Commissioner T.N Seshan ordered to issues voters ID. But not issued in Tamilnadu. Lawyer Rajini, Persident of Southern Women's Association, filed a case for TGs. It gives solution to annex TGs in election voter's list.

EMPLOYMENT

Though some TGs are educated and technically qualified, mostly TGs are not provided jobs. Public will not give jobs. They feel them as shy and worst people. NGOs and TGs organizations only provide jobs for them. In dancing and cooking, they are not treated well. They said if proper job is provided they will not go for prostution.

CASES IN THE NAME OF IPC 377

The section 377 of the Indian Penal Code is talking about unnatural sex offences. In this section only, Child abuse and others coming. It is a good section. Anyhow, it affects the TG marriage or TGs having sex with male.Rather than this police also file fake cases on TGs.

PUBLIC BEHAVIOUR

There is a law to control Eve teasing, but not for TGs. The Youths and culprits in the public teased them. There are problems for TGs in travelling in bus. No female is ready to sit or stand near TGs. When they go to public toilets, they could not enter in to women toilets. Even some women oppose their entry. Mostly TGs have problem in getting houses for rent. People think that they are worst people and if they live near or in their house, it is indecent for them even places, which are given by Government, are also opposed by the public for TGs living. The TGs are also one of the members of our community. Their social, psychological, political views are identified through the research. In Ayyanpettai, Villupuram District, TN Government provides land for free apartment. It was opposed by the area people.In pukkaathurai, kancheepuram District land for 15 flats is provided. This area people also opposed it. TGs were not able to get Insurance and they face problems in getting mobile sim cards. Like these, they suffer a lot due to the gender difference.

MEDIA ATROCITY

A TG, who is discriminated by the family, get out of her home and join in a TG community. There are ceremonies when joining the TG unit called 'Jamath'. After joining she will be adopted by a senior TG. She will be treated as daughter to the senior TG. It is like pseudo family system. After that the new TG will be castrated. The operations done by them are called thayamma operation and which done in hospitals is called Doctor Operation. Their religious beliefs are mostly in Hindu mythology. The worship of Arvan is the festival they mainly celebrate in Tamil month Chithirai. Aravan is the character who marries Krishna who changed as Mohini and sacrifices himself to Kali. The TGs thought that they were resembles of Lord Krishna. In Koothandavar temple in koovagam Tamilnadu, the 18 days festival is celebrated grandly. From all over India TGs arrive for this festival. There are temples rather than Koovagam for Aravan in Tamilnadu but they were not celebrated like this.

ECONOMIC LIFE

The economical life of TGs is not appreciable. They earn mainly by dancing, catering, begging and prostitution. Some also do other small business. Like other female they marry men. It is not legally permitted by our law. However most of their marriages are not successful. Psychological pressures which they faced from their family, school, society urges them to change as Transgender. These pressures even tend them to suicide. Rather than this media is focusing them as Sex vulgar people. It tends the people to tease them. But the scene has now changing. Now the Government has take steps for their uplift. The identity, sex reassignment operation, ration card, voter card are cared by the Government and Tamilnadu government has ordered to form a separate Welfare Board for TGs. TGs themselves unite as Association and fought for their rights. THAA as pioneer, nearly 12 associations work for them. Rather than these, NGOs also work for their welfare. The rights they got and the public view on them are the fruits of their Activism.

TRANSGENDER'S ACTIVISM

'Suppressing a people is teaching them courage'. Like this TGs who discriminated by others form a unite community. They fight for their rights. In North India TGs are very active in local policies. There a slogan arose 'There is one solution to useless politicians, give the mandate to eunuchs'. Sabanam Mausi became India's first TG M.P. fro Madhya Pradesh in 1999, as an independent only 5 years since the TG have been able to vote. Another TG Kamala Jaan was elected as mayor of Katni. Meena bai became the president of the Sehra town municipality. In 2000, Asha Devi was elected as Mayor of Gorakpur. In Tamil nadu there is not a situation of entry in politics. But there are many activists who work together for their rights. They form associations; they appeal government for their rights and try to change the view of the society.

CONCLUSION

The present study helped the researcher to know about the social status of the Transgenders in the contemporary society. At the end of the study the researcher found that there is a change in the views of people about the transgender but it is not enough for the upliftment of the Transgender. The change which is existing today helped only 5 to 10 percent of the transgenders to become great in life such as Kalki, Narthagi Natarajan, Rose, Vidya, and Priya Barathi and so on. They are working a lot to have Communal Identity. It is in hands of the public and in their perception for the development of rest of the Community.

REFERENCES

- www.imdb.com/keyword/transgender
- www.answers.com/topic/hijra-southasia
- www.transgendercare.com
- www.en.wikipedia.org/wiki/eunuch
- www.en.wikipedia.org/wiki/transgender
- www.geocities.com/leylasuhagi/hijraislam.html

- www.galva108.org/deities.html
- Krishnaswamy .O.R, Renganathan.M, Methods of Research in Social Sciences, Himalaya Publishing Home, Mumbai, 2006.
- Revathi, Unarvum Uruvamum, Adaiyalam & Sangama, 1205/1, Karupar salai, Puthanatham – 621310, 1st Edition 2005.
- Samuthram.S, Vaadamalli, Vanathi Pathippagam, T.Nagar, Chennai -17, 3rd Edition, Dec 2003.

16 SOCIAL EXCLUSION OF TRANSGENDER AND INCLUSION THROUGH SOCIAL WORK STRATEGIES

P.G.Nisha, Dr.K.Suryan

INTRODUCTION

Social exclusion and financial exclusion are relatively recent political concepts. The official definition of social exclusion is: 'Social Exclusion is a complex and multi-dimensional process. It involves the lack or denial of resources, rights, goods and services, and the inability to participate in the normal relationships and activities, available to the majority of people in a society, whether in economic, social, cultural or political arenas. It affects both the quality of life of individuals and the equity and cohesion of society as a whole. A large number of factors which lead to individual members of society feeling excluded from society have been identified. They are: having too little money, having poor mental and physical health, living in a poor quality neighborhood where there is a high risk of crime and a high fear of crime, not receiving the appropriate care, poor mobility and access to transport, a lack of good social or support networks, living alone without a family around them, living with a family but isolated from the gay community, not having the privacy of their own home, poor or limited access to suitable local services, low opportunities for civic participation and cultural activities, not having a bank account, limited use of basic financial services, poor employment, learning and skills opportunities, no opportunities to use digital technology, lack of transport, unsuitable, and poorly-maintained housing, no access to suitable information, advice, advocacy and redress, inability to afford and use common consumer goods, inability to plan and save for the future .In India has around 1billon population of transgender and in Tamilnadu theyare30,000 in number they live full or partially in the gender role. Generally they are described as transverse, hijras, Aravanis, jogappas.In Society transgender are excluded in many forms

WHO ARE THEY?

Transgender is a term used to describe people who may act, feel, think, or look different from the gender that they were born with. The word transgender is used to include many groups of people who share one important "trait" (a way of feeling or behaving) but may not be the same in other ways. The common trait for transgender people is that they call themselves "transgender" and feel that their given gender is not quite right. Sometimes the word "transgender" is also used by people who prefer it to the word "transsexual".Sex is assigned at birth, refers to one's biological status as either male or female, and is associated primarily with physical attributes such as chromosomes, hormone prevalence, and external and internal anatomy. Gender refers to the socially constructed roles, behaviors, activities and attributes that a given society considers appropriate for boys and men or girls and women. These influence the ways that people act, interact and feel about themselves. While aspects of biological sex are similar across different cultures, aspects of gender may differTrans" is crossing or to cross. And "sex" is sort of the scientific or biological classification of an organism's sex. So "transsexual" for me describes someone who is crossing from one sexual classification into another as well as they can, using current medical technology. So it sort of implies someone who's having surgery or taking hormones, or doing other medical interventions to align their body with their new sex. Transgender is a person whose gender identity, gender expression or behavior does not conform to that typically associated with the sex to which they were assigned at birth. Gender identity refers to a person's internal sense of being male, female or something else; gender expression refers to the way a person communicates gender identity to others through behavior, clothing, hairstyles, voice, or body characteristics. Transgender whose appearance or behavior is gender-nonconforming will identify as transgender person. The ways that transgender people are talked about in popular culture, academia, and science are constantly changing particularly as individual's awareness, knowledge, and openness about transgender people and their experiences grow. Transgender is a term that literally means--"trans" means "crossing" or "across" and "gender" is "gender"--so, transgender describes someone who is crossing gender boundaries. At its most broad definition it could be a woman with short hair or a man with long hair because typically in the past men have had shorter and women have had longer, so they are crossing gender boundaries. In a more precise sense a drag queen would be transgender because it is a male wearing and taking on the characteristics of a female, or a drag king is a female taking on the characteristics and persona of a male. Transgender just means you are crossing those artificial lines of what men and women are supposed to be like in society. Transgender and identity: In the medical world the transgender are called "gender Dysphoia", meaning those feel caught in the body of other sex (a women caught in the male body) may experience such intense and prolonged is comfort that they undergo a process of gender role transition in which they express their in gay gender identities called gender identity disorder. Gender and sex is not same. Gender is a social and cultural construct but sex is biological determination. But the fact is that transgender gender identity is different from their sexual identity. Their accepted sexual behavior doesn't match with their gender identity. The transgender are people who have a different gender identity in their body in a sense, born as boy feel as girl or vice—versa from adolescent period on wards due to biological cause related to the mind and body. People who are assigned a sex at birth based on genital, but who feel this is a false or incomplete description of them, so the work transgender/transgender in the inclusive for individual who challenge traditional gender roles and the assumption that sex determines gender.

TRANSGENDER DEFINED AS;

Transgender people have a gender identity that is different from their birth sex or express their gender in way that contrivance. Societal expectations of the range of possibilities for men and women. Some transgender people identify as men or women, while others have an identity that is not as simple as man or women. This an umbrella term may include cross dressers tag king queens, transsexuals people who are androgynous, two sprit people, and people who are bigendered or multigendered.

FEMALE-TO-MALE:

Female-To-Male or FTM is a sort of classification of a trans-person who was assigned the gender of female at birth and who is transitioning socially and, perhaps, medically and legally into living as male.

MALE-TO-FEMALE:

Male-To-Female or M-To-F identifies someone who was assigned the male gender at birth and who is transitioning socially (and perhaps medically and legally) to living as female.

GENDER QUEER:

Gender queer is a term that is used essentially by a lot of younger and up-and-coming people who just are not willing to play by the old game of what men should do and be and what women should do and be. Gender queer people just like sort of flouting those conventions and expressing themselves however they want and even specifically sometimes being a little shocking to sort of shake up the system.

TWO-SPIRIT:

Two-spirit is a term that was recently brought back into the lexicon by Native American indigenous people and Canadian indigenous people. It describes people in the indigenous cultures, way back when, who felt like they had both a male and a female spirit in their body. And those people were often revered and consulted as mystics and people of great value in those early cultures. The current native and indigenous people are reclaiming that identity and term, and bringing it back out as a way to sort of celebrate the way their culture views Tran's issues.

GENDER IDENTITY:

Gender identity is usually understood to be a person's own sense of their identity as male or female. You're - everyone is - assigned a gender at birth, usually based on just a cursory examination of their body. But most people end up feeling on the inside that that was the right, you know, identification. There are some people who just feel inside that they are a different gender, though, and that's where a term like gender identity becomes important.

BI-GENDER:

Bi-gender or bi-gendered is a term that some people use to describe a feeling that they embody both genders, male and female. They don't feel like they're one or the other, they feel like they're sort of everything in one.

CISGENDER:

Cisgender or cisgendered is a newer term that sort of came about, mostly it spread on the Internet. But if you just look at the root part of the word, the etymology, it means someone who is comfortable in the gender they were assigned at birth. So the majority of the people on the planet are cisgender or cisgendered. They're comfortable with their assigned gender.

ANDROGYNE:

Androgyny is somebody who embodies both male and female characteristics. Andro meaning male and gyno meaning female. It's often used to describe somebody who doesn't seem to embody either male or female characteristics as well, if you describe somebody as androgynous, it often means you can't tell what they are, or they are not very definite in their presentation.

TRANSWOMAN:

A transwoman is a term that a lot of people in the Trans community use as sort of a simple catch all to describe a woman who is transitioning from male to female. And she may or may not be undergoing medical, may or may not be undergoing legal, or she may or may not be undergoing social steps, but she's doing one or all of those.

TRANSMAN:

Transman is sort of a catch-all term for someone who is transitioning into the male gender and sex. But they may not necessarily be undergoing medical transition or they may not necessarily be going through legal. Trans is sort of a catch-all term that doesn't nail them down to either sex or gender.

TOTAL POPULATION OF TRANSGENDER

In Developed countries 1,000,000 (1 million) men in the U.S.14, 000,000 (14 million) men worldwide are transgender - not including women. About 9 million people across the United States identify themselves as lesbian, gay, bisexual or transgender.

Bangladesh - 300.000

European - 30.000 MTF

100,000FTM

Belgium - 12,900 MTF

33,800 FTM

U.K - 3, 00,000 to 5, 00,000

United states - 900,000 LGBT

Bangkok - 17,000

Thailand - 180,000

Indonesia - 20960 – 35300

Hijras have long been involved in the make-up of India, between 500,000 to 1 million, and are a caste unto them. Tamilnadu has an estimated population of 30,000 transgender people Social Exclusion Knowledge Network (SEKN) model, developed by Popay et al. assumes that social exclusion is driven by unequal power dynamics and operate in four interconnected and relational dimensions (e.g. cultural, economic, political, and social) at different levels (e.g. individuals, groups, households, communities, countries, and the world as a whole) The power dynamics construct a continuum: inclusion to exclusion along the line of inter-related and interdependent factors, such as cultural, economic, political and social issues. Economic aspects of exclusion include barriers to employment opportunities, constrained access to commodities, and livelihood opportunities, such as income, housing, land, and working conditions. Social aspects of exclusion refer to limited or no access to social, educational, legal and health services, resulting from ruptured social protection and social cohesion, such as kinship, family, neighborhood, and the community. Cultural aspects of exclusion refer to subordination of certain norms, behaviors, cultural practices, and lifestyles which exclude certain individuals or groups. Political aspects of exclusion refer to deprivations of citizens' rights, including restricted access to organizations, voter rights, legislations, constitutions, and decision-making in policy. This multidimensional model of social exclusion also frames analysis of the experiences of hijra. An explicit link between exclusion and rights encompasses discrimination on the basis of gender orientation. However, transgender population or others who prefer living with alternative gender and sexualities are not included in the list. Gendered exclusion was only considered in the case of women in various settings. SEKN model to guide theoretical and conceptual exploration of social exclusion in lives of hijra.

SOCIAL EXCLUSION OF TRANSGENDER:

Transgender communities have been excluded from effectively participating in social and cultural life, economy and politics and decision making processes. This paper illustrates the multiple forms of oppression faced by transgender communities.

SOCIO - CULTURAL PARTICIPATION;

Tolerance in Indian society is quiet common, languages and customs but the level of acceptance and tolerance are depending up on public knowledge and understanding of same sex sexual orientation and people whose gender identity and expression with their biological sex.A cultural aspect of exclusion refers to subordination of certain norms behavior cultural practices and lifestyles which excluded certain individuals or groups. Social aspects of exclusion refer to limited or no access to social educational legal and health services resulting from ruptured social protection and social ridicule gender- variant people for being different and they may even be hostile even from police they face physical and verbal abuse forced sex, extortion of money and materials assets on false allegation. They are easily target for extorting money and as sexual objects. A 2007 study documented that 75% of transgender reported; forced sex is 46% physical abuse is 44% verbal arouse is 56%, blackmail for money is and thereat to life is 24%. Exclusion of transgender from the family members. Like non-acceptance of their male child behaving like feminine or inappropriate to the expect gender role consequently family members may threaten, sex even assault their son/ sibling from behaving or dressing up like a girls or women. Some parents may outright disown and erect their own child for crossing up likes a girl or women. Some parents may outright disown and erect their own child for crossing the prescribed gender norms of the society. Reason for excluding the transgender from the family bringing disgrace and shame to the family, diminished chances of their child getting married to transgender women may find it difficult even to claim their share of the property. The child or teenaged may decided to run away from the family not able to tolerate the discrimination or not wanting to bring shame to ones family. So they find their way to transgender communities.

ECONOMIC EXCLUSION

Transgender communities face variety of social security issues. Since most hijras run away from the home, they do not expect support from their biological family. Subsequently they face a lot of challenges especially health concerns, lack of employment opportunities. Economic commodities and live hood opportunities. Such as income, housing, land and working conditions. Lack of living hood options: Most of employers deny employment for even qualified and skilled transgender people lack of live hood options is key reason for transgender people to choose or continue to be in sex work with its associated HIV and health related risks. Recently, transgender have been self employed who run food shop or organize cultural programs; qualified TG women became agents for life insurance Corporation of India. Lack of specific social welfare schemes and barriers to existing schemes; Social welfare department provide a variety of social welfare schemes for socially and economically disadvantaged groups. No specific schemes are available for hijras, except some rare case for providing land for aravanis in tamilnadu. Recently the state government of Andrpradesh had ordered the monority welfare department to consider hijras as minority and develop welfare schemes for them. Only the department of social welfare in the state of tamilnadu has recently established "Aravanigal/ Transgender women welfare board" to address the social welfare issues of Aravanis/Hijras.

POLITICAL EXCLUSION:

A political aspect of exclusion refers to deprivations of citizen's right, including restricted acess to organizations, voterrights, legislation constitutions and decision making in policy. In 1897, the criminal tribe's act of 1871 was amended and under the provisions of the statue "a eunuch (was) deemed to include all the members of the male sex who admit themselves or a medical inspection clearly appear, to be impotent." Under the section 377 of the Indian penal code according to the sections who appear dressed or ornamented like a women in a public street or who dances or plays music or takes part in any public exhibition should be arrested warrant and hijras were also reportedly harassed by the police by threatening to file a criminal case under sec-377 zpx. In July 2009, the Delhi high court ruled the consensual same sex relations between adults in private cannot be criminalized.

LEGAL EXCLUSION:

Legal issues can be complex for people who changes sex, as well as for those who are gender-variant. Legal recognition of their gender identity and same sex marriage, child adoption, inheritance, will and trusts, immigration, status, employer discrimination and access to public health benefits and private health benefits. Especially getting legal recoginisation of gender identity is complicated procees.Lack of legal recoginisation has important consequences in getting government rationcard, passport and bank account. Some of the legal provisions (e.g. Indian trust Act, society's registration act) that enable a group of individuals to form a legal association and it is challenges for transgender communications.

SOCIAL WORK INTERVENTION MODEL

Researcher adopted a systems approach (Carpenter and Treacher, 1993) to conceptualize the transsexual's problems. In the light of this approach, a transsexuals gender problem is not understood as an individual pathology but rather as a result of interaction between the individuals, family and societal system the overall goal of intervention is to help transsexuals improve their social adjustment .specific goals are formulated for each transsexuals is need of help, on the basis of the individualized social assessment. These goals can be roughly grouped as follows:

1. To help them improve their relationship with their family and to seek support from them.
2. To enable them to enhance their interpersonal relationships;
3. To help them live through their grief towards the loss of their love;
4. To link them with community resources

CRITICAL ISSUES RELATED TO SOCIAL WORK INTERVENTION:

Six issues were found to be important and pertinent to the success of social work intervention with transsexuals. First, the social worker does not consider transsexuals to be abnormal and adopts a new perspective; that is a system perspective, to view their problems and difficulties. As Carpenter and Treacher (1993, p.15) have said,' one of the power we have is the power to see things in different ways to help people to find new meanings- but we have start where they are and not where we are.' The interaction between the social worker and transsexuals is reciprocal. When transsexuals feel that the social worker traits them as normal people, they open up and trust the social worker. it is essential for the social worker to assess if transsexuals are ready to work on their own problems ,and to respect their choices accordingly ,rather than taking up a paternalistic view and making he decision for them. Second, although a structural family approach is used in working with transsexuals and their significant others; individual work is a part and a parcel of the intervention. Individual counseling was made available to the transsexuals before the family interviews. The individual work is systems oriented. The focus of intervention is to help transsexuals identify the sources of stress that have arises from the maladaptive interaction between them and their significant others. Motivating transsexuals to work on their difficulties is necessary, since they have avoided the problem for a long time. However, it is even more important for the social worker not to own their problems and to let them decide if they should disclose their secrets tot heir significant others. Motivation transsexuals to work on their difficulties necessary, since they have avoided the problem for a long time. How ever, it is even more important for the social worker not to won their problems and to let them decided if they should disclose their secrets to their significant others. Third, a structural family approach was found to be useful in working with transsexuals and their significant others. Most come from lower-middle or working-class families. It is easier for them to identify their difficulties in their family interests (e.g. losing 'face' for the family) than to work on their presumed intrapsychic conflicts. They are more receptive to action oriented and here-and-now intervention than to intervention characterized by abstract thinking and cognitive discussion. It provides a social context for transsexuals to over come their difficulties and to interact in a new way. Fourth, socio culture factors also shape the interaction between the transsexual, their significant others and health care services. The traditional cultural norms and expectations demand for conformity, the face of the family and the inseparable relation between the individual and family maters are important; these add to the psychological but of transsexuals in general. Because of this, help in their families to understand their difficulties in social context as an important part of the intervention to reduce their distress. Fifth in this case, social work intervention has been mainly confined to work at the family level. Not much has been done with the large system such as mass media. The societal pressure could be alleviated if the public exercise more understanding an acceptance towards transsexual when the mass media stops portraying transsexual's deviants and begins to report their pain and suffering, transsexual will be better able to person choice to decide what they believe to be the best course of their action for themselves. transgender forum gay movement advocates homosexuals human rights, works towards gaining the sympathy of society and is active in voicing their needs tobe treated as dignified citizens.Sixth,despite being in a hostile sociocultural environment such as Indian society provides, most transsexuals were able to pass muster with the public and adjusted well. A few failed to do so, partly because of inadequate family and societal support.

CONCLUSION;

To conclude, helping transsexuals to adjust themselves living condition can be achieved through the following: a shift of orientation from a pathological perspective to a systems perspective, the use of a structural family therapy approach: recognition of the roles played by sociocultural factors in shaping their interaction between families and the healthcare service; a genuine respect for transsexuals basic human rights.

17 PLIGHT OF FEMALE SEX WORKERS IN MADURAI TOWN

T.Kavitha, Dr.K.Suriyan

We are people.... and we want to be treated
With respect and dignity and
We want right the rest of your enjoy.

-Dina Chan, Sex workers Union of Toul Kork

INTRODUCTION

Sex trade is one of the oldest professions in the society. Sex work may be formal and informal in some instances; sex work is only a temporary informal activity. Women and men or Transgender who have occasional commercial sexual transaction or where sex is exchanged for food, shelter or protection would not consider themselves to be linked with formal sex work. The sex industry in Asia is changing rapidly. It is become increasingly complicated, with highly differentiated sub sectors. The majority of studies, together with anecdotal evidence, suggest that commercial sex is becoming more common and that it is involving a greater number of people in a greater variety of sites. Occasional sex work take place where sex is exchanged for basic, short term Economic needs and this is less likely to be formal, full time occupation. Commercial sex worker may be conducted in formally organised in formally organised setting from sites such brothels, nightclubs and massage parlours. Most women do not choose prostitution: They are forced into this type of work because of drug addition, poverty, Lack of education etc., [1]

In India until recently , the temple harboured dancing girl under the devadasi system Devadasi literally mean God's(Dev)Female servant(Dais),that persons called Religious prostitution.[2] Prostitution can be considered as sexual harassment, rape, battering, verbal abuse, domestic violence, a racist practice, a violation of human rights,

Children sexual abuse, a consequence of male domination of women a means of maintaining male dominating of women or all of the above. The commercial sex industry include street prostitution, message brothels, escort service, out call services, night clubs, lab dancing, phone sex adult and child pornography, peep shows prostitution tourism. Most women who are in prostitution for longer than a few month drift among these various permutation of the commercial sex industry. But for most of the women and child prostitution in India.[3]

SEX WORK AND PROSTITUTION

A broad meaning of 'sex worker' would be the exchange of money or goods for sexual services either regularly or occasionally involving female , male and transgender adults, young people and children where the sex worker may or may not consciously define such activity as income generating. But the are most women who enter in to the trade tend to come from urban slums and poor rural areas. High prostitute supply regions in India include Andhra Pradesh, Tamilnadu and West Bengal and some very poor North States.[4] an estimated 35 percent of prostitutes are young girl. In Bangalore, Calcutta, Delhi, Hyderabad, there are an estimated 10,000 girl prostitute. The girl tends to come from urban slums and poor rural area. High prostitute supply regions include. Andhra Pradesh, Karnataka, Maharashtra, Uttar Pradesh, Tamilnadu and West Bengal states. About 85 percent are Hindus and about 66 percent are from Scheduled Castes and tribes. Bangalore and Bombay have a higher proportion of girl prostitutes. The countries like Nepal and Bangladesh from their boarder from their were 50% poor migrants to India involving in sex trade.

'Prostitution' is the sale of sexual services such as oral sex or sexual intercourse for many persons. Prostitution the word itself speaks about the plight of women. Some women are entering as sex workers for their children's welfare. Their girl children are

Much more likely to get involved in this kind of field. The other reason for their involvement in this field of are ill treatment by the parents, family prostitutes, social norm, inability to arrange marriage, lack of sex education, early marriage, lake of recreational facilities, ignorance acceptance of the prostitution, economic causes like poverty, psychological causes like desire for physical pleasure, dejection etc.[5]

PROBLEMS FACED

The prostitution facing more problems such as sexual harassment, rape, battering, verbal abuse, domestic violence, a racist practice, a violation of human rights, childhood sexual abuse, a consequence of male domination of women, a means of maintaining male domination of women, all of the above the prostitutes faced in field.

SEX WORKERS TERMS

Sex workers known by different names in different areas. Jogan Shankar gives the names by which they are known in various parts, such a Mohair's in kerala, Nazis in Assam and Basavis in Karnataka. In Goa they 'Bhavanis' and Kudikar on the West-Coast, Bhogam-Vandhi or Jogin in Andhra Pradesh, Thevadiyar in Tamilnadu, Murali and jogateen and Aradhini in Maharashtra in Karnataka, Old Devadasies are called as jogati and young Devadasies as Basavi. The term Basavi refer to feminine form of Basava a bull which roams the village at will without any restriction. Hence Basavi allude to the foot loose positution.It is probably during this period that the ancient classical temple dance forms like Odissi (Jagannath Temple Oissa), Kutchipudi(Andhra Pradesh) and Bharatbnattiyam (Tamilnadu). The Devadai system is a form of open prostitution. The poor people dedicate their daughters to the system in the name of appeasing the gods. [6]

TYPES OF COMMERCIAL SEX WORKERS

Cage girls in Pillow houses

The worts brothel are called "pillow house", where prostitutes are separated by cloth dividers in tiny rooms. Visitors are charged $3 for a few minutes, and strict vigil is maintained to discourage prostitutes from talking to their customer. Payment is made to the brothel owner who keeps the money, and allows as many as forty visitors a day during "peak" season.

Point of no return

Escape is never an option because there is a nexus between criminal, pims, brothel owner and the local police who share the major part of the commercial sex worker income. What trickles down to the hapless woman is a mere pittance. It is an open secret that all important red light areas in India enjoy police protection, which means the policemen themselves go to the brothel for tea, snacks and girls. In return for favours, they inform the brothel keepers in advance about the raids that are scheduled to take place. A girl who escaped from her brothel and went to police was reportedly raped by them and brought back to her owner the following day. Most prostitutes do not even make the attempt to escape because they have nowhere to go, they are illiterate and have been smuggled into the city.

Call Girls

Call girls are commercial sex workers who are part-timers and are usually more educated, carry cell phones, and are well groomed and cannot be compared to those live in brothels. They have more mobility, earn higher incomes and have some freedom in choosing their clients who are mostly from the middle and upper classes of society. Generally, call girls are known to take good care of their health and visit doctor whenever necessary. Almost all of them want their client to use condom, though they most often comply when client offer a much higher amount for condom – free sex.

Escort Girl

The costliest end of the supply the high- class escort girls were recruited from women's college and from burgeoning fashion and film industries to commercial sex workers trade. For large sum of money and usually operate by way of a discreet introduction service. The boom in internet services has seen the emergence of several snazzy websites, openly advertising escort girl services.

Devadasi system

The devadasi system is still flourishing in parts of India, especially in the south and specifically in the states of Maharashtra, Andhra Pradesh, Tamilnadu and Karnataka. There are more than 450, 0000 Devadasie trapped in this form of prostitution. A Devadasies, in way is considered "Public property" in the village. Devadasies who do not become prostitute struggle to survive as agricultural labourer or maidservants. A report commissioned by the National Commission for Women in India reveals the shocking reality of how thousands of dalit women continue to be forced into the Devadasies system in several states of India.

Gigoglos

Call it role reversal or western influence or proof that sex revolution in India is in full swing-Indian gigolos or male prostitutes entertaining women for money have come to stay. Earlier a large percentage of male prostitutes were the eunuchs or hijras. Now it can be a well dressed male frequenting internet community groups, coffee house, swanky restaurants and multiplexes. Male prostitutes are known by various names and euphemisms including male escorts, gigolos, rent-boys, hustlers, models or masseurs. The term "rent boy" may be derived from the boys "renting" themselves out. A man who does not regard himself a gay, but who is prepared to have sex with male client for money, is sometimes called gay for pay or rough trade. Male prostitutes offering services to female customers are sometimes known as gigolos.

Child Prostitution

The ugliest face of the sex trade in many Asian countries is child prostitution. In the Nigerian milieu, prostitutes below the age of 18 are regarded as child prostitutes, since only persons above 18 years of age are statutorily regarded as adult .Child prostitution is the "Sexual exploitation of girls and teenagers" Awake February 2003, available data show that approximately 1.5 million children in India, 1 million in Asia, 10,000 children in United states and 5000 children in Latin America are engaged in prostitution. According to jubilee Action report (1995 to up 1 million female children join prostitution each year around the globe. Given the phenomenal increase in sex tourism, the number is bound to have risen to frightening proportion. Poor families are ticked into selling their children to such work for meagre sums as 4 or 5 USD. Their family member thrust sometimes girl children who are victims of incest into this trade.

Police as Pimps

A Part from the many child prostitutes working in Indian brothels, many more are tempted into the sex trade by sex tourism and pedophiles who offer children for money and other rewards into sexual activities. Just one Indian city Goa, sees as may as 10,000 pedophiles visit each year. 70%of the children who are victims of sex acts do not tell anyone. Though according to the Universal Declaration of Human Rights, the Convention on the Rights of the child, many other international treaties and agreements and local Indian laws, Child prostitution is strictly illegal, offences rarely end in conviction. The crime ring is well organized and police officer extorts money from trafficker and offenders and abets the system of prostitution by falsifying documents to prove that the children are not minors. In one case, a ten-year old girl prostitute who was rescued by a hawker after many attempts was returned to the brothel keeper by the local inspector on the same day. [7]

Sex Workers at Global Level

S.No	Place	Child Prostitutes	No. of Sex Workers
1	Wold wide	1.2	-
2	India	-	12,63 laks
3	Britain	-	30,000
4	USA	10,000	-
5	Asian	1million	-
6	Uk		4,000
7	Sirlanka	40,000	-
	Colombo	35,000	8,000
8	Hong Kong	-	20,000
9	Thailand	-	300,000 to 2.8 million
10	Vietnam	20,000	300,000
11	Burma	-	30,000
12	Malaysia	-	43,000
13	Indonesia	75,000	1,40,000 to ,230,000
14	Philipines	-	4,00,000
15	Bangladesh	-	2,00,000
16	Nepal	-	25,000
17	Peru	5,00,000	-
18	Brazil	2,000	-
19	Mexico	20,000	-
20	Oceania	4000	-
21	Kullalumpur	-	8000 to 10,000
22	Mumbai	25,000	1,00,000
23	G.B Rode	-	5000 to 6000
24	Sonagachi	-	5,000
25	G.B road	-	5000 to 6000
26	Himachalam	-	10,000
27	West Bengal	-	70,000
28	Karnadak	-	85,000
29	Andhra Pradesh	-	1,00,000

Source: World Health Organisation Regional Office for the Western Pacific

STI/HIV, SEX WORKER IN ASIAN, JULY, 2002

Statement of the Problems

Madurai Town is known for its own tradition and culture of Tamilnadu. Monogamy is the prominent way of life. Non-availability of any fruitful regular employments they migrate and opt employments. The women also tried to get some employment from the available sources with all means. The immediate available employment is street vender and needs of capital. Since, no capital they opt alternative as construction work. Here, there are lot of misuse prevails both in psycho-socialy and economically. Ignorance, non-accessibility of health and legal services and total stigmatization may add to the misery of the poverty driven rural families and migrated to urban areas and involving in sex work. They are not regular in practicing but it is seasonal. They are subject to illtreatment bu their family members, exploitaton from many sources, sexual violence, harassment, physical assault, victims to social services and denial of human rights. The risk of acquiring STD, HIV\AIDS opens up a new avenue to them.

The present study is mainly intended to protrude the socio-economic, psychological, political, cultural, legal problems of the women involving sex workers in Madurai Town. The near villages have been drastically affected by severe daughter and are poverty stricken. This has made the rural women to migrate to Madurai town and spreadover to bus-terminal like Mattuthavani, Periyar, Arapalayam, Anna Nilayam, Koripalayam, Anuppanadi (Theppakulam), Pudur, Mellur, Oothakadai, Annupanadi, Sellur and so on. The interviews were held with sex workers through structured inteview schedule with a view to focus and analyse the socio-economic background, sexual behaviour and mode of practices. Besides, the role of Governmental and Non-governmental organizations in reducing the sex trade and to control the HIV, AIDS\STD among the high risk women groups has also been investigated. The study also suggest for enhancing the living condition of the Female sex workers and rehabilitation measures for their welfare.

NEED OF THE STUDY

Prostitution is tolerated, rather accepted as an inevitable and integral part of civilization. On the whole, however, not much serious thought has been given to this social malady. It is both an indication of an unjust social order and an institution that economically exploited women. The public view the prostitutes as not the victims of society's apathy but the ones who are morally loose to get into this profession. This however, is untrue. Most of these women from the villages are purchased, kidnapped, drawn in through syndicates of organized crime or recruited by individuals with the promise of job, by friendship or love or with promises of marriage. There are a few who are inducted into prostitution by the parents. Among female vagrants are many adolescent girls abandoned by their relatives, they begin by begging and slip into prostitution. They face the danger of violence at the hands of police, customers, moneylenders the brothel keepers, rowdies and such other exploitative elements. They lack access to health care services, education, alternate job avenues, old age security, etc.

The women who are involving in sex work are facing the problems of poor environmental conditions, lack of proper nutrition and default in medical treatment, these women constantly suffer from health problem like fever, cold, dysentery, diarrhoea, ulcer, scabies, tuberculosis, anaemic etc. Many times, sexually transmitted diseases have been found among women. And of course they are under the risk of acquiring AIDS. Besides their own handicaps and proneness to deviation this segment constitutes the potential source of strength to those who are interested in the propagation of the trade.

OBJECTIVES

i) To profile the socio-economic conditions of female sex workers;

ii) to elicit the psychological feeling of the sex workers while on trade and off;

iii) to analyse the causative factors to involving the women sex workers, and

iv) to find the role of NGOs and GOs.

RESEARCH DESIGN

The data collected from the respondents through the field surveys was explorative in nature for the purpose of knowing socio-economic and demographic details regarding the sex workers, causative factors to involve in sex trade, their health status and future concerns for their inclusiveness in the normal society. Both the qualitative and quantitative data were collected and analyzed with an application of simple statistical methods like percentage, t-test, correlation, etc.

RESULT OF THE STUDY

Socio-Economic Profile of the Respondents

Table 1 Age wise Respondent

S.No	Age	No. of Respondents	Percentage
1	Below -15	7	14
2	16 to 20	15	30
3	21 to 25	20	40
4	Above 26	8	16
Total		50	100

Source: Computed from primary data

The above table shows about the age wise distribution of the respondents who involved in sex work. Out of 50 respondents the majority 70 percent of them were belonging to the age of 16 to 25 years; the remaining 16 percent and 14 percent of them were belonging to the age group of below 15 years and above 16 years category.

Table 2 Caste wise respondents

S.No	Caste	No. of Respondents	Percentage
1	BC	11	22
2	MBC	16	32
3	SC	23	46
Total		50	100

Source: Computed from primary data

The above table reveals about the caste wise distribution of the respondents. From the total respondents the majority 46 percent of them belonged to scheduled cast category followed by that 32 percent and 22 percent of them were belonging most backward class's category.

Distribution of the Respondents by their

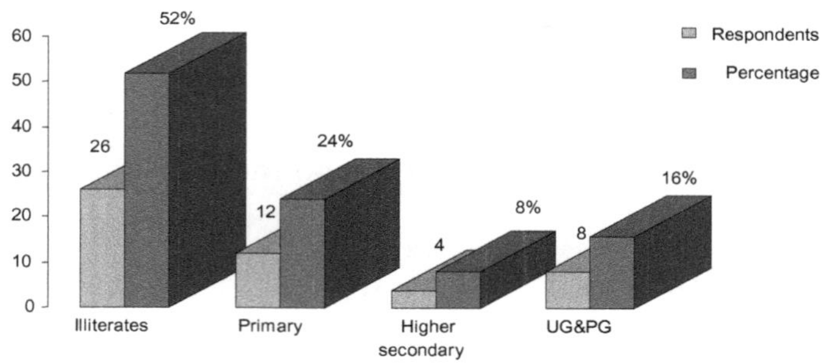

Source: Computed from primary data

The above diagram shows that the female sex workers in the education wise ,most of the 52 percentage respondents are illiterates, 24 percentage of the respondent are primary education8 percentage of the respondents are higher secondary education, another 16 percentage of the respondents UG&PG .

Distribution of the Respondents by their Monthly Income

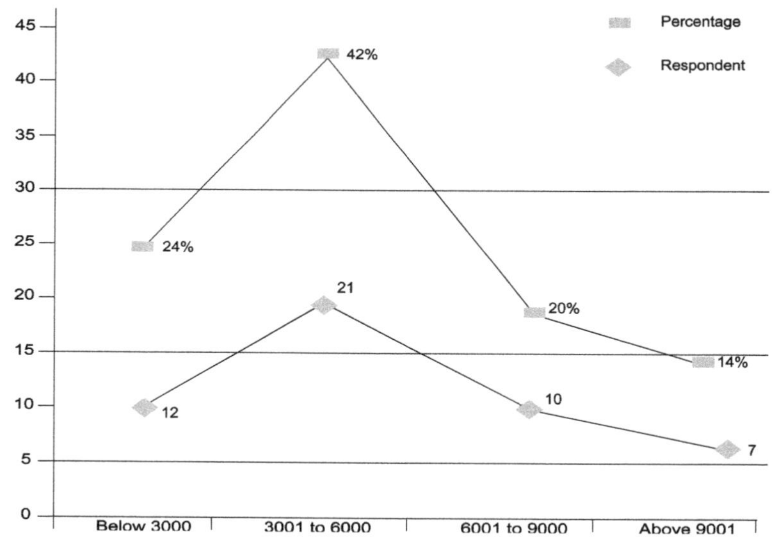

Source: Computed from primary data

From the total respondents the majority (60 percent) of them were able to earn below Rs 6000 per month, followed by that 20 percent 14 percent of them were able to earn upto 9000 and above 9000 respectively.

Mode of Expenditure of the Respondents

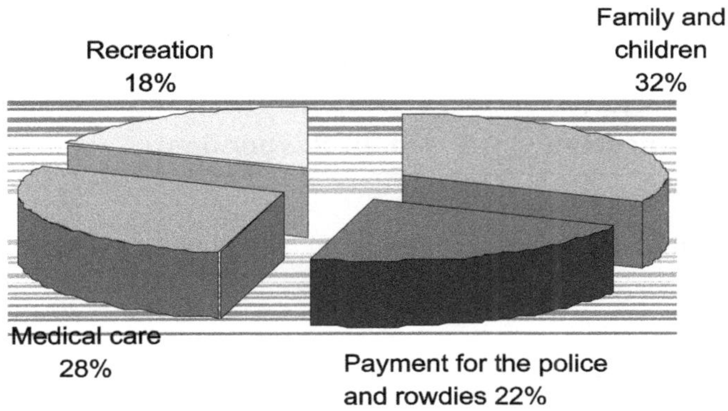

Source: Computed from primary data

As far as the expenditure of the respondents is concerned that the majority 36 percent of them spend their earnings for heir family and children particularly to meet out the basic needs and education of their children; the remaining 32 percent, 22 percent and 10 percent of them spent their earnings to meet out medical expenses, payment for the police and rowdies and recreation respectively.

Diagram 4 Economical factors

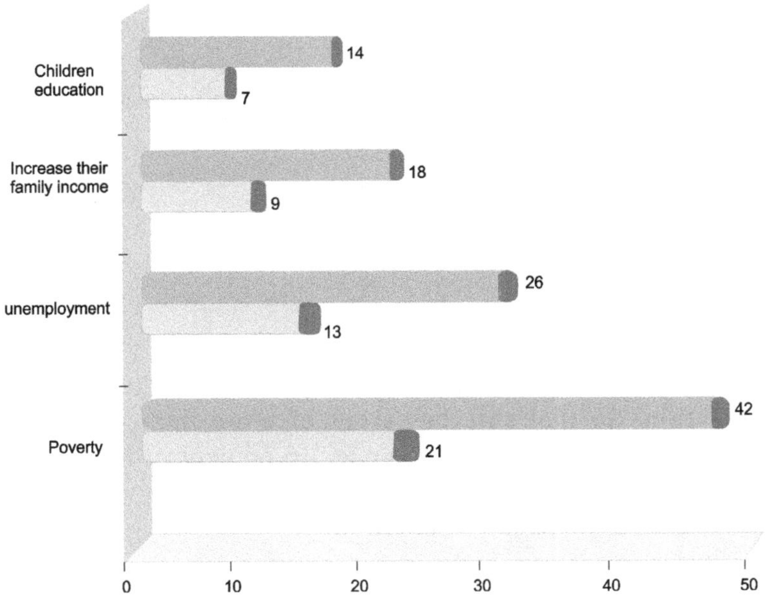

Source: Computed from primary data

The above diagram shows that the majority 42 percent of the respondents were forced to involve in sex trade due to poverty, 26 percent of them were involving due to unemployment, 18 percent of them were for their family income and 14 percent of them for children's education.

Table: 3 Educational Factors

S.No	Education	No. of Respondents	Percentages
1	Ignorance	14	28
2	Illiteracy	19	38
3	Lack of Sex Education	10	20
4	Inadequate Skills	7	14
Total		50	100

Source: Computed from primary data

The above table reveals that the education factors stressed the respondents to be in sex trade. From the total respondents 38 percent of them were illiterate, 28 of them were ignorance in the implication of the trade, 20 percent of them were lack of sexual education and remaining 14 percent of them were did not have adequate still to work and ear. And also they feel this is the way for easy earning without capital.

Table 4 Availability of Recreational Facilities

S.No	Recreational	No. of Respondents	Percentage
1	Absence of Proper Recreation	11	22
2	Pornographic	18	36
3	Modernize	21	42
Total		50	100

Source: Computed from primary data

The above table shows that Majority 42 percent of them were influenced with modernization. So that the they want of more money to compensate to live equality with high the economic people, 36 percent of them were watching movies in the forms of pornographic and 22 percent of them were involving in sex and feel it is for their time pause/ recreation.

Diagram: 5 Socio-cultural factors

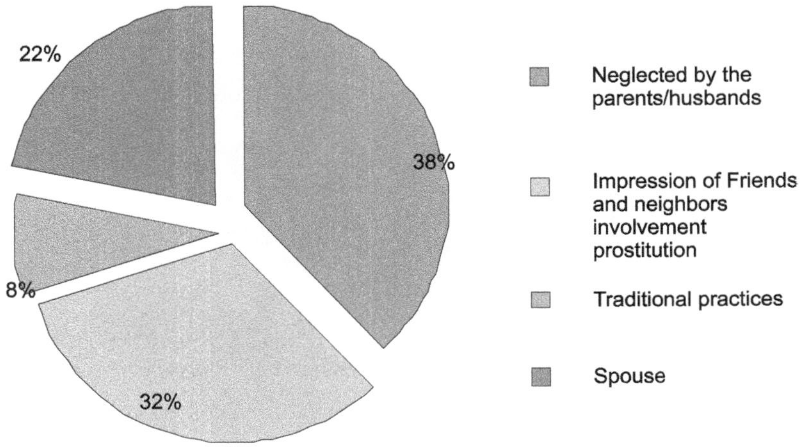

Source: Computed form primary data

The data presents in the table is that the 38 percent of the respondents were involving in sex trade sex trade because of the family dysfunction, 32 percent of the were influenced friends and neighbours, 22 percentage of them were expressed that due to their desertion/deception and there is no grip and safety in their life they had been with the selected individuals later with the many due to neglecting of the previous man/men; and few cases 8 percentage expressed that they were in the field because of their tradition like devadasi or underprivileged segment.

Table 5 Psychological factors

S.No	Psychological Factors	No. of Respondents	Percentage
1	Sexual urge	18	36
2	Sexual pleasure	23	46
3	Dejection and deception in love	9	18
	Total	50	100

Source: Computed from primary data

The above data indicates that the 46 percent of the respondents involving for the sexual satisfaction, 36 percent of the respondents were for their sexual urge, and the remaining 18 percent of them were due to dejection and deception in love emerged into sex trade.

Diagram: 6 General factors

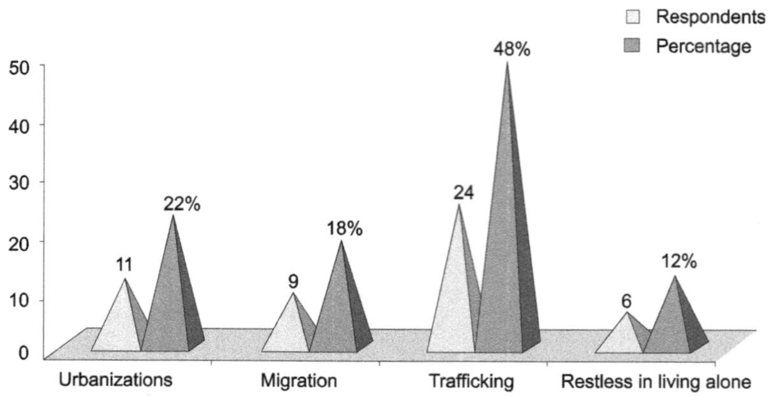

Source: Computed from primary data

The table above shows that majority 48 percent of the respondents involving in sex trade due to trafficking, 22 percent of them involved in this trade due to urbanization, 18 percent of them are due to migration, and 12 percent of them were restless at their life.

MAJOR FINDINGS

Personal Particulars

The majority 70 percent of them were belonging to the age of 16 to 25 years; belonging to scheduled cast category (46 percent); 52 percentof them were illiterates.

Economic Particulars

Very occasionally they involved in construction work and able to earn only Rs. 150 per day. But from the sex work theym were able to earn Rs. 300 -500 for a as total for a month was Rs. 6000

As far as their expences are concerned that generally 36 percent of them spend their earnings for their family to meet out the basic needs and children's education in very particular. Sometime they spend it for medical care, giving bribe for the police and the rowdies.

Causes for involving in Sex Trade

The majority 42 percent of the respondents were forced to involve in sex trade due to poverty, the others were due to family dysfunction, failure in affairs, influence of modernization, sexual satisfaction with their life partner, cheated by the employer, contractor and other persons like police, anti-social elements etc.,

Emergence of Women in Sex Trade

In the tenure of their trade they were facing lot of problems such as sexual harassment (54 percent), rape (42 percent), battering (66 percent), verbal abuse (44 percent), a racist practice (52 percent), violation of human rights (68 percent), childhood sexual abuse (30 percent) and domestic violence (58 percent).

CONCLUSION

The majority of sex worker enter into sex trade due to survival and meet their basic needs economic needs, family dysfunction, education of the off-spring, unemployed, and socially backward etc., They face many obstacles in their life such as Psychological, health, social-cultural and not able to fulfill their economic needs due to sharing of income to intermediate (brothels keepers, goondas, police, pimps). Around the world, millions of people are living in bondage. They labour in fields and factories under brutal employers who threaten them with violence if they try to escape. They work in homes for families that keep them virtually imprisoned. They are forced to work as prostitutes or to beg in the streets, fearful of the consequences. If they fail to earn their daily quota they can't get their and dependents and often held far from home with no money, no connections, and no way to ask for help. This is called modern slavery. Human trafficking is a crime with many victims: not only have those who are trafficked, but also the families they leave behind, some of whom never seen their loved ones again.

It has a broad global impact as well. It weakens legitimate economies, fuels violence, threatens public health and safety, shatters families, and shreds the social fabric that is necessary for progress. And it is an affront to our basic values and our fundamental belief that all people everywhere deserve to live and work in safety and dignity. Sex trade profession legalized is widely accepted in few counties but it was successfully implemented and practice through the NGOs and GOs. Different steps to prevent control and rehabilitate the female sex workers from different forum with a view to safeguard the society from all kind of evils.

REFERENCES

1. Sikka, P (1984), '***Prostitution : India perspective and Realities***', The India journal social work, Tata Institutes of Social Sciences, Mumbai.

2. Sex Work is Real Work (1997), '***We Demand Workers Rights***', Announcement of the Sex Worker Convention.

3. http:www.astudyongirls/womeninprostitutioninindia.

4. Mathur, A.S and Gupta, B.I (1965), '***Prostitutes and Prostitution***', Ram Pramod and sons, Agra.

5. http:// www.sikhspectrum.com/o520007/devadasi.htm

6. Agha, S (1999), '***Declines in Causal Sex in Lusaka***', Zambia.

7. http://blog4us.hubpages.com/hum/blog4us.

SOCIAL STRUCTURAL CONSTRAINTS IN EMPOWERMENT OF MARGINALIZED GROUPS – THE DALIT DIMENSION

18 SUB-PLAN FOR TRIBAL DEVELOPMENT IN INDIA

Dr.Neema Gnanadev

The tribals are the indigenous people of India who are called "Adivasis" which literally means original settlers. Under the constitution of India certain tribes have been specified as Scheduled Tribes (ST) and they are given special treatment or facilities or privilege especially who are most backward.

The Ministry of Rural development is implementing various programmes for providing employment to most disadvantaged sections of the society through special employment generation programmes and for improvements in quality of life in rural areas. The Ministry has made for specific provisions in the programmes being implemented to ensure adequate flow of resources to the SC/STs a special plan or sub-plan is a new approach for integrated tribal development. It represents total developmental efforts of the central Ministries, The State Government and by other financial institutions in the Tribal sub plan areas provides special assistance besides the Government of India to the State Government. It is ensured that TSP areas get at least 10 percentage of the total state plan. Elimination of exploitation has been accorded the highest priority in the Tribal sub-plan, review of excise policy, forest policy, credit and marketing, restorations of alienated land, debt redemption, administrative structure and personal policy and comprehensive time bound programmes were made an integral part of it. Credit requirements were another priority area and Tribal Development Cooperative Federation was set up in 1976 at the Tribal sub-plan level for regulating the flow of credit and marketing. LAMPS and PAC's were established to purchase minor forest and agriculture produces, provide consumer commodities at reasonable prices, providing productive and consumption loans and subsidies agriculture inputs and support for generating employment opportunites.

Integrated Tribal Development projects were formulated in the Tribal sub-plan area in 1974-75. On the basis of the objectives and contents, area specific, sectoral and group oriented programmes were formulated. Each has complement of the other laws. It focuses on welfare of the tribal communities living in it. The programmes include infrastructure and economic development in direct benefit programmes. The former two were emphasized during the 5th plan period while the latter is receiving increasing emphasis after the fifth plan period.

OBJECTIVES OF THE SUB-PLAN IS:

(i) To narrow the gap between the levels of development of tribal and other areas; and

(ii) To improve the quality of life of the tribal communities.

However, immediate objectives are as follows:

- Elimination of exploitation in all forms,
- Speeding up of the processes for social and economic development,
- Building up inner strength of the people
- Improving organizational capabilities among tribal

GENERAL STRATEGY TO ACHIEVE THESE OBJECTIVES OF SUB-PLANS

Keeping in view the special problems of the tribal region in each State entire legal, administrative and institutional frame as also inter-sectoral and intra-sectoral priorities required to be reviewed keeping the primary focus on the welfare and development of the people. No developmental activity for benefiting the tribal population will succeed unless exploitation in various forms is prevented. As the sub-plan will focus attention on the welfare and development of the people, special attention will have to be given to areas and groups facing special problems. These will include primitive tribal groups in extremely backward pockets, shifting cultivators and tribal application who are affected by major projects. The tribal sub-plan is formulated by the Tribal Development Department (TDD) according to the recommendations of the Sukthankar Committee since 1993-94. Planning Department communicates fixed outlays to the Tribal Development Department for formulation of TSP. The TDD decides the outlay for different schemes keeping in view the actual benefits accruing to the tribal people.

THE ESSENTIAL FEATURES OF TSP ARE:

In May 2003 the Ministry of Tribal Affairs issued fresh guidelines for release and utilization of Special Central Assistance (SCA) for Tribal Sub-Plan features of the new guidelines are:

(i) Recognise that there is no uniform solution to the variety of problems facing tribal regions and tribal communities; therefore, accept the uniqueness and formulate policies, programmes and schemes to suit each individual situation and especially for vulnerable sections like Primitive

Tribal Groups (PTGs), bonded labourers, shifting cultivators, forest villagers, displaced persons, etc.

(ii) Evolve appropriate frame for development with emphasis on tribal people at the national and State level through Sub-Plan exercise, ensuring adequate quantification from State and Central Plan funds, with budgetary mechanisms (Separate Demand / Major Budget Heads etc.) to ensure accountability, non-divertability and full utilisation. (iii) Accord highest priority to protective measures for elimination of exploitation of tribal people. (iv) Re structure the administrative and institutional set up to suit the local needs and aspirations. (v) Supplement State efforts substantially by the Union Government through Special Central Assistance (SCA)

The tribal development under TSP envisages their following

(i) Educational promotion schemes of schools, residential schools, hostels, scholarships, special coaching/training etc.(ii) Agriculture and allied activities by providing minor and medium irrigation facilities, animal husbandry, dairying, poultry etc. (iii) Improvised credit and marketing facilities for agriculture and minor forest products; (iv) Special training programmes to tribal farmers; (v) Irrigation and power facilities to promote agricultural production and small scale industry etc.;(vi) Provision of basic infrastructure for speeding up the socio-economic development of the tribal areas through community centres, communication network, schools, health centers, rural electrification, drinking water and other facilities etc. are to be provided to the tribals; (vii) ITDP, MADA, Cluster and Primitive Tribal Groups special comprehensive developmental projects to be prepared by the States/U.Ts.

FUNDING OF TSP PROGRAMMES

The Tribal Sub-Plan Programmes are to be financed by the following sources: (a) Tribal Sub Plan funds form State /U.T Plans and Central Ministries/Departments, (b) Special Central Assistance (SCA) to Tribal Sub Plan (TSP), (c) Grants under Article 275 (1) of the Constitution to the States/U.Ts, (d) Funds through Central Sector Schemes, (e) Funds from Centrally Sponsored Schemes and (f) Institutional Finance.

ALLOCATION OF FUNDS FROM THE STATES/U.TS PLAN TO THE TSP

State/U.T Governments are required to allocate the funds from the State/U.T Plan for tribal area development in proportion to the percentage of tribal population in the States/U.Ts. Similarly, Central Ministries/Departments should also allocate the funds for tribal development in proportion to the percentage of the tribal population in the country.

Table 1.1 Allocation of funds to TSP in Five Year Plans and Annual Plans (Rs. in crore)

Five Year Plan	State Plan Funds			Central Five Ministries Funds		
	Outlay	Allocation to TSP	percentage	Outlay	Allocation to TSP	percentage age
7th Plan	73953.35	7076.81	9.6	127519.6	-	-
8th Plan	174752.75	16902.66	9.7	247865.0	5517	8.0
9th Plan	296911.20	22314.22	7.5	1,10,454	6462	5.9
10th Plan	614811.10	46004.23	7.5	6,81,399	-	-

Source: Ministry of Tribal Affairs.

These funds were invested to be used for implementing development programmes in the tribal areas, primarily for the STs, in the fields of education, health, agriculture, horticulture, small industries, artisans and other income generating activities infrastructure. The guideline also stipulates 10% allocation of funds under this grant for innovative projects and proper adherence to the TSP adoption by the State/U.T. The Ministry is also providing funds for setting up 100 Ekalavya Model Residential Schools on the pattern of Navodaya Vidyalas in 24 States with both recurring and non-recurring expenses. During the last two years of 10th Plan, the Ministry has provided additional funds of Rs. 50 crore every year for minor irrigation facilities to STs lands. Ministry of Tribal Affairs had released Rs. 741.29 crore and Rs. 1302.7 crore during 9th and 10th Plan periods respectively as grants under Article 275 (1) of the Constitution to 25 States/U.Ts for tribal development activities. Though a good amount of fund has been released by the nodal ministry, the States/U.Ts was not strictly following the guidelines.

IMPLEMENTATION STATUS OF SCP AND TSP

The Strategies of TSP and SCP initiated in 1974 and 1979 respectively for achieving overall development of STs and SCs to provide basic minimum services, raise their socio-economic development and administration by allocating funds at least in proportion to ST and SC population from the annual plans of State/UTs. TSP approach applies now to 21 States and 2 UTs, where STs constitute a sizable population. 27 States/UTs have been allocating funds under SCP. The 10th plan Mid-Term Review has indicated that, only a few Central Ministries/Depts. Are allocating funds towards SCP and TSP. The allocations made by the States/U.Ts is not commensurate with the population in the State/U.T and are notional in nature as they indicate only the flow of funds by the various sectoral departments. The various reviews, reports and commission reports observed that SCP and TSP strategy is not being implemented properly and inter-sectoral allocation and prioritization is not being done. The SCP and TSP expenditure in many of the States/UTs was not even 50% of the allocated funds. No proper budget heads/subheads were created the funds were diverted to the other general sectors from SCP and TSP funds. Further, there was no effective monitoring to ensure that the allocation of SCP and TSP funds are being done and the allocated funds are not utilized effectively. Various State Governments are adopting their own mechanism for implementation of SCP and TSP in their States. The State Government of Maharashtra had initiated a mechanism for effective operationalisation of SCP and TSP strategy which is popularly known as 'Maharashtra Model' In the Annual Report of the Ministry of Tribal Affairs for the year 2002-03 it has been mentioned that among the initiatives taken by the Ministry a direction has been issued to the States for adoption of the Maharashtra pattern of planning and execution of funds earmarked for Tribal Sub- Plan areas. In Maharashtra, the funds earmarked for TSP are placed with the Tribal Development Department of the State Government which releases the funds to different line departments for execution of development works under TSP, and ensures utilization of TSP funds for tribal areas.

REFERENCES

1. Amar Kumar Singh M.K. Jabbi, (Development Deprivation & Discontent) Tribal in India editors Har. Anand publications, New Delhi, 1995
2. Tribe Rehabilitation and development, Rawat Publication, Alexander Delhi 1991.
3. A Montly Journal Kurushetra, A Jamal of RD, Education In India, Ministry of Rural Developpment 2004.
4. Satish, Tiwari, Rural Development, Enclyclopaedia of Indian Government Services, Anmol Public private Ltd., New Delhi, 2000.
5. Renu Jatana, Sweta Waldia, Tribal development Programmes, Mahamaya Publishing house New Delhi.2009
6. Niranjanm Pani, Jitendra Sahoo, Tribal Development, Mahamaya Publishing house New Delhi.2008.
7. Socio-Economic and Educational Development (SEEDS) Planning Commission, RRF-754/29 Rajnagar 11, Palani Colony, New Delhi, 2011.

19 EMPOWERMENT OF ELECTED DALIT WOMEN IN PRIS : ISSUES AND CHALLENGES

Dr. T. Sundara Raj

INTRODUCTION

Commitment of our nation to welfare of the poor and weak is well evident from the fact that "Justice, Social, Economic and Political" has been kept as the first among the objectives in the Preamble of the Constitution of India. This was considered both necessary and essential for constituting India into a sovereign, socialistic, secular, democratic, republic. On account of various historical and social factors, persons belonging to the Scheduled Castes, Scheduled Tribes and Other Backward Classes often referred to as "Dalits", have limited access to assets and opportunities. This has affected their achieving equality of status and opportunity vis-à-vis others, as envisaged under Constitution. With a view to overcome the constraints and achieve the desired objectives, several specific provisions have been made in the Constitution itself for empowerment of the weaker sections (Singh, S. K. 2007). the presence of 1.05 million elected women representatives in the institutions of local governance in rural India is truly an extraordinary phenomenon. What make it more extraordinary are the otherwise awfully poor human development indicators of rural women the social and economic opportunities available particularly to those belonging to socially disadvantaged groups such as Scheduled Caste and Scheduled Tribes (Planning Commission). The government has attempted to involve and encourage women in decision-making process by providing one-third reservation (including the number of seats reserved for Scheduled Castes and Scheduled Tribes) for them in Grama Panchayats to ensure their participation at the local and district levels of governance through the 73rd Amendments of the Constitution. The impact of reserving one third of seats for women in the Panchayati Raj Institutions has been immense, and has empowered women to a great extent both politically and socially. At present, there are approximately 260,000 Panchayat representatives in India, out of which around 75,000 are women (Hazra Anupam, 2011). This is the largest number of elected women in the world. It is true that the quota system has resulted in over 100,000 Dalit women elected representatives across the country today. Unfortunately, however, political representation through quotas has not led to effective political participation for the majority of Dalit women. The main obstacle is the multiple discrimination these women face arising from the entrenched caste hierarchy, chronic poverty and patriarchy (Jayshree Mangubhai, 2009). Representation of women in the formal structures of governance at the local level has recorded a steady increase. Besides that illiteracy, dominance of patriarchal values in the society, lack of access and control over income and other resources, restrictions to public spaces and insensitive legal systems continue to weaken their effective political participation.

The National Policy for Empowerment of Women 2001 has as its goal bringing advancement, development and empowerment of women in all spheres of life through creation of a more responsive judicial and legal system sensitive to women and mainstreaming a gender perspective in the development process. Government is working on three prong strategies a) Social Empowerment - Create an enabling environment through adopting various policies and programmes for development of women, b) Economic Empowerment – Ensure provision of training, employment and income generation activities with the ultimate objective of making them economically self-reliant. c) Gender Justice – Eliminate all forms of gender discrimination and thus enable women to enjoy not only de-jure but also de facto rights and fundamental freedom on par with men in all spheres, viz, political, economic, social, civil, cultural etc., (Planning Commission). With the concept of power, ideology, patriarchy and gender, we should be clear about the notion of empowerment. Empowerment is defined as the process- whereby the powerless or less powerful members of a society gain access and control over material knowledge, resources and challenge the ideologies of discrimination and subordination, which justify this unequal distribution. Empowerment manifests as a changing balance of power in terms of resource distribution and change in ideology, or ways of thinking (Srilatha Batwalia, 1994).

Women are the vulnerable sections of the society and the Scheduled Castes (SCs) and Scheduled Tribes (STs) women are more vulnerable. The Government has enacted several women specific and women related legislations to protect them against social discrimination, several harassment, dowry deaths, and child marriage, anti abortion laws, violence and atrocities and also to provide for equal pay to men and women for equal work. Article 243 D clearly states that the number of seats to be reserved in any Panchayat should be related to the proportion of SC population in that Panchayat area. However, it appears that some states have developed different formula for calculating reservation. They have instead taken state average for SC and reserved that proportion of seats/ posts for SCs. The reservations of seats can be seen as an instrument to facilitate the empowerment of SC, by first getting them elected to PRIs and then providing examples as role models, by way of a trickle–down effect, to empower all marginalized women and SC everywhere. According to the 2001 census, scheduled castes comprise 16.2 per cent of the total population of India, that is, they number over 17 crore. Scheduled tribes comprise 8.2 per cent of the population, that is, they number over 8 crore. Both together constitute 24.4 per cent of the Indian population, that is, they together number over 25 crore. While dalit women share common problems of gender discrimination with their high caste counterparts, they also suffer from problems specific to them. Dalit women are the worst affected and suffer the three forms oppression -- caste, class and gender.

As some of the above figures show, these relate to extremely low literacy and education levels, heavy dependence on wage labour, discrimination in employment and wages, heavy concentration in unskilled, low-paid and hazardous manual jobs, violence and sexual exploitation. In the process of empowerment, Dalit women have to face various problems associated with Panchayati Raj Institutions (PRIs) and these problems get tripled because of her triple roles like wage earner, a home maker and a Dalit woman. Since, Local Self Government (LSG) has been recognized as a means to ensure democratic functioning and decision-making, development of women through PRIs assumes importance. The idea behind LSG is that moving decision-making close to people. The purpose of this study was to assess the degree and nature of exclusion and inclusion of dalit women within PRIs. The simple reason is that this is the largest political space open for Dalit women today to participate in public affairs. Moreover, at this level, there are separate quotas for Dalit women, aside from quotas for Dalits and women in general, meant to facilitate their inclusion in local governance. This study examined only one of these domains- the participation and the factors which use an influence on inclusion in that sphere. Rates of participation are used as an indicator of inclusion (empowerment). The study seeks to understand how intensively dalit women participate in activities associated with PRIs. Why there are differences in participation levels and disproportionately in the activities and decision-making of PRIs.

Regarding Kerala, the relatively high status that women enjoyed in Kerala used to be traced to the incidence of Matriliny (Robin, Jeffrey), which was a unique feature of Kerala. Female friendly sex ratio, high women literacy rate etc was given a background, which was related to the matrilineal system that prevailed here. Kerala society is fast changing and legislative enactments have dramatically increased women's access to decision making structures in last decade. The 73rd and 74th Constitutional amendments passed in 1993 provide of reservation 33 per cent elected seats for women at the different levels of governance in both rural and urban local bodies. The Indian Country Report of the platform for action-10 years after, reports that participation in the decision making as elected women representatives has impacted on other aspects of capability development (Platform for action-10 years, 2006).

In Kerala, there has been proliferation of institutions at the grass root level on a scale not witnessed anywhere in the country since 1996, synchronizing with the ongoing decentralized participatory planning campaign for the ninth plan. One of the major goals for decentralization is to create institutions and groups, which provide an enabling environment for the functioning of the local bodies as agencies of self government and to ensure local level development on a sustainable basis. People's campaign has led to proliferation of institutions at the grass root level. The planning campaign since 1996 has brought a wider section of women hitherto excluded from Kerala's associational life into the centre stage of rural civil life (John, Chathukulam, 2002). This paper aims to examine the issues and challenges encountered by the elected Dalit women in PRIs. The study was conducted in Thiruvananthapuram district of Kerala State, which consists of seventy eight Grama Panchayats, four Municipalities and One Corporation. The total number of women representatives was 499 from Gramam Panchayats. Out of which 56 respondents are dalit women. There are 58 elected women, of which 5 are dalit women from Block Panchayts. Municipalities consisted of 8 dalit women and 3 dalit women from One Corporation. Purposive sampling method was used for the study. This study is currently very important since it is part of ongoing national efforts to eliminate gender disparities particularly among the marginalized communities. The intensive survey yielded a set of information that complemented the data from the extensive study. This allowed the researcher to reliably interpret final figures and better understand how dalit women's social and economic positioning ultimately affects inclusion and exclusion in PRIs. The empowerment of women has come from analyzing many sources. Particularly it has been prompted by the need to know certain facts such as attitude of the society, experience in party, family and LSG membership, personality development and LSG membership and the constraints faced. These are used as major indicators to measure the women's empowerment in PRIs.

MAIN CONSTRAINS FACED BY DALIT WOMEN REPRESENTATIVES IN THE STUDY AREA

In practice, multiple barriers structural, cultural and institutional continue to restrict the rapid advancement of women in elected office. Even though these women representatives have positive approach as members of LSG, they face some constraints also. Women representatives (64%) complain that, men never consult them in the panchayats regarding fund utilization. The women feel that they were not given due consideration in the local bodies. The traditional caste leaders and elites dominated the decision making by proxy functioning of the PRIs. The extreme form of patriarchal structure linked with caste, religion and other institutions in the society do not accept women's new role (Gail Omvedt, 2005). It brings a large number of hindrances in the way of representatives. Another factor is the expected loyalty towards the political party one represents.

Major (56%) political parties have tended to exercise rigid control over the elected representatives. Even if individual opinion differs, they are bound by party decision and they cannot take independent decisions. On the whole patriarchal structure, illiteracy, domestic responsibilities, male dominance, lack of support from the family members, lack of awareness about the procedures in PRIs etc., produce problems and tensions in the lives of women representatives. Sanchita's (2005) study also point out the same thing that lack of awareness about the systems and procedures regarding the functioning of gramamsabha and grama panchayats lead to subdued leadership on women's part. Problems faced by women representatives are mainly lack of personal security and risk of sexual harassment, low level of self confidence, social and cultural barriers such as exclusives responsibility for household work, restrictions on mobility. Inherent attitudes of a patriarchal society, that men are superior to women and that women are best suited to be home makers, create formidable challenges. Studies (Maitreyi, 2003) reflect another thing that due to their domestic responsibilities many are left with little time to participate in the affairs of the community and it is almost impossible for them to develop their own capacity through education and training. Women also receive little encouragement from some male family members (34%), resulting in limited spatial mobility and a lack of social capital. The main reasons of the challenges they face are the notions have caste and gender exclusively dalits, which place severe restrictions on their mobility and they are not allowed to work with men, which might cast doubts on their good reputation and reduce their marriage prospects in some dalit unmarried women. In addition to these problems, dalit women (55%) representatives also faced a shortage of peer support networks compared with men, which generally serve as a platform for women representatives to establish networks and exchange information and experiences as well as to get training programmes and to provide other means of support.

WOMEN'S EMPOWERMENT AND PRIS

Empowerment is a multidimensional social process that helps people gain control over their own lives. It is a process that fosters power in people for use in their own lives, their own communities and in their own society, by acting on issues that they describe as important. Above all, empowerment is a result of participation in decision-making (Saxena, N. C). Women's empowerment also refers to the process by which women acquire due recognition on par with men, to participate in the development process of the society through the political institutions as a partner with human dignity (Palanthurai, G, 2001). So, PRIs are one of the best ways to encourage empowerment of women.

ATTITUDE OF THE SOCIETY

Attitude of the society are helpful to know whether they face good or bad experiences from the society, whether these experiences affected their work, whether they are able to solve these problems, attitude of society towards them as a women member, support they are getting from the people, whether the people are treating them as their leader. This helps us to assess whether they get good or bad experiences and their ability to solve the problem and how the good experiences encourage them to work in a good manner. 76.65 per cent of the women respondents stated that their opinion were recognized by other members and had experience before entering the LSG. The majority of the respondents had positive attitude from the public, as well as some respondents stated that the public supported them. The candidates do all the needs to the society with good will. This gets promoted through Medias, so the public come to know the goodness of their leader and they support their representative. This shows the positive form the society. Public opinion is that when women have power in LSG accountability is ensured and corruption at the local level is controlled under women leadership. Hust (2004) also found that the corruption is less in PRIs due to the presence of women leaders. This shows the fact that women are struggling with men to assure their demands and it also reflects the reality that all women representatives are not passive leaders; some are dynamic, energetic and vibrant. It is also amazing to note that winning rate of women in election is high though the number of contestants is low.

EXPERIENCE IN THE POLITICAL PARTY

The question of experience in the political party help us to assess whether they have previous experience in party work, their decision making power, their confidence in working with other male members in the party, the attitude of other male members in own and opposition party. 68 per cent of the respondents do not have any prior experience before join the LSGs. 42 per cent members stated that they have the decision making power in the party at their level, because they have long members, good knowledge about functions and procedures of local bodies. These respondents were elected representative in the previous election. A small portion of women representative has experience harassment at the hands of political parties. A woman panchayats members husband assaulted by the members of own political party, only because she had questioned certain corrupt practices of the parties rank and file.

FAMILY AND LSG MEMBERSHIP

Family and member in local bodies help us to know whether they are satisfied in their family life, whether they get support from family, the role of the LSG members in decision making, attitude of the family members in social life of the LSG members and how far it affected their personal life. Family is an important part of a person's life and women have important role in it. This is helpful to get a general idea about the family life of the members and how they adjust with family life and social life. 75 per cent of the respondents were satisfied with their family life and other members of the family support them. The respondent's husband and family members share the workload at home. Then they face dilemma in their social life, their husband and family members console and favour very good support both mentally and physically. This type of attitude enhances their confident in the social life, so that it leads to empowerment.

PERSONALITY DEVELOPMENT AND LSG MEMBERSHIP

Personality development is one of the main factors in the empowerment process. Which is helpful to understand whether they have previous experience in social life and how the present post helps them to increase their abilities, the development of their skills and change in attitude? 71 per cent of the respondents do not prior experience as a leader before becoming members of the LSG. The achieved the leadership quality after joining as a LSG member, so that they face any issue more confidently and get mentally prepared. These respondents more conveniently approach any offices without males or supports help. So the women respondents gain the attitude of empowerment and get their personality development as an LSG member (Kerala Women's Commission).

CONCLUSION

To conclude that LSG is the best mechanism to elect women to execute various empowerment programmes. All the women members said initially they used to feel uncomfortable while attending local body meeting. But slowly they could overcome the shyness. Their LSG post gave them the sense of leadership and respect they did have earlier. They are now approached by all the people of their constituency for whatever they require. This gave them a sense of confidence they never had before only this can make the elected representatives accountable to the people. In the end of the study the fact that initially dalit women were not dynamic because of the unfamiliarity of the political field. But the involvement of them in PRIs changed a lot and also gained self confidence, political awareness and affirmation of their identity. Hence, we can say that reservation has considerably lighted up the lives of dalit women. But reservation does not prove to be the end of woes of all the dalit women and complete empowerment of these women, in fact there is another kind of power struggle that they go through.

SUGGESTIONS

The active participation of dalit women and incorporation of their perspectives at all levels of decision making is essential to meet the goals of equality, justice and development. Another important issue is the political empowerment of women. Thirtythree per cent reservation of women in legislatures still remains an unfinished task. Reservation in panchayats does not prove to be the end of woes of all the dalit women and complete empowerment of these women. It is only the beginning, the foundation. The struggle continues as this reservation is imperative for women's political participation in nation building and decision-making at all levels from Panchayats to Parliament. Women need to be trained to make better use of information technology including social media.

REFERENCE

1. Sing, S. K (2003), Micro Finance in Economic Empowerment of Weaker Sections, Yojana, Vol.47, March, 2003, New Delhi, p.21.
2. Planning Commission, Government of India, and Society of Tribal Women for Development, www.stwfd.org, New Delhi.
3. Hazra, Anupam (2011), Empowering Women in Rural India, Kurushetra, Vol.59 No. 11 September, 2011 Ministry of Rural Development, New Delhi.
4. Jayashree, Mangubhai (2009), Obstacle to the Effective Political Participation of Dalit Women, Geneva, 12 to 13, November, 2009, India.
5. Srilatha, Batwalia (1994), Women's Empowerment in South Asia, Concepts and Practices, FAO (FFHC/AD) and ASPBAE.
6. Robin, Jeffrey, Gender Profile in Kerala, Integrated Rural Technology Centre, Mundur, Palakkad, http://sakhikerala.org/downloads/Kerala%20Devt-%20a%20fem.perspective.doc
7. Platform for action-10 years after, Indian Country Report, Development of Women and Child development, Ministry of Human Resource Development, Government of India, 2006, pp. 49-53.
8. John. M. S and John Chathukulam (2002), Building Social Capital through State Initiative, Participatory Planning in Kerala, Economic and Political Weekly, New Delhi, May 18th, 2002, pp. 1939-1940.
9. Gail Omvedt (2005), Women in Governance in South Asia, Economic and Politically Weekly, New Delhi, October, 2005, pp.4746—47.

10. Sanchita, Tripati (2005), Women Leadership and PRIs, Kurushetra, Vol.54, No.1, Ministry of Rural Development, New Delhi, p.13.

11. Maitreyi, Chaudhuri (2003), Empowerment of Women through PRI, ed. Asha, Mukherjee and Kumkum Bhattacharya, Conditioning and Empowerment of Women: A Multidimensional Approach, Gyan Publishing House, New Delhi, p. 227.

12. Saxena, N, C, What is meant by people's participation, A note, Journal of Rural Development.

13. Palanithurai, G (2001), The Genre of Women leaders in local bodies: Experience from Tamil Nadu, Indian Journal of Public Administration.

14. Hust, Evelyns (2004), Women's Political Representation and Empowerment in India. A Million India's Now, Economic and Political Weekly, New Delhi, pp. 262-265.

15. Status of Women in Kerala, A Report based on sample studies, Kerala Women's Commission, Thiruvananthapuram.

20 SYSTEMATIC EXCLUSION OF DALITS IN TAMIL NADU

Dr.K.Suriyan

Indian castes are stratified into four groups on the basis of work and purity. Accordingly, in the Hindu hierarchy there are namely the Brahmins (Priestly caste), the Kshatriya (warriors), the Vaishyas (trades) and the Shudras (menial task workers). Among the four tier caste ladder another rung are called as untouchables (Punchamas) who are scheduled in the caste list called as scheduled castes. They are facing lot of problems even in the civilized society due to their poor quality of life. Now-a-days dailts have been little bit improved their quality of life by doing of several development activities and affirmative actions taken by both the central and state governments. On the other hand, the caste dominant venomous people who capture/hold the power through any other mode for vested mean and disguise systematically and exclude the dalits in many ways just like a 'cow skinned tigers' especially in Tamilnadu. Tamil Nadu covers an area of 130,058 sq km. It is the eleventh-largest state and the seventh-most-populous state in India; it has 32 districts. It is among the most industrialised states in the country. It also has a rich tradition of literature, music and dance. The climate ranges from dry sub-humid to semi-arid. Important rivers flowing through the state include Palar, Cheyyar, Ponnaiyar, Kaveri, Bhavani, Vaigai and Tamaraparani. Chennai is the capital city. Coimbatore, Madurai, Thiruchirappalli, Salem, Tirunelveli and Erode are some of the other key cities in the state. Tamil is the state language; English is also commonly used for communication and as a medium of education. But the exclusion of dalit also larger, especially in southern districts. Exclusion involves a systematic denial of entitlements to resources and services like place of settlement, availing of basic amenities, self respect, education, occupation, politics etc., and the denial of the right to participate on equal terms in social relationships in economic, social, cultural or political arenas. This process occurs at various levels – within and between households, villages, cities, states, and globally. This is an actor-oriented approach which is useful because it points to who is doing? What and in relationship with whom? It also provides information for international development agencies to identify those dynamic processes already extant which they could aim to strengthen or minimise. In a situation where there is a disparity in social power relationships, the question of who has the prerogative to define, who is the definer and who is the defined, becomes a site of conflict. The process of exclusion among the people of high class/caste society is systematic and more dangerous than the practice of untouchability practiced by a lay man. The fields of exclusion, impact among the dalits and society is inevitable, but it has to be eroded to protect the society from the internal war. It has to be discussed and find a suitable strategy to bring out for avoiding such inhuman activities through this paper under.

FIELDS OF SYSTEMATIC EXCLUSION

Social Exclusion

a) Caste

Issues pertaining to exclusion of scheduled castes on the basis of settlement are very common in India. Accordingly, they determined the `caste' which cannot be equated with `race' or covered and includes discrimination against members of communities based on forms of social stratification and analogous systems of inherited status. Caste is descent-based and hereditary in nature. It is a characteristic determined by one's birth into a particular caste, irrespective of the faith practiced by the individual. Caste denotes a traditional system of rigid social stratification into ranked groups defined by descent and occupation. Caste divisions in India dominate in settlement, housing, marriage, employment and general social interaction/divisions that are reinforced through the practice and threat of social stratums, economic boycotts, and physical violence. It is cruel, inhuman and injustice to social growth. Dalits have faced a unique discrimination in our society that is fundamentally different from the problems of minority groups in general. The practice of `untouchability' is highly prevailed in rural society which is not just social discrimination. They are not allowed to sit along with them there in the canteens of work place by occupying their own caste people. They cannot use upper caste water taps (Chellampatty block of Usilampatti Taluk). In schools the dalit children are not treated as the children of the other castes (Dharmapuri). They live in colonies of their own (in all villages of Tamilnadu) and testimony of scavengers in Tamilnadu. Caste still has limited social advancement, job and marriage choices. Since, the higher caste wealthy people construct their own temples, occupy the place of ropes, admit their own children at a larger extend and construct houses in the heart of the village in a well planned manner.

RELIGIOUS EXCLUSION

With a view to avoid discrimination of the upper caste people towards the dalits, they converted into Christian or Muslims and sometimes Buddhist. But their identity as dalit or out caste never was changed when they are with the local communities. They may not allow the dalits to worship in churches and mosques like others. They cannot enter into temples (Uthapuram), cannot touch ropes of temple car (Kanthadevi) while the upper castes pull.

GENDER EXCLUSION

Dalit women are the worst affected and suffer the three forms oppression such as caste, class and gender. These are related to extremely low literacy and education levels, heavy dependence on wage labour, discrimination in employment and wages, heavy concentration in unskilled, low-paid and hazardous manual jobs, violence and sexual exploitation, being the victims of various forms of superstitions (like the devadasi system) etc.

EDUCATIONAL EXCLUSION

There is a severe lack of public education and awareness of caste discrimination in India. In 2001, the literacy rate among SCs was 54.7 %. Among women, the literacy rate for SCs was 41.9 %. School attendance was about 10 % less among SC boys than other boys, and about 5 % less among SC girls than other girls. Several studies have observed discrimination against SCs in schools and colleges in various forms. Treatment of caste discrimination in admission in different courses that are highly having employment opportunities. In other Arts courses the dalits are highly admitted and calculating into overall percentage of the institution. Some institutions completely followed their own way of reservation which are least percentage of admission to the dalit students and passed in the academic council.

ECONOMIC EXCLUSION

In India 70% of the total scheduled caste households were landless or near landless (owning less than one acre). They don't have employment opportunities other than agriculture labour which gives very meagre earnings. It forced them to be in poverty. The largest incidence of poverty in rural areas was among agricultural labour followed by non-agricultural labour, whereas in urban areas the largest incidence of poverty was among casual labour followed by self-employed households. The monthly per capita expenditure (MPCE) for all household types was lower for SCs than others.

OCCUPATION

In 2000, 49.06 % of the working scheduled caste populations were agricultural labourers. They work from early sunrise to late sunset for a meager amount of coolie from the landlords with all painful experiences like less payment as coolie, sexual harassment, engaging their child as bonded labour for taking care of livestocks. It is reported that out of the 60 million child labour in India, 40 % come from scheduled caste families. Moreover, it is estimated that 80 % of child labour engaged in matchstick and firecracker industries come from scheduled caste backgrounds. The tanning, colouring and leather processing, lifting dead animals, clearing human excreta, cleaning soiled clothes, collection of waste in slaughter houses and sale of toddy are some of the hereditary jobs generally pursued by Dalit children.

EMPLOYMENT

Opposition to reservation for Scheduled Caste candidates in teaching faculty positions has much in common with widespread general opposition to reservations per se. The same argument of merit and excellence is adduced by anti-reservationists in all fields. Even those who believe that social exclusion, deprivation and discrimination are bitterly addressed in affirmative action like quota system which is never implemented or wrongly implemented even in so called Gandhian institutions. There are some stupites wrongly argued that it is okay to have quotas even in faculty positions, but only to the junior faculty level; let there be reservations for Assistant Professors but not for Associate Professors and professors. The junior faculty members are also engaged in teaching and research the seniors also in. In fact the juniors are engaging more classes (15 h/w) but the Professors harldly 5 hrs/w. As far as reservation is concerned that it should not be for traditions, but should be equal for all the citizens. Recently by December 6, 2005 directive from the Ministry of Human Resources Development (MHRD) and a subsequent order from the University Grants Commission (UGC) on the implementation of the 22.5-per cent reservation are legally binding.

POLITICAL EXCLUSION

With the onset of the imperialist-dictated political prevalence among the politician of liberalisation, privatisation and globalisation by the ruling classes of our country during the last decade and a half, the problems of dalits, adivasis, other backward castes and the working people as a whole have greatly aggravated. The drive to privatise the public sector has directly hit reservations for the SC/STs. The closures of thousands of mills and factories have rendered lakhs jobless and this has also hit dalits and other backward castes. The ban on recruitment to government and semi-government jobs that has been imposed in several states has also had an adverse effect. The growing commercialisation of education and health has kept innumerable people from both socially and economically backward sections out of these vital sectors. In this background, reservation in private sector has become very important because the joblessness among the SC and STs has witnessed a steady increase in the recent period. The most disastrous effects of these policies can be seen in the deep agrarian crisis that has afflicted the rural sector. Rural employment has sharply fallen and this has hit dalits, adivasis and women the most. Mechanisation of agriculture has further compounded the problem. The real wages of agricultural workers, of whom a large proportion are dalits, have fallen in many states. No efforts are made to implement minimum wage legislation even where it exists, and periodic revision of minimum wage is also conspicuous by its absence. The dismantling of the public distribution system has increased hunger to alarming proportions. An overwhelming proportion of the malnutrition-related deaths of thousands of children in several states is from dalit and adivasi families. Thus, the neo-liberal policies have accentuated both the economic as well as the social divide in the country.

LAW AND ORDER

There is a widespread of custodial torture and killing of Dalits, rape and sexual assault of Dalit women, and looting of Dalit property by the police "are condoned, or at best ignored." This problem is not a recent one. In 1979 India constituted the National Police Commission to analyze problems in police performance. Though the Scheduled Castes and Scheduled Tribes (Prevention of Atrocities) Act, 1989 (hereinafter Prevention of Atrocities Act, 1989) act passed it has not been practiced properly. They are vulnerable to arrest under draconian security laws. Additionally, under a theory of collective punishment, the police often target entire Dalit communities in search of one individual and subject the community to violent search and seizure operations. Dalit women are particularly vulnerable to sexual violence by the police, which is used as a tool to punish Dalit communities. Police also actively allow private actors to commit violence against Dalits with impunity, and at times, collude with private actors in committing such atrocities. Police systematically fail to properly register these crimes under the Prevention of Atrocities Act, 1989 and the Protection of Civil Rights Act, 1995.According to the reports of several forums, India failed to protect Dalits from discrimination in the distribution while celebrating their leaders birth day at Paramakudi, Ramnad District (September 11, in the eve of a dalit leader Mr.Immanuel Sekaran).

LESSONS FROM PARAMAKUDI

In any society with a history of caste oppression and conflict, the slightest provocation can sometimes set off a sequence of deadly attacks and reprisals. Law enforcement officers cannot prevent all acts of provocation, but what they can do is to anticipate and contain the resultant social tensions before they explode. Failure to do this at Paramakudi in Tamil Nadu proved tragic; with the protest by supporters of a Dalit party turning violent and the police opening fire and killing six persons.

HEALTH

In 2000, the Infant Mortality Rate (child death before the age of 1) in SCs was 83 per 1000 live births as against 61.8 for the others, and the Child Mortality Rate (child death before the age of 5) was 119.3 for 1000 live births. These high rates among the scheduled castes are closely linked with poverty, low educational status and discrimination in access to health services. In 1999, at least 75 % of SC women suffered from anaemia and more than 70 % SC womens' deliveries took place at home. More than 75 % of SC children were anaemic and more than 50 % suffered from various degrees of malnutrition.

BASIC SERVICES

From the total population of the scheduled caste only 11% of them were accessable to sanitary facilities and 28 % of they were able to use electricity as source of lighting during the nights.

STRATEGIES TO OVERCOME

The following are the strategies to ensure a better life for the crores of dalits in our state and it calls upon them to join the common movement of all toiling, oppressed and exploited sections to win these demands and also to effect a radical social, economic and political transformation.

LAND REFORMS

The central and state governments must immediately set in motion a process of land reforms whereby land will be redistributed to the landless agricultural labourers and poor peasants gratis. All loopholes in the present laws must be plugged. All schemes to reverse land reform legislation and give away land to multinational corporations and big business houses should be scrapped forthwith.

RESERVATIONS

All the backlogs in reserved seats and posts and in promotions for scheduled castes must be filled forthwith special recruitment drives. The three Constitutional amendments made to correct the three OMs issued in 1997 diluting reservations for scheduled castes should be implemented. The pre-1997 vacancies based roster should be restored. A comprehensive legislation covering all aspects of reservation for scheduled castes in employment and education both public and private institutions should be enacted.

SPECIAL COMPONENT PLAN

Special Component Plan should be properly implemented in all the states with proper allotment of funds according to the population of dalits. A National Commission should be set up to assess the real position of dalits including reservation. The state level commissions should be set up to oversee the implementation of all schemes connected with the SCs including reservation.[1]

INFRASTRUCTURE DEVELOPMENT

Infrastructure development in the scheduled caste areas like road, water, health, culture and other needs has to be given proper importance. When allotting fund for infrastructure development, a separate allotment for scheduled caste areas should be provided. A comprehensive National Programme of Minor Irrigation for all irrigable but unirrigated lands of scheduled castes through wells, community wells, bore-wells, community bore-wells and tube-wells, bandheras, check-dams, lift, etc., should be immediately undertaken and implemented.

ROOTING OUT UNTOUCHABILITY

All forms of untouchability must be rooted out of the country by strengthening the relevant laws, ensuring their strict implementation and most importantly, by launching a mass movement of the people.

PROTECTION FROM ATROCITIES

The Central Government should amend and strengthen the SC and ST (Prevention of Atrocities) Act 1989, providing for special courts with judges, investigating officers and public prosecutors unburdened by any other work. Social and economic boycott and blackmail should be included as substantive crimes. Full economic rehabilitation of victims and their survivors must be ensured.

EDUCATION

The commercialisation of education should be stopped since the massive fee and donation structure of private educational managements is something that socially and economically backward students cannot afford. For this, the central government must increase its own outlay on education to 6 % of the GDP. SC/ST students should be given special scholarships to pursue their studies. The stipends in Social Welfare hostels should be raised and the quality of these hostels improved. Steps should be taken to universalise primary education and expand secondary education. Special measures to curb the drop-out rate among SCs should be undertaken.

EMPLOYMENT

The privatisation drive should be stopped as it leads to loot of national assets, greater unemployment, a curtailment of reservations and also a spurt in corruption. The Central Government should enact a bill to provide reservations in the private sector, which has been a long-standing demand of SCs and STs. Special schemes to provide self-employment to SC youth should be started. The Right to Work should be incorporated as a fundamental right in the Constitution.

AGRICULTURAL WORKERS

The Minimum Wages Act for agricultural workers must be stringently implemented throughout the country. A comprehensive bill for agricultural workers is another long-standing demand and it must be enacted without delay. Homestead land must be provided for SCs, STs and agricultural workers.

RURAL EMPLOYMENT GUARANTEE SCHEME

The National Rural Employment Guarantee Act must be strictly implemented all over the country by involving the people, their mass organisations and the panchayati raj institutions. It should be extended to all districts and also to urban areas of the country.

PUBLIC DISTRIBUTION SYSTEM

The public distribution system must be universalised to ensure food to all. Until this is done, BPL ration cards must be issued to all poor families, many of whom are from SCs and STs. The grain under the BPL scheme should be made available at Antyodaya prices.

CREDIT

Agricultural credit to peasants and agricultural workers must be made available at 4 % rate of interest. For SCs and STs in both rural and urban areas, credit facilities should be expanded and the credit given at concessional interest rates.

BONDED LABOUR AND CHILD LABOUR

The total liberation and full rehabilitation of bonded labourers must be ensured. The pernicious practice of child labour must be abolished and children properly rehabilitated and educated. Similarly, total liberation and full rehabilitation must be ensured for Safaqi Karmacharis who are engaged in scavenging.

SCAVENGERS

Ensure total liberation and full rehabilitation for scavengers (safai karamcharis), ban engagement of contract labour in safai services and other services where scheduled castes numerically predominate and instead introduce necessary improvements by involving such Karamcharis; and reactivate the Central Monitoring Committee for Liberation and Rehabilitation of Safai Karamcharis and State, Municipal and District Level communities.[2]

INTERCASTE MARRIAGES

Intercaste marriages should be encouraged by giving special subsidized housing and other facilities to married couples immediately after their marriage. We should consciously try to uphold such inter-caste marriages and make them an event of big social participation and sanction.

CONCLUDING REMARKS

The overview of systematic exclusion of dalits till 65th independence is a comprehensive one; though there are some constitutional provisions in the form of reservation for at least 65 years since independence, contrary to expectations, while sections of the OBCs have made rapid progress but the dalits haven't. The bureaucracy has not been addressed the dalits but support the upper caste people in the form of non-implementing any constitutional provisions and adopting lot of formalities while availing their own rights in either getting admission in educational institutions, getting loans for their education, agricultural activities, start a self-employment, contracts and license for running any business like petrol bunk, schools, colleges or any other service institutions. There are so many educational, employments, political and economic institutions that violate the norms of reservation while admitting, appointing, allocating and offering such constitutional provisions. The politicians, bureaucrats and judiciary machineries are not able to be very genuine to protect and safeguard the rights of dalits in the constituent India. If continued to be the same, there will be an internal war to protect their self-self by dalits. Hence, the law makers and the rulers should take necessary steps to keep India in peace rather to be piece ...peice...

REFERENCES

1. Report (2007), Planning Commission, New Delhi

2. Pramode Dasgupta Lecture (13/07/2010), Kolkata

21 ROLE OF NGOS IN PROTECTION OF HUMAN RIGHTS SYSTEMATIC EXCLUSION OF DALITS IN TAMIL NADU FOR DALITS TO REMOVE SOCIAL EXCLUSION- A STUDY

Dr. A. Balakrishnan, R. Vettriselvan and S. Krishnan

INTRODUCTION

"On the 26th January, 1950 we are going to enter into life of contradictions. In politics we will have equality and in social & economic life we well have inequality. In politics we will be recognizing the principle of one man, one vote, one value. In our social & economic life we shall by reason of our social and economic structure, continue to deny the principle of one man, one value, how long shall we continue to deny it for long we will do so, only by putting our political democracy in peril. We must remove this contradiction at the earliest possible moment"

-Dr. Babasaheb Ambedkar....

The constitutional and statutory laws in India establish a comprehensive list of human rights. Many laws have been adopted to remove discriminatory practices towards ex-Untouchables/Dalits. Most of these international human rights documents not only provide a detailed catalogue of human rights to which everyone is entitled to enjoy but also categorically proclaim that the principles of "equality" and "non-discrimination" constitute the dominant themes of the modern international human rights law (Vijapur, 1993). The term "Untouchables" is not an appropriate word recent days, as the practice of Untouchability has been legally restricted. Untouchables are known by different names in India; Mahatma Gandhi called them Harijan, children of god. Religious books of the Hindus called them Sudras; Ambedkar called them "depressed classes". However since 1970 the term "Dalit" has been widely used. Dalit is a Marathi word, first used by Mahatma Jotiba Phule, a 19th century social reformer who led a movement for the upliftment of Untouchables, which means "broken people." In official documents they are designated as the Scheduled Castes (SCs). Human rights violation may take place in the every level of the nation for downtrodden people by treating those poor and blocking them to get their basic rights from government. Central government may introduce number of policies, programmes, Acts and schemes to prevent the Dalit people from social exclusion to create a healthy inclusive society. But mostly government has failed to achieve the full aim of the plans implemented for them. Those times government may get the assistance from NGOs for to reach the last citizen of the nation to make the plan effective and create inclusive society. NGOs are the voluntary organization that may come forward and take actions against the social exclusion issues to help the excluded people to get their basic rights and subsidiaries from the government to uplift the socio-economic condition and make the equal society by include all the people.

STATEMENT OF THE PROBLEM

The caste system was the foundation for the traditional social stratification, the problem of exclusion practices in rural community of India was more complicated as it was not simply a socio-economic phenomenon but, and more importantly. Mostly the way of scriptures, we can trace that; Indian society could be broken into a number of different groups on the basis of varnas. The dalits who constitute one fifth of India's population had a historically suffered from caste and untouchability based exclusion. There is a number of evidences shown that many cases results that there is a lot of discrimination was practiced with regard to wage, education, employment, property ownership and political partnership etc., Most of the SC and ST communities are still striving to fulfill their basic needs of food, clothing and shelter. Besides these, today they require better opportunities to live in dignity and self-respect. Hence, ample opportunities should be made available to them, which would ensure them a secured and dignified life in this 21st century. After independence, the Constitution of India piloted by Dr. Babasaheb Ambedkar prescribed certain protection and safeguards for the SCs and STs with the objective of promoting their educational, economic and political interests. The Government has yet so far provided various plans and programmers offering them opportunities to develop. It provided general infrastructure and resource development-like providing educational facilities, health services and building communication networks etc.

It is observed that the Government programmes - especially those pertaining to SC and ST welfare are never taken seriously, and there are no effective monitoring systems to pinpoint the failures of the plan objectives. There are diversion of resources and lack of utility of the schemes. Therefore, the condition of these communities is still remained very miserable. Therefore, the present effort suggest suitable remedial measures to ensure the effective implementation laws against human rights violation for the development and inclusion of the depressed excluded sections.

RELEVANCE OF THE STUDY

India has a rich and glorious cultural legacy, but it should be noted that nowhere in the world. Caste system is a unique feature of Indian life we find the extent of discrimination that is perpetuated by one group of people against the other, as it is done in case of low caste Untouchables by the high caste Hindus in India. It is believed that originally there were only four broad/main castes the Brahmins (the priestly class), the Kshatriyas (the warrior class), the Vaisyas (the merchant and peasant class), and the Sudras (the Untouchable class). But over the last two thousand years, these four castes have been astronomically sub-divided into thousands of castes and sub-castes. The 2011 census revealed that there were two thousand three hundred and seventy eight "main Castes" and tribes in India. The official list of "scheduled castes" prepared by the then British authorities of the Government of India in 1935 contained four hundred twenty nine Untouchable castes. Thus, traditionally Sudras/Dalits were excluded from engaging themselves in reading and learning profession and participating in Aryan religious customs and ceremonies. In principle, marriage was permitted within one's own caste. This rule was often broken, but any Brahmin male who took a Sudra to be his wife would become the object of particular scorn. If a Brahmin male had only one wife and she was of Sudra status, he would be considered to be in a state of ritual impurity and would be forbidden to attend family ceremonies like *sradha* (rites for the dead) ancestor worship. On the other hand, any Sudra male who approached a Brahmin female, behaved like a Brahmin caste, or did any harm to a Brahmin person would be subject to serious punishment, sometimes even death (Yamazaki 1997, 5). Another scholar (Zinkin 1962, 59) cites a rule from scriptures, which stated: If dalit assumes a position of equality with high caste men, either in sitting, or going along the road, they shall receive corporal punishment. A Sudra committing adultery with women of the first three castes shall suffer capital punishment, or shall be burnt alive tied up with straw. If a Sudra intentionally reviles a Brahmin or criminally assaults him; the limb with which he offends shall be cut off. For centuries, and even now, these Untouchable castes have been subject to various restrictions in their movements or relationships with other people, especially the high caste persons. They still face many social disabilities, like denial or restriction of access to public facilities such as wells, schools, roads, post offices and courts; denial or restriction of access to temples where their presence might pollute the deity as well as the higher caste worshippers; and from rest-houses, tanks and shrines connected to temples. They have been denied access to services such as those provided by barbers, laundrymen, restaurants, shops and theatres, and are required to use separate utensils and facilities within such places. They face a lot of restrictions on style of life, especially in the goods indicating comfort or luxury. Riding on horseback, use of bicycles, umbrellas, footwear, the wearing of gold and silver ornaments (in fact, their abject poverty could never afford them to do so), the use of palanquins to carry bridegrooms were all forbidden for these people. Traditionally, they were required to have their homes/huts constructed outside the village and quite away from the high caste families; this practice is followed even now in almost all villages. This segregation is believed to have a divine sanction. While the touch of an animal was not considered polluting, the very sight of an Untouchable was enough to pollute and called for the performance of special cleansing ceremonies. Domestic and agricultural animals could live and eat in the same house with high caste Hindus but the Untouchables could not even live in the same town. For many orthodox Hindus the cow dung is ritually so "clean", that a Brahmin priest will use it to wash away his impurities. Even now untouchability continues to be widely prevalent and is practiced in one form or another in most of the villages in India. This fact has been empirically established by a recent study of Action Aid India. (Shah, et al. 2006). Here, the attempt was made to analyze the role of NGOs to remove the social exclusion practices in Tamil Nadu with some recent cases to give a better suggestion to government for using NGOs to create an inclusive society for all the people and protect the Dalit people from human rights violation.

OBJECTIVES OF THE STUDY

- To study the role of NGOs practices adopted for Inclusion practices in Tamil Nadu.
- To understand the problems faced by the Dalit people in the process of inclusion by violating human rights.
- To analyses the selected cases of the excluded communities with reference to human rights violation.
- To suggest the suitable measures to overcome the problems faced by dailt in the inclusion to engage NGOs to protect the Dalits from human rights violations

NON GOVERNMENTAL ORGANIZATIONS IN INDIA

In the past decade, India has witnessed the emergence of an enormous organization such as community-based organizations, self help groups, cooperative and trade unions in the various sectors of the economies. These organizations of the poor have developed strategies for addressing poverty at the local level with an objective of improving their living and working conditions and enhancing their bargaining power. These experiences have been restricted to limited areas and have not been replicated on a large scale. Nevertheless, enabling the poor to form their own organizations has, in many cases, proved to be the most successful and sustainable strategy for fighting conditions of deprivation and poverty. Today, a lesser role is being argued for the state and greater role for non-state actors, which include the institutions of the market as well as non-government organizations (NGOs). Voluntary organization is a group of persons who organize themselves on the basis of voluntary membership with external and State control, for the furtherance of some common interests of members. They can pursue a general interest or interest of the group which formulated the organization. Briefly, the absence of external or state control defines the inherent strengths and weakness of the voluntary organizations at the same time.

NGOs are expected to play a critical role in all conceivable aspects of development. In fact, the role of NGOs itself is changing over the years due to change in the function and philosophy of other development organizations. The role of government has changed from a police state to welfare state and subsequently to a development state. Correspondingly, NGOs had undergone various generations of changed role such as charity, relief, welfare, development and empowerment. The mainstream thinking on the role of government and NGOs in poverty alleviation and social inclusion has changed through the decade at both international and national level. Through a well defined policy towards NGOs rarely existed, NGOs were approached by Central Governments and funding agencies to assist in implementation of the community development and social welfare programmes. In the field of development, NGOs range from large charities to local self-help organizations, coordinating bodies as well as lobby groups (ODI, 1998). During the 20th century, NGOs have earned for themselves a rich, respected, revered and reliable place in the history of development both in India and globally (Ditcher, 1988., Ramaswamy, 1991 and Fowler, 1992). In India, NGOs are called by different names likely voluntary organizations, non-party processes, social action groups and so on. And it will differed from others by an activity, method of approach, welfare measures and sources for getting funds and so on.

SOCIAL EXCLUSION IN INDIA

In India, there is a distinct and all-pervasive system of discrimination based on caste. The United Nations and its agencies refer to it as "discrimination based on work and descent". What it means is that people who are born into specific groups, trades or castes are unable to escape from the stigma of their background or their origins. Hence those born as leatherworkers, barbers, agricultural workers or manual scavengers (toilet cleaners) will remain in those employment sectors all their lives. Sometimes people escape from the system by moving to the large towns or cities, but overall the system remains heavily in the same position. "Dalit" is a term which has had increasing currency in recent years. Literally, it means "the oppressed". It encompasses peoples who used to be called "untouchables", or "Harijans"; who are often also referred to as "Scheduled Castes", because the way they are referred to in the constitution of India. "Adivasi" is a term which refers to those who are members of "Scheduled Tribes". That is, individuals who are racially distinct, as indigenous peoples, in contradistinction to the Caucasian peoples who invaded and settled India centuries ago. Government frame many policies and implements a number of schemes and programmes to empower the 'dalits' but still there is a lot of gap between the normal people and oppressed community. Still many Medias were pointed out the lot of issues related to the discrimination every day. Higher education is a dream for lower caste children still now; mostly they are engaged only for the casual employment. The basic rights for the downtrodden people were still denied. They are expecting some support from externally to meet their things and still there are lot of excluded practices was identified in the rural areas in various formats. The local body dalit representatives are having the power only for namesake, but originally the power owned by the upper caste people of that locality (The Hindu., 22-2-2012).

ROLE OF NGOS FOR SOCIAL INCLUSION

Many number of issues related to social exclusion were identified only by the NGOs working in those locality. Majority of the NGOs were started with an aim of creating inclusive society and remove the discrimination from the modern world. Traditionally the first effort of every reform activity may take only by the NGOs and then the government come forward and takes action for those problems some of the efforts taken by the NGOs along with the help of the government to bring the suppressed and depressed section to the higher level and thereby involve them in the process of inclusion.

- The welfare funds for the socially oppressed people were distributed by NGOs
- Identification of local problem for the downtrodden people
- Identify the obstacles to meet out their basic rights
- Help to reach the government schemes to the appropriate people
- Create awareness about the basic education and self empowerment
- Planning and implementing the welfare schemes for the development of the socio-economic condition for the oppressed community
- Mobilize all the available local resources and take initiative to improve the local standards
- Build the self reliant and sustainable self developed community
- Mediate the needed people and government or other agencies

- Create people participation towards the needed government programmes and policies.
- Motivate and articulate priorities to the needed social service action
- To strengthen the civil society to provide equal rights to all
- To increase the bargaining power to empower the downtrodden people
- Arranging micro credit to develop the entrepreneurial skill for the oppressed community people

Dimensions of NGOs Involvement in Social Inclusion Process

Educational Dimension: Exclusion also results from denial of rights to have education and poor access to education and uneconomic employment opportunity are traditional characteristics of Indian society for the socially excluded people. Lack of access to education and occupational structures for various reasons especially the state's failure to provide free or affordable education and generate adequate employment opportunities in the past. In hill and remote areas were taken care by the NGOs. In order to provide education to the poor they take effort to construct and run the schools for the welfare of the Tribal students to empower them by improving their literacy level. These actions were taken by the many of the NGOs especially religion based missionaries which they all focused for the tribal welfare and tribal development. In Tamil Nadu the Districts namely, Theni, Dindigul, Nilgiri and Coimbatore are the most benefited areas for the welfare activities taken by the NGOs. Especially this effort has helped the excluded people to home better and higher education opportunities to increase the inclusive process among the student community.

Economical Dimension: The main moto of the NGOs is to eradicate the poverty. In almost all the districts the NGOs arrange micro credit for poor which cover a sizable portion of rural dalits. Further to empower them by creating skill among them for taking up of business opportunities in order to improve the economic standard in rural area of their life. Many of the NGOs undertake the economic activity like formation of SHGs providing micro credit for the rural people to reduce the role of money lenders and the poverty. This facilitates to reduce the level of economic backwardness of the oppressed people in the society and to make them following economically equal on par with other communities in the society.

Social Dimensions: The famous issue near Madurai i.e Utthapuram which was published in almost all the daily News papers/Magazines more than a year has explored to the world by the local NGO. Last century the fore fathers were built the discrimination wall in the Utthapuram village near to Madurai. The village was cutted into two parts and one is for upper caste people and another part for dalits. No dalit people was allowed to cross the wall, this was identified by the NGO namely Theendamai Olipu Munnani Madurai Region (Discrimination eradicating Frond) exacted near Madurai has explored it and information disseminated to the world and it helped to remove the discrimination wall and took a step to enter dalit people into the temple in the village and it take effort to get their rights for the local people and for construct the inclusive society.

Fragmented labor: Exclusion may also be the result of the disappearance of well-organized industrial structures. In the process they have fragmented industrial labor and weakened the organizational ability and their bargaining power of the working class from oppressed community. The NGOs related to industrial labourers was involved to create the balanced society by creating awareness about their rights in the working places. More number of NGOs is run only with the aim to uplift the dalits and protecting the Human Rights among them namely Tamil Nationalist Groups, Dalit Outfits and Human Rights Organization, Council for Professional Social Works, Peoples Watch, Human Rights Watch, and Theendamai Olipu Munani and so on. They are all fight against the social exclusion by protecting the human rights of the excluded and downtrodden people to create the inclusive society in Tamil Nadu.

MAJOR FINDINGS

- The inequality practices in recent period in terms of education and economic status of Dalit people in the study area.
- The power politics practiced into the Dalit representatives from their constituency.
- NGOs are plays the vital role in removal of social exclusion and creation of inclusive society.

SUGGESTIONS

- The group action (three party participation models) will introduce and encourage the inclusion practices (Government, NGOs and People).
- NGOs must give more attention to implement the economic measures to uplift the Dalit people to protect their human rights.
- Introduce new combined economic development model as a tool for Dalit empowerment to reduce the human rights violation against the Dalit people.

CONCLUSION

With the words of great social reformer, Dr. Babasaheb Ambedkat that, "turn in any direction you like, caste is the monster that crosses your path. You cannot have political reform; you cannot have economic reform, unless you kill this monster". Human Rights are a human dignity to prevent that is very important to take actions without any denies. Exclusion operates at the level of individual, group, institution, locality, and region and so on. It is both cultural and material, and is hierarchical in terms of needs and intensity. Therefore, there is a need for a disaggregated approach in understanding the patterns and processes of exclusion and the nature of the excluded, taking into account historical and contemporary disabilities, and problems of lack of integration of particular groups. Inadequate social and economic infrastructure in areas that have insufficient resources for participation in mainstream development also has been at the root of various "sub-national movements". People respond to social exclusion in various ways, ranging from passivity to group action. Because of a long history of fatalism, which is embedded in the caste system, it is more often than not the case that the excluded themselves are not aware of their exclusion, and even if they are aware, they do not act. Economic development is a tool for dalit empowerment to reduce the human rights violation against the dalit people. There is a need to raise awareness of exclusion, leading to mobilization and group action. Disadvantages arising out of exclusion in India take multiple forms namely economic, educational, social, political and cultural and are all deeply rooted in traditional society. The group action is only possible with the help of fullest involvement of NGOs. In recent days the exclusion by education, employment, economic status and gender is more popular in society. Government, NGOs and interested people may join together to fight against social exclusion to create an inclusive society. NGOs need to give more attention to implement the economic measures to uplift the vulnerables in the society to protect their human rights.

REFERENCES

Dr. Babasaheb Ambedkar., writing and speeches, vol.1, published by Government of Maharashtra, 1979

Dr. Babasaheb Ambedkar., writing and speeches, vol.1, published by Government of Maharashtra, 1987

Ditcher, T.W., 1988, The Changing World of Northern NGOs – Problems, Paradoxes and possibilities, Development, Vol.4, pp.36-40

Fowler, S., 1992, New Forests of the Kerandimal Khondha, Melbourne, Community Aid-Abroad, p.186

ODI., 1988, Development Efforts of NGOs, Development, Vol.4, pp.41-46

Ramaswamy .U., 1991, Non-Governmental Organizations: a Perspective, Friedrich Elbert Stiffing, New Delhi.

Shah, Ghanshyam, et.al., 2006, Untouchability in Rural India. New Delhi: Sage Publications.

The Hindu., 2012., Daily News paper, Madurai Edition dated 22-2-2012.

The Laws of Manu. 1997. Translated by Doniger, Wendy and Brian.K.Smith. New Delhi: Penguin Books.

Vijapur, Abdulrahim P. 1993. "The Principle of Non-discrimination in International Human Rights Law: The Meaning and Scope of the Concept", *India Quarterly* (New Delhi), 49 (3).

Yamazaki, Gen'ichi. 1997. "Introduction: Social Discrimination in Ancient India and its Transition to the Medieval Period" in Kotani, Hiroyuki, editor. *Caste System, Untouchability and the Depressed*. New Delhi.

Zinkin, Taya. 1962. *Caste Today*. Oxford: Oxford University Press.

22 HEALTH STATUS OF RURAL MARRIED WOMEN IN THANTHONIMALAI BLOCK OF KARUR DISTRICT

S. Menaka & Dr. M. Hilaria Soundari

Health is a common theme in most cultures. Infact, all communities have their concept of health, as part of their culture. In spite of that, health continues to be a neglected entity. At the individual level, it cannot be said that health occupies an important place; it is usually subjugated to other needs defined as more important, such as wealth, power, prestige, knowledge and security. Health is often taken for granted and its value is not fully understood until it is lot. During the past few decades, there has been a reawakening that health is fundamental human rights and worldwide social goal, essential to the satisfaction of basic human needs and to an improved quality of life, and that it is to be attained by all people. The widely organization (1948) in the preamble to its constitution. "Health is a state of complete physical, mental and social well being and not merely an absence of disease or infirmity".

INDIA'S HEALTH SCENARIO

The tragic loss of ideals in public conduct and policy within India is nowhere more obvious than in the area of health. The women's health movement in India is fast gaining momentum although there continues to be a vast gap between ground relatives and women's aspirations. Women's groups are extremely active and are working towards the betterment of health care services ration wide. In any community, mother and children constitute a priority group. They are also a vulnerable or special risk group. The risk is connected with child bearing. Much of the sickness in women is largely preventable. By improving the health of the mothers, we contribute to the health of the general population. Despite, a current effort, the health is mother and child still constitutes one of the most serious problems affecting the community in developing countries.

Women often work more hours per day and more days per year in their fields than their men folk and they are directly responsible for producing more than half of all the food grown. After feeding the men and seeing that the children have eaten, the women herself eats the left-over food. Many millions of the world's women suffer due to poor health, almost half of them are anemic and among pregnant women this rises to over 60% or more.

Women have different hormonal and structural constitution than men. There are differences in their nutritional, functional and emotional buildup. Even the environmental and social surroundings affect the two sexes differently. In developed countries women make up thirty to forty percent of the labour force and their numbers are rising. In India, they make 19 to 23% of the main workers. Employers are taking on more and more women of various are groups. This has brought a new sense of identity, financial security, sense of worth and relationship outside the domestic sphere. While it has meant an improved standard of living and greater financial independence for them on the one hand, it has brought out many hazards to their health due to hostile environment and exploitation on the other hand.

WOMEN AND WORK RELATED HEALTH PROBLEMS

Women's work is different from that of men (both within and outside home); women perform tasks which are often valued less. Often, they have to combine jobs with domestic chores, childbearing and nurturing and they have less access to resources necessary for their well being. Therefore, the health risks that women are exposed to as well as their impact on their lives and health are different.

Vast majority of women are employed in the informal sector, with some also taking in work to be performed at home. Women are segregated into certain kinds of jobs, and in certain levels within each occupational category, because they are considered more suitable for women. Women often have a double workday i.e., having to attend to a wide range of domestic responsibilities often in addition to an entire day's work in a remunerative activity. Work related health problems are given below:

- Dust inhalation
- Exposure (e.g) work environment, physical workload working postures and place of work
- Accidents and injuries
- Exposure to disease causing pathogens or
- Violence in the workplace, including sexual harassment.

STATEMENT OF THE PROBLEM

Health is considered as a fundamental human rights and a world wide social goal. It is essential to the satisfaction of basic human needs and improves the quality of life. There are groups that would be termed 'vulnerable' with regard to their physical, mental, social, spiritual or economic status within community. It has been recognized that women all over the world are a vulnerable groups with regard to their health status. A World Bank Report on Women's Health in India released in 1996 has grimly catalogued the variety of ways in which women are discriminated against. They get less education and less nutrition then their brothers. On the other hand women are often over worked and undervalued. Our society is tradition bounded where women have been socially, economically, physically. Psychologically and sexually exploited from time immemorial, sometimes in the name of religion, sometimes on the pretext of writings in the scripts and sometimes by the social sanctions.

Even now a day also, gender inequalities prevail in our society. It becomes great threat to women far accessing their health status. They are getting mental torture/disorder due to gender inequalities. A woman cannot receive the needed health care services because she is not allowed to travel anywhere alone. So, the social economic and cultural inequalities affect the status of women health, particularly married women.

The present study highlights the socio, economic conditions, basic health problems, health status of rural married women and also explains the role of Government and NGOs for improving their health status. Further the study suggests various remedial measures for improving upon the health status of rural married women.

OBJECTIVES OF THE STUDY

- To study the socio-economic conditions of rural married women
- To identify the health status of rural married women
- To find out health problems of rural married women
- To identify the role of government and NGOs to promote the health status of rural married women
- To find out solutions for the health problems confronted

METHODOLOGY OF THE STUDY

Descriptive method has been adopted for the present study. Area of the present study is Velliyanai village Panchayat located in Thanthonimalai block in Karur District. The Universe of the study area is velliyanai village panchayat covering married rural women in the age group of 18-59, and the total no of women in the said are group comes to 1,500 women. For the purpose of the study 10 percent of Rural Married Women have been selected through proportionate sampling method. Accordingly the sample size constitute150 rural married women are the respondents for the present study.

The finalized interview schedule was administered among the respondents for gathering different information from them. The data are collected through observation and interview by the investigator. The collected data was tabulated and analyzed by percentage tables.

DATA ANALYSIS AND INTERPRETATION

This chapter seeks to present a comprehensive discussion and analysis of the data collected from 150 married women respondents in rural area. The data are obtained with the help of a well structured interview schedule by the investigator

Table: 1 Socio, Economic Background of the Respondents

N= 150

Particulars	Distribution of the Respondents	Numbers	In Percent
Age (Years)	20-29	40	26.7
	30-39	67	44.7
	40-49	32	21.3
	50-59	11	7.3
Education	Illiterate	30	20.7
	Primary	40	26.7
	Middle	29	19.3
	High school	27	18
	Higher secondary	18	12
	UG degree	6	4
Caste	SC	45	30
	BC	98	65
	MBC	7	4.7
Religion	Hindu	148	98.7
	Christian	2	1.3
Type of Family	***Nuclear family***	39	26
	Joint family	111	74

Particulars	Distribution of the Respondents	Numbers	In Percent
Occupation	Agricultural labour	37	24.7
	Own cultivators	20	13.3
	Bus body	4	2.7
	Construction workers	5	3.3
	Private teacher	5	3.3
	Government employee	5	3.3
	Textile Worker	10	6.7
	Home Maker	64	42.7
Respondents Annual Income	Below 10,000	40	26.7
	10,000 to 20,000	60	40
	20,000 to 30,000	35	23.3
	30,000 to 40,000	10	6.7
	40,000 and above	5	3.3

The profile of respondents selected from Velliyanai village panchayat in Karur district. It described the distribution of age, education, caste, religion, type of family for 50 respondents who were selected from villages.

The sample constituted women of 20 years and above. The details break-up of the sample by age group is given in the table no 1. It is seen from the above table, majority 44.7% of the respondents belong to the age group of 30-39 years, 26.7% of the respondents belong to 20-29 years, 21.3% of the respondents belong to 40-49 years and the remaining 7.3% of the respondents come under the age group of 50-59 years.

Education is considered a catalyst and forerunner of change among the Dalits. Education acts as and carrier of upward mobility. In order to improve the educational status of the Dalits, the governmental and non-governmental functionaries have come out with financial assistance; in educational institutions; etc. out of the total respondent's majority 26.7% of the respondents have primary level of education, 20% of the respondents are illiterate, 19.3% of the respondents have middle level of education, 18% of the respondents have high school level of education, 12 percent of the respondents have higher secondary level of education and the remaining 4% of the respondents have UG degree level of education. So this clearly mentioned that, only a little more than one fourth of the respondents have primary level of education, whereas on fifths of them are illiterate.

While coming to the community of the respondents, majority (65.3%) of the respondents comes under BC, 30% of the respondents belong to SC, and 4.7% of the respondents belong to MBC. So this table concludes that, majority 65.2% of the respondents comes under backward class.

Regarding religion, out of the total no. of respondents 150, majority 98.7% of them belong to Hindu, and the remaining 1.3% of the respondents are Christians with no respondents from other religious group.

Regarding Type of family, according to the data, majority of the respondents (74%) are in nuclear family and the remaining 26% of the respondents belong to joint family. So majority of the respondents are hailing from nuclear family.

The primary occupation of the Dalit women seeking agriculture. The majority of the women do not going for work, they comes under home maker, followed by 'agriculture labourers' (24.7%), 'own cultivators, '(13.3%) 'Textile worker (6.7%) and private teacher, government employee and construction workers (3.3%), so this table clearly found that, majority of the respondents are home makers.

The poverty line in India, calculated by the National Planning Commission as the cost of a fixed all-India average consumption basket that meets calorie norms of 2,400 calories in rural areas and 2,100 in urban areas, was Rs.328 per person per month (Rs.3,936 annual income) for rural India in 1999-2000. The rural poverty line in Tamil nadu is set at slightly less, Rs. 307.64 per capita monthly income (Rs.3, 691.68 per year). Poverty ratio for Tamilnadu stands at 17.8% and 32.6% respectively. However, this estimation and the method of government calculation of poverty have come under persistent criticism and this estimation arguably constitutes more of a survival line.

According to the data, in the present study says that, 40% of the respondents get annual income of Rs.10,000 to 20,000, followed by below Rs.10,000 (26.7%), 'Rs..20,000 to 30,000' (23.3%), 'Rs.30, 000 to Rs. 40,000' (6.7%) and 'Rs.40,000 and above' (3.3%). So this table, indicates that, 40% of the women respondents earn their annual income is Rs.10, 000 to 20,000.

Table: 2 Health Status of the Respondents

N= 150

Particulars	Distribution of the Respondents	Numbers	In Percent
Having Food Regularly	Always	142	94.7
	Some times	6	4
	Not always	2	1.3
Having Nutritious Food Regularly	Always	35	23.3
	Sometimes	115	76.7

Particulars	Distribution of the Respondents	Numbers	In Percent
Frequency of Food Consumption per day	Two times a day	7	4.7
	Three times a day	143	76.7
Regular items of Food Consumed	Fruits	39	26
	Vegetables	150	100
	Leafy vegetables	60	40
	Cereals	57	38
	Egg	22	14.7
	Milk and Milk Product	141	94
	Fish and Meat	9	6

Health is a common theme in most cultures. Infact, all communities have their concept of health continues to be a neglected entity. At the individual level, it cannot be said that health occupies an important place; it is usually subjugated to other needs defined as more important, such as wealth, power, prestige, knowledge and security. Women's health is not only influenced by genetics, biology and physiology but also by women's role in society. The field of women's health was developed in response to increasing knowledge of the non-reproductive differences between men and women, administrators collaborating in a multidisciplinary effort to understand and promote women's health and general well being. The above table says that, respondents by their health status. Out of the total respondents 94.7% of the respondents having food regularly and the remaining 4% and 1.3% of the respondents have taken food only for sometimes not always. While coming to the having nutritious food regularly, majority of the respondents (76.7%) having nutritious only for sometimes and the remaining 23.3% of them taking always nutritious food.

Regarding the frequency of food consumption per day, according to the data, out of the total no. of respondents, 76.7% of the respondents frequency of food consumption per day is three times a day and the remaining 4.7% of them have the habit of two times per day, followed by regular items of food consumed , all the respondents took vegetables for regular items in their food, 94% of the respondents taking milk and milk product as a regular items in their food, 40% of the respondents taking leafy vegetables as a regular items in their food, 38% of the respondents taking cereals as a regular items in their food, followed by 26% of the respondents taking 'fruits' as a regular items in their food, 14.7% of the respondents take 'egg; as a regular items in their food and the remaining 6% of the respondents take fish and meat as a regular items in their food.

Table No.3 Health Problems of the Respondents

N= 150

Particulars	Distribution of the Respondents	Numbers	In Percent
Health Problems during Rainy Season	Fever	129	88.9
	Cold	129	89.9
	Head pain	39	26.8
	Cough	37	25.5
	Back pain	9	6.2
Health Problems during Summer Season	Head pain	56	39.4
	Eye irritation	27	19
	Heat	96	66.6
	Heat pricking	38	26.8
Major Health Problems	Stomach pain	40	40
	Blood Pressure	20	20
	Diabetes	8	8
	Ulcer	25	25
	Others	60	60

According to the data, the above table says that, respondents by their health problems. Out of the total no. of respondents, during the rainy reason 89.9% of the respondents affected by cold problem, followed by 88.9% of the respondents affected by fever and the remaining 25.5% and 6.2% affected by cough and Head Paid. So majority of the respondents are affected by fever and cold during rainy season. Regarding health problems of respondents during summer season, out of the total respondents, 66.6% of the respondents are having heat problems because they do not take enough water during summer season, followed by 'head pain' (34.4%), 'back pain and giddiness' (26.8%), and 'eye irritation' (19.0%).

While coming to the Major health problems of the respondents, 66.7% of the respondents stated that they are having major health problems as posted in the above table whereas only 33.3% of them reported in the negative. Among these stated in the positive, 60% of them had other health problems such as back pain, leg pain, kidney problems, skin problems and head problems followed by 'stomach pain' (40%),' ulcer,' (25%),' blood pressure' (20%) and 'diabetes' (8%). The above table reveals that health problems such back, leg, head pain, skin problems and also kidney problem are reported by respondents as their major health problems.

Table No.4 Knowledge about Family Planning

S.No	Knowledge about family planning	No of respondents	Percent
1.	Yes	142	94.7
2.	No	8	5.3
	Total	150	100

Out of the total no. of respondents selected for the study, 94.7% of them have knowledge about family planning and the remaining 5.3% of them stated in the negative. So this concludes that majority (94%) of the women respondents have knowledge about family planning method.

Table No.5 Knowledge about the type of communicable diseases

S.No	Knowledge about communicable diseases	No of respondents	Percent
1.	HIV+	41	97.6
2.	Sexually transmitted diseases	11	26.2
3.	Sexually transmitted infections	4	9.5
4.	Reproductive tract infections	3	4.8
5.	Urinary tract infections	2	7.1
	Total	42	100

The above table shows that respondents by their knowledge about type of communicable diseases, of the total no. of respondents interviewed for the study, 97.6% of them have knowledge about HIV+ followed by 'sexually transmitted diseases' (26.2%), 'sexually transmitted infections' (9.5%), 'reproductive tract infections, (7.1%) and 'urinary tract infections' (4.8%)

Majority of the respondents have knowledge about HIV+ compared to other communicable diseases.

Table No.6 Knowledge about the type of non-communicable diseases

Sl.No	Knowledge about communicable diseases	No of respondents	Percent
1.	Diabetes	107	91.7
2.	Blood Pressure	104	69.3
3.	Cancer	102	68
4.	Heart attack	99	66
5.	Total	N=108	100

An analysis of the present table reveals that, 91.7% of them have knowledge about diabetes, followed by 'blood pressure' (69.3%),' cancer (68%) and 'heart attack' (66%) Majority of the respondents have knowledge about diabetes, cancer, blood pressure and heart attack.

Table No.7 Rating of awareness about environmental sanitation

Sl.No	Category	No of respondents	Percentage
1.	High level	82	54.7
2.	Middle level	68	45.3
3.	Low level	39	26
	Total	150	100

The present table indicates that rating of awareness of environmental sanitation is said to be as middle level according to 38% of the respondents followed by 'high level' (36%) and 'low level' (26%). From the above table it is clearly understood that, more no. of (38%) respondents have rated their awareness of environmental sanitation as middle level.

Table No.8 Suggestions for Improvement of their Health Status

Sl. No	Category	No of respondents	Percentage
1.	Take food three times per day	116	77.3
2.	Use locally available at low cost	129	86
3.	Must have nutritious food three times	123	82
4.	Bring boiled water during rainy season	129	86
5.	Drink a lot of water during summer season	105	70
6.	Rest during heavy work load	71	47.3
7.	Must know about family planning method	81	54
8.	Avoid heavy works during pregnancy period	78	52
9.	Attend health related awareness programs conducted by panchayat and NGOs	99	66
10.	Must know about chronic diseases through mass media	76	50.7
	Total	N=150	100*

The present table reveals that distribution of respondents by suggestions for improvement of their health problems, among the total no. of respondents, 86 percent of them stated that, use locally available vegetables at low cost and having boiled water during rainy season, followed by must have nutritious food three times per day (82%), 'take food three times per day' (77.3%), 'drink a lot of water during summer season' (70%), 'attend health related awareness programs conducted by panchayat and NGOs etc' (66%),' must know about family welfare method' (54%),' avoid heavy works during pregnancy period' (52%), 'must know about chronic diseases through mass media' (50.7%) and 'having rest during heavy work load (54%).Majority (86%) of the women respondents suggested that, locally available vegetables must be used and boiled water must be drunk all the time for improvement and solving their health status.

MAJOR FINDINGS, SUGGESTIONS

- It has been observed that more no. of respondents belong to 30-39 years.
- Majority (98.7%) of the respondents are Hindus and backward community (65.3%)
- A little more than one fourth of the respondents have primary level of education, whereas one fifth of them are illiterate.
- Majority (94%) of the respondents are hailing from nuclear family
- Majority 42.7%) of the respondents are home maker
- The respondents with family annual income of Rs.10,000 to Rs.20,000
- Majority of the respondents are members in SHG in their villages and treated equally on par with men.
- 94.7% of the respondents have sufficient food always in their family.
- 76.7% of the respondents are able to get nutritious food only for sometimes.
- Only a few of them had food two times a day.
- 95.3% of the respondents take vegetables and milk and milk products in their food items
- 96.7% the respondents have health problems during rainy season
- Health problems such as back, leg, head pain, skin problems and also kidney problem are reported by respondents as their major problems.
- 94.7% of the respondents have knowledge about family planning methods.

- Majority of the respondents have knowledge about non-communicable diseases.
- 38% of the respondents have rated their awareness of environmental sanitation as middle level.
- The government and NGO have conducted health related awareness programmes to the benefit of majority of the respondents
- 86% of the respondents suggested that, locally available vegetables must be used and boiled water must be drunk all the time for improvement of their health status.

SUGGESTIONS

- The local bodies should be encouraged to implement national health policy
- The local self government should provide a better set of administrative arrangements for the implementation of the schemes as well as streamlined health delivery system.
- The government spending on health sector should be increased and government hospitals should be made more efficient to cater to the needs of poor people.
- More and more government doctors should be encouraged to work in rural areas and quality of services should be improved.
- There is a need to encourage community participation to bring accountability to staff and to improve the maintenance.
- The provision for health services to women should not only focus on reduction of fertility or child survival but also on all groups including adolescence and old age.
- The need is to urge women to be more open about their ailments without any hesitation or shame.
- Doctors should be trained to be more sensitive towards women's special needs.
- There is a need to encourage women to take proper nutrition in order to avoid anemia and other deficiencies.
- Health education should be imparted to women for developing attitude towards their health needs.

CONCLUSION

The present study concludes that, the study population comprising rural married women is hailing from backward community with primary level of education and family annual income of Rs.10, 000 to 20,000. Regarding health status of rural married women, they study shows that, the married women have health problems during rainy season affected mostly by fever and cold. For improvement of health status of women, locally available vegetables should be used and boiled water must be prepared and drunk all the time.

Still, there is a vast scope for the improvement of health status of rural married women provided that GOs, NGOs and Social Action Groups bestow their attention on this issue jointly.

REFERENCE

Books

- Devi Lakshmi, *"Encylopedia of Women Development and Family Welfare Services"*, Anmal Publications Pvt, Ltd, New Delhi, 1998.
- Marsorie Agosin , *"Women, Gender and Human Rights: A Global Perspectives"*, Rawat Publications, Jaipur New Delhi.2001
- Mira Seth, *"Women and Development – The Indian Experience",*, Sage Publications, New Delhi.
- Neeraja, *"Rural Women", "Maternal, Child Health and Family Planning Services"* Discovery Publishing House, New Delhi, 2003
- Savita Thakur Joshi,*"Women and Development- The Indian Scenario"*, Mittal Publications, New Delhi, 1999.
- Vibhuti Patel, *"Women's Challenges of the New Millennium"*, Gyan Pubishing House, New Delhi, 2002.
- Chakraborthy singh mandal, *"Sexual Health Problems and Treatment Seeking Behaviour among Rural Women in India"*International Conference AIDS, july 11-16; 15, Abbstract No.C 11462. International Institute for Publication Sciences, Mumbai India, 2004.

JOURNALS

- Anuratha Mathu, *"Women's Health – A Major Area of Concern"*, Social Welfare, Vol.52, No.1, April, 2005.

- Jenifer Hass et.al, *"Changing in the Health status of women during and after pregnancy"*, The society of General Internal Medicine, Journal List, vol. 20(110, January 2005.
- Jacop.M, et..al., *"A community health programme in rural Tamil Nadu, India. The need for gender justice for women"*, Reproductive Health Masters, Vol. 14, issue 14, page 101-108.
- Mahisha Bhatia, Ranbir Randhawa and Manjit Kanur, *"Improving Health of Rural Women"*, Social Welfare, Vol.51, No.4, July 2004, Annual Publishing.
- Meenu Anand, *"Women's Reproductive Health – Dismal Reality"*, Social Welfare, Vol.52, No.1, April 2005.
- Peter Perman, Rajee Ahuja, "The role of government in health", Economic and Political Weekly, June 28-July 41, Vol.XLIII, No.26 and 27, 2008.

23 DALITS – INCLUSIVE APPROCH FOR EMPOWERMENT

S. Raja, Dr. S. Gurusamy

INTRODUCTION

Indian social structure marked by inequality, injustice, discriminations, oppression exploitation, etc., against the weaker sections namely, Dalits who mostly belong to scheduled caste which constitute considerable size of populations of the country and also in Tamilnadu. Obviously Dalits in the contemporary society by asserting themselves seek, social justice. However the problem of untouchably perpetrated by Hindus on Dalits victims are more in size. A study is dealing with future by inequality due to caste, gender, culture based segregation and segmentalization of society. Socio-economic disparity identity with segments that are hierarchical placed in the system of social system. Dalits are people in the lowest stata or social satisfaction this people are subjected many social caste Hindus particularly in the rural community Dalits are exckle, marginalize and also human rights violations, the atrocities against dalits have implementation for pursuing inclusive growth in the society.

DALITS

The word dalit comes from the Marathi languages and means "ground" "suppressed" "crushed" or broken to pieces. It was first used by "Jyotirao Phul" in the nineteenth century in the context of caste oppression faced by the erstwhile untouchable caste from the twice-born Hindu castes. Dalit is a term for a group of people traditionally regarded as untouchable or low caste. Dalits are mixed population of numerous caste groups all over south Asia and speak various other caste groups on the basis of phenotypes or genetics. As a result population statistics remain controversial and are often subject to political agendas. The caste system in a social construe among south Asia people and has no genetic basis. A large majority of social groups have encountered proactive provisions in the constitution to improve the conditions of dalits through reservations in educational institutions welfare schemes and government jobs. Scheduled castes constitute about 16.8 percent of Indian population. In spite of substained and consistent efforts on the part of the government to ameliorate. The condition of SCs the social group continues to be categorized amongst the "poorest and most subordinated in Indian society by any measures of human development" more then half the SC population is concentrated in the five states of Uttar Pradhash, West Bengal, Hihar, Tailnadu and Andra Pradhash.

WHO ARE THE DALITS?

The government of India Act 1935 determined these forms of deprivations, particularly social and economic on the basis that:-

- The occupy a low position in Hindu social structure.
- Their representation in government services is inadequate.
- They are inadequately represented the fields of trade, commerce, and industry.
- They suffer from social and physical isolation from the rest of the community.
- There is a general lack of educational development amongst the major section of this community.

DEFINITION OF SCHEDULED CASTE

According to Dr.D.N. Majumdhar the term "scheduled castes refer to the untouchable castes". The untouchable caste are those who suffer from various social and political disabled many of which are traditionally prescribed and socially enforced by higher caste. We can define scheduled castes as those economically, socially education, politically backwardness caste which are kept a distance by other caste as an untouchables.

EMPOWERMENT

Empowerment means to increase the spiritual, political, social, or economic strength of individuals and communities. It often involves the empowered developing confidence in their own capacities. Empowerment is then the process of obtaining these basic opportunities for dalit people either directly by those people, or through the help of non-dalit others who share their own access to these opportunities. It also includes actively thwarting attempts to deny those opportunities. Empowerment also includes encouraging, and developing the skills for self-sufficiency, with focus on elimination the future need for charity or welfare in the individuals of the group. This process can be difficult to start and to implement effectively. But there are many examples of empowerment projects which have succeeded.

REVIEW OF LITERATURE

1. Gurusamy S. (1996) in his book entitled "development of sociology" – A reader has highlighted the systematic exclusion of dalit in resources sharing social participation, etc., at grassroots level due to structural inequalities and emphasized the need for pursuing policies of inclusive growth towards ensuring social equilibrium.
2. Suriyakant Wag More (2005) article on decentralized governance in has society implication for Dalit empowerment discusses the importance between good governance and decentralized governance with its essential component for the development of dalits Further they commended the intention of NGOs in the development of dalits also presented the status of dalits in the contemporary society.

OBJECTIVES

- To study the social structure in the study area.
- To expose the problems encountered by dalits.
- To analysis the empowerment initiatives among dalits in the study area.
- To examine structural constraints of dalits.

METHODOLOGY

Selection of study area

This study is conducted in a village panchayat Cheyur in Tirupur dist. Of Tamilnadu.

SAMPLING DESIGN

Simple random sampling procedure shall be adopted to conduct the structured interviews in a selected area.

UNIVERSE OF SAMPLE

The universe of study that belong to six villages of the selected panchayat. Accordingly the village of dalits in the study is contained 302 persons. It was decided adopt 10% as sample for this study. According sample size is 60.

TOOLS OF DATA COLLECTION

An appropriate personal interview schedule will be constructed for the purpose of data collection. The data will be collected through personal interviews, focused group discussions, observation etc.,

SOURCES OF DATA

Data for the study will be collected from both primary and secondary date (books, journals, articles) sources.

RESEARCH DESIGN

The research design of the study shall be descriptive.

Analysis and interpretations

1. Age 40% of the respondents belong to the age group between 36-45 years, 25% if respondents belong to the age group of 26-35, and 20% of the respondents were belong to the age group of 46-55 and remaining 15% of the respondent age group between 66 and above. Majority of the respondents (46%) belong to the age group of 36-45 years.

2. Marital status of the respondents among the 50% of the respondents was married, 35% of the respondents were unmarried and 10% of the respondents were widow. 5% of the respondents are separated and remaining of respondents was widower. The majority of the respondents 50% were married.

3. Educational status wise distribution of the respondents 5% of respondents were studied upto primary and 20% respondents were illiterate. 15% of the respondents were completed the middle schooling and 10% of the respondents were studied upto high schooling. It is conclude the majority of the respondents 55% were completed upto primary school.

4. Occupational status of the respondents 5% of the respondents were working in companies and 55% of the respondents were daily wages workers and 10% of the respondents were government employees. The more number of respondents 55% were daily wage workers.

5. Annual income of the respondents 50%of the respondents were below Rs.10000-20000, and 25% of the respondents were above 30000, and 35% of the respondents were below poverty line.The majority of the respondents 50% are belong to the category or below Rs.10000-20000.

6. Type of houses of the respondents among 20% of the respondents is lived in the pacca house, and 55% of the respondents are lived in the thatched houses and 25% of the respondents were livening in hut house. Majority of the respondent (55%) are living thatched type of houses.

7. Type of family-wise distribution of the respondents 78% of the respondents were belonging to nuclear family and 22% of the respondents were living in the joint family.The majority of the respondents (78%) were living in the nuclear family.

8. Distributions of respondent's savings 50% of the respondents have the saving in SHG, 40% of the respondents have the saving by themselves and only 10% of the respondents have the savings in the bank.More number of the respondents (50%) have the savings in the SHGs.

9. Distribution of respondents by problems in working place 40% of the respondents stated that over burden has given in the work place, 30% of the respondents expressed that working conditions were not favorable, and 20% of the respondents viewed that work has been given without leave and remaining 10% of the respondents replied that wages problem was prevailed in the work place. More number of the respondents (40%) were expressed that over burden has been given in the work place.

10. Distribution of respondents by SCs SHGs More than half of the respondents (65%) were member in SHGs both men and women. 25% of the respondents were not member in the SHGs and remaining 10% of the respondents were not interested in the SHGs. Majority of the respondents (65%) were member in the SHGs.

11. Distributions of respondents by participation in the Election More than 50% of the respondents were participate in the election. 30% of the respondents were not participated in the election and remaining 20% of the respondents do not aware about the election. More number of the respondents (50%) were participated in election.

FINDINGS

1. Majority of the respondents are having sufficient infrastructure facilities.

2. Majority of the Dalit community faced it s problems like untouchable, unemployment, harassment to place of work.

3. Members of Dalit experienced physical exclusion and subjected to social discrimination.

4. The programmes of empowerment are not fully reaching the dalit community.

5. Majority of the respondents were involved in agricultural labor work.
6. Majority of the respondents are facing conflict problems.
7. Majority of the respondents are not having good economic condition.
8. Majority of the respondents are facing problem their festivals.

SUGGESTIONS

1. Skill training programme should be given to the self-help groups and prepares them to start their own business or trade.
2. The bankers may provide financial assistance to the SHG started by the Dalit people without hesitation and try to promote their economic power.
3. Providing employment opportunities to the dalit people of improving their standard of life for that they must be organized and trained in income generating activities.
4. The dalit problems may be eliminated only through collective social actions for with GOs, NGOs, and corporate sectors should involve and contribute towards effective empowerment.
5. Greeting awareness among dalit about their rights provision of legal aid for the production and development of the dalit people.
6. The victims of human rights violation should be properly compensated.

CONCLUSION

1. Dalit they are called as Dravidians, they are the original inhabitants of the Tamilnadu. But they are living under poverty and low socio-economic status the face lot of problem in society. The government of India creates various commissions for the dalit people. But it deviated from its goals.
2. The several structural constraints serve as obstacles to effective empowerment. Empowerment of dalits is possible only by undoing the already existing structure of power which has inherent class, caste, and gender pieces. The problem of unemployment, illiteracy and caste discrimination are main reasons for the low socio-economic status of dalit.
3. The dalits problems may be eliminated only through collective social action for which the GOs, NGOs, corporate sector should involved and contribute towards effective empowerment of dalits.

REFERENCES

1. Pullaguras (2008) “Professional Work & Battle Against Untouchability”, Fight agsinst untouchability.htm. not dated.
2. Ellyn Artis, Chad Doobay and Karen Lyons (2003) Economic social and cultural rights for dalits in India: Caste study on Primary Education in Gujarat, Workshop on Human Rights: from Grassroots Courage to International influence the Woodrow Wilson School of public and international affairs, Princeton University, Liam Mahony.
3. Yuwaraj K. Narnaware, (2000), Human Right Violations against India’s Dalits, Electronic, not dated.
4. Thind G.S. our Indian sub-continent heritage, Vancouver, BC: Crosstown Press Ltd. n.d.
5. Narula S. (1998) “Broken People” caste violence against India’s untouchables, human rights, watch, Electronic, not dated.
6. Human rights of the Dalits in India, (2007) official journal of the European Union, C250/E87.
7. India practices ‘Hidden apartheid” against Dalits: report, www. infochangeindia.org.
8. Pullaguras (2008) the dalit human rights situation: A brief overview, fight against untouchability, just another wordpress.com weblog, Electronic.
9. Prabha Tirmare, Violation of human rights of dalit wowen: issues, factors and concerns, www.infochangeindia.org. not dated.
10. Jogdand P. (1995) dalit women, issues and perspectives, Gyan Publications, New Delhi.
11. Omvedt, G. (1995) dalit women and communalism, edited in Jogdand (1995) dalit women, issues and perspectives, Gyan publication, New Delhi.
12. Pal R. and Bhargav G. (1999) human rights of dalits: societal violation, Gyan publications, New Delhi.
13. Violence against women, Wikipedia, the free encyclopedia, Electronic not dated.

24 ISSUES IN SOCIAL INCLUSION OF SCAVENGERS IN TAMIL NADU

Dr. C.Kubendran

INTRODUCTION

"It is inhuman to witness a human being cleaning the other man's excrement" – The Author of the article. Mahatma Gandhiji himself cleaned the latrines in the ashram. All his followers followed it. But manual scavenging is in existence in India even after 65 years of Independence India. It is a shame for the Nation whose father is Mahatma. Inclusion after libration and rehabilitation of socially suppressed people like scavengers into the main steam of the society is not a easy task. Neither the government nor the scavengers were not ready for completely change of their life leading to integration of these scavengers into main stream of the society, as both of them depend on each other for smooth running of family and government respectively. A "SCAVENGER" means a person irrespective of sex who is partially or wholly involved in the obnoxious and in human occupation of manually removing night soil and filth. A vast majority of the scavengers belong to SC followed by STs. Though the reservation system is fooled in the recruitment of scavengers, generally people, belong to upper caste don't prefer their occupation. Due to their food habits caste culture, we feelings pig rearing activities, government provides cite and accommodations separately little far away from the main habitations of other people. Mostly nearby Graveyards burial ground. Drainage Tank, either side of the canal.

This arrangement was made because the government wanted that the scavengers should not be disturbed by other and they should not disturb others. Scavengers are the government servants starting their work regularly by 5.30 am. The role and contribution has been crucial in keeping the environment, social life of the people clean and peaceful. But they are not given due respect, recognition by the public. Scavengers had always been looked upon down by the general public because of their appearance in uniform, nature of work, personal habits and social life and caste to which they belong. The pitiable part of their life is that majority could not see occupational motility from scavenging to any other non scavenging occupation for generations. It is estimated that, there are 7, 70,338 Scavengers and their dependents unemployed children about 18 years. The numbers of scavengers vary from state to state.

WORK PLACE

Dry latrines, either sides of the canal, used for open defecation, open drainages, public urinals and toilets, bazaar streets and bus stops and bus stands located within the municipality limit are the official work places of scavengers. Men and women and children belong to lower castes are generally employed at all level of government administration and elected bodies. Valkimi and a sub caste of SC Arunthathiar are considered to be the lowest among the settlement lower in the caste hierarchy in India and Tamilnadu respectively. The perception of pollution and impurity imposed upon them forced to live in a isolated and remote areas mostly a corner in the municipal burial ground or near by garbage ground. As they are the workers at lowest level in the municipality and numerically minority, the facilities like schools, health centres and public distribution system, are not access to them. Their children generally could not continue their education even up to high school level. The prejudices existing in the Indian society, keep always the scavengers far away from all the basic rights, privileges enjoyed by the people of other communities. The nature of work they are engaged is so dangerous that the frequency of death even before reaching the age of 45 is more. To cite an example, out of 6826 scavengers in Pune Municipal Corporation within three years, 327 persons were died from various diseases acquired at work.

Steps taken: Since 1947 several committees and commissions were set up by the government to conduct empirical study on scavengers and recommend to the government measures to stop the manual scavenging. To quote, the Barve committee of 1949 the scavenging conditions enquiry committee of 1957, the national commission of Labour committee of 1968 and the National commission for Safari Karmachari of 1957 have recommended several new strategies to ban scavenging in our country. The national planning commission of India declared that it would initiate actions to eradicate manual scavenging by the end of 2007. But there was no impact on scavenging. The standard of life of scavengers remains unchanged. They are not treated at par with other caste groups. They are officially and unofficially excluded for various reasons. A man treating his fellow man as very much inferior is not sign of a liberated and civilized society. They also need to be given equal treatment with due respect. They should also become part of the society. All the steps taken by the government and leading NGOs and Dalit organizations like Navsarjan and National Council for Dalit Human rights etc., working towards the protection of their rights and engaged in campaign against manual scavenging in India. Yet the scavengers are isolated and excluded from the society. What is harmful aspect of exclusion of scavenger is that if the present trend continues there is no chance for the younger generation too to mingle with the main stream of the society which will affect the social fabric of the society. The urgent need of the hour is to understand the stumbling block in the way to integrate the scavengers into main stream of the society and to evolve suitable strategies to the same so as to create an equalitarian society.

PROBLEMS FACED BY THE SCAVENGERS

The problems faced by the scavenger in all walks of life are many but similar to all the states. Men, women and children particularly Schedule Caste and Schedule Tribes are generally employed as manual scavengers in India. Even among the scavengers there is a hierarchy between the two sub-castes within the Schedule Caste. The Parayars are the Sub-Caste at the lower level in the category who is allotted some specific activities like cleaning of public toilets, removal of human excreta, air the street, where as removal of cabbage, clearing of stagnated drainage, cutting of tree branches, emptying of septic tanks are carried out by the upper group within the SC caste. These sections are socially politically, culturally excluded from the main stream of the society for generations. Inclusions of these excluded regiment of the society needs to be given due importance in a country like ours, which ensures equal rights and opportunities to all its citizens. Growth of any nation can be fully realized only when there is inclusion of development of marginalized, disadvantaged by adopting conceptual approach which provides emphasis on equal nondiscriminatory access to growth and disadvantage – reducing growth. Scavengers are one of the groups of disadvantaged which is a powerless and less access to infra structure facilities, In order to they lead life far away from the life of even the groups considered to be lower strata of the society. In order to integrate these excluded and disadvantaged section and empirical study was needed to find a suitable ways and means. Accordingly a study was conducted among the scavengers working in municipality in Tiruvarur. This paper honestly attempts to analyse the problems faced and issues involved in inclusion of scavengers into the main society with some practical solutions.

OBJECTIVES OF THE STUDY

The major objectives of the study were

1. To study the living conditions of the scavengers
2. To understand the nature of work and problems faced in the work
3. To identify the issues in social inclusion of scavengers into the main stream and

4. To suggest suitable measures to integrate the scavengers

RESEARCH DESIGN

Study area: Tiruvarur Town in Tamil Nadu was the study area

SAMPLING PROCEDURES

There are four decisions' was 146 Male, Female 25 members from each sex was selected by the researchers using simple random sampling. Hence the sample size was 50.

DATA COLLECTION:

The researcher administered an interview schedule as the chief tool for collecting primary data from the scavengers. Participatory observation method was also used to gather information on the living conditions and nature of work of the scavengers Apart from primary data, Secondary data, Such as, Municipality records related to scavengers like attendance leave late, punishment, No of working days, Salary and other allowances, housing rent loan etc.

DURATION OF THE DATA COLLECTION

This study was carried for three months from November 2011 to January 2012

FINDINGS

Demographic Details of the Scavengers:

1. Men scavengers are out number (74%) in the municipality work
2. With regard to community of the scavengers 92% of the scavengers belonged to SC followed by ST, 87% and 13% respectively.
3. More Number of scavengers 68% belonged to the age group between. 30-45.
4. 77% of the percent of the scavengers are illiterate and educate with primary education.
5. 100% of the permanent employers are married
6. In respect of the size of the family, Majority of the scavengers was medium followed by larger size between 6-9. There were two families having 10 children.

7. The age of the mother was only 46 and 47. 72% of scavengers do not know their date of birth and It may be due to their illiteracy

8. 92% of the men and 64% of women scavengers hard the habit of consuming alcohol. Many do not know the standard of education of their children.

9. 85 and 60% of both sexes consume regularly. The age at which they started this habit was between 17-20 for majority of the scavengers

10. Petal chewing is another personal habits of 86% of the total scavengers.

11. Borrowing loan from money lenders at high rate of interest ie. 10% to 15% on emergency had been the practice for majority of the scavengers(78%) 68% of scavengers do not have the habit of savings. Though they know of it.

12. The main reason for borrowing money at a high rate of interest was to celebrate family life cycle ceremonies like ear boring, daughter's puberty marriage and death of relatives. It was observed that all these expenses are in productive and over and above the economic capacity of the scavengers.

13. 70% of the scavengers pay only the interest between Rs.5,000 and 10,000/- every month from their salary

14. 60% of the scavengers have surrender their Bank Pass book and ATM card to the money lenders early for easy repayment of interest

15. It was understood through focus group discussion that though there is reservation for BC and MBC in the recruitment of scavengers' none from these communities preferred to engage in scavenging activities. With inadequacy of scavengers, the municipal administration had to engage temporary scavengers either from their community or partners of the permanent scavengers. There is no promotion, or incentives or profession based bonus for these scavengers.

Though there is more possibility for accidents during the scavenging activities yet there are no medical allowances, sick leave or etc. There is no provision for compassionate Job for the son and daughters of the deceased and sick persons. Pig rearing had been the additional source of income for almost 60% of the scavengers which fetched more income in the short period of time without any risk involved. But in the recent times, the municipality had strictly warned the scavengers not to continue the rearing of pig which affected their additional income to then family to manage the social and cultural affairs. Now, they are struggling hard to fond alternative source of income as already mentioned majority or scavengers are illiteracies and killed other than scavenging and pig rearing activities.

2) Living Conditions & Infrastructure facilities

The scavengers' settlement was established , little fare away from main town some 60 years ago it was surrounded by graveyard, garbage ground and drainage tank. Later,. Municipality had constructed 40 houses in small size with similar structure. The monthly rent of which, according to the work experience around, Rs.400 will be deducted from their salary. The settlement is thickly populated as the numbers of families living in the settlement are two to three times the available houses. Since most them were neither highly educated nor technically qualified and in ability to start own business they could not integrate in to the main society. They are left with no option but to settle with the parents and started scavenging activities. Above all the rent rate out side is much higher'

- 74% of the Scavengers live in colony house (Called Pettai) constructed by the municipality rent of which would be detected from their salary.
- 92% of the houses don't have separate toilets.
- 75% of the houses do not have both room facilities attached in the houses. They use open place for defecation and take both in a place semi covered mostly with banners and / or cloths. Palm leaves on coconut leaves at the back of houses. There was public toilet; locally available constructed by was out of usage.
- Children defecate on the bank around the drainage pond situated in front of the colonies.
- 95% of the houses were in dilapidated conditions and need a overall correction of repairing.
- 60% of the parent scavengers have school dropouts, unemployed sons and daughters in the house. Who are used as substitutes for scavenging work in the absence of the parents?
- 90% of the scavengers lack access to use the infrastructures like, public distribution system, Health Centre, Noon meal centers', even tea shops and Tiffin centre's.
- 74% of the scavengers wanted their sons and daughters to engage in scavenging activities as there was no guarantee for them to get govt. employment. During the study, it was observed that a father of a B.Tech. Graduate had been insisting that his son should be observed in municipality scavenging work. When cross checked with his son about the plan of his father it was confirmed.

NATURE OF WORKS

Any kinds of manual work that was refused and could not be done by the educated, decent and civilized people are the work of scavengers. For the government scavengers the work starts by 5.30 and ends the first shift of work by 11.30. Then second shift starts by 2.30 and ends around 6.00 O' Clock. All the scavengers are required to entry the time of incoming and out going to the work in the respective division allotted to the scavengers within the municipality limit.

REGULAR WORKS

The regular official work of the scavengers are cleaning the public toilets and the urinal basins and floors and , application of bleaching powder and phenol, in the bus stands, government hospitals etc., cleaning of streets, clearing up of drainage, removal of garbage and plastics blocking the drainage in the streets and in the bazaars. Cleaning of septic tanks collecting the waste materials and dumping into the lorry,

SEASONAL WORKS

- When needed, cutting the branches of trees encroaching the road and streets, spraying the anti mosquito smoke/fogging,
- Spraying of larvaecide
- it is this scavengers who have to carry out the preparatory work prior to the commencement of any program being organized by the district administration through municipality .like administering polio drops , distribution of tablets,
- On the occasion of area visit of VIPs like collectors, secretaries, Ministers the scavengers do the area cleaning and spreading bleaching powder and wait till the program is over.

ADDITIONAL WORKS:

- Disposal of debris in the event of natural calamities like tsunami and floods even in the out side district ie. Anywhere in the state. Recently, the scavengers in Tiruvarur went to Cuddalore district and involved in the disposal of debris in Thaaney, flood.
- Sometimes they also involve in the disposal of dead animals on the streets, like dogs, cats, rat Doing post mortem works, pigs, goats, chicken etc. Sometimes the abandoned human body found unidentified in the bushes or in the canals and also burying them

- On account of these kind of more pains taking work in unhealthy environment, with the stinking and the fouling smell emanated from the drainage septic tank, and handling of dead bodies of animal and human, and the process of carrying and burying them or burning them, they developed the regular habit of consuming alcohol during the execution of work even in the working hours.
- What is strange here is that the drinking habit of both the scavengers has been, accepted officially by the other workers and officials including the chairman and the commissioner of the municipality.

THE RISKS INVOLVED IN SCAVENGING ACTIVITIES.

Taking into account the nature works, there are more chances of frequent occurrence of minor and major wounds, chronic sick accidents leading to disability even deaths during the works. To quote some examples

i) In the process of cleaning of septic tank, while lifting the cement plates, used to cover the septic tank, the plate may fall either on the hands or legs causing severe wound sometimes fractures

ii) The hands, feet and legs get wounded while collecting the garbage, medical wastes, by syringes, broken bottles, glasses from TASMAC when involved bare footed and empty hands.

iii) It was told that there was a 'drainage pest' in all the drainages. , the scavengers believe that the pest bite causes paralyzing the legs of the victims. The scavengers involved in these activities with bare legs are more prone to this disease. The belief of the scavengers needs to be medically proved. The researchers witnessed two such cases in the study area.

iv) While applying a chemical acid to remove the strain in cleaning the latrines and urinal basins, they suffer from eye irritation, wounds on the legs and feet. And they are also affected by severe suffocations.

PROBLEMS FACED BY THE SCAVENGERS:

i) Early death of the parents

It was identified that most of the scavengers particularly the fathers die of the sickness even before reaching 45 years. It was said that the early start of drinking habit and slowly leading to regular drinking and ended in drug addiction without taking adequate food in time and taking all types of non- vegetation food and not given importance to medical care and living in the highly polluted , filthy and unhygienic conditions for many years were the main reasons for the early death of the parents who had a lot of debt borrowed at high rate of interest from the money lenders for very survival and to conduct marriages to the son and daughters, and to meet the expenditure related to social and relative functions. Sudden demise of parents forces to discontinue the schooling and go for cooly work as child labor in the unskilled labour in the unorganized sectors and exploited thoroughly till reaches the age eligible to get compassionate job. There starts the scavenging work of the next generations. It was also understood when the fathers died, Majority don't leave the property and any other assets for the generations but they leave only the debts at high rate of interest and scavenging occupations. This cycle continues for generations. More frequent occurrence of death among the scavengers in the place is due to suffocation during the cleaning of the septic tank, from which emanates poisonous gas. News items of the incidents took place in different parts of the county is published in dailies and weeklies.

ii) Frequent fire in the garbage ground;

There is frequent fire accidents in the garbage ground where all the waste materials collected within the municipality limit and carried through the Lorries are dumped into. The frequency is more during the summer seasons all the waste were dried and become the material more prone to burn. Fire accident is not only natural sometimes some ant-social elements set fir in the night. By the time the scavengers reached the spot the severity of the fire would be more. In the process of putting off the fire the scavengers are likely to get wounded severely.

iii) Head loading and unloading of garbage onto the lorry;

While dumping the waste materials like soil, sand and big stone and iron rode, broken glasses and broken branches of trees steel materials and other hard and thick materials with heavy weights materials on the to the lorries on head load , it may fall on the heads or any parts of the body of the scavengers standing below the lorries . it had many times caused to severe fracture on the leg and hands leading to disabled or required a long medical treatment.

ISSUES ON INCLUSION OF SCAVENGERS;

Though there were a number of steps taken by the government to uplift the standard of life aiming at the inclusion of the scavengers in to the main stream of the society, yet there are some issues identified which prevent them from integration. They are as follows;

i) Mono-caste settlement:

It was nearly 60 years passed since their settlement was established. The scavengers had developed a soil cult with their settlement. They feel more comfortable even though there were no basic facilities,. Since majority of the neighbors are from the same caste and one way or the other related to each other by the long time practice of endogamy, the scavengers were not ready to change their place of residence from their settlement to any other area.

ii) Settlement is the right of the scavengers:

The scavengers felt that the allotment of government houses specifically for the scavengers is a symbol of recognition given by the government to the scavenging work. It is a identity and safety area to live with all the member of the family and community in one place Whatever the facilities available outside the settlement, the displacement of this area to the other area is not imaginable.

iii) Only suitable place for pig rearing:

Pig rearing is the only known traditional and additional occupation of the scavengers. It needs broad space for grazing, wide drainage or cement tank for pig fodder which are mostly the market wastage and hotel waste like the left over of the food items and banana leaves etc., Pig rearing is not possible in the main society because the very appearance of the black pigs, the grazing area, pig fodder, only drainage with stinky and disgusting smell its of its ugly environment. More over crossing of pig on the street while people go for an auspicious work is considered to be bad omen and it has also been a customary practice of Tamil people, for generations that the owners of the vehicle, be it two wheeler or four wheeler will sell off their vehicles immediately after it dashed with the pig as it was believed that dashing of vehicle with pig is a symptom given by the God to indicate that there is a big lose of property or life of the owner in the days to come. Which is not accepted by the main society needs a place fare away from the main society without any scientific proof

iv) Cost of land and living outside are high:

The settlement was allotted only for municipal scavengers. The settlement was quite remote. Now due to urbanization and rapid growth of real estate, the non-scavengers from other caste people also started coming in to the settlement area to start various petty businesses like Tea shop, Ironing shop, Tiffin centre, Barber shop, money lender shop.

v) Hoping to get a permanent housing:

Scavengers are on the hope that the houses in which they have been living on rent for more than 60 years, almost two generations, may be allotted permanently to the occupants as in the case of Nagapattinam municipality where all the rented houses were allotted to the respective occupants.

vi) Community monthly meeting;

The scavengers meet once a month in the settlement itself on any convenient holydays particularly on no moon day in the night. And share their experiences and family problems, economic dispute among the members are discussed and settled. they don't generally go to police station or court to get justice to the problems all the problems would be solved within the caste panchayat. Even the problems lime love affaire, inter-caste marriage, eloping with lover, extramarital relationships, premarital relationships and wife beating problems related to drinks, suspicion of either of the partners separation of the partners even divorce cases are dealt with by the community panchayat in the monthly meeting. It is unwritten law that all members from all the family should attend the monthly meeting without fail. Failing which the family who don't attend the meeting would be punished by excommunication of levying fine.

vii) Frequent Get together with pig eating:

The scavengers, living in the settlement are mono caste, mono culture and with mono-occupation They have a habit of organizing a get together exclusively for their own people in general Once or twice a month preferably on Sun day where they one or two pigs is cut into pieces and distributed to all the participants members along with alcohol which they considered a delicious feast longing for. What is important here is that the pig is the unique, traditional food of scavengers and they could not give up eating of pig meat and Pig meat is not available in the main society as the pig eaters are considered as polluted and looked upon down as a barbaric behavior. Only scavengers are the big pig eaters. There is no pig meat shop in the main society. Purchase of pig meat in one kg or two in retail in the main society is not possible as in the case of goat meat or chicken which are widely available in the shops The concentration of people eating pig meat is more only in the scavenging settlement .

One family can not take full meat of the pig. So there needs more than two families to share the full pig. Almost all the members of the scavengers are fond pig eating. It is possible only more people join together to share the full pig. So Sunday is the only day convenient to all to meet. It is not possible in all the Sundays. And they spent times happily. Such get together would not be possible if all the scavengers are scattered to different places. So the scavengers are particular in settling in the same area.

viii) Non acceptance of other people:

Scavengers are very rigid in practicing the age old customs and traditionally followed ceremonies and rituals of the caste system in a traditional way of life. That was not possible in the main society which is fast moving into highly civilized and rational way of life, in face, the scavengers lead a village and tribal life within the city limits. Neither the scavengers could give up their traditional rituals ceremonies nor can the main society tolerate it, that's the same case with regard to food habits. 100% of the scavengers are non-vegetations and eat all types of domestic and wide animals like cow, buffalo goat, pigs, cat, and tortoise alive, rabbits etc., that food habit can't be followed in the midst of main society. Social security and caste panchayat living together, the scavengers feel secured and safety to their property and sons and daughter who are non schooling manual labour. If any thing goes wrong within the caste members or between two castes the caste panchat will involve and solve the problems if they go out of their caste settlement. There is no safety mechanism. So they don't want to go away from the settlement it is also one of the issues on social inclusions

ix) Nearer to the workplace:

The scavenger's settlement is located very nearer to the municipality office and bus stand which is very convenient to attend the work in time which is very much essential in the occupations.

x) Homogenous groups with strong occupational identity:

The scavenger's settlement is the place of identity for them in municipality. For any urgent meeting related to occupation or any family dispute could be solved with the occupations identity with their own caste panchyat people. It is easy for the private people to approach the scavengers in a particular junction point. The scavengers also feel living together is convenient to share their works as most of the works they undertake from the private establishments and official need more manpower from the scavengers.

xi) No alternative employment:

As scavenging has been the traditional and caste based occupation for generations together, they started claiming that scavenging work was meant for this caste and government t should appoint only SC/ST people to this work. The government should also increase the number of houses in the colony proportionate to the number of scavengers in every municipality. It was also understood through the focus group discussion that the scavengers, on seeing the difficulties and problems faced by the people in the main society after higher education and huge money spent and used influential personalities in getting government job, the scavengers fully realized with the illiteracy and unskilled and from the lowest strata of the society decided that the only government optioned for them was scavenging and were very particular in getting government job to lead a economically guaranteed and happy independent life. No matter how much risk, dangerous, and inhuman the nature of occupation of scavenging. They also think that the possibility of getting government job is more if they live in the settlement arranged for the So, they do not want to change their occupation and place of residence due to the feelings of in secured employment and expectation to get government job. This is one of the issues in integration of the scavengers in to the main stream of the society.

SUGGESTIONS:

The followings are the suggestions given for the betterment and prosperity of the scavengers.

1. Ensure the Issue of caste certificate to all the Scavengers belong to SC/ST.
2. Provide protective adequate device like face mask, hand glows, rough cloths, foot wear and modern equipments during the scavengers' activities.
3. Identify and introduce necessary technological changes which will render the occupation humane, dignified and safe, avoiding any direct human contact with excreta, in a maximum of five years.
4. There must be immediate liberation and demolition of the latrine and the full rehabilitation package, within a very short defined time frame.
5. Appoint a female health assistant from the same scavenging group for providing first aid in case of accident.
6. Both manual scavenging and dry latrine should be banned immediately
7. Next generation should be freed from all sorts of atrocities and inhumane occupation for which quality and professional education should be assured.
8. admission to the job oriented courses in the government and private colleges and universities be ensured with adequate financial assistance in the form of special stipend and monthly scholarship and free hostel facilities should be offered.
9. Medical leave and allowances permanent employees in case of accident, chronic disease caused by scavenging work.
10. Conduct resurvey on the exact number of Scavengers and their dependents, unemployed children with above 18 years and aged, sick, parents or in laws.

11. Provision of medical allowances for the needy in the family.
12. Permanent house, at least assurance to housing fill the member from the family is engaged in Scavenging activities.
13. Import social, health and moral education to all the members of the scavengers in their settlement.
14. Provide vocational training – with stipend involving specialized training institutions. It possible outside its state for alternative employment followed by loan and subsidy to the dependent of the Scavengers.
15. Encourage pig rearing activities and provide them loan facilities followed by proper cattle medical care.
16. Observe the dependent as temporary Scavengers officially and give them preference at the time of permanent employment.
17. Formation of SHGs among men and women dependent be mandatory and they may be given group loan. Up to Rs.5.00 lakhs for start of small business not related to Scavenging.
18. Special supplementary education centre should be established within the Scavengers settlement area to prevent school dropouts' and engorge them for higher education.
19. Change the colour and quality of uniform suiting to the taste and nature of work of the scavengers. They may be a change from men trousers to full pant.
20. Drug – de – addiction Centre be established within the settlement and relieve them from addiction and take steps to prevent the younger generation from becoming addicts.

REFERENCES:

1. ***"India, Manual Scavenging, a shame on the nation"*** – Human Rights Council, Ninth Session, Aug.25, 2008.
2. ***"A report – Eradication of in Human practice of manual Scavenging and Comprehensive Rehabilitation of Manual Scavengers in India"*** – by Rashtriya Garima Abhiyan – 2010.
3. ***"The HINDU, Chennai Edition"*** – 18.01.2012.
4. ***Scavengers Records,*** Tiruvarur Municipality.
5. ***A Manual Employment scheme for rehabilitation of Scavengers*** – 2010.

6. The Hindu, bare foot A law for atonement by Harsh Mander Sunday, March 25, 2012.

25 INCLUSIVE EDUCATION IN INDIA: THE VOICE FOR VOICELESS AND MARGINALIZED TRIBAL PEOPLE IN INDIA

K.Thamizhiniyan, S.Naseema

INTRODUCTION TO INCLUSIVE EDUCATION:

Inclusive education systems recognizes the uniqueness of each learner, the heterogeneity of learners and provide a platform with a variety of measures to respond to the needs of all, without sacrificing each one's uniqueness, constitutes a good model for inclusive education. In inclusive it is vital that challenges and changes are effected in Organization, content, assessment, approaches, strategies, staff quality, community participation, teacher educators etc. inclusive education for tribals is leading to a feeling of oneness, equality, fraternity, learning to live together and learning to be which are the focuses of UNICEF in life skill development. Inclusion of tribals in mainstream education system is a developmental process which strengthens the capacity of the education system to reach out to all heterogeneous learners. In India major tribal communities have still remained invisible and voiceless for many of the developmental activities of Indian government due to illiteracy. The present Indian development status alarms the state and central government to have inclusive experience in education which is unavoidable not only for the future classrooms but also for the development of nation.

Inclusive Education policy,

- Acknowledges that everyone can learn.
- Acknowledge and respects differences in children: age, gender, ethnicity, language, disability, etc
- Enables education structures, systems and methodologies to meet the needs of all children
- It is a part of a wider strategy to promote an inclusive society, etc.

According to UNESCO, inclusion "is increasingly understood more broadly as a reform that supports and welcomes diversity among all learners". This definition should be kept alive for all diverse learners including Scheduled Tribes and proper systematic steps must be taken to eliminate the concept of discrimination and provide healthy platform for all diverse Scheduled Tribes who are highly vulnerable.

WHY INCLUSION FOR STS CHILDREN?

- Every ST children has the right to learn together
- ST children should not be devalued or discriminated against by being excluded because of their learning disability
- ST people can rediscover their own strenths and greatness
- Research shows children do better academically and socially in integrated setting
- ST children may miss the social skills if they are segregated
- ST children may have a chance to understand the outer world around them
- Segregation og children may have fear, ignorance, lack of life skill and skill development
- Inclusion can help the ST children to adapt themselves in the mainstream life style
- ST children can place their roles in national development with the government schemes
- ST children can fix their voice for the development of their people with the help of outer world

SCHEDULED TRIBES IN INDIA – AN UNDERSTANDING

India accounts for 2.4 percent of the world surface area and supports 16.7% of the world population. India's more than 1.28 billion people live in 28 States and 7 Union Territories. The uniqueness of our society is its 'Unity in Diversity' which is visible with a population mix of Hindus 80.5 percent, Muslims 13.43 percent, and Christians 2.3% and 3.77 percent. The Scheduled Tribes population of our country as per the 2001 census is 8.43 crore, constituting 8.2% of the total population of India. More than half the Scheduled Tribes population is concentrated in the status of Madhya Pradesh, Chhattisgarh, Maharashtra, Orissa, Jharkhand and Gujarat. No community has been specifies as Scheduled Tribes in relation to states of Haryana and Punjab and Union Territories of Chandigarh, Delhi and Puducherry. The Scheduled Tribes live in about 15% of the country's areas in various ecological and geo climatic conditions ranging from plains and forests to hills and inaccessible areas. They are at different stages of social, economic, linguistic and educational development. Among the tribal communities some have adopted mainstream life and many communities are still vulnerable tribal groups (earlier known as primitive Tribal Groups-PTGs) who are characterized by Government of India as

- A Pre-agriculture level of technology
- A stagnant or declining population
- Extremely low literacy, and
- A subsistence level of economy

The essential characteristics, first laid down by the Lokur Committee for a community to be identified as Scheduled Tribes are,

- Indications of primitive traits
- Distinctive culture
- Shyness of contact with the community at large, and
- Backwardness

Article 366(25) of the constitution of India refers to Scheduled Tribes as those communities, who are scheduled in accordance with Article 342 of the constitution.

According to the 1991 census, 42.02% of the Scheduled Tribes populations were main workers of whom 54.50% were cultivators and 32.69% agricultural labourers. Thus, about 87% of the main workers from these communities were engaged in primary sector activities. The literacy rate of Scheduled Tribes is around 29.60% as against the national average of 52 %(as per 1991 census). In 2001 the literacy rate of ST is 46.8% against 65.4% national average. More than three quarters of Scheduled Tribes women are illiterate. The estimate of poverty made by Planning Commission for the year 1993-94 shows that 51.92% Scheduled Tribes were still living below the poverty line, as against 37.3% of the total population living below the poverty line.

Table 1 Distribution of ST Population in Different States/UTs

S.No	States of India	% of ST Population in No. States/UTs to the total ST population of the country (Descending Order)
01	Madhya Pradesh	14.51
02	Maharastra	10.17
03	Orissa	9.66
04	Gujarat	8.87
05	Rajasthan	8.42
06	Jharkhand	8.40
07	Chhattisgarh	7.85
08	Andhra Pradesh	5.96
09	West Bengal	5.23
10	Karnataka	4.11
11	Assam	3.92
12	Meghalaya	2.36
13	Nagaland	2.10
14	Jammu & Kashmir	1.31
15	Tripura	1.18
16	Mizoram	1.00
17	Bihar	0.90
18	Manipur	0.88
19	Arunachal Pradesh	0.84
20	Tamil Nadu	0.77
21	Kerala	0.43
22	Uttarakhand	0.30
23	Himachal Pradesh	0.29
24	Dadra & Nagar Haveli	0.16
25	Sikkim	0.13
26	Uttar Pradesh	0.13

Source: Annual Report 2010-11/ 41, Ministry of tribal affairs, Government of India

While the tribal population in some states is low when calculated as the percentage of the total tribal Population of India but it constitutes the majority within the state or UT itself (e.g. in Lakshadweep, Mizoram, Nagaland, Meghalaya, Arunachal Pradesh and Dadra & Nagar Haveli). A very sizable segment of tribal population, as stated earlier, resides in the states of Chhattisgarh, Gujarat, Jharkhand, Orissa, Rajasthan, Maharashtra and Madhya Pradesh. The tribal population of each State/UT as a percentage of the total tribal population of the country is given in table 1 above. There are over 700 Scheduled Tribes notified under Article 342 of the Constitution of India, spread over different States and Union Territories of the country. Many tribes are present in more than one state. The largest numbers of scheduled tribes are in the states of Orissa (i.e. 62). The synonyms of these 700 or so tribes are also vary many a times and are listed in the Schedule. As compared to the sex ratio for the overall population (933 females per 1000 male), the sex ratio among Scheduled Tribes is more favorable, at 977 females per thousand males (2001 Census), though also declining. In all States except Andhra Pradesh, Tamil Nadu and Uttarakhand, the ST sex ratio as per 2001 Census was better than the general sex ratio.

Tribal Literacy in India: The literacy rate for the total population in India has increased from 52.21% to 64.84% during the period from 1991 to 2001 whereas the literacy rate among the Scheduled Tribes has increased from 29.60% to 47.10%. Among ST males literacy increased from 40.65% to 59.17% and among ST female literacy increased from 18.19% to 34.76% during the same period. The ST female literacy is lower by approximately 21 percentage point as compared to the overall female literacy of the general population. However, the increase in total as well as female literacy among STs is significant. Literacy rate has increased from 8.53 percent in 1961 to 47.10 percent in 2001 for STs While the corresponding increase for total population was from 28.30 percent in 1961 to 64.84 percent in 2001. The details are given in

Table 2 Literacy among STs and all Social Groups

Year	Scheduled Tribes			All Social Groups		
	Male	**Female**	**Total**	**Male**	**Female**	**Total**
1961	13.83	3.16	8.53	40.40	15.35	28.30
1971	17.63	4.85	11.30	45.96	21.97	34.45
1981	24.52	8.04	16.35	56.38	29.76	43.57
1991	40.65	18.19	29.60	64.13	39.29	52.21
2001	59.17	34.76	47.10	75.26	53.67	64.84

Source: Annual Report 2010-11/ 41, Ministry of tribal affairs, Government of India

Literacy Rate increased by 17.5 percentage points from 1991 to 2001 for STs and increased by 12.63 percentage points for total population during the same period. Male-female gap in literacy rate increased from 22.46 percentage points in 1991 to 24.41 percentage points in 2001 for STs while it declines from 24.84 percentage points in 1991 to 21.59 percentage points in 2001 for total population.The percentage of literacy gap between STs and all population various from 0.5 to 31.9 percentage point during 2001. The States like Tamilnadu, Kerala, Karnataka, Goa, Andhra Pradesh, Maharastra, Gujarat, Madhya Pradesh, Orissa, West Bengal, Uttar Pradesh, Bihar and Jammu & Kashmir are having more than 17.7 (i.e. literacy gap at all India) percentage gap of literacy rate between STs vis-a-vis total population during 2001. All States registered a decline in literacy gap between 1991 to 2001 except in Uttar Pradesh, Bihar and Dadra & Nagar Haveli. Although Uttar Pradesh and Bihar maintained almost the same gap as compared to census 1991 but the gap was widened in case of Dadra & Nagar Haveli. States like West Bengal, Orissa, Goa, Kerala and Tamil Nadu are having more than 25 percentage point gap of literacy between STs and all population in these states. State-wise details are given in

Table 3 Literacy Rate Of Total Population and Scheduled Tribes Population and Gap In Literacy Rate -India /States/Union Territories: 1991-2001

ST code	India/ State/UT	Gap In Literacy Rate in 1991 of total population and STs	Literacy Rate 2001		Gap In Literacy Rate
			Total	ST	
1	2	3	4	5	6
	India	22.6	64.8	47.1	17.7
1	Andaman & Nicobar islands	16.4	81.3	66.8	14.5
2	Arunachal Pradesh	41.6	54.3	49.6	4.7
3	Assam	3.7	63.3	62.5	0.8
4	Andhra Pradesh	26.9	60.5	37.0	23.4
5	Bihar	18.6	47.0	28.2	18.8
6	Chandigarh#	-	81.9	NST	-
7	Chhattisgarh	16.2	64.7	52.1	12.6
8	Dadra & Nagar Haveli	12.5	57.6	41.2	16.4
9	Daman & Die	18.3	78.2	63.4	14.8
10	Delhi#	-	81.7	NST	-
11	Goa	32.6	82.0	55.9	26.1

12	Gujarat	24.9	69.1	47.7	21.4
13	Haryana	-	67.9	NST	-
14	Himachal Pr.	16.8	76.5	65.5	11.0
15	Jammu & Kashmir	NA	55.5	37.5	18.0
16	Jharkhand	13.9	53.6	40.7	12.9
17	Karnataka	20.0	66.6	48.3	18.3
18	Kerala	32.6	90.9	64.4	26.5
19	Lakshadweep	1.2	86.7	86.1	0.6
20	Madhya Pradesh	26.3	63.7	41.2	22.5
21	Maharashtra	28.1	76.9	55.2	21.7
22	Manipur	6.3	70.5	65.9	4.6
23	Meghalaya	2.4	62.6	61.3	1.3
24	Mizoram	0.4	88.8	89.3	0.5
25	Nagaland	1.0	66.6	65.9	0.7
26	Orissa	26.8	63.1	37.4	25.7
27	Pondicherry #	-	81.2	NST	-
28	. Punjab	-	69.7	NST	-
29	Rajasthan	19.2	60.4	44.7	15.7
30	Sikkim	2.1	68.8	67.1	1.7
31	Tamil Nadu	34.8	73.5	41.5	32.0
32	Tripura	20.0	73.2	56.5	16.7
33	Uttar Pradesh	20.7	56.3	35.1	21.2
34	Uttarakhand	16.6	71.6	63.2	8.4
35	West Bengal	29.9	68.6	43.4	25.2

1. Excludes Jammu & Kashmir where 1991 census was not conducted.

2. Excludes figure of Paomata, Mao Marm & Purul Sub divisions of Senapati districts of Manipur; for 2001.# NST = No Notified Scheduled Tribes in the States.

Source: Annual Report 2010-11/ 41, Ministry of tribal affairs, Government of India

The proportion of STs in enrolment at higher education increased from 2.1 percent in 1990-91 to 4.3 percent in 2005-06. It shows that their share in enrolment in higher education is still less than their share in the total population. Though Indian higher education system is considered to be the largest system in terms of number of institutions, only a smaal proportion is enrolled in higher education, year wise enrolment of STS in higher education given in table 4 below.

Table 4 Enrolment STs in Higher Education (Share of Enrolment of STs (%))

year	PG and Ph.D	Graduation	B.E	B.Ed	MBBS
2000-01	2.6	3.0	3.3	5.3	3.6
2002-03	2.7	3.7	3.2	5.0	4.9
2003-04	2.8	3.8	2.0	5.5	4.5
2004-05	4.0	4.4	3.1	5.9	3.7
2005-06	3.2	4.6	3.5	4.7	6.2

Source: Prakash, Ved, 2008 based on selected Educational Statistics (Various years), MHRD.

INCLUSIVE EDUCATION IN HIGHER EDUCATION

The objective of inclusiveness in higher education will be achieved through the following.

1. Reduction of regional imbalance

2. Support to institutions located in border, hilly, remote, small towns and educationally backward areas

3. Support to institutions with large student population of SCs, STs, OBCs, minorities, and physically challenged

4.Support to the SCs, STs, OBCs, minorities, and physically challenged, and girl student with special scholarships/fellowships, hostel facilities, remedial coaching, and other measures

5.Setting up of an 'Equal opportunity Office' in all universities to bring all schemes relating to this group under one umbrella for effective implementation

Source: 1.3.25 of XI Plan Document, p 26 Vol, II, GOI, 2008

SUGGESTIONS:

The following suggestions may help inclusion of STs in mainstream education in a successful wasy.

- Identifying barriers to access and quality education
- Assessing the barriers including physical, social, institutional etc.
- Identifying new strategies to address the barriers

- Improving learner-friendly curriculum
- Enabling tribal- friendly environment and promoting mental health and welbeing of STs.
- Identifying new policies of inclusion for STs
- Assessing the existing policies
- Strengthening institutional arrangements
- Removing the fear for language system in official set up
- Undertaking assessment of schools
- Improving civil society poarticipation
- Assessing parental and commun ity involvement in schools
- Promoting participation of children, people, parents and community
- Assesing teacher quality and attitude issues
- Planning strategies to make changes in curriculum to enhance inclusion
- Utilising the alloted funds properlu and fully
- Enhancing the political will towards inclusion of STs.

CONCLUSION:

India is very conscious that all its dreams for national development will remain incomplete until weaker sections of the society also benefit from the developments. india should act highly committed to mainstreaming the marginalised Scheduled Tribes in the process of economic growth through systematic Inclusive education. Though education is one of the most important sectors in the Eleventh Five Year Plain to actualize this vision, still the reality shows that Inclusion of Scheduled Tribes is miles to go in india. Right to Education with the inclusion of STs in mainstream can be the voice for voiceless scheduleld tribes in India. With this attitude Indian Education System has to extend the educational opportunities to the vulnerable STs and it has been considered an antidote to the longstanding discrimination and exploitation.

REFERENCES:

- Fifth Survey of Educational Research.(1988-91) New Delhi: National Council of Educational Research And Training.

- Govinda, R (2007) India Country Case Study, "Country Profile commissioned for the EFA Global Monitoring Report 2008, Education For All by 2015: Will We Make It?, UNESCO, Paris.
- Govt. of India (1966) Education and national Development: Report of the Education Commission 1964-1966, New Delhi.
- (1991) Census of India, New Delhi.
- (2001) Census of India, New Delhi.
- (2006) Selected Educational Statistics: 2004-05, MHRD, New Delhi, 2007.
- (2007) Education in India, prepared by National University of Educational Planning and Administration for the Department of Higher Education, Government of India, October 2007.
- Mukhopadhyay, S. (2001) Inclusive Education in the context of EFA, Sub-Regional Orientation cum Training Workshop on Planning and Monitoring of EFA in South Asia jointly organized by NIEPA, New Delhi, IIEp, Paris and UNESCO, New Delhi, 22 October to 3 November 2001, Document 4.2d p 154(Mimeo)
- Prakash, Ved (2008) " Education, Equality and Social Justice" , paper presented in the II International Symposium and Public Forum organized in Brasilia and Campo Grande, from April 24, 2008 (Mimeo)
- Pratham (2011) Annual Status of Education Review (ASEr – 2011), New Delhi, 2011.
- UGC (2010) Annual Report: 2009-2010, New Delhi.
- UGC (2011) Annual Report: 2010-2011, New Delhi.
- Devy, G. (2008) "The Tribal Situation in Higher Education." Concept Note
- Kothai, K.(2007) " Seasonal Migration hinders Education in India". One World South Asia. October.
- Ministry of Tribal Affairs (2011) Annual Report: 2010-2011, New Delhi
- National Tribal Commission (2008) "Education of Tribal People in India". March.

SOCIAL STRUCTURAL CONSTRAINTS IN EMPOWERMENT OF MARGINALIZED GROUPS – THE ELDERLY PERSONS DIMENSION

26 LIFE AT ELDERLY: A SITUATIONAL ANALYSIS

Dr. S. S. Vijayanchali, Dr. E. Arumuga Gandhi

INTRODUCTION

Old age, also referred to as one's eld, consists of ages nearing or surpassing the average life span of human beings, and thus the end of the human life cycle. Euphemisms and terms for old people include seniors (American usage), senior citizens (British and American usage) and the elderly. Old people have limited regenerative abilities and are more prone to disease, syndromes, and sickness than other adults. For the biology of ageing, see senescence. The medical study of the aging process is gerontology. The boundary between middle age and old age cannot be defined exactly because it does not have the same meaning in all societies. People can be considered old because of certain changes in their activities or social roles. Examples: people may be considered old when they become grandparents, or when they begin to do less or different work—retirement.

AGEING

Ageing is a natural process that begins at birth, or to be more precise, at conception, a process that progresses throughout one's life and ends at death. It is a constant, predictable process that involves growth and development of living organisms. Aging can't be avoided, but how fast we age varies from one person to another. How we age depends upon our genes, environmental influences, and life style. Ageing can also be defined as a state of mind, which does not always keep pace with our chronological age. Attitude and how well we face the normal changes, challenges and opportunities of later life may best define our age. Growing older cannot be prevented. We begin aging at the time of conception and continue aging one day at a time. However, some of the effects of aging can be slowed and even prevented. Prevention in later years requires participating in health education and health promotion activities designed to reduce the risk of disease. Prevention also involves engaging in interventions that improve outcomes in the event an illness does occur and includes efforts that reduce the risk of progressive disability and decline of function. In later life the goals of prevention also include maintaining function, vitality and quality of life. According to *Towards Enriching Years* during the process of ageing, physical functions of the body slowly deteriorate demanding greater coping skills on the part of the ageing person to adjust to the environment. In addition, there are problems caused by others in the society because of their unfavorable attitudes. Ageism, like sexism or racism, is a concept pertaining to prejudice or a negative attitude towards a particular group. Ageism implies that the old are perceived as sick, unhappy, empty and useless, and are discriminated against. As ageing is a continuous process in the structure and functions of the body, the physical abilities of the former tend to slow down with the passage of years. It is an impoverished environment, poor nutrition and diseases that break down the nervous system's natural potential resistance against deterioration. As far as the psychological structures and functions are concerned, there need not necessarily be deterioration. Cicero, the Roman statesman and philosopher of first century BC, writing in his treatise On Old Age said that old people could retain their intellectual abilities by engaging their minds fully and actively and that old age was respectable as long as the elderly asserted themselves and were not dominated by anyone else. He supports his statements by referring to the death of Plato, the fifth century BC Greek philosopher. When death occurred, Plato was writing at his desk, at the age of 81 (Encyclopedia Brittanica, 1963). Ageing is any change in an organism over time. Aging refers to a multidimensional process of physical, psychological, and social change (Hultsch and Deutsch). Some dimensions of aging grow and expand over time, while others decline. Reaction time, for example, may slow with age, while knowledge of world events and wisdom may expand (Schaie). Research shows that even late in life potential exists for physical, mental, and social growth and development. Aging is an important part of all human societies reflecting the biological changes that occur, but also reflecting cultural and societal conventions. Age is usually measured in full years — and months for young children. A person's birthday is often an important event. Chronological aging, referring to how old a person is, is arguably the most straightforward definition of aging and may be distinguished from "social aging" (society's expectations of how people should act as they grow older) and "biological aging" (an organism's physical state as it ages). Stuart-Hamilton also notes distinction between "proximal aging" (age-based effects that come about because of factors in the recent past) and "distal aging" (age-based differences that can be traced back to a cause early in person's life, such as childhood poliomyelitis).

PHYSICAL CHANGES

There is often a general physical decline, and people become less active. Old age can cause, amongst other things:

- Wrinkles and liver spots on the skin
- Change of hair colour to gray or white
- Hair loss
- Lessened hearing
- Diminished eyesight
- Slower reaction times and agility
- Reduced ability to think clearly
- Difficulty recalling memories
- Depressed mood
- Lessening or cessation of sex, sometimes because of physical symptoms such as erectile dysfunction in men, but often simply a decline in libido
- Greater susceptibility to bone diseases such as osteoarthritis.

Declaring Elderly Incompetence

In almost all cases in which elderly persons are declared mentally or physically incompetent to adequately take care of themselves, state laws require that a minimum of two doctors, or other health professionals, vouch for evidence of such incompetence. Only then can legal supervision by a loved one or caretaker be initiated, including power of attorney, guardianship and conservatorship. If doctors' corroboration cannot be obtained by interested parties, then other proof must be proffered to support the case for incompetence, including outstanding bills and financial debt, or substandard living conditions that would be deemed unsafe or hazardous to the elderly person(s).

THE PROBLEM OF OLD AGE IN INDIA

A man's life is normally divided into five main stages namely infancy, childhood, adolescence, adulthood and old age. In each of these stages an individual has to find himself in different situations and face different problems. The old age is not without problems. In old age physical strength deteriorates, mental stability diminishes; money power becomes bleak coupled with negligence from the younger generation. There are 81million older people in India-11 lakh in Delhi itself. According to an estimate nearly 40% of senior citizens living with their families are reportedly facing abuse of one kind or another, but only 1 in 6 cases actually comes to light. Although the President has given her assent to the Maintenance and Welfare of Parents and Senior Citizens Act which punishes children who abandon parents with a prison term of three months or a fine, situation is grim for elderly people in India.

India is a vast country both in terms of area as well as population. It has a total area of 3,288,000 square kilometers. Its present population is estimated to be over 850 million. The total working population is estimated to be about one-third of this number. Dependency ratio is therefore about 1:2. The per capita income at current prices during 1988-89 was Rs.4250 ($280 based on rate of exchange of Rs.15 per one U.S. dollar). About 25.8 per cent of the people are reported to be living below the poverty line (Subrahmanya, 1994). India, a sub-continent that carries 15 per cent of the world's population, is gradually undergoing a demographic change as a result of many factors including specific development programs. With decline in fertility and mortality rates accompanied by an improvement in child survival and increased life expectancy, a significant feature of demographic change is the progressive increase in the number of elderly persons (accepting 60 years as a practical demarcation for defining the elderly). In 1951, the sixty plus population was around 21 million. Three decades later in 1981, it was a little over 43 million , a further decade later in 1991, this had increased to 54.7 million and for 2001 it is projected to be nearly 76 million (medium projections). Calculations also based on census reports show the decadal rate of growth of the population in the age category sixty plus to be higher than that of the general population.

It is estimated that the decadal growth rate for 1991-2001 (medium projection) in the age group 0-14 years (which for most national planning such as policies such as education, welfare, and health is an important target group) will be only 6.7 per cent while that of the 60 + population will be 38.4 per cent. These demographic facts and trends make the elderly in India an increasingly important segment of the population pyramid in the coming years (Shankardass, 1995).

TABLE 1 Growth of Elderly Population of 60+ in India

Year	Male	Female	Total Population
1901	5.50	6.56	12.06
1911	6.18	6.99	13.17
1921	6.48	7.00	13.48
1931	6.94	7.27	14.21
1941	8.89	9.15	18.04
1951	9.67	9.94	19.61
1961	12.36	12.35	24.71
1971	16.87	15.83	32.70
1981	22.49	21.49	43.98
1991	28.23	27.07	55.30
2001	38.22	37.71	75.93

Source: Ageing in India: Occasional Paper No.2 of 1991, Office of the Registrar General & Census Commissioner, India.

TABLE 2 Characteristics of Ageing Population

Variables Dependency Ratio	1950	1990	2000	2025
Total Population	1.22	1.10	0.94	0.75
Children	1.09	0.94	0.77	0.50
Old (60+)	0.12	0.15	0.16	0.25
Sex Ratio				
Total Population	117.46	106.98	106.40	104.40
Children	102.96	107.38	106.43	104.65
Working Group	110.12	107.67	108.15	105.98
Old	89.90	100.28	96.15	95.65
Median Age	19.95	22.31	25.03	33.65

Source: Calculations based on World Demographic Estimates and Projections, 1950-2025, United Nations, New York, 1988.

TABLE 3 Economically Dependent Elderly and Supporting Persons

Supporting Person	Rural Elderly		Urban Elderly	
	Male	Female	Male	Female
Spouse	7.06	11.51	6.14	11.30
Own Children	74.95	73.84	78.03	72.32
Grand Children	6.24	6.38	6.11	6.52
Others	11.78	8.27	9.72	8.86

Source: Sarvekshana, Volume XV, No.2, Issue No.49, Oct.-Dec. 1991.

DEPENDENCY

Little evidence exists on the income of the elderly individuals or of households with elderly heads, due to the difficulty of obtaining accurate (or any) responses to survey and census questions on these issues. Even if respondents were willing to report incomes, several factors complicate data gathering: seasonal variations in income; self-employment in agriculture; the extent of the informal or non-monetized economy in many countries; and the frequent pooling of household resources. The human life cycle begins and ends with stages of dependency, in the sense that consumption exceeds labour earnings. This generalization applies on average to age groups, but not necessarily to individuals so far as old age is concerned. The average shape appears to be universal, although ages and extent of dependency may vary widely from population to population. It arises from the combined influence of physiology, culture, institutions, and economic choice, in ways that we take as given (Martin and Preston, 1994). Majority of the elderly in both rural (50.78 per cent) and urban (57.35 per cent) areas are totally dependent on others for economic support. About 15.20 per cent of the elderly in rural areas and 13.71 per cent of the elderly in the urban areas are partially dependent on others. The lower rate of total dependency among the elderly in the rural areas can be explained by the fact that the rural families are more supportive to the elderly. There are many reasons for this phenomenon. In rural areas, there is a greater continuity in the occupational and familial roles of the elderly, particularly among the males. They continue to be active until physical incapacity prevents them from working. Whether a man is self-employed as a cultivator, or an artisan, or is working as a farm laborer, the chances are that he will continue to remain 'employed' longer in the rural areas than in urban areas (Gore, 1992).

TABLE 4 Economic Dependency among the Elderly

Sex	Totally Dependent		Partially Dependent		Non Dependent	
	Rural	Urban	Rural	Urban	Rural	Urban
Male	32.74	37.39	16.20	16.90	51.06	45.71
Female	77.51	86.04	13.71	9.13	8.78	4.84
Total	77.51	86.04	13.71	9.13	8.78	4.84

Source: Sarvekshna, Vol. XV, No.2, Issue No.49, Oct.-Dec. 1991.

LIVING ARRANGEMENTS

Several authors have addressed the question of what it is about different living situations that causes them to be valued more or less highly, most comprehensively by Burch and Matthews (1987). Burch and Matthews note that each potential household living situation available to an individual conveys a distinct array of "component" household goods, including physical shelter; storage of property; domestic services (meals, laundry, cleaning); personal care (including, of special relevance to the elderly, assistance with everyday tasks including hygiene, locomotion, and so on); companionship (both social and sexual); recreation and entertainment; privacy; independence/autonomy; power/authority; and the benefits of economies of scale can take the form of a larger share of personal money income left for discretionary uses, after paying for market inputs to the production of household goods (Martin and Preston, 1994). The National Sample Survey data for the year 1986-87 reveal low percentages of institutionalization among the elderly (0.68 per cent of persons aged 60 years and above in rural areas and 0.40 per cent in urban areas). About 7.31 per cent of the elderly in rural areas as against 5.54 per cent of the elderly in the urban areas are living alone. This is quite contradictory to the popular notion that the rural families tend to keep their elderly relatives with them more than their urban counterparts. However, this trend is quite consistent with the finding that living with children is more common among the urban elderly (50.97 per cent) than the rural elderly (48.57 per cent). On the other hand, percentage of elderly living with spouse is more in the rural areas (37 per cent) than in the urban areas (35.26 per cent). These data reveal that majority of the elderly do not have the plight of living alone during their twilight years. However, we should not lose sight of the fact that living alone does not necessarily mean that the elderly experience loneliness. Similarly, living with spouse or children does not necessarily mean that the elderly do not experience loneliness.

HEALTH PROBLEMS AND PHYSICAL DISABILITIES

Ageing is associated with the decline in physiological effectiveness, which affects us all sooner or later and is an intrinsic part of growing old. Unlike the universal changes of sensescence, disease is sporadic, a particular disease affecting only certain members of the population. However, multiple pathology is a characteristic feature of old age. Not only are the elderly persons at risk of particular age-related diseases; they may also suffer from a combination of several diseases and senescent changes. In addition to the multiple disabilities caused by the diseases themselves, complications may arise due to the complexity of drug treatment prescribed (Bond et al, 1994). The analysis of National Sample Survey data for 1986-87 reveals that about 45 per cent of the rural elderly are chronically ill among whom 45.01 per cent are men and 45.85 per cent are women. In the urban areas, 44.82 per cent of the elderly (45.49 per cent women and 44.34 per cent men) are chronically ill. Cough and problem of joints are the most common health problems. High blood pressure, heart disease and urinary problems are more common among the elderly in the urban areas. As far as physical disabilities are concerned, in the rural areas, 5.4 per cent of all the elderly (6.8 per cent females and 4.4 per cent males) are physically disabled while in the urban areas, 5.5 per cent of all the elderly (6.7 per cent females and 4.7 per cent males) are physically disabled. In both rural and urban areas, more females than males are physically disabled (Kohli, 1996). The official statistics reveal that large segments of the elderly in India are illiterate, out of work force, partially or totally dependent on others and suffering from health problems or physical disabilities. A review of the Indian government's Five Year Plans shows very limited and inconsistent concern for the elderly. The only welfare measure for the elderly considered by the government until the Seventh Five Year Plan was the running of old age homes. The Eighth and Ninth Plans, however, incorporated fairly more specific and comprehensive welfare measures for the elderly such as provision of old age homes, day care centres, Medicare and no institutional services. However, the issue of older persons' learning has not been given any importance in the government policies and programs.

STATEMENT OF THE PROBLEM

Unfortunately old age has now become a prevalent social problem in our society. It is strange no one wants to grow old but everyone wants to live long. In our modern society, where money is the scale of everything, the old age people are measured as an economic liability and a social burden. Old age is observed as an ineluctable, undesirable, problem-ridden stage of life that we all are compelled to live, marking time until our final exit from life itself. Many people get extremely fearful when they become old. Distinguishing old age with fear is in fact a rather recent phenomenon. It seems to intensify as each day passes and the world become more difficult and less comprehensible. Old age is a stage of life, where one needs to learn certain things afresh and get hold of new skills, mind-sets and socialization norms. In this lens, we present some useful information that would be of use to our senior citizens and also for the one who care for them.

OBJECTIVES OF THE STUDY

The prime objective of the present empirical study is to elicit the social life of the elderly people and carried out with the following sub-objectives:

1. To understand the socio-economic status of the elderly people;
2. To know their living pattern;
3. To probe the health status among the elderly people;
4. To explain their participation in the decision making process in their family;
5. To elicit their day-to-day activities viz., leisure time and physical activities;
6. To assess the food consuming pattern found among them;
7. To suggest ways and means influence inclusive policies for elderly people thereby to improve the quality of life of elderly people.

SETTING OF THE STUDY

To achieve the objectives of the present study a total of 100 elderly people were included in the present study and they were selected from Dindigul by using purposive random sampling technique. To collect systematic and unambiguous data from them a structured interview schedule was prepared. By keeping the study objectives in mind and particulars regarding their present socio-economic profile with living patterns, health status, dietary pattern, problems that they faces due to elderly, leisure time and day-to-day physical activities were collected. Both to avoid others interruptions and to elicit free responses from them all they were met alone while they were free. Since the present study was descriptive in nature no attempt has been made to form hypotheses and that no necessity has been raised to test them accordingly. To arrive at general conclusions the collected data were processed and converted into percentage and interpreted by using descriptive methods. To throw more light on the generalizations and to make the present study as valid and reliable one mean was computed to some selected variables and presented in the summary form.

SUMMARY OF THE STUDY

Social Profile of the Elderly

To analyse the socio-economic status of the elderly their sex, age, religion marital status, educational level, present as well as previous occupational status, and family type were concerned. As far as sex of the elderly people included in the study is concerned more than three-fifths (62%) in the total were males while the rest 38 percent constituted by females. While grouping on the basis of their age-group more than half of them (52%) were in the age-group of 60-64 years followed by another one-fourths (24%) who were in the age-group of 65-69 years. The rest were belonging to 70-74 and 75-79 years age-group elderly people and their proportion in the total was 14% and 10% respectively. The mean age for them was 66.1years. Nearly three-fifths (58%) of the elderly people included in the study were Hindus of which majority of them constituted by Most Backward Castes (69%) while the rest constituted by Backward Castes (17.2%) and Scheduled Castes (13.8%) followed by Christians (36%) and Mohammdens (6%). Hence, it is found that majority of the elderly people included in the study were Hindus. While probing the educational status of the elderly people a mixed pattern has been observed. It was found that graduates constituted 30 percent in the total followed by another 6 percent post-graduates whereas the rest elderly people's educational level remained Primary (20%), and Secondary (4%). However, illiterates constituted the rest one-fourths (40%).

Living Pattern

As far as the living pattern of the elderly people included in the present study is concerned nearly one-thirds (32%) of them were living in joint families while another 28 percent of them found in extended families. However, the rest one-fourths were in nuclear families. It was found that 29 percent of them were one amongst 5 – 8 members' family while another one-fourths (24%) were in the families which included of more than nine members. However, majority of the elderly people were in five members families. Hence, it was found that their household includes an average of four members. It has to be noted that a large majority (82%) of them were living with their sons.

ECONOMIC CONDITION

The occupational status of the elderly included in the study revealed that of the total 21 percent of them were retired Government employees while another one-thirds (24%) were self-employed and involved in tailoring, small business-petty shops, grocery shops, and such as whereas the rest all (55%) found as farmers and agricultural labourers. The Hence, it was found that all the elderly people contributed an average of Rs.4, 342/- per month to their family. In other words, they contributed two-fifths in total family monthly income (Rs.10, 842/-) that shows the indispensable role played by elderly people so that they would not be considered as a burden to their family.

HEALTH STATUS AND CARE

The analysis of health status among elderly shows that of the total elderly people interviewed a large majority (83%) of them were suffering of any one health problems and amongst asthma, diabetes, blood pressure, and body ache were more prevailed problems. It was found that they were suffering of these problems for an average of 13.4 years. While probing the type of treatment preferred by them it was found that majority of them preferred invariably allopathic (72%) whereas homeopathy and ayurvedic kind of treatments preferred by 16% and 12% each respectively. It was found that majority of the elderly (69%) people seek assistance while visiting physicians while the rest were managing themselves. They seek the company of either their sons (57%) or daughters (23%). However, the rest one-fifths (20%) were accompanied by their neighbours that shows the pivotal role played by the neighbourhood communities in taking care of the elderly and emphasizes the importance of neighbourliness. All they said that they were taking medicines properly and receiving proper care while they feeling not well. Figure 1 depicts this.

FIGURE 1 Person Accompanies the Elderly during sick to the Hospital

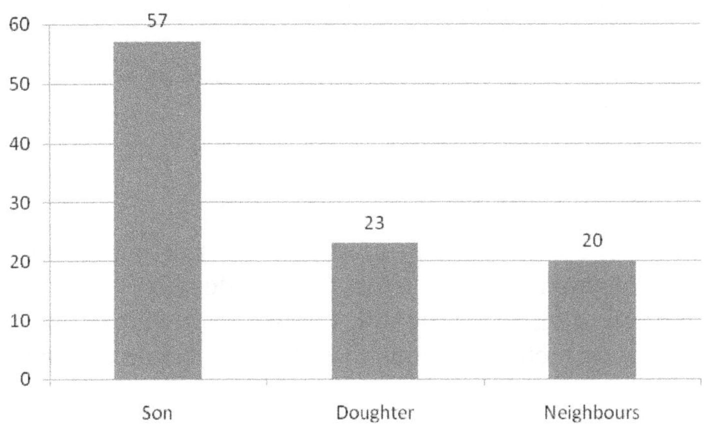

Dietary Pattern

It was found that of the total elderly people a large majority of them (78%) follows three-time meal pattern while another 17 percent were found with two-time meal pattern. The rest 4 percent followed four-time meal pattern in a day. Either idly, dosa or poori or pongal sometimes were taken at breakfast while chappati, idly, dosa or rice with sambar stands for dinner. All they preferred rice with sambar, one vegetable and butter milk for lunch. It is noteworthy to be mentioned that all that almost all the elderly people were non-vegetarians (92%). Their pattern of preference toward non-vegetarian items revealed chicken (52%), fish (23), mutton (12%), and fish (6%), chicken, mutton and fish (5%) and chicken and fish (2%). It was observed from their responses that all they preferred any one of the above said once in a week, particularly during the week-end. Figure 2 portrays this.

FIGURE 2 Consumption Pattern of Non-Vegetarian Items

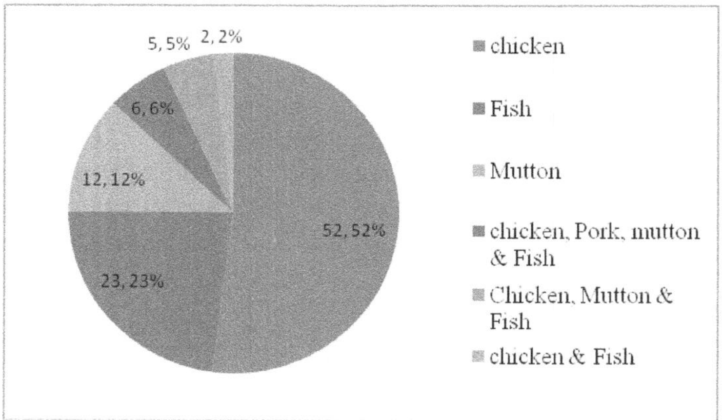

It has to be noted that a large majority of the elderly were found with the habit of taking fruits at night after dinner. As far as possible almost all they tried to follow the words of the physicians regarding the food pattern and then only all they were able to realize homeostasis in their health, according to them. Invariably all they were in strong belief that they follow a healthy eating habit. Hence, there is no need to mention that all they were in satisfaction as far as dietary pattern is concerned.

PROBLEMS FACED DUE TO ELDERLY

While probing that did they face any problems due to their elderly status nearly three-fifths (58%) of them said 'yes' while the rest denied (42%). They face many problems and among them social, health, financial and emotional problems were predominant. As far as social problems that they faced due to their elderly status were disrespect, ignorance, avoidance, not listening their words etc. which led them to fall in emotional problems such as isolation, aggressiveness, stress, etc.

As far as health problems that they face is concerned as discussed above many of them were not free from any one kind of elderly related ailments. They themselves manage the requirements for their well-being. Invariably all they felt that though they contribute to the total family income their words in many occasions being ignored; they have no control over the money that they add to the family's total monthly income; almost in all occasions they were not being consulted and being informed. Hence, it is very obvious that all the elderly people were depressed and being with the attitude of ignored or neglected. None of them received any old age benefits from government; and few of them (23%) protected through the means of life insurance.

LEISURE TIME ACTIVITIES

Leisure time activities of the elderly people is concerned it was found that many of them spent their leisure time through watching T.V. (71%) reading newspapers (11%) spending with younger generations-grand children (15%) and chatting with their friends/neighbours (3%). Either evening or whenever they were free they spent an average of 1.40 hours for such leisure time activities in a day in their home itself. It was found that the day for them starts at 5-6am with a small walk for males while cooking process for females. Few of the males only involved in exercises in the form of walking for an average of half an hour and stated that no need of assistance while doing exercises. Many of them were doing exercise because of either doctor's strict advice or their friends' suggestion; only few of them personally motivated regarding this.

TABLE 5 Mean for some selected Indicators

Indicator	Mean (N = 100)
Age	66.1
Monthly Income	Rs. 4,342/-
Household Size	5
Family Monthly Income	Rs. 10,842/-
Health Problems Faced	13.4 years
Time spent for Leisure Time Activities	1.40 hours/per day
Time spent for Exercise	0.5 hours/per day

CONCLUSION

While concluding the present study on the situational analysis of life of elderly people it is to be highlighted that many of the elderly included in the study were in their early elderlyhood; majority of them were Hindus and belong to Most backward Castes. Illiterates constituted more in the study followed by retired some graduates. Many of them were involved in agriculture and related activities. They played an indispensable role in the total monthly income of their family by adding more than one-thirds in the total income. Many of them were not free from health problems and they themselves manage their health care needs. Many of them consult physicians regularly with the help of their sons, daughters or even with neighbours. It is to be noted that due to elderly state many of them faced social, economic and psychological problems. Almost all they followed three-meal pattern and found as non-vegetarians. Many of their leisure time activities included watching T.V at their home. Hence, it has to be suggested that to make the elderly free from health problems awareness education has to be given to overcome the problems; to avoid the sense of being isolated and depressed their part in decision making process shouldn't be ignored. In other words, elderly people also have to be included in the process of decision making. Then only the state of well-being which includes social, economic, psychological and physical state would be achieved.

REFERENCES:

1. Kohli, A.S. *Social Situation of the Aged in India,*. Anmol Publications Pvt. Ltd. New Delhi, 1996.
2. Martin, L.G., and Preston, S.H. *Demography of Aging*, National Academy Press, Washington, 1994.
3. Shankardass, Mala Kapur. Towards the Welfare of the Elderly in India. *Bold*, Vol.5, No.4, 1995, pp 25-29.
4. Subrahmanya, R.K.A. (1994) Income Security for the Elderly in India. *BOLD*. Vol2, No.4, p 28.
5. Rowan H Harwood, "Commentary: Disability amongst Elderly People World-wide: The need for Multi-dimensional Health Assessment (International Journal of Epidemiology, 32 (6), 2003.
6. World Demographic Estimates and Projections. 1950-2025, United Nations, New York, 1988.
7. Kulkarni, J., Bharati, V., and Rekhade, N. "Adjustmental Problems of Old Persons," *Shodh, Samiksha aur Mulyankan*, Vol. II Issue 9-10, Oct-Nov., 2009.
8. Kujur, D., and Ekka, R. P. "Socio-Economic Status of Elderly People in India," Shodh, Samiksha aur Mulyankan, Vol. II Issue 15, April 2010.

9. Krishnaswamy, B and Usha, G. "Falls in Older Prople: National/Regional Review" Working paper, Madras Medical College and Government General Hospitalm Chennai, 2008.

10. Leena, A, Ashok, K., Padma, M., Kamat, V., and Kamat, A. "Health and Social Problems of the Elderly: A Cross-Sectional Study in Udupi Taluk, Karnata," Indian Journal of Community Medicine, Vil. 34, Issue 2, April 2009.

11. Sivamurthy, M. and Wadakannavar, A. R. "Care and Support for the Elderly Population in India: Results from a Survey of the Aged in Rural North Karnata, India," (Unpublished paper submitted to the IUSSP General Population Conference Held at Salvador, Brazil, 18-24, Aug. 2001).

12. Jhilam Rudra De. "Management of Old Age – A Critical Problem in Indian Perspective across Culture and Time," (Unpublished Paper).

27 SOCIAL VULNERABILITY AND DEPRIVATION AMONG ELDERLY WOMEN IN MELUR BLOCK, MADURAI DISTRICT: A STUDY

T. Augustus Julian Lazmey

'Old age is shamefully seen like head lice in children
And venereal disease in their older siblings' (Stott, 1981: 3).

INTRODUCTION

Population aging is a worldwide phenomenon with a consequence of lengthening life expectancy and decreasing fertility and India is no exception. The 2001 census has shown that the elderly population (60+) of India accounted for 77 million and census 2011 projections indicate that elderly population has crossed the 100 million mark. The life expectancy has also gone up to over 70 years today. The transition to a modern society and the disintegration of the joint family system led to the loss of the traditional authority of older people. The perception of ageing differs from place to place, time to time and people to people. It purely depends upon the social, cultural and economic conditions of factors. Because every individuals activity, lifestyle, expenditure, occupation etc are determined and influenced by these factors only. The problems faced by the aged largely depend on the socio-economic conditions and environment in which they live. Aged people need intensive and long term care, which increases the stress and burden on the family. The need and problems of the elderly vary according to their age, health, living style and other circumstances.

STATEMENT OF THE PROBLEM

Ageing implies a greater increment in the number of elderly women, 55 % of the world's elderly are women. The demographic shift towards elder women population, need to focus attention on their physical and psychosocial well-being. Indian society is moving towards industrialized urban society where changes are causing adverse effects on psychological well–being of aged women. Older women are a growing presence in the developing countries. Indian older women face triple jeopardy: that of being old, of being women, and of being poor. An important contemporary aspect of aging is the gender composition among older persons. Women tend to marry older men, hence, women are more likely to be widowed and live in the widowed state for longer periods and the earning capacity of women their ability to maintain themselves is less than that of men. As the result, the majority of older Indian women they live as widows, live in poverty, and frequently live as dependents of their children or extended families. Being an elder woman, caring for other older persons and other members in the family may affect various aspects of their life, such as physical and emotional health, decreased time for respite, which in turn affects the social life among caregivers and contributes to social isolation. Moreover, Abuse and violence against women in Indian homes has been largely hidden and widely denied by all communities due to the fear of assault on the integrity of their families. Elder abuse is a part of the intra-familial violence even though society as a whole has been acknowledged and accepts this as a problem. Elder women also face the economic problems they are deprived in terms of access to economic activities too.

REVIEW OF LITERATURE

William F. Benson (2004), According to the respondents, neglect and exploitation are the most common forms of abuse. They further indicated that those elders most likely to be abused are: 1) women, 2) very old, 3) socially isolated in their own homes, 4) perceived as burdens to their families, 4) living with their abusers, 5) in poor physical condition, and 6) likely to have become dependent on others suddenly. The respondents characterized abusers as: 1) family caregivers, 2) likely to be unemployed, 3) poor and in need of money, 4) feeling burdened by care giving, and 5) depressed. They did not believe that abusers were likely to have been abused by others in the past or to have histories of abusing others. They were also in agreement that abuse was repetitive. http://www.nationalcenterdvtraumamh.org, "Psychological abuse" Perpetrators of psychological abuse against the elderly often take advantage of their vulnerability in ways that control and/or humiliate the victim, including: Denying or creating long waits for food, medication, heat, or basic care. Taking the victim's walker, glasses, or dentures and intentionally failing to follow medical, therapy, or safety recommendations.

M. SIVAMURTHY et-al (2001), that the care and support for the elderly population in India is becoming an important issue, is apparent from the growing number of the elderly in the population. The Government of India has expressed its concern in this regard by preparing the National Policy on the Older Persons and by constituting a National Council for the Older Persons (NCOP) to oversee the implementation of the policy. The Central and the State Governments have already introduced a number of schemes to provide care and support to the elderly. The Non-Government Organizations (NGOs) are also undertaking the work of taking care of the aged mostly in urban areas, although in a limited way. But, it is the family that is found to be playing the most vital role in India in this respect, especially in rural areas. This is in fact what the elderly persons seem to want also. The Indian culture emphasizes the reverential treatment to be given to the aged persons in the family. It is therefore necessary that efforts must be made to strengthen the family support for taking care of the elderly population.

Madhu Mathur, Depression and Life Style in Indian Ageing Women, 2009, Females are the worst sufferers due to lack of education and less stable economic base. Apart from economic constraints in patriarchal society, the marital bond and stability of the family relationship is on the shoulders of women in the family. Women need to be assimilated in the mainstream by educating them, equipping with skills and encouraging them to become economically independent. An independent financial status contributes to mental satisfaction otherwise unconsciously their thoughts undermine the sense of confidence. Mental health depends on social harmony, social support, sound family relations and independent financial status. Loneliness is a deadly enemy during old age.

Syam Prasad, http://www.igidr.ac.in/pdf/publication/WP-2011-013.pdf (2011), Deprivation is a much broader term than poverty that includes all kinds of denial or being excluded from a minimum standard of living. It is a position in which the people are denied of the basic needs, i.e., both economic and social necessities that enhance the capability and thus the wellbeing of individuals. The process of ageing is always accompanied by a decline in the wellbeing of the human beings that results in the rising economic, health and social insecurity among the aged. The aged generally suffer from economic dependency, physical immobility and insecurity in the form of access to health care and also from social isolation. In the West, most of these insecurities are looked after by the state in the form of social and institutional arrangements. In India, where the incidence of the public provision of the old age care is less, the family system played a key role in the protection of the old. Here we looked at the deprivation of the aged in the context of changing intergenerational balance with a rapid growth of the aged. The elderly in India are generally suffering from economic, health and social insecurity. Majority of the elderly are reported to be in a bad condition in terms of deprivation measured as generalized deprivation

AIM OF THE STUDY

The study aims to explore the various determinants of vulnerability factors and aspects pertinent to deprivation among the elder women in Melur Block, Madurai District.

OBJECTIVES

- To examine the various determinants of vulnerability factors among the elder women in the study area.
- To analyze the aspects pertinent to deprivation and its impact among the elder women in the study area.

METHODOLOGY

a) Area of Study

The study was conducted in 2 panchayat villages in Melur Block, Madurai district, Tamilnadu. The selected panchayat villages are Navinipatti and Vellalur.

b) Selection of respondents

The respondents were elderly women whose age is above 60 years. By using the conventional method of random sampling method, 10 respondents were selected from these villages, 5 from each village.

c) Tool for the study

The tool used to collect the data from the respondents is Focus Group Discussion method (FGD) which will reflect the on in-depth gathering of information in a collective manner reflecting the issues relating elderly victimization and deprivation. Two Focus Group Discussions, group consisting of 5 women elders women from each selected village was selected and conducted. The data was collected during the month of February 2012.

RESULTS, DISCUSSIONS, ANALYSIS AND INTERPRETATION

Women are the essential source for the development of the society. In India, for Indian women ageing is not a trauma. The problems of the elder women are not much a product of aged process rather they are a product of subordinate status of women through their life cycle. According to the deliberations through Focus Group Discussion, it recognized that the problems of ageing are increasingly the women's problem. Elder women are more likely than elder men in terms of illness, poorness, loneliness and care givers and psychosocial status. The aged are not homogenous even within the well defined group like family and society by large.

SOCIAL VULNERABILITY AND DEPRIVATION

The elder women people are more emotionally and socially dependent as well in nature. The facts are these elder women are vulnerable because of their unproductive nature in the old age. The Elder women are socially vulnerable, economically vulnerable and emotionally vulnerable. Social vulnerable the perception about the elder among the younger generations is elderly life is a burden. When the family members feel or perceive them as a burden automatically deprivation alienation and marginalization happens and finally they are excluded. The elderly people they prefer whether to stay within the home or move away from home to seek asylum. But the present living condition itself makes them to stay with in the family will the self determination for survival and upholding the family values and traditions. Status and recognition of elder women with in the family is also slowly degrading. Elder women are socially dependent on their spouse and family members for better quality of life. They seek some kind of help in order to fulfill their needs from other member especially the family members which is deprived to them. In this regard they are forced to be victimized both directly and indirectly. They also adapt to the situation with tolerance, patience and perseverance in the deprived social setup. The relationship with In-laws also becomes unhealthy in many situations some times leads to deprivation for food, care and support to them which leads to frustration and anxiety

(a) Economically Vulnerable

According to the elder women, they are restraining themselves in order to survive within the family even there is loss of dignity, disrespect and abuse. Since they are dependent they are vulnerable to victimization. Economic repercussion, when their economic condition deteriorates drastically they become cheap labours in near by cottage industries, engage in paid domestic house servants, work in MGNREGP etc to meet their economic and medical needs. They are victimized in the work place. ***Denial*** that is denial of basic need and rights of the elderly people, which leads to destitution at times and creates dependency syndrome among them. They depend upon their self capacity up to a physical bearable level for the economic survival otherwise they seek asylum from their spouse, sons and daughters and in-laws.

(b) Emotionally Vulnerable

Women among the aged are the worst victims of apathy (lack of concern), denial and neglect. Elder women mostly live with their spouse. The elder men are been taken care by these elder spouses but the either way is not possible many times for various reasons. Denial and Neglecting attitude among the family members leads to subordination of women's right especially elder women right under prevailing patriarchy system in rural areas. These denial, discrimination and devaluation leads to major psychological problem. When elder women are victims of psychological problems they are abused to the extent. Simply elderly are emotionally dependent, they depend for love, care and support, for the fulfilling their day to day routine etc which becomes a burden to the present day young generations. When these factors are deprived they are vulnerable to all factors of alienation and isolation.

CONCLUSION

In the nit shell women gets the secondary status in the society. By becoming old, her life experiences combined with socio-economic factors lead her to a miserable state of existence. Poor health, poverty, isolation, neglect, vulnerability and deprivation prove to be the hard facts of her life. However, the government agencies, NGO's, social workers, social scientists and policy makers all must join hands to these issues to support in away for pave way for establishing the fundamental requisites for social justice, gender justice and protection of human rights of the elder women.

REFERENCES

1. Benson, Williams, (2004), "Elder Abuse in Indian Country - Research, Policy, and Practice" – A Research study, NATIONAL INDIAN COUNCIL ON AGING for the National Center on Elder Abuse

2. Liebig, Phoebe, Rajan, S. Irudya (eds.), (2005),"An Aging India", Rawat Publications, New Delhi

3. Ramaiah, A, "Developing Supplementary Indicators from social inclusion perspective towards the achievement of MDGs: Some Key Issues based on Indian Experiences"

4. Sen, Amartya, "Social Exclusion: Concept, Application and Scrutiny", Social Development Paper 1, June 2000

5. Sharma, K.L, (2009), "Dimensions of Ageing: Indian studies", Rawat Publications, New Delhi

6. SIVAMURTHY, M & WADAKANNAVAR, A.R "A Study on Care And Support For The Elderly Population In India: Results From A Survey Of The Aged In Rural North Karnataka (India)", 2001

7. Srivastava, Vineeta, (2010), "Women Ageing: Social work Intervention", Rawat Publications, New Delhi.

8. http://www.harmonyindia4ever.com/

9. http://www.un.org/ageing/coverage/indiaE.htm

10. http://www.globalaging.org, http://www.oldagecare.nic.in/

11. http://www.igidr.ac.in/pdf/publication/WP-2011-013.pdf

12. http://www.nationalcenterdvtraumamh.org

28 INDIA AND AGEING

M.Jeyaseelan

INTRODUCTION

Age is natural and universal process. Old age is synonymous to rich experience and wisdom. The people earn great reverence and respect due to their age. In India, the popular saying *old is gold* rightly pointed out the significance of getting aged. Alas these are all gone of the days. The above proverb is now applicable only to the abiotic structures like buildings, monuments etc., the biotic organisms are thrown away as useless and waste when it is getting aged. In India the size of the elderly population, i.e. person s above the age of 6 0 years is fast g r o w in g although it constituted only 7.4 % of total population at the turn of the new millennium . The downward trends in fertility and mortality coupled with long life expectancy the elderly population is being increasing. Now a day the ageing is not only individual problem but also social problem all over the world. The government as welfare state is in the position to design the appropriate policy and social security measures towards these marginalized sections owing to the traditional age old joint family system and dilution of kinship bonds fails to provide safety measures.

DEMOGRAPHIC PROFILE OF AGEING POPULATION IN INDIA.

As far as the elderly population (aged 60 years or above) is concerned it accounts for 7.4% of total population in 2001. The grey population which accounted for 6.7% of total population in 1991 is expected to increase its share to more than 10% by the year 2021. The share of the elderly in India constitutes 13% of the world's total elderly population. India has acquired the label of "an ageing nation" with 7.7% of its population being more than 60 years of old. According to the Central Statistics Office Ministry of Statistics & Programme Implementation Government of India (Situation Analysis of the Elderly in India, 2011) the following are the salient features of demography profile of elders.

- For males it was marginally lower at 7.1%, while for females it was 7.8%. Among states the proportion vary from around 4% in small states like Dadra & Nagar Haveli, Nagaland Arunachal Pradesh, Meghalaya to more than 10.5% in Kerala.
- Both the share and size of elderly population is increasing over time. From 5.6% in1961 it is projected to rise to 12.4% of population by the year 2026.
- The sex ratio among elderly people was as high as 1028 in 1951 but subsequently dropped to about 938 in 1971 and finally reached 972 in 2001.
- The life expectancy at birth during 2002-06 was 64.2 for females as against 62.6 years for males. At age 60 average remaining length of life was found to be about 18 years (16.7 for males, 18.9 for females) and that at age 70 was less than 12 years (10.9 for males and 12.4 for females).
- There is sharp rise in age-specific death rate with age from 20 (per thousand) for persons in age group 60-64 years to 80 among those aged 75- 79 years and 200 for persons aged more than 85 years.
- The old-age dependency ratio climbed from 10.9% in 1961 to 13.1% in 2001 for India as a whole. For females and males the value of the ratio was 13.8% and 12.5% in 2001.
- About 65 per cent of the aged had to depend on others for their day-to-day maintenance. Less than 20% of elderly women but majority of elderly men was economically independent.
- Among economically dependent elderly men 6-7% were financially supported by their spouses, almost 85% by their own children, 2% by grand children and 6% by others. Of elderly women, less than 20% depended on their spouses, more than 70% on their children, 3% on grand children and 6% or more on others including the non-relations.

IS AGEING PROBLEM IN INDIA?

The ever rise of ageing population in western countries is perceived as great problem. The family is the universal social institution which provides social security to the vulnerable sections like aged. But in the western culture, the family is no longer act as social institution and it is merely association of man and woman. Since there is no relatively permanent social institution like family, the state is in the position to provide social security to the aged people. On the other hand, in the developing countries like India, the traditional joint family looks after the welfare of the all dependents. The dilution of the so called joint family into nuclear family owing to the force of modernization results in the physical and emotional deprivation of elders. The failure of agricultural economics and the emergence of industrial economics lead to migration of young generation in search of livelihood to urban areas. The high costs of living of urban areas not favor to keep the aged persons along with them. So they are forced to remain in the rural area itself. The woman is the prime care provider in the family settings. Unfortunately the demographic shift in the work force changed the role women. This shift favor for the institutionalized care of elders. As far as India is concerned, the concept of old age homes is eccentric in nature. It is perceived as cultural shock. Is old age really problem in India? It is not perceived as problem. The most of the Indian populace are still living in rural India. The kinship bond and community bond is not fully diluted. In developed countries, the state looks after all the social security measures meant for the elders. But they are emotionally deprived. Though the government has implemented so many policies and programmes for the sake of aged person, in India the role of family is not yet fully replaced by the government. The problem of ageing is relatively less in rural India than urban India.

HAPPY AGEING

The man made problems are having some solutions. On the part of ageing, it is natural problem. Essentially, happy aging consists of three cardinal aspects viz., maintaining physical and mental health, good adjustment and life satisfaction. If these are ensured, life in old age becomes mere enjoyable bringing greater happiness to the individual. "It is the mind that makes the man" and "So you think. So you are". The old aphorisms rightly pointed out the fact that if only the mind set is make the men very happy by having a positive and confidant out look. Regarding the ageing, we should accept it is part of life and stage of the life span like adolescence and adulthood.. The changes consequent on aging are a part of our good self and there is no use of fighting with our self on the contrary, there is need for a better understanding of us and view the aging process in the right context and perspective. Research has consistently shown that those, who adapt aging changes as part of the growing self, enjoy a happier: old age than those who fight against them with anxiety. One has to say to one self "Yes, I am aging. So what? Even the youngster of today will be aging tomorrow and it is not something that has only be fallen us the aged. I am old, but I have gained so much experience and knowledge through my life, understood so many things for better than what I did as a child". This sort of a self-enhancement exercise is a sure way to boost our own self-image with enhancement and with improvement of our self-image comes peace and happiness. Positive self-perception of health is one of the basic components for happy ageing. Fretting never helps to solve the problem. The mind acts on the body and helps or hinders the physical condition, depending upon the nature of the mental outlook; therefore, one needs to cultivate a positive and confident view on the progress or outcome of an illness. Here is an attitude that should be cultivated as frequently as one can so that it would, become habitual. This variable of positive perception of one's health correlates well with happy aging. It is common understanding that at the onset of old age one has to make several new adjustments and modifies others. Flexibility as a trait developed throughout life, pays rich dividends in old age in adjusting to the changed conditions. Since life is characterized by frequent changes rather than by stability. It is essential that capability to adapt to changing conditions is an asset to be cultivated. Flexibility is a trait that correlates positively with happy aging. Different generations may act as different sub culture groups and what may hold good for one generation may not hold good for another. Sticking to prestige and reaching with a sensitive ego may not help in old age. Smooth satisfying intergenerational and familial interaction contributes substantially to happy aging. The idle man's brain is the devil's workshop. Lot of leisure time is possible during old age. It is better to have a hobby or indulge in income generating activity or past- time activity. If nothing else becomes available servicing others or extending a helping hand to those in need makes their lives more useful and purposeful. At home too, help in home making functions. (Baby sittings, teaching and engaging children care taking, house keeping or doing the odd job) makes the elderly contribute to the home functions and gives a sense of participation to the elderly and makes the care giver a feeling that the elderly are after all helpful at home. The ageing is always associated with diseases and injuries. It can be preventable through some practices. If you keep and arrange your furniture, appliances, electrical goods intact in the respective places then chance for injuries are less. Most of the injuries are occurred at bathroom during old age. So you have safe and vigil attention at bathrooms, then we can have a safe ageing. There are several other variables whose active practice adds to happy aging. "A sound mind in a sound body" is the key to happy aging. So happy aging is not utopia. We can experience happy aging.

CONCLUSION

Ageing is part of our life. Many of the people are not blessed with this stage of life. Ageing have the more positive aspects. The elders are backbone of the family and they carry the culture, tradition and values of the family. In a way they can play the role of historian, role model and can mentor the youngsters by their valuable experiences. In our traditional value system, ageing is considered as accumulation experiences and wisdom. Since ageing is natural problems, we have to get along with problem with appropriate adaptation of change. As far as in Indian context, the ageing is blessing not cursing.

REFERENCES

Ajaya Kumar Sahoo. Gavin J.Andrews. S.Irudaya Rajan.2009. *Sociology of Ageing A Reader*.Jaipur: Rawat Publications

Anoop Kumar Bhartiya.2008.The Aged in India: Policies and Programmes, Social Welfare,Vol.55.No.7

Anupam Hazra.2009. Status of Elderly in India, Social Welfare,Vol.56. No.7

Bali. Arun.P (ed).1999. *Understanding Greying People of India*. New Delhi: Indian Council of Social Sciences research.

Bhat, Anitha Kumari and Raj Dhruvarajan.2001. "Ageing in India: Drifting Intergenerational Relations, Challenges and Options" in *Ageing and Society*, vol. 21.

Gurusamy.S.2001. Age for to aged, *Social Welfare*, Vol.48, No.7.p.3

Gurusamy.S.2002. Plight of the aged in Rural Tamilnadu, *Journal of Extension and Research*, Vol.IV, No.1&2.,pp106-112.

Helpage India.2004. Promoting productive ageing, *Health action*, February, pp.9-10.

Irudaya Rajan, S. and Kumar, Sanjay.2003. Living Arrangements among Indian Elderly: Evidence from National Family Health Survey. *Economic and Political Weekly*, 38(1), 75-80.

Seval GÜVEN, Arzu SENER.2010. Family Relations in Aging, ***International Journal of Business and Social Science***, Vol. 1 No. 3; (www. Ijbssne.t com)

29 THE PROBLEM OF AGED PEOPLE IN THE SOCIETY

V. Seethalakshmi

India is a land of culture and tradition. The family is most important primary group in society. It is an organization par excellence. Family is an instrument of culture transmission and an agent of socialization. The joint family is the bedrock, on which Hindu values and attitudes are built. It is found in almost all the parts of India. "Old age is an incurable disease" – said the Roman Emperor Seneca. The traditional Indian family structure, the older persons had enormous authority and power over family members through control of family. Family productive resources such as the family enterprise of land. Caring for older persons in the family does not appear to be a tenable system. Joint families that ensure a secured life for the aged are fast disintegrating. A nuclear family will not be able to take care of the older persons. It will be simply impossible if the older person concern is mentally and physically disabled. Ageing is a natural and irreversible process of human life. It is an inevitable, obiquitous and universal phenomenon of our life cycle. It brings about certain anatomical, physiological, psychological changes in life. Ageing is a part of life but no one is eager to explore this stage and we are living in a youth culture that glorifies the young and neglects the old. Elderly people constitute precious human resource reservoir gifted with knowledge of various arts. Our elders have given everything to the children, family, society and nation. Now it is our turn to give love, affection, care and respect. Earlier family members used to believe that a person status increased with the age because of his experience. Elderly people provide useful advice in family decision.

The global population of elderly has constantly being increasing

Census year	Total population (in million)	Population of elderly 60 + (in million)
1951	361.1	19.8
1961	439.2	24.7
1971	547.3	32.7
1981	685.9	41.5
1991	846.3	56.7
2001	1027	77

The transition of Indian society from the traditional pre-Industrial to Modern Industrial led the emergence of nuclear families. These changes have seriously affected the social context of the aged, thereby exposing them to several serious problems. Insecurity, health and functional problems are the major area in which the elderly have needs and face problems and require help. The traditional modes of family support decline and more and more children abandon their old folk to migrate in search of better opportunities. A new and frightening social malaise in pervading Indian life - the social and emotional isolation of elderly people. In many cases, the elderly are pressurized in myriad ways by their grown up children to transfer all the properties immediately. If the old person hesitates he invites many troubles including physical torture. If they don't resist and smoothly transfer their properties and bank balances etc in the name of the children, there is hardly any assurance that their needs and aspirations would taken care of properly. Elderly persons due to retirement from job and due to reduction in income have a feeling of loneliness, rejection and insecurity. This creates various problems in the elderly people such as

- Ageing
- Chronic disease
- Psycho-social problem
- Feeling of worthlessness
- Feeling of tiredness and tension
- Loss of appetite
- Trouble in sleeping
- Dependency
- Increased expenditure
- Problems in concentration

- Headaches and vague aches and
- Pain all over the body

Of all problems faced by the aged people psychological problem occupies formost place due to urbanization and industrialization most of the elders are left alone. They face exploitation, abuse and desertion. With none to live with and care for them elders have to look for an alternative home for security, companionship, care and a life of dignity. Economic problems are also faced by the aged with the superannuation a person has to retire from service, which not only results into loss of employment and social status, but also substantial deduction in his income level. This economic insecurity leads to dependency which in turn leads to their loss of self respect and consequently and more vulnerability. Elders are repository of culture, tradition and indigenous knowledge. They transmit family values to the younger generation through stories, song and cultural practices. They are also the sage counselors and in the mad rush of life, the cool shade of their presence is the most soothing and calming influence. We forget to recognize their experience, knowledge and unqualified love. We fail to treat them as the most valuable treasure of the nation and give them their due.

The fast track changes and westernization of Indian society have resulted in the degeneration of the Joint family system, dislocation of cultural and familial bonds loss of respect for the aged. Nowadays the youth and the middle aged persons are seen to be driven more by the individualistic ideals of the west. Their selfishness and careerist attitude do not permit them to spare a bit of their valuable time, energy or resource for the care of the elderly in their household.

It is very difficult for an individual to psychologically endure the problems of dependency on family members, relatives, friends and society which may have been caused by the loss of economic and social status due to retirement. Loss of employment transformed the aged from the independent self supporting individual to a dependent and helpless individual. Consequently they suffer loss of status in their family also. It may degenerate from the status of a breadwinner to a neglected one in the family. They have to experience reversal of roles which qualitatively redefines their status and role in their own family. Many at times the ole persons find it difficult to adjust to the changed environment, status or situation, more so when the old are only tolerated and not treated well by their own family members. Generally speaking elderly live in a lonely life most of the time especially in nuclear families. During the empty nest stage the aged couples are left to fend for themselves. Because of their helplessness and dependency and fewer social contacts the aged feel lonely, insecure and unloved. Loneliness is painful. It is said that most serious disease for older person is not cancer or heart disease, it is loneliness. Being alone is different loneliness.

Loneliness said to be the leading cause for depression as there is a general decline in health, the elderly tend to have fewer interest. When the elderly do not have anything to do worthwhile, their thoughts ramble and often culminate in feelings of guilt or uselessness. Suicide thoughts might also enter their minds. Health problems, isolation, reduced sense of purpose in life, worries, anxiety and fear may all lead to depression. With the tradition joint families now mostly gone and a simultaneous increase in the number of middle class women seeking jobs and professions, the need for providing care for elderly relatives and led to old age homes being setup. In the west care system for elder is well defined. An institution for elders is well organized and state controlled. Old age homes new concept to us is coming up in large number today. Indian society is getting more and more conscious about the problems of the older persons. Many organizations are active in the field of welfare activities for this elderly people. But most families shy away from this concept. On the one hand elderly parents think that their offspring are abandoning them and failing in their filial duties. On the other the children developed guilt feelings about abandoning their parents to old age homes. Psychological problems are more common in old age which includes cognitive impairment depression, dementia, death anxiety etc. Many organizations NGO are active in the field of welfare activities for the older persons. Government of India endorsed national policy for the older persons and constituted council for older persons to execute their endorsed policy matters. National policy is framed to generate and secure adequate and improved service system for all older persons of the country. The old age homes are homes which provide residential care for elderly who are destitute or homeless and for people who are not able to function independently in all aspects of their daily living. At present there are more than 800 old age homes in India. The national policy of older persons was formulated in 1999, declared as the International Year of Old Persons by the Government of India. The national policy on older persons in comprehensive document with far reaching possibilities. The national policy recognizes NGO sector as an important institutional mechanism that can provide user friendly affordable services to complement the endavour of the state. The national council for older persons has been constituted by the ministry of social justice and empowerment to operate for the welfare of the older persons. Through the national coordinating bodies are doing social service, NGOs are doing laudable work in caring for the aged.

Provisions under National Policy of Older persons cover

- 60+
- Persons below poverty line.
- Rate of monthly pension to be revised.
- Pre-retirement counseling

- Provision of tax relief.
- Income generating programmes.

The concept of old age homes came into existence before independence; very few around 15 were established. The number of old age has been increasing in the recent past. We come to know about the rising figures of old age homes. The Government of India approved the national policy for older persons on January 13th 1999 in order to accelerate welfare measures and empowering the elderly in ways beneficial for them. This policy included following major steps

- Setting up of a pension fund for ensuring security for those persons who have been serving in the unorganized sector.
- Construction of old age homes and day care centres for every 3 – 4 districts.

Year of establishment	No of old age homes	Percentage
Before independence	51	7.1
1950-60	38	5.3
1961-70	65	9
1971-80	139	19.4
1981-90	174	24.2
1991-2000	183	25.5
2001-present	800	-

It is evident that the establishments of old age home has been increasing every year, 50 – 60 % of old age home provide free accommodation. Majority of old age home vegetarian food. Medical and other services such as running of day care centres have been undertaken by the old age homes to improve the quality of the living. Volunteer organizations and philanthropists should start counseling centres in different localities. It will help in developing healthy mental attitude towards life and that will be a positive step towards happy ageing. Old age home with spiritual atmosphere and sincere service by organizers and workers are providing very useful for satisfactory and peaceful life of elderly. Growing old with dignity needs the help of voluntary social welfare organizations and devoted workers dedicated services can infuse a sprit of joy, hope and happiness in the life of the aged. At the government level ageing should be recognized as a development issues and strategies should be worked out to meet the challenges in the light of growing consumerism and globalization. Old age must be recognized as a mark of triumph, intelligence, reflection. Judgment resides in old people. The ageing people are longing to get love and affection from the family members especially from their grand children without giving respect to their expectation we are sending them to the old age homes.

The existence of old age homes in large number resulted in the establishment of crèche. When old people are at home they imbibe the values of life to the younger generation through short stories from our epics Thus we are loosing our culture, tradition, values, moral and other aspects of human life.

REFERENCES:

1) Bali Arun.1994 "Ageing and Social Care:Trends and Policies"-Help Age India

2) John Bgraham(1998) " The supportive network coping with old age"

3) Mishra P (1987) "Social adjustment in old age " B.R publishing coperation New delhi

4) PRB report, world population data sheet 2002

5) Rokach.A (2004) "coping with loneliness and oldage"

30 LIVING CONDITION OF AGED WOMEN IN MODERN ERA

Balamurugan. J, Dr. G. Ramathirtham

INTRODUCTION

Ageing is a universal process and it affects each human being in the world. It is a byproduct of demographic transition, i.e.; the change from high fertility and mortality rates to low fertility and mortality rates. This phenomenon is more evident in developed countries but recently it seen to be increasing more rapidly in developing countries. Ageing is generally associated with fatigue and decline in the functional capacity of the organs of the body due to physiological transformation. The definition of ageing is a matter of debate, especially with regard to public policy (Neugarten, 1982). Also ageing is relative and varies from society to society and region to region. The different terms used in the gerontological literature, to refer to old persons symbolically indicate the uncertainty associated with the later years of life in all societies. Commonly used terminologies in these literatures are old, older people, aged, elderly, mature, senior citizens, etc. Some prefer to use the adjective 'older' to 'old' which is falsely suggestive of the existence of a group clearly distinctive from the non-old (Rao, 2007). Old age is not a problem of 'age' but the intermingling of socio-cultural and other demographic variables. There is a continuous interplay between adult development and social forces; and gender is a potent social factor in determining ageing experience. 'Gender' and 'ageing' have become the core of any genuine development concern at national and international levels (Srivastava, 2010).

REVIEW OF LITERATURE

Living condition is very important in term of providing support for the elderly and can, in general, guarantee their well-being. In India, where the family has an obligation to care for the elderly, the consequences of rapid decline in fertility and mortality on elderly living arrangements are in interesting issue in the field of population and development. Populations are ageing, with changes in the living condition of the aged occurring in most countries, as a result of lower fertility, higher mobility, changing attitudes about family structure & function and increasing life expectancy, especially mortality declines in later life (Muthukrishnaveni, 2010).

In India, gradually the sex ratio is getting evened out. India was one of the few countries with the dubious distinction of having an unfavourable female to male ration in the population with demographic changes. Now there will be older women in India too. But the bad news is that they are likely to be more vulnerable due to socio-cultural reasons. Older women are likely to have more health problems, less likely to be financially independent and have less power and status compared to old man. India lives in her village, old people in rural areas face several hard ships while being deprived of basic amenities that take granted with migration and urbanization depriving rural areas of its able to bodied empty young people, rural areas will become packets of poverty living conditions also change leading to problems in providing security to elderly (Prakash, 2001).

A study on the living condition of elderly revealed that except a few (7 percent), all most live with their children. These few are living by themselves in single household because of not having any children. Among the others, 73 percent live with their sons whereas 20 percent with their daughters (Dharmalingam, 2001). A study on the level of life satisfaction among the elderly people according to their age and type of family found that the younger respondents had greater life satisfaction and the respondents who were living separately from their children were more satisfied than those who were living with their married or unmarried children (Hosmath, 1993).

Most of the elderly staying with their unmarried children, when it comes to sharing their inner feeling of life, likes joys and sorrows. They preferred and considered their wife as their close and intimate person in the family. It is also pointed out that the respondents have maintained friendly relations with their grown-up-children (Jayashree, 1999). In a study on living condition of aged found that on an average the Indian elderly are residing in a household where at least seven members are living. Interestingly, only 2.4 percent of the elderly are living alone and another 3.5 percent are residing with others relatives or non-relatives. More elderly female (3.49 percent) are living alone compared with males (1.42 percent). In other worlds, only 6 percent of elderly in India are living in a family where their immediate kinship is not present in the household (Rajan, 2003).

METHODOLOGY

Descriptive research design with purposive sampling purposive sampling method, 400 respondents from Puducherry municipality have been taken for this study. An interview schedule method has been used to collect the primary data for the study. The present paper describes the problems of living condition faced by elderly women.

DATA ANALYSIS

The study has analysed and profiled the socio-economic back ground and problems of urban elderly women, impact of the problems among the elderly, evaluate the different welfare programmes The paper also suggest some remedial measures that can be taken to eradicate the problems of elderly women. The study has been carried out with broad-based objectives. This study has been conducted by using pre-tested interview schedule among 200 aged women as respondents from retired person and 200 housewives as respondents. The sample of the respondents is selected by purposive sampling technique. The socio-economic profile of the respondents in this study presented below.

Table 1 Socio-economic profile of the respondents

	Number of respondents	Percentage
Age (in years)		
- 65	186	46.50
66 - 70	117	29.25
71 - 75	58	14.50
76 - 80	22	05.50
80 and above	17	04.25
Education		
Illiterate	104	26.00
Primary	48	12.00
Middle	52	13.00
High school	34	08.50
Hr. Secondary	30	07.50
Graduate	22	05.50
Post Graduate	22	05.50
Others	80	22.00

	Number of respondents	Percentage
Marital status		
Unmarried	15	03.75
Married	170	42.50
Divorce	2	00.50
Widow	195	48.75
Single	2	03.00
Deserted	6	01.50
Type of house		
Pucca	192	48.00
Tiled	14	03.50
Kutcha	174	43.50
Old age home	20	05.00
Monthly income (in Rs)		
Below 2,000	189	47.25
2,001 – 4,000	61	15.25
4,001 – 6,000	64	16.00
6,001 – 8,000	35	08.75
8,001 – 10,000	48	12.00
Above 10,000	3	00.75
Total	**400**	**100.00**

The table 1 indicates that socio-economic profile of the respondents, the majority 46.5 percent of the respondents belong to age group is 61 to 65 years. Regarding the religion of respondents, it has been found that majority (62.5 percent) is Hindus, 27.75 percent are Christian and 9.75 percent are Muslim. Educational attainment of the elderly people was very low and deplorable. Among the total respondents, 46 percent illiterate, 41 percent of respondents studied upto higher education, Graduates are 7.5 percent and the remaining respondents are completed their Post Graduate (5.5 percent). Considering to the marital status of respondents, 96.25 percent of them were married but 48.75 percent of the respondents belong to the category of widow. Most of the respondents prefer to stay in their own house regardless of the size of house. Among the total respondents, 48 percent are living in good condition with pucca house and 54 percent of the respondents residing in their own house. It has been found from the study that in the matter of monthly income as living status it is seen that,

47.25 percent of the respondents have a low monthly income of only less than 2,000 rupees from Government Old Age Pension scheme and lead a low living status. Moreover, it is seen that 52.75 percent of the respondents get financial help from their Retirement Pension Schemes and rent.

It is seen that 30 percent of the respondents who are elderly are found to migrate from rural and settle in urban area for their children's education, job and also to increase their economic status. Most of the respondents want to live with their spouse and children only. Nevertheless, 42 percent of the respondents living with their spouse and 44.00 percent of the respondents were living with their children. The children with limited income often cannot meet even the basic needs of the parents. They are economically insecure. Considering the dependency, 67.25 percent of the respondents are dependent on others for their needs and also insufficient income and illness. Regarding the loneliness of the respondents, it is found that 50 percent of the respondents suffer. Moreover respondents between the age group of 61-70 years are found to face more suffering compared to their older group. The main reason of the loneliness of 49.75 respondents shows that they belong to nuclear family where they feel more individualism and detached from others. Misunderstanding within the family member is main causes for loss of security and love of aged. However, 46.50 percent of the respondents, irrespective of their family were found satisfied with fulfilling their basic needs

Table: 2 Distribution of the respondents according to their Nature of Residence

Sl. No	Nature of Residence	Number of respondents	Percentage
1	Home	368	92.00
2	Old age home	20	5.00
3	Others	12	3.00
	Total	**400**	**100**

Family structure that has existed in India some long past as a unit of social bondage and economic constituent among the people in the family system. It has proving social and economic and moral support to members in the family. This situation may occur when they are staying in the house either aged (or) not. This table 2 shows that 95 percent of the respondents were staying their own house (or) relative houses. Followed by 5 percent of respondents were staying in old age home and they are hanging for getting affection and support from their family even they are having good economic background.

Table: 3 Distribution of respondents in terms of their Living with the relationship

Sl. No	Relationship	Number of respondents	Percentage
1	With Husband	170	42.50
2	With children	176	44.00
3	Others	54	13.50
	Total	**400**	**100**

This table 3 shows that 42.50 percent of respondents were living with their spouse. Followed by 44.00 percent of respondents were living with their children, 13.50 percent of the respondents were living with Grand Children, other relatives houses and also aged home. Among the 400 respondents only 20 respondents are stayed in old age homes. However, overall picture of the table reveals that 0.75 percent of respondents were staying in old age home due to not supporting of their children and 0.75 percent by misunderstanding with daughter in law. Followed by 0.5 percent of respondents are reported that they are facing economical problem, 0.5 percent of respondents are due to mental and health problem and 0.5 percent of respondents don't have any caretaker. Remaining 0.5 percent of respondents feel that due to loneliness, 0.50 percent of respondents due to their death of spouse and 1 percent of respondents in aged due to migration of their children.

It indicates death of spouse makes the problem during aged condition. Migration of children from one place to another because of their Job, economic status etc. This time some aged parents are avoidable one and lead to Aged Home. Also it explains that husband and children's are the most responsible relations of women and aged.

Table: 4 Sources of Financial support

Sl. No	Financial support form	Number of respondents	Percentage
1	Husband	101	25.25
2	Son	59	14.75
3	Daughter	14	3.50
4	Grand children	5	1.25
5	Own	131	32.75
6	Others	90	22.50
	Total	**400**	**100**

Finance is must to meet out our daily needs and development of family either by own earning or from other family members. The table 4 shows that 25.25

percent of the respondents depends their husband for financial support, 14.75 percent of sons and 3.50 percent of daughter rendering financial support to their aged mother. Some son in law and daughter in law are not willing to do financial support, but 25 percent of the respondents are getting finance support from their grand children. However, 32.75 percent of the respondent meet out their financial needs by own. Followed by 22.5 percent of the respondents are getting financial support from combine by husband with relatives, friends and grand children's.

To maintain self-respect and status, one should not be economically dependent on others, and should have some personal income. Income flows from assets, past savings, pensions and gainful work. Some activities such as household work though may be supportive and hence very necessary, do not yield independent income. In India, assets, past savings and pensions account for income only in respect of a few. It is the gainful work, which is a source of income for a vast majority.

Table: 5 Distribution of the respondents according to the dependency

Sl. No	Dependent	Number of respondents	Percentage
1	Dependents	269	67.25
2	Independents	131	32.75
	Total	**400**	**100**

A person after losing her vim, vigour and vitality in the old age becomes utterly helpless is forced to depend on others to fully or partly. The growth rate of aged population increased is steadily increasing the dependency ratio also. Erosion of status of the aged person due to the role reversal from "provides" to "dependent" and faced failed to discharge their duty. This table 5 shows that 67.25 of the respondent were dependent to others. 32.75 of the respondent were independent.

Table: 6 Reasons for respondent's dependency

Sl. No	Reasons for dependency	Number of respondents	Percentage
1	Insufficient income	190	47.50
2	Illness	30	7.50
3	Others	49	12.25
4	Not applicable	131	32.75
	Total	**400**	**100**

Table 6 indicates that majority (47.50 percent) of respondents were dependent to others because of insufficient income. 18.75 percent dependency due to insufficient income, 7.50 percent of dependency due to illness and 12.25 percent of respondents are dependent to other for combined problem of insufficient income and their health problem.

The aged are liked by members of their family. But it is human nature to develop emotional attachment to a close one in the family who is more helpful and cares them during the sufferings. The aged are conservative in nature, having their own norms and values. They appreciate the obedience, respect good habits and kind words next to their children they love their grand children whom they consider as the future pillar of their family. In the company of children, the elder forget their worries and enjoy the life with them. Marriages in the relatives also encouraged to strengthen the family ties and reinforce the love and affection among its members.

Regarding the responses of respondents on family member love and affection with elder persons reveals that 37.75 percent of respondents only having chance to getting love and affection from their family members. But 62.25 percent of respondents were hanging for getting love and affection from their family members.

Table: 7 Opinions of the respondents about family members not expressing their love and affection

Sl. No	Reason for not Express love and affection	Number of Respondents	Percentage
1	Because of the small family size	11	2.75
2	Lack of personal income	21	5.25
3	There is nobody to show love and affection	30	7.50
4	Misunderstanding	75	18.75
5	Other reasons	112	28.00
6	Not applicable	151	37.75
	Total	**400**	**100**

This table 7 shows that 2.75 of respondents are not in the position of getting love and affection from their family members because of their small family size. Followed by 5.25 percent are due to lack of personal income, 7.5 percent of respondents are thinking aged is a problem one and burden to them. Also 18.75 percent of the respondents are loss affection due to misunderstanding with the family members, 28 percent of respondents reported that they have loss affection due to combined effect of misunderstanding with insufficient income and nobody ready to give love and affection.

Meagre income on one hand, increasing necessities on the other hand and lack of employment opportunity to meet their needs making the life of the elderly is miserable. Rigidity attitude selfishness, suspicion of younger generation also leads to neglecting of elder. Regarding the neglection of the respondents shows that 43.25 percent of the respondents were neglected by their family members. Retired respondents are also suffering by neglection. Followed by 56.75 percent of the respondent was not neglected.

Aged women's feels frustrated and become subordinate to their daughter-in-law and behaviour of children also makes frustration to aged. Clutch of home management comes into the other hand also causes frustration. In this study indicates that 49 percent of respondents were suffering by frustration and 51 percent of the respondents were not suffered by frustration.

Table: 8 Distribution of respondents according to their Reasons for the feeling of frustration

Sl. No	Reasons	Number of respondents	Percentage
1	Retirement	21	5.25
2	Age factor	25	6.25
3	Insufficient income	30	7.50
4	Children's Behaviour	44	11.00
5	Illness	26	6.50
6	Others	50	12.50
7	Not applicable	204	51.00
	Total	**400**	**100**

This table 8 shows that 11 percent of the respondents were frustrated due to their children education and other behaviour of children. Parents are incurred for more money to their education, but some students have not realised their family situation and necessity. Some children misbehaviour with family and they are not adjust with family members. Most of the sons forget to give respect to their old parents and rejected in many occasion by their son after his marriage. It was severely affecting the aged health and mind and get frustrated severely. It indicates that problem by daughter of aged is very less when compared to male children. 7.5 percent of aged frustrated due to their insufficient income. 6.50 percent of the respondents were suffered by their illness and it make dependent to others. Followed by 6.25 percent of the respondents are frustrated by their ageing factor, 5.25 percent of the respondents frustrated after retirement and 12.50 percent of the respondent suffered by misunderstanding with daughter-in-law.

After retirement, she has to face loss of regular income, and also cope-up with a lower status. She may not able to getting same respect either from her family members (or) from society. Before retirement, the aged is considered useful for the society and financially helpful to his family. But after retirement, the same individual is regarded as a useless old and became burden of the family.

DISCUSSION

The forces of modernization, technological change, mobility and the explosion in the lateral transmission of knowledge are making changes in life styles and values to adjust to the changing circumstances. Individuals and modernity, which sometimes lead to ambivalence in attitude towards the use of the knowledge and experience of the past in solving problems of the present, tend to make old people feel less valued.

The shortage of housing accommodation in the cities and high rentals act as a severe constraint in common residence of the aged with their sons, particularly for migrant families. The migration of younger people increases the vulnerability of the old who stay behind, particularly for families, which do not have independent production assets such as land, livestock or household industry and are dependent primarily labour. Increasing employment of women outside the home in offices and in factories implies that they can spend less time for taking care of the older members, especially those who required constant care. Further, the relatively independent status acquired by a white-collar woman worker, who has her own carrier and aspirations, sometimes leads to demand on the husband for setting up a separate nuclear family.

There is now a great investment by the family on education and upbringing of children, which affects the intra-family distribution of children, which affects the inter-family distribution of income in favour of the younger generation. The joint family system, an important sustaining factor of which is the common ownership of the means of production, is gradually breaking down. This has increased the vulnerability of the old, particularly those with no children or immediate kin, as there is lesser readiness in discharging long-term social obligations towards such members.

REFERENCE

1. Dharmalingam, B. And Murugan, K.R. 2001. 'Elderly Widows and their Place in the Family', *Social Welfare*, 48(1), 1012-1020.

2. Hosmath, S., Revati, V., Gaonkar and Khadi, P.K. 1993. 'Life Satisfaction during Later Years'. *Man in India*, 73 (3), 229-232.

3. Jayashree. 1999. 'Living Arrangements Enhance Quality of Life', *Social Welfare,* 50 (1).

4. Muthukrishnaveni, S. 2010. *Living Arrangements and Health Conditions of Elderly in Rural India,* New Delhi: Serials Publications.

5. Neugarten, B. 1982. *Age or Need Public Policy for Older People.* Baverly Hills, Clifornia: Sage Publication.

6. Prakash, I.J. 2001. 'Health Concerns of Older Women in India', *Research Development Journal,* Help Age India, 10 (3).

7. Rajan, S.I. 2003. 'Living Arrangements Among the Indian Elderly Evidence from National Family Health Survey', *Economic and Political Weekly*. 38 (1), 75-80.

8. Rao, K.V. 2007. *Ageing in Rural India.* New Delhi: The Associate Publishers.

31 PROBLEMS OF ELDERLY PERSONS IN URBAN SOCIETY: A STUDY

T.Murugesan, Dr.I.Singaram

INTRODUCTION

In urban areas the problems get further accentuated. Community support is weak and the kin network is diffused over a large area and relatively ineffective. The entire responsibility of support and care of the ageing falls on the male children with whom the ageing live. The composition of the family in urban areas is becoming nuclear and smaller, as a result of which there are fewer people available in the house to provide care and comfort to the ageing. Those who are available are torn apart by the stresses of urban living. Women too in the urban areas are now working outside the family. They have fixed schedules of work and have other pressures on them. Children are loaded with their studies, competitive examinations and concerns for making their careers. Problems of the Aged as follows:

(i) Economic problems include such problems as loss of employment, income deficiency and economic insecurity.

(ii) Physical and physiological problems include health and medical problems, nutritional deficiency and the problem of adequate housing etc.

(iii) Psycho-social problem which cover problems related with their psychological and social maladjustment as well as the problem of elder abuse etc. The paper deals with based on secondary sources.

ELDERLY IN URBAN SITUATION

The place of living, Socio-cultural, political and economic characteristics and other similar factors influence the well-being of the aged. Likewise, rural-urban characteristics also play a salient role. Needless to add, urban family groups markedly differ from rural family groups. These differences are noticeable in terms of structure, size, mode of production and consumption, interpersonal relations, etc. Generally speaking members of these groups differ from each other in terms of capabilities, resource-generation and social likes and dislikes Equally important is the consideration of impersonality, almost inherent in urban environment, in contrast to cohesion and bonding on rural community. Commercialization, industrialization and political changes have accelerated the pace of urbanization. India has been no exception to this. The Urban component, in its population, has been steadily growing decade after decade. In 1991, almost one-fourth of India's population was classified as urban. In 2001, the corresponding figure has risen to 28.1 percent. Also, the proportion of elderly men, living on rural areas, tends to increase with age. In contrast, greater proportions of elderly women are living in urban areas. The reason may be that elderly women are more vulnerable to chronic illnesses and widowhood, and social services (vijayanunni, 1997). The trend from the above data of gradual increase in the proportion of the elderly females in urban areas puts forth the challenge to the urban governance to meet the needs of senior citizens.

AGEING IN URBAN REGION

In urban areas the problems get further accentuated. Community support is weak and the kin network is diffused over a large area and relatively ineffective. The entire responsibility of support and care of the ageing falls on the male children with whom the ageing live. The composition of the family in urban areas is becoming nuclear and smaller, as a result of which there are fewer people available in the house to provide care and comfort to the ageing. Those who are available are torn apart by the stresses of urban living. Women too in the urban areas are now working outside the family. They have fixed schedules of work and have other pressures on them. Children are loaded with their studies, competitive examinations and concerns for making their careers. The authority that the ageing exercised on their children in the past as a result of greater experience has almost vanished, and the aged are now told, 'You don't know'. There are several reasons for this admonishment. First, the children of the ageing are not in the same profession. Second, the quantum of information which their children claim to have makes the ageing look almost primitive. Third, the whole techno-economic situation has now completely changed, which leaves the ageing bewildered and redundant. When paucity of accommodation, high cost of living, general stress and tensions at all levels are added to these, the problems of the aged are extremely serious.

A GLOBAL PROFILE OF AGEING WOMEN

For multiple reasons the feminization of ageing has important policy implications for all countries: Ageing women make up a significant proportion of the world's population and their numbers are growing. The number of women age 60 and over will increase from about 336 million in 2000 to just over 1 billion in 2050. Women outnumber men in older age groups and this imbalance increases with age. Worldwide, there are some 123 women for every 100 men aged 60 and over while the highest proportions of older women are in developed countries, the majority live in developing countries, where population ageing is occurring at a rapid pace. The greatest growing group within ageing women is the oldest-old (age 80-plus).worldwide, by age 8o and over, there are 189 women for every 100 men. By age 100 and over, the gap reaches 385 women for every 100 men. while most ageing women remain relatively healthy and independent until late in life, the very old most often require chronic care and help with day-to-day activities. Older women are a highly diverse group. Life at age to is obviously very different from life at age 85. Although cohorts of older women may experience some common situations, such as a shared political environment, exposure to war and the arrival of new technologies, their longevity has given them more time to develop unique biographies based on a lifetime of experiences.

CURRENT STATUS OF ELDERLY PEOPLE

Women comprise by far the greater number and proportion of older population in almost all societies; this disparity is increasing with advancing age. In India, while the sex ratio favors men at all ages, the trend reverses in favour of females above the age of 70 years with the number of women exceeding the number of men in this age group. Sex ratio in elderly population, which was 928 in the year 1996, is projected to become 1031 by the year 2016. More often than not, women are over burdened with cumulative inequalities throughout the life cycle from womb to tomb as a result of socio-cultural and economic discriminatory practices leading to a secondary status. Thus, a longer life span is directly correlated to greater morbidity and higher incidence of health related problems among the older women. In comparison to men, women are also denied access to opportunities for personal growth and social development, in education, employment, professional and political life. Furthermore the patriarchal system and preoccupation with sexual and reproductive functions during adult age, perpetuates the subservient role of women in the family and in the society. Women also spend majority of their working hours in domestic labour, which is usually unpaid and unrecognized.

THE PROBLEM IN ELDERLY PEOPLE

Due to the progress made in the fields of technology, economic development and public health longevity has increased and has to an increase in the number of elderly people in good health. Although very few people live to the upper limit of the human life span, a good many are living into their eighties and nineties. Percentage of the aged living up to that ripe age is higher among the westerners.

Living to a "grand old age" is a source of personal and family pride; however, there is a cost: the onset of physical or mental disabilities that may limit one's Anatomy. Many seniors are more afraid of dependency than of death. The thought of dependency conjures up images of being powerless, of becoming a burden on others and of being kept alive by artificial means some will prepare meticulously for disposal of their property and of their body after death but may hesitate to plan for the weeks, months or even years prior to death. Although some people remain physically and mentally able until they die, the prospect of developing a more or less disabling condition becomes more probable in later years. The best strategy is to anticipate adapting one's life situation to one's changing needs. Some individuals chase the thought away, others adopt a fatalistic attitude, and a few just hope to die in bed suddenly before they become too frail or disabled. Retirement or old age is considered as having arrived at a "golden" period of life, a period of self awareness, wisdom, reflection, and adventure and sharing, it offers an opportunity to humanize the present sick and clean eyed wisdom of age. In India, the aged have traditionally been considered as wisdom banks, are the best source of social education, for solving social problems and developing national integration. The age structure of population in any society depends on its birth rates, death rates and net migration. Throughout the world and women empowerment went only to the segments of younger generation. Thus most elderly women were terribly marginalized, first as women, second as aged women and third as widows.

HEALTH IN OLD AGE

Advances in health care are resulting in a rapid increase in the number of older people and in their proportion relative to entire population. Society is faced with increased financial and social burden because of the greater number of physical, psychological and social problems the older group is experiencing. Equally serious and frequent are mental health problems. Among the aged, anxiety states, depression, phobia, senile dementia and several other symptoms and diseases are reportedly wide spread. Worse still, often at times, mental symptoms are passed over for hypochondriacs. Mental health cannot be ignored in the old. Since it is not the focus of the present study, it is not discussed here.

COMMON MINOR HEALTH COMPLAINTS OF ELDERLY:

Certain so-called common 'minor' health problems are discussed below;

HEARING IMPAIRMENT

The loss of hearing occurs progressively over many years as the person ages. There are different causes for this. Sensori-neural deafness is particularly common and important. This is due to a combination of degenerative changes in both the cochlea and the auditory nerve. It typically results in preferential loss of high frequency hearing, Hearing problem hinders communication with others, limit social activities and reduce constructive use of leisure time. Such people often withdraw from others to avoid frustration. Occasionally they become suspicious of relatives and friends.

EYE IMPAIRMENTS

These are major causes of disability in older people, especially in developing countries where there are fewer resources for prevention and treatment. At present, about 25 million older people are blind; the number is expected to double by 2020 (WHO, 1998). There is a gradual increase in the incidence of eye ailments with increase in age.

CATARACT

It is a very common eye change in old age. It is the occurrence of opaque areas in part of the lens or whole of it in the eye. Cataract can occur in one eye or both eyes. When it forms, light cannot easily pass through the lens and this affects vision. Cataract may develop without any sign of pain, redness and tears etc. in the eye.

GLAUCOMA

It results from too much pressure inside the eye from the fluid within, which damages the eye and causes a loss of vision. This relates to deficient drainage of aqueous humour. As the process progresses, the angle of vision becomes increasingly narrower, until the victim is effectively looking down a narrow tunnel.

EXCESSIVE TEARS

It may be caused due to a sign of increased sensitively to light, wind or temperature changes. Protective measures such as sunglasses may help the patients. Sometimes eye infection or a blocked tear-duct may also cause excessive tears and need treatment.

EXCESSIVE DRYNESS

Dried eyes result from the tear glands producing too few tears. It causes irritation, burning of eyes or a poor vision.

RETINAL DEFECTS

It results from Senile Macular Degeneration, Diabetic Retinopathy and Retinal Detachment.

SENILE MACULAR DEGENERATION

It is a condition in which macula (a specialized part of the retina, responsible for sharp, central and reading vision) loses its function. The early signs of causing it are-blurring of reading matter, loss of central vision, a dark spot in the center of field of vision and distortion in vertical lines.

DIABETIC RETINOPATHY

It is a serious complication in the elderly. The vessels that nourish retina fail to do so or there may be a leak from the blood vessels, which interfere with vision. In latter stages new blood vessels may grow and release blood into the centre of the eye resulting in serious loss of vision.

RETINAL DETACHMENT

It is a separation between inner and outer layers of retina. Detached retinas can be surgically reattached with a good or partial restoration of vision.

BLOOD PRESSURE CHANGES WITH AGE

The systolic and diastolic blood pressures generally increase with age.

HYPOTENSION

Distributions of autonomic functions are common in old age and postural hypertension is common. It is often worse in the morning and occurs when the person stands up from the sitting or lying position. Its onset is favoured by exertion such as walking. The initial blood pressure may be raised on to normal but falls to levels where cerebral perfusion is adversely affected and giddiness, vertigo, faintness and even transient syncope result and the patient exhibits pallor and a thin pulse that may become virtually undetectable.

HYPERTENSION

High Blood Pressure (BP) is called hypertension. It tends to rise with age although the rate of increase seems to fall off beyond 65 years of age and may even be reversed in the oldest age groups.

SOCIAL WELFARE SCHEMES FOR ELDERLY

Bismark first introduced some sort of an old age pension in Germany in 1893. The social insurance programme came into operation in 1889. The basic law on social security was enacted in 1935 in USA and in 1922 in USSR. The Asian countries made a late start, the year of such enactment being 1941 in Japan and in 1951 in China. Steps have been introduced in several countries to provide free/ cheap medical care for the aged. Social welfare schemes are a strategy designed to redistribute power and resources. It is a group activity dedicated to increasing political and social consciousness, grounded in a belief in the essential need for self determination, and designed around a continuing cycle of reflection and action. The women in question usually live in third world countries or in areas of the industrialized world where similar conditions of deprivation prevail. They face many difficult circumstances, including cultural norms that often denigrate women and accord them very low status, lack of legal safeguards and rights to property, lack of political power or access to those with power. Women in general and older women in particular have lower status in the family and society thereby having restricted access to family or social support system. They continue to remain care providers until such time that they are physically active. *Widows are the worst affected by social customs.* Lack of education during early years deprive the older women from having access to latest information and knowledge intensifying their social isolation and widening the generation gap. In sum, older women are marginalized by the family, society and the Government and are not integrated in the development process. In a developing country like India, multigenerational living arrangements have been an integral part of the rural and urban scenario. However, due to migration, industrialization and modernization, several young adults prefer to live in nuclear families even in rural India. This shift in the trend leaves older women to fend for themselves particularly after their husband's death. It may be because they are no longer considered productive, useful and are considered to be interfering, a burden or old fashioned.

CONCLUSION

In India the situation is far more complex. An overwhelming number of people live in rural areas but migration from rural to urban areas is substantial, which creates problems for the ageing at both ends. If children go to urban areas leaving behind the aged in the rural areas, that creates one set of problems, and if the old are taken along, it creates another set of problems. The growth of the urban population and urban centres has been haphazard, and there are acute shortages of housing and other facilities. The health care system is woefully inadequate and there is hardly any specialized agency focusing on the old. There are no programmes available to train people taking care of the aged. In other words, the entire responsibility of taking care of the old continues to be with the traditional institution of the family.

REFERENCE

1. Archana Kaushik Panda (2005) “Elderly women in Mega polis” Concept publishing company New Delhi.
2. Bhatla, P.C. (1998). Terminal Care; An Analytical study. In P.C.Bhatla (ed) Aged Women; Coping with life (113-117). National Institute of Primary Health Care, New Delhi.
3. Carrol L.Estes and Associates (2001) “Social policy & Aging – A Critical perspective, Inc, Sage Publications.
4. Gore, (2004) “Aged in India” (J.P.Yadhav ed) Anmol Publications pvt Ltd, New Delhi.
5. Joseph, James (1991) Aged in India: Problems and personality, chugh Publications. Allahabad.
6. Joshi, Pratap, (2000) “Old Age care and Welfare Administration” Kanishka Publishers Distributors, New Delhi
7. Muttagi P.K. (1997) “Aging issues and old age care”-Book (A Global perspective), Classical publishing company, New Delhi.
8. Nayar, P.K.B (July 1999). Problems and Needs of Aged Widows; Some Neglected Dimensions. Paper presented at the International Conference on Women’s health- The Nations Gain, Singapore.
9. Pappathi .K (2007) “Ageing scientific perspective and social issues”, A.P.H.publishing company, New Delhi.

SOCIAL STRUCTURAL CONSTRAINTS IN EMPOWERMENT OF MARGINALIZED GROUPS – THE WOMEN DIMENSION

32 CHALLENGES OF MUSLIM WOMEN IN KERALA

Dr. K. Suriyan, Beena M.N.

INTRODUCTION

The origin of Islam can be traced back to 7th century in Saudi Arabia. Islam is the second largest religion in the world. The central theme of Islam is that there is only one god. Muslims are the followers of Islam. Historically the interpretation of Islam has been largely a male endeavour. Women played an important role in the transmission of Islam religion. Although the first convert to Islam was a women (Muhammad's fist wife, Khadijah).

CHALLENGES IN FAMILY LIFE

The Muslim women are one of the weakest social groups. The status of women was inferior to that of man and for the same reason she has less rights woman has been created for the comfort and enjoyment of man, men are made governors over women, hence it is the duty of women to obey their men. The duties of women are only to please their husband, to breed children and to do the drudgery of the home. There for they do not require any education. In Muslim society an educated women is look upon with suspicious and anger. The transition of the status of Muslim women has begun. In fact, it has begun since independence. This is because of the influence of communalism. This is because of the influence of communalism. Presently in changing society, the muslim women try hard to get rid of the burden of traditionalism and ritualism by way of getting themselves educated, participating in societal tasks, earning through occupying gainful employment and thus becoming self reliant.

CHALLENGES IN EDUCATION

Muslim women have calliber and understanding to interpret complex knowledge. Their capabilities and skills are same as of women in different societies. Muslim women have good mind and willingness to educate themselves. They are being deprived of poor education. Religion Islam has laid a lot of importance to education. Holy prophet (SHW) emphasized that both men and women should get education when the women will be educated; she will participate in the economic activity. Islam focuses a lot on education. Change never comes outside, but it starts with in you. Change the thinking and then implement new ideas. Muslim women find themselves doublely marginalized. The educational status of Muslim women is very low. In higher education representation of Muslim women is even worse than SC/ST women. The greatest obstacle to education for girls is the financial constraints of the parents. Socio-economic deprivation of families clearly makes it more difficult for girls to get education than for boys. Girls are often taken out of school the earliest.

SOCIAL AND CULTURAL CHALLENGES

The growing influence of numerous Islamic movements in different part of India today is a major force shaping prospects for Muslim women's mobilization for their rights some of these are actively involved in promoting girls education. Muslims are the most marginalized communities in the country and then the position of Muslim women was pathetic. The community of Muslims is not a monolith. There are women belonging to different social groups and different occupations. There is a tremendous variation in the status of various types of Muslim women. The caste system percolated the traditions in-marriages, child marriage, dowry system, veiling, polygamy, oral and oneside talaq-in significant status in women in patriarchal society, a small proportion of fields of education, employment, minimum role in decision making in the family economic dependency one will clearly notice the lower status of the women in Muslim communities. The image of the Muslim women in popular media and even academic discourse revolves around stereotypes. The scholar committee report find that poverty is extremely high in the Muslim society. Muslims fare only slightly better than SC/ST in this regard. In urban area, Muslims seem to be more deprived as compared to other socio-religious community. Muslim women's efforts for gender justice as distinct from gender equality, in that sameness in status and roles between genders. The term 'justice' is more fuid. Muslim women are routinely portrayed in the media s helpless creatures and a cruelly oppressed by their men. Muslim women must necessarily be part of a wider struggle against the overall marginatization of the Indian Muslim as whole.

ECONOMIC CHALLENGES

In 2001 census will show a sharp increase in the rate at which Muslims are demographically chatching up with majority. The disapproval of family planning is highest among Muslims. The practice of family planning methods in 1980 was lowest among Muslims. It will badly affect the economic security of Muslim families. The average Muslim is poorer and less educated. The poverty and low education both happen to lead to a higher birth rate. The population growth (28.74%, 1981-1191) in the Muslim majority distrit of Malappuram (with female literacy at 75.22% for higher them among other states) is more than twice as high as the average of Kerala (13.98). This will reveal a general reveal a general rule that at any give level of literacy and economic status Muslims will have a markedly higher birth rate.

RELIGIOUS CHALLENGES

Muslim women are suffering both from internal and external oppression. Muslim men practice what they themselves believe is Islamic and press their women and refuse to entertain any thought of change. May educated Muslim women thus start believing their can be no liberation with in Islam and seek their freedom through secular law. Men are thought to be bread winner and decision maker.

MARRIAGE PROVISIONS

The issues in the provisions for divorce in the Muslim personal law and that of the destitution of the Muslim divorce women have two aspects. Firstly, the provision for divorce is male dominated and one-sided as the provision for women to divorce her man in hardly practiced. The Muslim personal law explicitly results in the exploitation of Muslim women: and brings about in equalities in the status of Muslim women. The law provides no definite provisions for proper maintenance amount for the Muslim divorce women from her husband. The Muslim divorce women could demand a maintenance from her husband and in laws under the provision of the criminal procedure code 125. To overcome here issues and challenges forefronted the following points. The role of men and women are complimentary to each other especially in building as a society based on equity and justice. There is strong evidence in history that this complementarily and not competition has brought about creativity and cohesion in the human kind. Better awareness and understanding about Islamic teachings on the position and role of man and woman will help remove mis-conceptions about gender justice and empowerment men and women are not rivals but partners in the process of social progress and harmonious co-existence. The status of Muslim women is affected by the mis-interpretation of Islamic laws on women's rights. There is also the problem of influence of Indian patriarchal system on the role of women in society. There is notable increase in the violence against women especially those belonging to urban and rural poor and marginalized section of the population domestic violence has also become a matter of great concern.

EFFORTS TO UPLIFT THE STATUS OF MUSLIM WOMEN

Muslim women's NGOs have come together and formed 'Bharatiya Muslim Mahila Moriha'. They have decided to operate with in Islamic frame work on one hand, and Indian constitutional frame work on the other. It is held its first convention in Delhi in early December.

MEASURES OF EMPOWER MUSLIM WOMEN

To empower Muslim women, to reduce rate of child birth, to usher the religious and social reforms, there is great need to improve general economic condition which in turn to improve educational status of Muslim women and that in turn will bring in greater awareness for change. There is also great need for internal critique and at least educated Muslim women should attempt an honest criticism of condition of women in their community and consolidate efforts for change and reform. They also tend to be defensive and reactive. Time has certainly come to be proactive for improving Muslim women's status.

CONCLUSION

The Muslim women did have the rights and privileges in Islam. But their rights were interpreted by selfish patriarchs in male dominated societies for their own interest. Different variables liked education; age, family structure, income, duration of stay in town, exposure to mass media etc. have contributed significantly in changing the attitude of Muslim women towards the process of modernization and social change. A transition is taking place in the status of Muslim women due to her own individual and group efforts and the liberal democratic set-up around.

REFERENCES

Dr. Babasaheb T. Kazi – Muslim women: Challenges and Opportunities – 2006.

Prof. Z.M. Khan – Indian Muslims: Profile and Challenges – 2006.

Eric Zuellke – Changes in fertility rates among Muslims in India – 2010.

Rifu Menon, Zoya Hassan – Status of Muslim women in India – 2010.

Asgar Ali Engineer – Muslim women in Indian Society – 2007.

*]Associate Professor, Department of Sociology, Annamalai University, Annamalai nagar – 608 002.

** Ph.D. Research Scholar Department of Sociology, Annamalai University, Annamalai nagar – 608 002.

33 SOCIAL AND STRUCTURAL CONSTRAINTS IN THE EMPOWERMENT OF WOMEN IN INDIA

P.M. Anu Rama

INTRODUCTION

'One could judge the degree of civilization of a country by the social and political position of women'- Nehru. Women constitute nearly half of the world's population, perform two third of its working hours, earn one fourth of the world's income and one tenth of the world's property. This statistics itself portray the subordinated position of women. The women's subordinated existence could be amplified by measuring their disproportionate representation in the fields of education, health, employment, politics etc. Though India's progress in the female literacy rate, maternal mortality rate are somewhat better when compared with the past, it is necessary to realize that we still lag behind many underdeveloped nations. Our claim as largest democracy and our pride as a nation emphasizing gandhian values would all be futile if we fail to realize and recognize the need for empowerment of women. Though their representation is minimal, one cannot dny that the education and employment have put the women in an economically advantageous position. Marginalization, deprivation and discrimination faced by Indian women are serious threats to the values enshrined in the constitution. The social constraints faced by Indian women are realities, the structural constraints by and large play a vital role in the contemporary status of women. These constraints are to be analysed and atleast to be reduced, if not removed. Recognition of these constraints requires a greater commitment and responsibility from the nation. Women empowerment as well as their participation on the basis of equality in all spheres of society is fundamental to the advancement of human rights, social justice, and sustainable development.

EMPOWERMENT

Empowerment is seen as a process by which the one that is without power, gain greater control over their lives. This means control over material assets, intellectual resources and ideology. It involves power to, power with and power within. Some define empowerment as a process of awareness and conscientization, of capacity building leading to greater participation, effective decision-making power and control leading to transformative action. UNDP report in the year 1995 was devoted to women's empowerment and it declared that if human development is not engendered it is endangered. Equality, sustainability and empowerment were emphasized and the stress was, that women's emancipation does not depend on national income but is an engaged political process. History proves that societies where men and women have played equal roles have been more balanced and prospered faster than those which have been either patriarchal or matriarchal. Hence the role of women in shaping the future can never be underscored. All discriminations and deprivations always couple with gender bias. If caste is the root of conflicts, then dalit women are tortured and raped. If women are to find refuge in religion, they are placed in subordination and subjugation. Even in ethnic conflicts, war crimes, women undergo cruel torture and inhuman treatment, since women are viewed and victimized as the weaker targets.Women were denied voting rights, property rights, and education rights for a long time.

SOCIAL CONSTRAINTS IN INDIA

In India the gender construct is so rigid and it sometimes becomes shackles. Patriarchal Social structure accepted the secondary status given to women. Violence in all forms, against women reflects the inherent discrimination against women in our social structure. Violence and violation of rights may start even from birth. But for Indian women, it starts even before birth. Economic conditions and cultural ethos have forged an invisible combination that threatens even the women embryo. Female foeticide denies the right to be born and thereby ruling out the right to live. If female foeticide is the starting point, then with female infanticide, eve teasing, sexual harassments, domestic violence, dowry deaths, rape and trafficking, the list goes endless. Though Indian constitution guarantees right to equality, liberty and justice, Indian women need to go a long way to achieve these ideals. Poor women workers face constraints and oppression in their occupation, barriers of caste, class, gender which further marginalise their position both at home and workplace. Caste affiliation restricts their mobility, formulates cultural norms for their social behaviour; class membership limits their access to productive resources and makes them invisible in the economic sphere. The gender roles compel the poor woman to a low-productive occupation near the household, minimising her economic role as only an extension of her domestic chores. Women workers thus are undermined as workers defined as homemakers and forced to a status of invisibility even living in subsistence and marginal survival conditions. Their vital contribution to the productive process and to the nation's economy remains unnoticed. Therefore, the nation's planning process never makes the requisite allocation for the growth and development of the poor working women.

A recent report published by the Ministry of Statistics and Programme Implementation, Government of India in 2011 observes that India ranks 134 in 2009 among 178 countries in terms of the UNDP Human Development Index (HDI) and 114 in terms of Gender Development Index (GDI). Women work longer hours than men, and carry the major share of household and community work that is unpaid and invisible. In no State in India, do women and men earn equal wages in agriculture. Also, women generally works in the informal sector where wages are lower and they are not covered by labour laws.Women workers are also engaged in piecework and subcontracting at exploitative rates. The report further states that the majority of women in India go through their life in a state of nutritional stress i.e., they are anaemic and malnourished. Poverty, early marriage, malnutrition and lack of health care during pregnancy are the major reasons for both maternal and infant mortality. The average Indian woman bears her first child before she is 22 years old, and has little control over her own fertility and reproductive health. In rural India, almost 60 per cent of girls are married before they are 18. Nearly 60 per cent of married girls bear children before they are 19. Almost one third of all babies are born with low birth weight.

STRUCTURAL CONSTRAINTS IN REALITY

Every day, around the world, women and girls face persistent structural constraints that prevent them from fully enjoying their human rights and hamper their efforts to improve their lives as well as those of others around them. Rural women spend more time than urban women and men in reproductive and household work, including time spent obtaining water and fuel, caring for children and the sick, and processing food. This is because of poor rural infrastructure and services as well as culturally assigned roles that severely limit women's participation in employment opportunities Faced with a lack of services and infrastructure, rural women carry a great part of the burden of providing water and fuel for their households. In rural areas, there is often a greater prevalence of social and cultural barriers, labour requirements and distance "penalties," that keep girls out of school. In Pakistan, a half kilometre increase in the distance to school decreases girls' enrolment by 20 percent. Decreasing the distance to school raises girls' enrolment and attendance. Building local schools with basic facilities in rural communities can increase girls' enrolment. The cost of education is another barrier, particularly for rural poor families. Women make up over two-thirds of the world's 796 million people who are illiterate, and many of them live in rural areas. As far as literacy rate of women is concerned, according to the report of United Nations Organisation, except Africa, Only 5 nations are lagging behind India in female literacy- afghanisthan, Bhutan, Pakistan, Yemen, puuppu New

Guinea. Infant mortality rate is high in India after Afghanistan, Cambodia, Myanmar, Pakistan.We are one the Fast developing economies. But Inspite of two decades of development we are still an underdeveloped nation. Though nations like Nepal and Bangladesh are less developed economies, with low per capita income, their social factors far ahead of India. If our heavy population is cited as an excuse, then here is a comparison between India and china: Infant Mortality Rate in India in 1990 was 81 and in 2010 it was 48 whereas in China it was 38 in 990 and 16 in 2010.Female literacy rate(age 15 to 24) is 74% in India and 99% in China.Even in the comparison with china the political structure may be quoted as a reason. But democracy cannot be an excuse for malfunctioning or misappropriation of funds or to the shirking of responsibility in a country like India where we have largest democracy in the world inspite of all social problems. People still have faith in democracy. What is required in India is political will and commitment in translating the economic progress of India into social progress.

SUGGESTIONS

In the last few decades women literacy is slowly increasing but still gender coupled with caste, gender coupled with religion and gender in combination with poor economic status act as a stumbling block to attain education. Illiteracy among Indian women can have devastating consequences on many sectors. Many studies have shown that illiterate women have high level of fertility and mortality, poor nutritional status, low earning potential and little autonomy within the household. A women's lack of education has a negative impact on the health and well being of her children. Survey results have proved that infant mortality rate is inversely related to mother's educational level. Maternal mortality is also less among literate woman. Education gives courage, independence and empowerment to women. But the social tendency to view these values against the tradition still oppresses the Indian women. In a society where women receive less health care than men, where overwork is burdened on women, where crime against women are increasing, where the patriarchal traditions make the women powerless, where women are treated as secondary citizens, where women are treated as a property and commodity, education only can empower them. Though Indian constitution guarantees free primary school education for both boys and girls upto age14, India has the largest number of none school going working girls. This situation needs to be changed. As women receive greater education and training, their economic status and social status would rise. As women's economic power grows, it will be easier to overcome the tradition of "son preference" and thus put an end to the evil of dowry and hence female infanticide & foeticide will be drastically reduced.

CONCLUSION

A key to ensuring rural women's empowerment and eradicating poverty is to address inequitable gender power relations and persistent norms and beliefs that maintain gender-based violence and harmful traditional practices Efforts to promote women's empowerment need to do more than give individual women economic or political opportunities. They need to tackle deeper-rooted structural constraints that perpetuate inequalities. Changing attitudes and values is as important to bringing about women's empowerment as changing women's material circumstances and political opportunities. Until we address the structural constraints that lead to women being treated in ways that undermine their dignity, deny them respect and perpetuate their disempowerment, efforts to empower women stand a far better chance of achieving success. Policies, programmes and systems are to be established to ensure mainstreaming of women's perspectives in all developmental processes, as catalysts, participants and recipients. Wherever there are gaps in policies and programmes, women specific interventions need to be undertaken to bridge these. Women's issues and concerns as a result are to be specially addressed and reflected in all concerned laws, sectoral policies, plans and programmes of action.

REFERENCES:

1. A.S.Dasan and Bhamy V.Shenoy, ed, India A People Betrayed, Mysore, Goodwill Fellowship Academy, 1993.
2. Ghosh Jayanti., Impact of Globalisation on Working Women in Unorganised Sector, First Vimal Ranade Memorial Lecture, Akhbar: A Window on South Asia,No.4, December, 2001
3. Saffioti,H., Women in Class Society, New York, Monthly Review press, 2001
4. Sharma,S.L, Globalisation and Its Socio-Cultural Discontents in Development, Gender and Diaspora, Jaipur, Rawat Publications., 2003.
5. Women and Men in India,13th Issue, Ministry of Statistics and Programme Implementation, Government of India, 2011.

34 MICRO FINANCE IS A BOON FOR WOMEN EMPOWERMENT AND SUSTAINABLE DEVELOPMENT:

Dr.Subash Chandra Bose

Microfinance is emerging as a powerful instrument for poverty alleviation in the new economy. In India, Microfinance scene is dominated by Self Help Group (SHGs)-Bank Linkage Programme as a cost effective mechanism for providing financial services to the "Unreached Poor" which has been successful not only in meeting financial needs of the rural poor women but also strengthen collective self help capacities of the poor leading to their empowerment. Rapid progress in SHG formation has now turned into an empowerment movement among women across the country. Self-help groups (SHGs) play today a major role in poverty alleviation in rural India. A growing number of poor people (mostly women) in various parts of world are members of SHGs and actively engage in savings (in actual term Thrift) and credit (S/C), as well as in other activities (income generation, natural resources management, literacy, child care and nutrition, etc.). The S/C focus in the SHG is the most prominent element and offers a chance to create some control over capital. The SHG system has proven to be very relevant and effective in offering women the possibility to break gradually away from exploitation and isolation. Almost all major donor agencies support SHGs in one way or another and many success stories are available, describing how membership in a SHG changed the life of a particular individual or group for the better. Many NGOs are promoting the SHG mechanism and linking it to various other development interventions. Whereas there is ample evidence that the SHG approach is a very effective, efficient and relevant tool for organizing and empowering the poor, do arise with design, development and introduction of programmes to promote income generating activities (IGAs) that will generate sufficient, sustainable and regular income. The approach towards poverty alleviation is based on the formation of self-help groups at the grass root level. This brings about the necessity for organizing them in a group by which they set the benefit of collective perception, collective decision-making and collective implementation of programme for common benefits. This organization holds the power and provides strength and acts as an anti dote to the helplessness of the poor.

EMPOWERMENT: Empowerment in its broader sense refers to an individual's or group's increased "power". Whereas power means access to and control over material, intellectual and ideological resources (Batliwala, 1994). In a development context, it refers both to "internal" change within an individual's sense of self autonomy, and "external" change in social status and basic power relationships in society (MkNelly and McCord, 2001). Rowlands, (1995) and Mayoux's (2000) stated that the definition of empowerment relates more directly with power. Discussion on empowerment reflects that it is a process through which people gain control over the variables that hinder their choices, and holds them back from exercising their choices towards enhancing the quality of their life (Ravallion and Shaohua, 2001; Economic power means access to income, assets, food, markets and decision-making power in the economic activities. Social power means access to certain bases of individual production such as financial resources, information, knowledge, skills and participation in social organizations. Political power means the access of individual household members to the process by which decisions, particularly those that affect their own future, are made. Psychological power means the individual's sense of potency, which is demonstrated in self-confident behaviour and self esteem. In connection with these four kinds of power Kumar and Sreedhara, (2004) identified three main variables of empowerment as: general, economic and social empowerment. But on the other hand Fayyaz (2002) divided women's empowerment into three categories as: economic, social and political.

SHGS AND WOMEN EMPOWERMENT:

A multidimensional and interlinked process of change in power relations; ***Power within:*** enabling women to articulate their own aspirations and strategies for change; ***Power to:*** enabling women to develop the necessary skills and access the necessary resources to achieve their aspirations; ***Power with:*** enabling women to examine and articulate their collective interests, to organise to achieve them and to link with other women's and men's organisations for change; ***Power over:*** changing the underlying inequalities in power and resources, which constrain women's aspirations and their ability to achieve them. These power relations operate in different spheres of life (eg economic, social, and political) and at different levels (eg individual, household, community, market, institutional). Sewant and Dewan (1979) the impact of economic development in rural women particularly on their employment and reported that declining work participation, the widening made female wage deferential and substantial improvement in female literacy were associated with the force of development. Rose K.D (1980), the status of women is enhanced by employment. The power in family is very important aspects from the point of empowerment of women.

MICRO FINANCE AND EMPOWERMENT:

The term micro finance is of recent origin and is commonly used in addressing issues related to poverty alleviation, financial support to micro entrepreneurs, gender development etc. There is, however, no statutory definition of micro finance. The taskforce on supportive policy and Regulatory Framework for Microfinance has defined microfinance as "Provision of thrift, credit and other financial services and products of very small amounts to the poor in rural, semi-urban or urban areas for enabling them to raise their income levels and improve living standards". Concern with women's access to credit and assumptions about contributions to women's empowerment are not new. From the early 1970s women's movements in a number of countries became increasingly interested in the degree to which women were able to access poverty-focused credit programmes and credit cooperatives. In India organizations like Self- Employed Women's Association (SEWA) among others with origins and affiliations in the Indian labour and women's movements identified credit as a major constraint in their work with informal sector women workers. The problem of women's access to credit was given particular emphasis at the first International Women's Conference in Mexico in 1975 as part of the emerging awareness of the importance of women's productive role both for national economies, and for women's rights. This led to the setting up of the Women's World Banking network and production of manuals for women's credit provision. Other women's organizations world-wide set up credit and savings components both as a way of increasing women's incomes and bringing women together to address wider gender issues. From the mid-1980s there was a mushrooming of donor, government and NGO-sponsored credit programmes in the wake of the 1985 Nairobi women's conference (Mayoux, 1995a)

MICRO CREDIT AND EMPOWERMENT:

Micro-credit schemes are thought to be potent agents of social change in impoverished settings where women lack access to resources. In the modern world micro-credit, micro-finance and enterprise development are now seen as effective poverty alleviation mechanisms, especially for poor women. Zaman (2001) reported that micro-credit played valuable roles in reducing the vulnerability of the poor, through asset creation, income and consumption smoothing, provision of emergency assistance, and empowering and emboldening women by giving them control over assets and increased self-esteem and knowledge. Several recent assessment studies had also generally found positive impact in this connection (Simanowitz and Walker 2002; Lalitha & Nagarajan, 2002 and ESCAP, 2002). A primary function of offering women credit in this way is to enhance their economic status, that enables women to earn extra income through which they can gain greater financial autonomy. Within the SHG approach, empowerment is embedded at many levels. The impact of SHG on the various dimensions of women empowerment depends on the backwardness, prevailing cultural practices, and demographic profile of the area.

Micro Credit and Empowerment

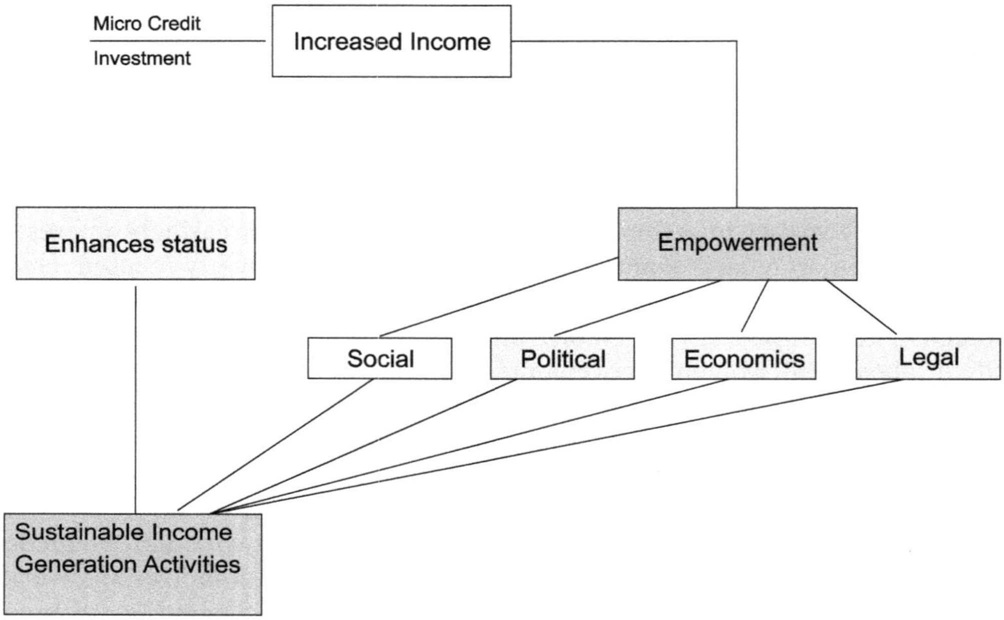

Analyzing Impact on Empowerment

Type of Indicator	Level at which impact on empowerment may be assessed
Economic	Increase in savings Increase in income Increase in assets Repayment rates & repeat loans Skill development
Social	Increase in self-confidence Change in attitude to women's role Improvement in communication skills and in social outlook
Political/Legal	Increase in participation in political process Removal of legal discrimination against women

ECONOMIC AND FINANCIAL EMPOWERMENT:

Economic empowerment is a necessary condition for enabling women to seek justice and equality. Without economic strength, women cannot be able to exercise their guaranteed rights. It is, therefore, necessary to seek participation of women as equal partners with men in all fields of work, equal access to all positions of employment, equal opportunities for work related training and full protection of women at work place. Economic empowerment of women, including reduction of female poverty require programmes that focus on identifying, developing and promoting alternative approaches to increase women's access to and control over the means of making a living on a sustainable and long term basis (Srivastava, 2001). It necessitates supporting their existing livelihood, widening choices and building capacity to take advantage of new economic opportunities. Its strategies to advocate that the government undertakes legislative measures to speed up women's participation in economic life, including the right of equality in property ownership and inheritance and access to credit, financial service and assistance in entrepreneurial development.

The basic requirements of women's empowerment strategy are;

(i) Introduction of special measures to increase the proportion of women involved in decision making;

(ii) Establishment of specific training programmes, especially for women living in extreme poverty, to improve their condition;

(iii) Creation of equal employment opportunities for educationally, technically and professionally qualified women by dismantling the forbidding walls of silent discrimination in their recruitment and related process;

(iv) Encouragement to women's entrepreneurship and other self-reliant activities, particularly in the informal sector;

(v) Integration of gender perspective into all economic structuring;

(vi) Elimination of all forms of discrimination in employment, including wages and breaking down of gender based occupational segregation;

(vii) Initiation of measures to improve working conditions of women in the informal sector, particularly, by encouraging them to organize so that they know their rights and are able to obtain necessary support to exercise them;

(viii) Mobilization of banking sector to increase lending on easier terms to women entrepreneurs and producers, especially in the rural areas; and

(ix) Activisation of enforcement machinery to ensure that the interest of women workers are protected, especially in the informal sector where large scale discrimination persists

The status of women is intimately connected with their economic position, which in turn depends on opportunities for women for participating in economic activities. Women's ability to save and access to credit would give them an economic role not only within the household but, may be, outside it as well. Type of Indicator Level at which impact on empowerment may be assessed Economic increase in savings increase in income increase in assets repayment rates & repeat loans skill development Social increase in self-confidence Change in attitude to women's role Improvement in communication skills and in social outlook Political/ Legal increase in participation in political process Removal of legal discrimination against women would improve employment opportunities for women and thus have a "trickle down and out" effect.

INCOME-GENERATING ACTIVITIES AND INCREASE IN INCOME:

In the Micro Credit Summit Preparatory Meeting (1995), Hillary Clinton said: "it is called micro, but its impact on people is macro. We have seen that it takes just a few dollars, as little as $10, to help a woman gain self-employment to keep her family out of poverty. It is not a hand out – it is a helping hand". It is widely accepted that the returns from the economic activity are used not only for women's welfare but also for the welfare of their children and the family and the community at large.

CONTRIBUTION OF IGA TO THE FAMILY INCOME:

The basic assumption underlying the provision of micro-credit is that the investment made with that credit would generate income, adequate to contribute significantly to family earnings. After joining a SHG, though the returns from IGAs taken up under it remain irregular and in many cases unstable, they would make a lot of difference to the lives of the poor. The increased incomes have helped to supplement the incomes to reduce the levels of poverty to a great extent in several families. Some members take up more than one activity (goat rearing and tailoring, for example) to make up the loss during off-seasons. It could be inferred that in case of 80 percent of the members with economic activities, their incomes from micro enterprises contributed considerably to the family incomes directly or indirectly.

AWARENESS AND CAPACITY BUILDING:

SHGs are generally found to be very effective in improving the levels of knowledge and skill of the rural folk through informal education and training programmes.

The success depends on the type of training, number of training sessions attended and also the quality of training. Political and legal empowerment: Women's participation is now recognised universally as a crucial element in augmenting the cost effectiveness of any plan for socio-economic progress. Social empowerment: This is a gradual process, which would take place only when the functioning of the group becomes sustainable. The extent of empowerment varies with the age of the group. Members in older groups show a high degree of social and psychological empowerment than their counterparts in infant groups.

SOCIAL AND POLITICAL EMPOWERMENT:

A combination of women's increased economic activity and control over income resulting from access to micro-finance with improved women's skills, mobility, access to knowledge and support networks. Status within the community is also enhanced. These changes are reinforced by group formation, leading to wider movements for social and political change. The financial self-sustainability paradigm and the poverty alleviation paradigm assume that social and political empowerment will occur without specific interventions to change gender relations at the household, community or macro-levels. By contrast, the feminist empowerment paradigm advocates explicit strategies for supporting women's ability to protect their individual and collective gender interests at the household, community and macro-levels. There have been positive changes in household and community perceptions of women's productive role, as well as changes at the individual level. In societies like Sudan and Bangladesh where women's role has been very circumscribed and women previously had little opportunity to meet women outside their immediate family there have sometimes been significant changes. It is likely that changes at the individual, household and community levels are interlinked and that individual women who gain respect in their households then act as role models for others leading to a wider process of change in community perceptions and male willingness to accept change (Lakshman, 1996).

Micro-finance has also been strategically used by some NGOs as an entry point for wider social and political mobilisation of women around gender issues. For example SEWA in India, CODEC in Bangladesh and CIPCRE in Cameroon, indicate the potential of micro-finance to form a basis for organization against other issues like domestic violence, male alcohol abuse and dowry. However there is no necessary link between women's individual economic empowerment and/or participation in micro-finance groups and social and political empowerment. These changes are not an automatic consequence of microfinance per se. As noted above, women's increased productive role has also often had it costs.

EMPOWERMENT PARADIGM:

Microfinance as an entry point for women's economic, social and political empowerment. Economic empowerment results in women's ability to influence or make decision, increased self confidence, better status and role in household etc. Micro finance is necessary to overcome exploitation, create confidence for economic self reliance of the rural poor, particularly among rural women who are mostly invisible in the social structure.

CONCLUSION:

It is concluded that micro finance and micro-credit programmes had the potential and powerful impact on women's empowerment. Although these were not always empowering all women, most women did experience some degree of empowerment because it was a complex process of change experienced by all individuals somewhat differently and varied from culture to culture. Micro-credit programmes had both positive and negative impacts on women's empowerment and eradication of poverty throughout the world. The positive aspects were enhancement in *Expanding women's mobility, Expanding women's control over labour, Expanding women's control over public resources, Expanding women's control over produce and income, Expanding women's participation in community institutions and decision making, Expanding women's exercise of political power,* women's ability to influence family affairs and decision making; increased self-confidence; improve their status, increased gender relations in the home and reduction in domestic violence; improve status within the community and accelerate economic empowerment. On the other hand negative impact of micro credit was of highly restrictive environment for women along with the increased workload and responsibilities as a result of their involvement in income generating activities other than their traditional responsibilities.

REFERENCES

1. Ackerley, B. (1995). Testing the Tools of Development: Credit Programmes , Loan Involvement and Women's Empowerment. World Development, 26(3), 56-68.

2. Fisher, Thomas and M.S. Sriram ed., 2002, Beyond Micro-credit: Putting Development Back into Microfinance, New Delhi: Vistaar Publications; Oxford: Oxfam.

3. Harper, Malcolm, 2002, "Promotion of Self Help Groups under the SHG Bank Linkage Program in India", Paper presented at the Seminar on SHG-bank Linkage Programme at New Delhi, November 25-26, 2002.

4. Kabeer N (2001),"Conflicts Over Credit: Re-evaluation the Empowerment Potential of Loans to Women in Rural Bangladesh": World Development,Vol.29,No.1.

5. Kamal, G.M., M.B. Rahman and AK.MA Ghani. 1992. Impact of credit program on reproductive behaviour of Grameen Bank's Women Beneficiaries, Associates for Community and Population Research, Dhaka.

6. Karl, M. 1995. Women and empowerment: Participation and decision making, Zed Books, London.

7. Khondkar, M. and D. Hulme. 2000. Micro-credit narratives and women's stories, IDPM Discussion Paper Series, Paper No. 62, Institute for Development Policy and Management, University of Manchester, UK. pp. 1-20.

8. Kumar, MAU. and T.N. Sreedhara. 2004. From passive participation to effective leadership: A study on the advances in women leadership in Dakshina Kannada, India. Sixth International Conference of International Society for Third Sector Research (ISTR) Ryerson University and York University Toronto, Canada. July 11-14. pp. 1-12.

9. Lalitha, N. and B.S. Nagarajan. 2002. Self-help groups in rural development. Dominant Publishers and Distributors, New Delhi, India.

10. Malhotra, A, S. Sidney and B. Carol. 2002. Measuring women's empowerment as a variable in international development. Paper commissioned by the Gender and Development Group of the World Bank. Washington, DC.

11. Mayoux, L. 1998a. Women's Empowerment and Micro-finance programmes: Approaches, Evidence and Ways Forward. The Open University Working Paper No 41.

35 DEVELOPMENT OF DISADVANTAGED WOMEN – INCLUSIVE PRACTICES FOR HEALTH PROMOTION

H. Usha

Each year as many as 27 million women give birth in India, of these, some 136,000die because of complications in their pregnancy and delivery. There are preventable deaths. In the year 2000 India pledged to bring down its Maternal Mortality rate (MMR) to 109 per 100,000 live births as part of its Millennium Development Goals. Although India has made slow progress in reducing maternal mortality, progress in Tamil Nadu has been rapid. The XI Five year plan (2008-12) included a goal of reducing M MR to under - 100 per 100,000 live births. Tamil Nadu ranked among the best states in India in terms of human development. This paper shows how Tamil Nadu has taken initiatives to improve maternal health services as part of inclusive practices for health promotion of Disadvantaged women leading to reduction in Maternal Mortality from 380 in 1993 to 90 in 2007. Tamil Nadu, the Southern - most state of India, comprises 31 administrative districts, 73 revenue divisions, 10 municipal corporations, 385 blocks and 17,244 villages. The purpose of this paper was to understand how Tamil Nadu has been able to reduce the MMR so rapidly. Maternal and neonatal health has been priorities for the Government of Tamil Nadu for over a decade. Tamil Nadu is the sixth most populous state of India. The state of Tamil Nadu has given more importance to the health programme in order to achieve the wholesome development of women. Various initiatives include establishment of maternal death registration and audit, establishment and certification of comprehensive emergency obstetric and new born – care centres, 24 hour x 7-day delivery services through posting of three staff nurses at the primary health centre level and attracting medical officers to rural areas through incentives in terms of reserved seats in postgraduate studies and others. This is supported by the better management capacity at the state and district levels through dedicated public-health officers.

Tamil Nadu's new initiative – Comprehensive Emergency obstetric and new born care centres (CEmONC) – could not only help India come closer to its 2015 Millennium Development Goal of reducing maternal mortality, it also sets an example for other states. CEmONC's are changing the face of mother and child care in public health institutions in the southern state. S.Vijayakumar, special secretary to the Tamil Nadu Health and Family Welfare Department and Project Director of Tamil Nadu Health Systems Project (TNHSP) has pointed out "Bridging the gaps in service delivery is crucial to saving the lives of mothers, newborns and the very young. You may set up a health centre in every village .... But if you cannot make the essential services easily accessible and available within the golden hour, all the efforts can go waste. A pregnant woman may be able to reach a primary Health Centre but the nurse may be missing, there may not be adequate blood availability, there may not be transport available to take her to a bigger hospital. These are the gaps that need to be urgently filled to save lives" These in fact are the critical service gaps CEmONC is fulfilling with efficiency. Sponsored by the World Bank CEmONC is an initiative of the TNHSP in its third phase of implementation. World Bank has funded then TNHSP for a five year period (2005 – 2010). The main objective of the project is to support the efforts of the Government for improving healthcare in the state. The TNHSP is supporting these CEmONC centres with additional buildings, equipment and manpower. Equipment costing three million dollar are being provided to the comprehensive CEmONC centres. Under this district and sub-district hospitals are now being staffed with experts like obstetricians, gynaecologists, paediatricans and general surgeons. Each CEmONC is equipped with an operation theatre, a blood bank and diagnostic laboratory. In addition, an emergency ambulance service is also just a phone call away. CEmONC services are presently available at 80 Government district hospitals and there are plans to many more sub-district hospitals and private health institutions in the rural areas. The TNHSP has also connected remote tribal villages to CEmONCs in the Kolli Hills, Kothagiri, Gudalur and other remote areas. Today, 1,539 PHCs across the state have 24x7 facilities to assist would be mothers. A special emergency ambulance service has been made available to take women to CEmONCs. Rural women in the state of Tamil Nadu in India can now reach a CEmONCs within a half an hour from their homes. Presently there are 400 vehicles in the service and additional 200 are being added. Apart from the emergency ambulance service, the on-site blood banks at CEmONC have proved vital in saving lives. It is a must in rural areas. Normally 60 percent of the pregnant women are anemic. A concerted effort has also been made to upgrade the skills of staff nurses by providing training in better birthing practices. In Tamil Nadu the PHCs reported 160,000 normal deliveries in 2008-2009, in 2009-2010this number rose to 250,000 indicating an increase in institutional deliveries. Now there is 99.5 percent institutional deliveries in the state of Tamil Nadu Maternal deaths were 74 for 161,000 live births in 2009-2010. Promotion of institutional deliveries was a conscious effort of the Government of Tamil Nadu along with improvement in the quality of care given to pregnant women during the antenatal, natal and post natal periods. As per the national norms, the Government deployed qualified Auxiliary Nurse Midwives (ANMs) Village Health Nurses (VHNs) at the rate of one for 5,000 rural people and one for 3,000 people in tribal areas. Tamil Nadu is one of the states in India, which follows the national norm strictly. The Government also strengthened the infrastructure of the sub centres for conducting antenatal care clinics, deliveries, and immunization services, treatments for minor ailments and for provision of spacing methods of contraception. The Directorate of Public Health and preventive medicine periodically conducted various skills – building training programmes.

The Government also strengthened primary health centres (PHCs) and community Health Centres. 229 of 1539 PHCs were upgraded as 30 bedded PHCs with five medical officers, three staff nurses, an ECG machine, laboratory equipment and other basic services: staff nurses in these facilities were trained to conduct normal deliveries independently and to refer women to a higher level without much delay by giving some first-aid in case of complications. A large proportion of the PHCs in Tamil Nadu have two medical officers posted in the facility, one of which is a female doctor. Posting of female doctors at the periphery is assumed to have played a major role in the increased use of health services by rural women. Poverty is one reason for high MMR and reducing poverty is listed as the first goal among the MDGs. For many welfare programmers' the State Government identifies families below the poverty line. Women of these families get those benefits. Besides the CEmONC, another state sponsored initiative for expectant women is the Muthulakshmin Reddy Maternity Benefit scheme under which a cash assistance of Rs.6,000 is given to pregnant women living below poverty line to compensate the wage loss during pregnancy and enable them to get nutritional food and give birth to healthier babies. Since 2006, Rs.10.64 billion has been spent to benefit more than 2 million women in the state. The scheme has been playing a vital role in promoting woman and child welfare. To identify the reasons behind maternal deaths, the state started compulsory audit of all maternal deaths. The system become fully established when the Government of Tamil Nadu issued an order in 2004, stating that all maternal deaths should be audited. It mandates that each maternal death be reported to the MCH commissioner within 24 hours of occurrence, irrespective of place of death – public facility or private nursing home or during the time of transit. Investigations of maternal deaths are carried out. Information on maternal death is obtained through telegram /fax/e-mail and medical officers perform the follow-up investigation within 15 days. This investigation tries to document specific circumstances that led to maternal death. The second part of the review of maternal death is carried out in the facility where the woman was treated and / or had died. The cause, treatment given and circumstances of deaths are investigated to see whether these deaths could have been avoided. The findings of these reviews are placed before the Medical audit committee on a monthly basis. Minutes of the committee meetings are placed before the District Reproductive and Child Health (RCH) Committee chaired by the District Collector, who also received relatives of the deceased who give their account of the events. Minutes of the review meetings are sent to the

MCH commissioner. Based on the reviews of maternal deaths and other evidence of how to reduce the MMR, the Government of Tamil Nadu has initiated various programmatic improvements.

Generally medical officers of PHCs do not stay at the PHC village and hence are not available for conducting deliveries during the night. To overcome this problem and to promote safe deliveries at the institutional level on a 24 hour basis the Government of Tamil Nadu piloted a scheme of appointing and contracting with three staff nurses (3 1/2 years trained with diploma in general nursing) to provide 24 hour delivery services in 90 PHCs in remote rural areas. They assist normal deliveries. They get incentives also for each delivery. These staff nurses will be absorbed into regular employment in the health department after 2-3 years of service in the PHC. To support the staff nurses, two cleaning staff members are posted on the basis of a consolidated salary and one driver is available round the clock to transport women with labour pain cases to a referral site in the case of complications during delivery at the PHC. The services of skilled birth attendants (SBAs) are made available especially in the villages. Tamil Nadu has taken the lead in this service. The state has filled 24,064 vacancies in the last four years including more than 7,000 hospital nurses and 3,000 hospital workers and 6,000 paramedics. Under the Tamil Nadu Health system project (TNHSP) funded by the World Bank in 2005, the state Government developed a public-private partnership with several NGOs to provide emergency transportation service in many districts. Under this, TNHSP provided equipped ambulance and running costs to the selected NGO. Other minor expenses are borne by these NGOs. In addition to the rural health programme, the state has given importance to the urban health programme to look after the health of urban people in the six metropolitan cities. The Chennai Municipal Corporation runs its own urban welfare clinic, which functions like a sub district hospital. The Government of Tamil Nadu has established a Tamil Nadu Medical Service Corporation (TNMSC) which became functional in Jan 1995. It is structured as a Government – owned company and registered under the Companies Act. It renders services like purchase, storage, and distribution of medicines for various government medical institutions in the state. It maintains the website of the Ministry of Health and Family Welfare where the public can interact with doctors and other medical staff through health-chats. Managing Director looks after the day-to-day administration of the corporation. No state other that Tamil Nadu has such an efficient and transparent medicine supply.

The state issues official orders for all activities carried out for improvement in maternal healthcare. The public are made aware through various advocacy campaigns. The state has undertaken various initiatives to reduce the MMR and hence, it has come down to 90 per 100,000 live births, one of the lowest in India. The state of Tamil Nadu provides better health services. The state is not only implementing various national health programmers' in maternal health but also adding its own innovations to improve the programmers'. This has resulted in lower maternal mortality rate. It can provide a good role model for various states in India that want to reduce maternal mortality. It is team effort that is slowly changing the picture in Tamil Nadu.

REFERENCES:

BOOKS

1. Socio Economic Backwardness in women - Anindita Mukherji and Neelam Verma, Ashish Publishing House, Delhi, 1987.
2. Women's Development problems and prospects - Shamim Aleem (ed) APH Publishing Corporation Delhi, 1996.

JOURNALS

1. Social Welfare - Volume 58. No.2 April 2011.
2. Social Welfare – Volume 57 No.4 July 2010.

WEBSITES

1. Government of Tamil Nadu official website (http.//www.tn.gov.in/government.htm, accessed on 27 November 2007).
2. Tamil Nadu.in.WIKIPEDIA(http.//en/Wikipedia.org wiki/Tamil Nadu Demographics and human riughts accessed on 27 november 2007).

36 IMPLICATIONS OF WOMEN EDUCATION IN RURAL AREAS: A FUTURISTIC APPROACH

A.Kubendran

INTRODUCTION

Women's education assumes significance from the point of view of enabling them to effectively participate in the developmental process as well as in changing their subjugated position in the society. However, the prevailing educational system is not found to be conducive for most women, especially those from a rural background. In India women in general and those particularly from the rural regions do not get a fair deal from the educational system. The low literacy level of 24.9 per cent among women in general and the still lower level of 16.3 per cent among rural women even after more than four decades of independence clearly indicate the biases of the educational system toward this section of the population. Education even at the basic level is found to be highly inaccessible to a large majority. Even when it is accessible to a few, it is not found to be conducive for their survival. As a result many drop out at the earliest stage itself. And for those who make it to the top, their attainment in general is found to be far from satisfactory owing chiefly to its discriminatory tendencies in terms of its form, content and practices. On the whole the educational system tends to perpetuate inequalities across gender and social groups instead of helping to bridge the gap between different groups.

WOMEN AND EDUCATION

Education is one of the most crucial instruments of empowerment of women. It is generally accepted that literacy and education helps in enlarging the capability of a person and it serves as the first defence in the struggle towards existence. According to notable economist Amartya Sen "Education may enhance a young women's decisional power in the family in many way. These include its effect on her social standing, her ability to be independent, her power to articulate, her knowledge of the outside world and her skill in influencing group decisions".

Empirically strong linkages have been established between education and improvements in levels of human wellbeing. Through education learning and skill formation, women can be much more productive over a period of time, which adequately contributes to the processes of economic expansion.

WOMEN OF RURAL INDIA

Women; the word sounds so powerful. Since eternity, women have played a role more important than men and that is no exaggeration. The world would not have been the same lovely adorable and liveable place without wonderful contribution so selflessly made by women. It has been said that, you teach a female and you build up a nation and truth can't be closer than that. Women have always carried the burden of being a wife, mother, sister all on their own and we need not to explain how magnificently they have carried this position. Men and women complement each other. If men were supposed to handle outside stuff then women were more responsible for internal affairs. The only difference in this notion is, today women are equally competent behind the veils and outside world. They are more confident and one can find them in every possible sphere of human's life. No male bastion is untouched by females and that's a wonderful sign of strides made by women. Urban women in India always had more advantages and opportunities than women residing in rural places. Better education, better economic resources, and more availability of required things for urban women and yet rural women have made rapid improvements despite lacking in basic facilities.

EMPOWERING RURAL WOMEN

Lack of formal education limits rural women's opportunities for independent action, including income generation, and adversely affects the health and development of children. It puts women and their families at greater risk of sickness and disease because of poor hygiene, inadequate nutrition and unsafe activities, including unprotected sex. If you've never been to school you can't count money, read notices and signs or write your name; and you cannot understand or help your children with their homework. You may well have low self esteem. Lack of schooling also means that women live in ignorance of their legal rights, including rights over their children and property, and their rights within marriage, and this in turn can lead to neglect, abuse, and too often domestic violence. It should be noted also that very few women in the region are in positions of authority in government, business or the professions, and there are no women Section or Paramount Chiefs (as there are in the south), so there are few role models for young girls to emulate. Equal access to education for women and girls will be ensured. Special measures will be taken to eliminate discrimination, universalize education, eradicate illiteracy, create a gender-sensitive educational system, increase enrolment and retention rates of girls and improve the quality of education to facilitate life-long learning as well as development of occupation/vocation/technical skills by women.

Reducing the gender gap in secondary and higher education would be a focus area. Sectoral time targets in existing policies will be achieved, with a special focus on girls and women, particularly those belonging to weaker sections including the Scheduled Castes/Scheduled Tribes/Other Backward Classes/Minorities. Gender sensitive curricula would be developed at all levels of educational system in order to address sex stereotyping as one of the causes of gender discrimination.

GENDER INEQUALITY

It is well known that both the structure of the Indian economy, education, polity and society and path of development pursued so far have served to sustain exuberant inequality among dimensions. One such important dimension is gender inequality.

Table 1 Gender Ratio in India, 1901-2001

SL.No	Year	Gender Ratio
1	1901	972
2	1951	946
3	1961	941
4	1971	930
5	1981	934
6	1991	927
7	2001	933

Source: Census of India 1991, General population, Part II B(1), Vol,1.

Sex ratio is a crucial indicator of development in a population. The analysis is mostly used in sociological analysis. India is an exceptional country where females are less in number as compared to males, up to the last century. Women are fewer than men in almost all the states in India except Kerala. However, the expectation of life for females crossed males in the recent years. In India discrimination against female sex is prevailing centuries together and the situation has detoriated over time.

The table: 1 reveals that this has declined to 927 in 1991, and increased slightly to 933 in 2001. This is a peculiar manifestation of continuing gender inequality and its accentuations are clearly observed in the Indian scenario.

Table: 2 Gender-wise Rural-Urban Literacy Rates (in percentage)

Particulars	1951	1991	2001
Male			
Rural	19.02	57.87	66.13
Urban	45.06	81.09	83.21
Total	24.95	64.13	70.85
Female			
Rural	4.87	30.62	44.36
Urban	22.33	64.05	69.34
Total	7.93	39.29	51.17

Source: Selected education statistics, Ministry of Human Resource Development, Dept.of Education, New Delhi, 1997 and Census Report, Govt.of India, New Delhi, 2001.

It can be seen from Table 2 that the rate of female literacy rate over a period of 50 years is more than six times and it is higher when compared to the rate of growth of male literacy during the same period. Similar trend can be noticed in rural as well as in urban areas. However, gender disparities prevalent in both rural and urban literacy, thus, gender disparities in literacy rates and sharp rural-urban divide continued to be the serious problems.

Impact of education programme on women

Due to the growth of educational level among the women there was a positive impact on women. Educated women could lead new social and economic life by acquiring and attaining in the following aspects.

Heightened social awareness

Education has heightened social awareness among women both for themselves as well as for their children. As women come out of their homes to become literates, they acquire a heightened sense of self-awareness and desire to gain knowledge of host of women's issues.

Increased social enrolment

The education has motivated and encouraged women to educate their children particularly girls by enrolling them in formal schools. An evaluation study of the literate women shows that the biggest achievement of the adult literacy programme has been its impact on girl's education.

Increase in self-confidence and personality development

The education made women to break the isolation which is socially structured into their lives, giving them a chance to meet other women and learn collectively rather than learn simply as individuals. The newly acquired skills have enhanced their ability to solve family problems and learn new skills. Women are communicating how they have started feeling more confident and knew they have learnt to function independently.

Gender equity

Education promoted gender equity and have sought to empower them as to decision-making about themselves, their families and their communities.

Status in the family

Education played a significant role in improving the status of women within their families... whereas traditionally, women have little say in the family decision-making, but participation in literacy programmes have begun to express their newly found self –belief in having say both within and without the family.

Women as entrepreneurs

It has opened several opportunities for educated women to step out of the households and involve themselves in some enterprise or a new vocation.

Household savings and access to credit

Educated women could enhance knowledge and skills for better management of expenditure and improving earning capacities and also begun to set-up thrift societies.

Health and hygiene

Education have helped them to spread knowledge about health care and nutrition, thereby enabling mothers to keep their family in better health and to care better for their children. Education also disseminated information for creating awareness about problems of early marriage, spacing and small family norms.

Future Directions:

The process of rethinking or revaluation of rural women's situation and roles has to begin from the earliest stages of education. In order to achieve that, however, efforts have also to be mounted to reorient higher stages of education. This calls for

a) Higher level of investment in research on rural women's issues;

b) Inclusion of rural women's issues as an integral part of the teaching curriculum in various disciplines;

c) Increasing rural women's participation in the implementation of these activities. The group believes that this will also facilitate needed reforms in education systems".

EMPOWERMENT APPROACHES

Several approaches are used for the Empowerment of poor and marginalized. The focus is both individual growth and development and macro-system change, using interventions at the individual, interpersonal, marginalisational and community levels. This multiple approach of empowerment is accomplished through interventions like self-help groups, which target individuals, groups, families and communities to become more effective in their social and educational environment.

EXISTING APPROACHES

The government has continuously stressed the importance of education and also adopted measures to increase literacy among women. The HRD Ministry has introduced strategies such as 'Operation Blackboard' free education for girls, Navodaya Vidyalayalaya, District Primary Education Programme (DPEP), Total Literacy campaign, and National Literacy Mission has also been introduced. The thrust of these strategies has been universalisation of education, where enrolment of all children in schools and re-enrolment of dropouts have been encouraged. Education for girls has been free up to the primary level and in some states up to higher levels, and UGC scholarship to women for higher education especially for rural women.

EDUCATION AND TRAINING

Although the gender disparity in the level of literacy both in urban and rural areas continues, the urge for women's literacy has taken the shape of a movement throughout the length and breadth of the country.

THE SARVA SIKSHA ABHIYAN

This aims to provide useful and quality elementary education to all children in the age group of 6-10 and bridge the gender and social category gaps at primary level by 2010. This mission should also be broken down into measurable goals to be achieved by the end of tenth plan in 2007. Focus should be on reducing the gender gap in secondary and higher education and on the special category groups including SCs/STs, OBCs and minorities of both urban and rural areas.

ADULT EDUCATION PROGRAMME

This strategy aims at increasing the educational infrastructure and thus the people's access to education. However social aspects such as socialization patterns, disregard for educated, if universalization of education is to be achieved.

OTHER APPROACHES

- There is a need to constitute village committees with the representatives of Panchayati Raj Institutions to pay the attention to increase the enrolment among the girls and reduce the dropout rate in their respective villages and to provide necessary amenities and facilities.
- Special emphasis has to be laid provide free cycles to the girls who go to high schools in case if it is from village.
- Government should provide scholarship to study beyond secondary school level free education has to be offered at least up to degree level.
- Steps should be initiated to utilise the services of faculty of social sciences in universities and NGOs for arranging seminars, workshops to sensitise and orient the women in different areas, to implement education programmes more effectively. Further , Universities should be entrusted with the responsibility to carryout research on women's education and to monitor and evaluate the programmes to know its impact in empowering women.
    - Removal of traditional disabilities suffered by different sections of population on various counts and elimination of exploitation in all forms, particularly the overt ones.
    - Government should advance the goal of equal access to education by taking measures to eliminate discrimination in education at all levels on the basis of gender , race, language, religion, national origin, age or disability, or any other form of discrimination and, as appropriate consider establishing procedures to address grievances. We need to improve the quality of education and provide equal opportunities for women and men in terms of access in order to ensure that women of all ages can acquire the knowledge, capacities, aptitudes, skills and ethical values needed to develop and to participate fully under equal conditions in the process of social , economic and political development.

- We need to create a gender-sensitive educational system in order to ensure equal educational and training opportunities and full and equal participation of women in educational administration and policy and decision-making
- Develop human rights programmes that incorporate the gender dimension at all levels of education, in particular by encouraging higher education institutions.

CONCLUSION

Structurally, pedagogically and philosophically educational institutions need to play a far more active role in the development of a new cultural ethos that can contribute to the realisation of the goals of comprehensive development of human material and this also requires that they internalise the concern for the equality of women and the enhancement of their role - in their curricula, method, organisation and research agenda ... the promotion of new knowledge about women and new perceptions of the role of women in development should be viewed as an instrument for educational and cultural development for the younger generation. If education is to become an active agent for ending gender inequality, it requires a new perspective, new methods and tools, and new knowledge - (a) about the centrality of women's role to correct the peasant iniquitous and destructive path of development; and (b) about the origin of women's subordination in society. It is the contention of this paper that the key to these two critical issues lie in the past and contemporary histories of rural women, to a far greater extent than in the experiences of their counterparts in urban areas, because one finds far clearer gender differentials in the assessment of problems, priorities, values and demands in rural than in urban areas in developing countries.

REFERENCES

1. M. D. Usha Devi "Research Perspective for Understanding Women's Education", Economic and Political Weekly, Vol. 27, No. 24/25 (Jun. 13-20, 1992), pp. 1279-1282.
2. *New Delhi Document on Women and Development* - Report of the Ministerial Level Conference of Non-aligned and other Developing Countries on Role of Women in Development, New Delhi, 1985, paragraphs 229 and 232.
3. Lakshmipathi Raju.M. Women Empowerment: Challenges and Strategies, Regal Publications,2007,New Delhi
4. Linga Murthy.N, Jyothi Rani, Towards gender equality, India's Experience, Serials Publication 2007, New Delhi,PP-105

5. Singh,O.R., "Education and Women Empowerment", social welfare, Vol.48 No.1, April 2001.

WEB SOURCE

http://www.indianchild.com/women_of_rural_india.htm

http://www.powerfulinformation.org/page.cfm?pageid=pi-empowerwomen

37 CONFLICT RESOLUTION MECHANISM AMONG WOMEN SHGS IN DINDIGUL DISTRICT

Dr. M. Mallammal, Ms. M. Priyadharishini

Indian villages are facing with problems related to poverty, illiteracy, lack of skills, social disparity, inequality, gender discrimination, health care etc. The intensities of the problems are different and vary from state to state. These problems cannot be tackled by individual or by state machineries alone rather they can be solved through group efforts such as mutual support and participation. In many parts of the world, effective ways to tackle poverty and to enable communities to improve the quality of the life through social mobilization of disadvantaged people are being experimented with. Keeping these ideas in mind, women self help groups have been started in villages and now they have become the vehicle of economic development and social change for the poor and marginalized. Women Self Help Groups (SHGs) have become a widespread, successful component of both rural and urban development in India. Women band together in groups and motivate each other to create new opportunities for income generation and interdependence on socio-economic development. A Self Help Group can be defined as a supportive, educational, change oriented and mutual aid group that addresses life problems or conditions commonly shared by all members who have no other resources other than their hard labour. These SHGs enable the poor to collectively identity priorities and tackle the problems they face in their socio-economic environment.

SELF HELP GROUP (SHG)

A Self-help Group (SHG) is a small voluntary association of poor people, predominantly from the same socio – economic background. They come together for the purpose of solving their common problems through self-help and mutual help. The SHG promotes small savings among its members. The savings are kept with a bank. This common fund is in the name of the SHG. Usually, the number of members in one SHG does not exceed twenty.[1]

ORIGIN OF SHGS IN INDIA

The origin of Self Help Group can be traced to the early 1980s.An experimental attempt was made in the neighbouring country of Bangladesh by Dr. Mohamed Yunus, former Head of the Department of Economics, Chittagong University to encourage landless and marginalized www.westgodavai.org women known as beggars to undertake petty trade with small loans given from his own pocket at the initial stage. This effort was turned into an effort of a grand success with its renovation approach to motivate the rural poor and disadvantaged women to inculcate banking habits through small savings and credit activities which at present has attained a global campaign as " Bangladesh Grameen Bank".[2] India has adopted the Bangladesh's model in a modified form. To alleviate the poverty and to empower the women, the micro-finance has emerged as a powerful instrument in the new economy. With availability of micro-finance, Self-Help Groups and credit management groups have also started in India. And thus the movement of SHG has spread out in India. In India, banks are the predominant agency for delivery of micro- credit. In 1970, llaben Bhat, founder member of 'SEWA' (Self-Employed Women's Association) in Ahmadabad, had developed a concept of 'women and micro-finance'. The Annapurana Mahila Mandal in Maharashtra and 'Working Women's Forum' in Tamilnadu and many National Banks for Agriculture and Rural Development (NABARD)-sponsored groups have followed the path lay down by 'SEWA'. 'SEWA' is a trade union of poor, self-employed women workers. Since 1987 'Mysore Resettlement and Development Agency' (MYRADA) has promoted Credit Management Groups (CMGs). CMGs are similar to self-help groups. In 1991-92 NABARD started promoting self-help groups on a large scale. And it was the real take-off point for the 'SHG movement'. In 1993, the Reserve Bank of India also allowed SHGs to open saving accounts in banks. Facility of availing bank services was a major boost to the movement.

The movement of SHG was nourished in the states of Gujarat, Maharashtra, Andhra Pradesh, Rajasthan, Tamilnadu and Kerala. Now nearly 560 banks like NABARD, Bank of Maharashtra, State Bank of India, Cooperative Banks, Regional rural banks, the Government institutions like Maharashtra Arthik Vikas Mahamandal(MAVM), District Rural Development Agency(DRDA), Municipal corporations and more than 3,024 NGOs are collectively and actively involved in the promotion of SHG movement.[3]

ORIGIN OF SHGS IN TAMIL NADU

In Tamil Nadu the SHGs were started in 1989 in Dharmapuri District. They were earlier Called as 'Madarsangams'. The Rural Development Department of Government and a large number of NGOs initiated the formation of these sangams.

2. Unpublished thesis work of Ms. A. AlarmelMangai, "A study on men and women self-help Group" (2008) P.12.

3. www.isrj.net

Of late, however, under the newly initiated Swarna Jayanthi Gram Swarozgar Yojana (SGSY) the District Rural Development Agencies of State Governments have initiated the formation of what are called Self Help Groups(SHGs),having specific features . At present 1.40 lakhs groups are functioning with 23.83 lakhs members. So far it has been utilized by the women members only. [4]

CONFLICT:

"Conflict is both destroyer and creator

Conflict is both changing and opportunity"

Conflict is defined as an incompatibility of goals or values between two or more parties in a relationship combined with attempts to control each other and antagonistic feeling towards each other.[5]

DEFINITIONS OF CONFLICT

According to Fink, conflict is defined as any "situation or process in which two or more social entities are linked by at least one form of antagonistic psychological relation or at least one form of antagonistic interaction".[6]

NEED FOR THE STUDY:

The emergence of SHGs in many villages in India is bringing about positive change in the attitude of women towards economic development and social relationship. A woman as a member of the self-help group has an important place and role in family and society as an individual and a member of the SHG. In her different capacities, she plays the role of a daughter, sister, wife and mother in her family and that of a responsible member in her group and in the village community. In this process she also experiences different kinds of conflicts within herself, in her family, within SHGs and the community that makes her feels uncomfortable and insecure. As a result she may fail to work efficiently both within the groups and in the community. Some of the specific conflicts noted in the field situation relate to the caste differences, methods or pattern of interactions during meetings and group activities and handling of government subsidies.

4. www.tamilnaduwomen.org

5. Fisher .R.J. "The Social psychology of intergroup and international conflict Resolution ,Newyork, "Springer – Verlrag,(1990).p20

6. William Baskaran, "Role of Academics in conflict Resolution Institute of Gandhian studies, Gopuri (2007) P.140.

Women SHGs have more chances of facing different kinds of conflicts because of their greater social, political and economic interaction. Conflict reduces unity among the members of the SHGs and in the village also. It may also prevent overall development of community and also makes them weaker in solving their common social and other deep-rooted problems. One can see the cumulative nature of the conflict in society. Once conflict begins it is difficult to stop it.Each aggressive act provokes a more intense and severe antagonism and leads to cyclic reaction. These conflicts can be solved effectively without affecting the goals of SHGs, when she herself understands the causes of conflict and the methods of dealing with them peacefully. Women have their own experiences in dealing with conflicts and resolving them at home, in society and in the village.

While these processes have been going on for many years, systematic efforts to study the causes, dynamics and the ways of dealing with the conflicts peacefully among SHGs for further development are very few and scattered.

OBJECTIVES OF THE STUDY:

- To study the socio-economic status of self help group's members.
- To identify various types and causes of conflicts and their dynamics among self-help groups.
- To study different types of conflict resolution mechanism existing among the SHGs and in their society.
- To examine the prevalent methods used by the SHGs towards managing the conflict in the present society.
- To explore new ways and methods of dealing with future conflicts.

RESEARCH DESIGN OF THE STUDY:

The present study adopted the analytical and descriptive methods. It has identified the reasons attributed towards conflicts within and among SHG members in the village.

SAMPLE SIZE:

In 10 panchayats 30 SHGs were selected purposively. Among 30 SHGs 150 members were selected, five members from each 30 SHGs, 2 of them were leaders and the remaining 3 of them as members in the group have been chosen as sample for the study.

SAMPLING TECHNIQUE:

In this research study the researcherers selected Purposive random sampling as a sampling technique

SOURCES OF THE STUDY:

The study was mainly based on both primary and secondary sources of data. Primary data had been collected from the members of SHGs by using interview schedule.

The Interview schedule consisted of five parts,

- Socio economic status of women self-help group members.
- Conflicts faced by women members in their family.
- Conflicts faced by women members in their groups.
- Conflicts faced by women members in their community
- Conflicts resolution mechanism among members in their families, groups, community.

The secondary data related to the study have been collected from studies already made on the subjects and from service providers, NGOs, Journals, reports, books, research articles and research organizations. The researchers used existing data as a base to explore further information related to this study.

RESULTS AND DISCUSSION

SOCIO ECONOMIC STATUS OF MEMBER IN THE SHGS

S.NO	PARTICULARS	NO.OF RESPONDENTS	PERCENTAGE
1	AGE GROUP		
	20-25	5	3.3
	26-30	32	21.3
	31-35	25	16.7
	36-40	46	30.7
	>40	42	28
2	RELIGION		
	Hindu	135	90
	Christian	15	10

S.NO	PARTICULARS	NO.OF RESPONDENTS	PERCENTAGE
3	COMMUNITY		
	SC	47	31.3
	BC	67	44.7
	MBC/DNC	36	24
4	EDUCATION		
	Illiterates	36	24
	Primary	58	38.7
	Higher Secondary	26	17.3
	Technical	27	18
		3	2
5	OCCUPATIONAL STATUS		
	Agriculture	7	4.7
	Daily wage	84	56
	Tailoring	12	8
	Weaving	2	1.3
	Mill worker	6	4
	Others	39	26
	Total	**150**	**100**

Source: Computed from the field data

Most of the respondents (30.7%) belonged to the age group of 36-40 years, 90% were Hindus, this might be due to a large segment of Hindu population in the Indian community. Majority of the respondents (44.7%) came under backward class, 38.7% were having primary level of education and 56% were working as daily wagers.

FAMILIAL CONFLICT AND THEIR RESOLUTION

S.NO	PARTICULARS	NO.OF RESPONDENTS	%
1	FAMILIAL CONFLICT		
	YES	118	78.7
	NO	32	21.3

S.NO	PARTICULARS	NO.OF RESPONDENTS	%
1	Fight between father and son	4	3.4
2	Fight between brothers	7	5.9
3	Fight between Husband and wife	76	64.4
4	Fight between mother-in-law and daughter-in-law	19	16.1
5	Fight among wives (in case of two wives)	10	8.5
S. NO.	**Methods**	**No. of Respondents**	**%**
1	Negotiation	33	28.0
2	Mediation	19	16.1
3	Consultations with aged persons	39	33.0
4	Threatening	7	5.9
5	Keep quiet	18	15.3
6	Others	2	1.7
	Total	**118**	**100.0**
Source: Computed from the field data			

Majority (78.7%) of the respondents were facing conflicts in their families.64.4% have faced conflicts between husband and wife in their families,33% of the respondents had solved their conflicts through consultations with aged and experienced people in their families (Traditional way).

CONFLICTS FACED BY WOMEN IN THEIR SHGs

S. NO.	Reasons	No. of Respondents	Percentage
1	Not attending meetings	37	24.7
2	Non-repayment of loans	61	40.7
3	Not participating important functions	17	11.3

S. NO.	Reasons	No. of Respondents	Percentage
4	Delay in paying savings	12	8.0
5	Unaware of condition of groups	6	4.0
6	Non-cooperation	11	7.3
7	Sharing Government subsidies	1	.7
8	Unaware of overdue, income and expenditure	2	1.3
9	Communication gap	2	1.3
10	Fulfilling Self needs	1	.7
	Total	**150**	**100.0**

Source: Computed from the field data

Among 150 members 40.7% of the respondents said that the main reason for the conflict within SHGs was non-repayment of loans 24.7 % of the respondents told that many of the members were irregular in attending meetings that lead to conflicts,11.3% of the respondents said that the members did not attend or cooperate with the group in organizing a

S. NO.	Impact of conflicts	No. of Respondents	Percentage
1	Not coming to groups	97	64.7
2	Discontinuing from group	15	10.0
3	Complaining the group with others	27	18.0
4	Joining with other group	1	0.7
5	Dividing friends from the group	2	1.3
6	Preventing relatives to join in the group	1	0.7
7	Establishing new group	7	4.7
	Total	**150**	**100.0**

Source: Computed from the field data

programme, 8% of the respondents told that delay in paying savings was another reason, 7.3% of the respondents told non-cooperation among the members in the group was the reason for the conflicts, 4% of the respondents were unaware of the conditions in their groups, 2.6% of the respondents explained that reason for the conflicts was unawareness about their account maintenance and 1.4% of the respondents told that at time of sharing subsidies, they could not think about the other situation and they wanted to fulfil their own needs. Majority (40.7%) of the respondents were of the opinion that the reason for conflicts with in SHGs was mainly due to non-repayment of loans.

IMPACT OF CONFLICTS IN SHGS

Among 150 members 64.7% of them said that if conflict arised among members in SHGs they would not come to groups properly, 18% of the respondents told that they would complain about the group performance to others, 10% of the respondents said that they would withdraw from the group, 4% of the respondents said they would establish new groups, 7% of the respondents said that they would join another group, 7% of them told that they would prevent their relatives to join in their groups and 1.3% of them told that they would divide their friends and form a fraction within a group.

From the above table it is inferred that 64.7% of the respondents reported that the disputants did not attend the group meetings due to the conflicts among the members of group.

S. NO.	Resolution Mechanism	No. of Respondents	Percentage
1	Negotiation	95	63.3
2	Mediation	28	18.7
3	Elder s' advice(Arbitration)	2	1.3
4	Terrorizing	6	4.0
5	Postponing	12	8.0
6	Withdraw	7	4.7
	Total	**150**	**100.0**

Source: Computed from the field data

Conflict Resolution mechanisms used among members in the group

Among 150 members 63.3% of them said that they solved their issues through mutual discussion (negotiation method), 18.7% of them said that they solved their conflicts through third parties like NGO, organizers, counselors etc. (Mediation method), 8% of the respondents said that they dealt with the problems by postponing the issues, 4.7% of them said that they handled their problems through avoidance (withdrawal approach), 4% of the respondents told that they tackled the problem by using threatening method and 1.3% of them said that they dealt with their conflicts by the advice of the senior members.

From the above table it can be concluded that majority of the respondents (63.3% of them) used to deal with their conflicts among members through negotiation method.

Types of problems faced by Women in society

S. NO	Social conflicts	No. of Respondents	Percentage
1	Domestic violence	36	24.0
2	Dowry	19	12.7
3	Sexual abuse	9	6.0
4	Female infanticide	4	2.7
5	Gossiping	60	40.0
6	Social insecurity	5	3.3
7	Divorces	13	8.7
8	Others	4	2.7
	Total	**150**	**100.0**

Source: Computed from the field data

Among 150 members, 40% of the respondents explained that gossiping was the major problem faced by women in the society, 24% of the respondents reported domestic violence caused by drunken husbands economic disparities etc.,12.7% of them, dowry problem was a big problem for women in their society, 8.7% of them, the problem of divorce due to misunderstanding and suspicion between husband and wife, 6% of them, sexual abuse faced by women in family and society (i.e) in working places, 2.7% of them, female infanticide and 3.3% of them, sexual discrimination within the families and society.

Table showing the respondents opinion about the solving of social problems through SHGs

S. NO.	Solving of Social problem	No. of respondents	Percentage
1	Dowry	11	7.3
2	Water problem	90	60.0
3	Caste problem	1	0.7
4	Abolition of alcohol	11	7.3
5	Female infanticide	5	3.3
6	Divorce	2	1.3
7	Making roads	20	13.3
8	Others	10	6.7
	Total	**150**	**100.0**

Source: Computed from the field data

The above table reveals SHGs involvement in solving of social issues. Among 150 members, 60% of them said that through SHG and its members the problem related to drinking water scarcity could be solved, 13.3% of them explained that SHGs could make roads in their villages, 7.3% of them said that the dowry problem and the problem of alcoholism could be solved and the remaining 5.7% of the respondents said that divorce cases could be solved through SHGs.

Table showing respondents' opinion about the mechanism of solving Social Problems

S.NO.	Methods	No.of Respondents	Percentage
1	Dialogue	12	8.0
2	Negotiation	56	37.3
3	Through rules and regulations	16	10.7
4	Solving through panchayat (Arbitration)	36	24.0
5	Joint agitation	23	15.3
6	Rally/Peace rally	1	0.7
7	Writing petition	6	4.0
	Total	**150**	**100**

Source: Computed from the field data

The above table explains the respondents' opinion about the methods used to solve the social problems. Among 150 members, 37.3% of them said through Negotiation, 24% of them through panchayat (Arbitration method),15.3% of them through joint agitation,10.7% of the respondents through legal measures,8% of them through Dialogue and the remaining 7% of them said by creating awareness about the issues through peace rallies.

MAJOR FINDINGS, SUGGESTIONS AND CONCLUSION

I.PROFILE OF THE SHGs

- Most of the respondents (50%) were members of SHGs for a period of 4-6 years.
- Majority (50%) of the groups conducted meetings monthly.
- (70%) of the respondents saved their income on monthly basis while they were meeting once in a month.
- Among 30 groups, 83.3% were affiliated with Mahalir Thittam.

- The NGO/Charitable Organization had a great influence as to form new groups. The contribution of friends, relatives, other media were also significant.
- Majority of the respondents (40.7%) felt that Self-Help groups are useful for women, because it is the main source through which their economic needs are being satisfied by getting loans with least interest.
- 40% of the respondents joined SHGs for economic development.

II. OPINION ABOUT CONFLICTS

The most of the respondents' (22.7%) opinion about conflict was misunderstanding-Misunderstanding between the members of their group and family which lead to conflict.

Majority of the respondents (58%) felt that conflicts arised among two or more individuals.

Majority of the respondents (56%) understood that the occurrence of conflicts in family and society was natural.

III. FAMILIAL CONFLICT FACED BY SHG MEMBERS

- Majority (78.6%) of the respondents were facing conflict in their families.
- Majority of the respondents (64.4%) have faced conflicts between husband and wife in their families.
- 33% of the respondents had solved their conflicts through consultation with aged and experienced people in their families (Traditional way).
- Among 150 members (54%) of the respondents faced conflicts in their families while going for meetings and to training programmes organized by SHGs.
- 53.1% of the respondents could not attend the meetings and training programmes due to their husbands' intervention to attend these programmes.

IV. CONFLICTS FACED BY WOMEN IN THEIR SHGs

- It is clear that majority of the SHGs (65.3%) f aced conflicts due to non-repayment of loans.
- Majority of the respondents (62.7%) explained that the conflicts arised occasionally in their SHGs.

- Majority of the respondents (40.7%) were of the opinion that the reason for conflicts within SHGs was mainly due to non-repayment of loans.
- Majority of the respondents (58%) found that frequent conflicts arised among the members in the groups irrespective of their position.
- 64.7% of the respondents reported that the disputants did not attend the group meetings due to the conflicts among the members of group.
- 63.3% of them used to deal with their conflicts among the members through negotiation method
- Among 150 members, 96% of the respondents had membership in one group and the remaining 4% of the respondents had membership in more than one group.
- Most of the respondents (80% of them) received loans from internal sources (among SHGs).
- Most of the respondents (45.5%) received loans amounting of more than Rs.20, 000/- from their group.
- Majority of the respondents (54.7%) received loans from the other institutions.
- Majority of the respondents (39%) got loans from other NGOs and (33%) of them received loans ranging from Rs.20, 000-30,000.
- Most of the respondents (35%) used loans for various expenditures of their families.
- 55.3% of the respondents faced problems in repaying the loans.
- Majority of the respondents (57.3%) cited that the economic problem was the main reason for the non-repayment of loans.
- (37.3%) of them used dialogue method (Persuasion) for resolving the conflicts arised due to non-payment of loans.
- 41% of the respondents told that they faced conflicts with other SHGs due to differences of opinion.
- Majority of them (60.7%) solved their personal problems through SHGs.
- Most of the respondents (44%) expressed that their economic problems were solved through SHGs.

V. CONFLICTS FACED BY WOMEN IN THEIR SOCIETIES

- 40% of women felt gossiping as the major problem in the society.
- 60% of the respondents opined that the problem related to water scarcity could be solved through SHGs.
- 37.3% of the respondents solved the social conflicts and problems through negotiation methods
- Among 150 members, 60.7% of the respondents stated that legal aspects (i.e.) courts/police are could not solve conflicts and 39.3% of them said that legal aspect of resolving the conflict was the right way to solve conflicts.
- Among 59 respondents who opined legal measures, 74.6% of them said that they are based on law.
- Among 91 respondents who were not in favour of legal measures, majority of them (35.3%) opined that the legal system was prejudicial towards rich.

SUGGESTIONS

The following suggestions are offered on the basis of the findings for improvement of self-help groups through conflict management.

- Everyone should co-operate with each other.
- Timely loan repayment and it should be in proper manner.
- Clear /open management should be practised in the groups.
- Group members should be transparent to each other.
- There should be co-operation with the head of group.
- Rules and regulations must be followed and maintained in a clear manner.
- Group activities should be in unity.
- SHGs should take inititativeness in the group entrepreneurship activities.
- Everyone should be an active partner in all the aspects of their groups work (i.e. social, economic, and political).
- Savings and their debts should be repaid at the right time.
- Group meetings should be held in good manner.
- They should adjust themselves to all circumstances of the group.

- Negotiation is the best way to resolve conflicts.
- Understanding any situation makes the group a healthy one.
- Proper maintenance of the accounts and auditing records.
- There should not be any caste /religion /race differentiation between the group members.
- The members of the group should try to understand the concepts expressed by group leader.
- The loan should be released according to the repayment capacity of the receiver.
- Identifying the needy people and help them accordingly.
- The account records should be clear and everyone should be aware about it.
- The members should make their own efforts in bringing up their group.
- They should be helpful in bringing growth and development for the group and try to avoid unnecessary debates among them.

CONCLUSION:

The study analysed the various problems faced by SHG members in the families, within the SHGs, and in the society. The majority of the problems were solved by the members by applying the different conflict resolution techniques like dialogue, negotiation, getting opinion/ suggestions from the elders etc. If proper training is given to them by organizing workshops, training programmes etc., they could solve all their problems. When conflicts get reduced they could do better work and thereby it will bring good economic development in the villages.

REFERANCES

BOOKS

1. Aloysius Parkas Fernandez, "Alternate management system for savings and credit-of the Rural Poor", SRS Publications, Bangalore, 1998.
2. Karmakar, K.G., "Rural Credit and Self-help groups: "Micro Finance Needs and Concepts in India", Sage Publications, New Delhi, 1999.
3. N.Lalitha, "Micro Finance and Rural Development", Gandhigram Rural Institute, Gandhigram (2005), P.25

4. Pratima Chaudhry,"Conflict Management and Organizational health", Vista international Publishing house, Delhi, 2006

5. Rajendran, K.K., "Self Help Groups and Co-operative Banks", Prentice Hall of India Pvt. Ltd., New Delhi, 1998.

6. Stephen P.Rabbins "Organizational Behaviour" 9th edition, Prentice Publication, 2003, pp.383 – 385.

REPORTS

1. All India Debt and Investment Survey – 1991.

2. Census Commissioner of India, Indian Census 2001.

3. NABARD, Annual Report 1990-91.

4. NABARD, "Financing of Self Help Group -A Reference", 1998.

5. Tamil Nadu Corporation for Development of Women Ltd., – Credit Guidelines for SHGs, Handbook -2007.

6. Unpublished Records of Mahalir Thittam Office, Tirunelveli – 2008.

38 INCLUSIVE GROWTH OF WOMEN UNDER MGNREGS

M.Suresh, Dr. R.Subburaman

INTRODUCTION

Creation of employment opportunity has always been one of the important objectives of sustainable development in Indian planning. Because of higher growth of population and the volume of unemployment from one plan period to another, the tenth five year plan (2002-2007) aimed at bringing employment into longer focus with the goal of reducing unemployment and its associated problems. It is for this purpose, the National Rural Employment Guarantee Scheme (NREGS) was launched in 2005. The basic objective of the scheme is to enhance livelihood security in rural areas by providing at least 100 days of guaranteed wage employment in a financial year to every household whose women voluntaries to do unskilled manual work. It was renamed as Mahatma Gandhi Rural Employment Guarantee Scheme on 2nd October 2009. The MGNREGS made provisions such as equal work to both men and women in gender biased society. The question arises whether the "Gender Justice" given by Act 'equal wage for equal work' is accepted by the society? What is the gender perception among both men and women working under the MGNREG scheme regarding the provision? Does it enable the rural people to have better livelihood condition? Hence, the proposed study aims at exploring the above provision of the act in a gender perspective from the view point of MGNREG scheme. Priority was given to women and in such a way that at least one third of the beneficiaries shall be women (Schedule 2(6) of the Act).

STATEMENT OF THE PROBLEM

The concept MGNREGS in the present study refers to Mahatma Gandhi National Rural Employment Guarantee Schemes being implemented in the entire district by government of India through Panchayat Raj Institution. The concept perception in study refers to the view point of the job card holders who will be selected for the study regarding the role of MGNREGS in the matters relating empowering of rural people, rural-urban migration and social equity. Women have continued to speak out for policies and practices that threaten them and there well-being. They continue to fight for improved living standards and protection. In almost all countries, women are disproportionately represented among the poor, and studies have found that the poor, in urban and rural areas of rich and poor countries, bear the greatest burden, in almost all countries, women have the primary responsibility for nutrition, child care and household management. In most developing countries, women play a major role as farmers, animal tenders, and water and fuel collectors. Despite their roles, women are not adequately represented in the decision-making.

OBJECTIVES OF THE STUDY

1. To study the overall performance of Women workers under the MGNREGS
2. To examine the perception of the beneficiaries regarding the role of MGNREGS in empowering rural women, and fostering social equity,
3. To study the gender equity and empowerment through women participation,

IMPLEMENTATION OF MGNREGA

This scheme was implemented in phased manner. It was introduced in 200 most backward districts of the Country in phase I (February 2006). It was implemented in 130 districts in phase II during 2007-08. The scheme was further extended to the remaining 285 rural districts of India from April 1, 2008 in phase III in order to bring the whole nation under its safety net. This programme was implemented on first in Andhra Pradesh. The MGNREGS was covered totally 615 district in the year of 2008-09.

Map 1.1 The MGNREGS: Implementing Districts

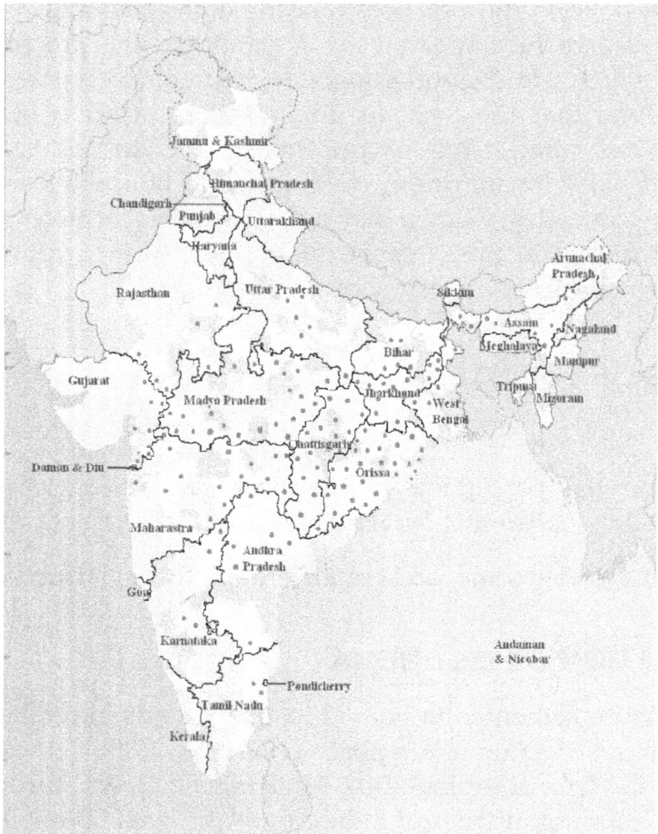

Source: Ministry of Rural Development, Government of India.Total District: 615 Districts

Phase I MGNREGA (200Distrcts) (commenced on 2.02.2006)

Phase II MGNREGA (130 Districts) (extended on 1.4.2007)

Phase III MGNREGA (285 Districts) (notified on 28.9.2007)

• Most Backward Districts

Table: 1 Performance of The Mahatma Gandhi NREGA (National Overview)

Performance Indicators	(FY 2006-07) 200 Districts	(FY 2007-08) 330 Districts	(FY 2008-09) 615 Districts	(FY 2009- 10) 619 Districts
Employment Generated:				
Employment provided to households	2.10 Crore	3.39 Crore	4.51 Crore	5.26 Crore
Person-Days (In Crore):				
Total	90.52	143.59	216.01	283.59
SCs	22.98 (25.36%)	39.36 (27.43%)	63.39 (29.28%)	86.45 (30.49%)
STs	32.98 (36.43%)	42.07 (29.29%)	54.78 (25.45%)	58.74(20.71%)
Others	34.56 (38.21%)	62.16 (43.28%)	97.84 (45.27%)	138.40(48.80%)
Women	36.79 (40.64%)	61.15 (42.58%)	103.41 (47.87%)	136.40 (48.09%)

The above table: 1 to examine that the Employment generated under MGNREGS in National level in every financial year. 2.10 crore households employment provide for only 200 back ward districts. Further to increasing for every year, followed by 3.39 crore in 2007-08, 4.51 crore in 2008-09, and 5.26 crore in 2009-10. Finally to cowered for entire country, totally 619 districts cowered in the financial year 2009-10. 5.26 crore employment was provide for households the financial year 2009-10.

PERSON DAYS

Distribution of the job card holders based on community like SCs, STs, and Others. The majority of the job card holders 38.21 percent belong to others community in the year of 2006-07, followed by 36.43 percent for STs and 25.36 percent for SCs was getting employment for during the year 2006-07. In the year 2006-07 total person days was 90.52 cror for only 200 districts. Further to increased for ever year followed by 143.49 cror in 2007-08, 216.32 cror and 2008-09. 283.59 cror cror person days of employment was generated during the financial year 2009-10. The participation level of SCs and Other community was to increasing for ever year, followed by participation of SCs was the year of 2007-10, 25.36%, 27.43%, and 29.28 precent. Others community participation was during the year of 2006-10, 38.21%, 43.28%, 45.27%, and 48.80 percent. The STs Participation level also decreased for every year 2006-10, 36.43%, 29.29%, 25.45%, and 20.72 percent.

WOMEN PARTICIPATION:

The NREGS made provisions such as equal work to both men and women in gender biased society. Only 40 percent of women were get employment in the year 2006-07, followed by women participation level during the year 2007-10, 43%, 48%, and 48 percent. Women participation was increasing for ever year to reason about due to more than wage. Totally high level of women gets employment 48 percent in the year of 2009-10. The average person days of household only 43 days in the year 2006-07, followed by in the year 2007-10, 42 days, 48 days, and 54 days in the financial year 2009-10.

OVERALL PERFORMANCES OF WOMEN WORKER UNDER THE MGNREGS

Table: 2

S.No	Financial year	Women persons Days (in crore)
1	2006-07	36.79 (40.64%)
2	2007-08)	61.15 (42.58%)
3	2008-09	103.41 (47.87%)
4	2009- 10	136.40 (48.09%)

Table 2 the national level of women participation under the MGNREGS the women's worker force participation was 40.64 percent in 2006-07, and has further increased to 48.09 percent during 2009-10. The participation of women level to increased for every year. The majority of the women worker got employment under the MGNREGS for every year. The MGNREGS was motivated for rural Economy and women empowerment.

Chart: 1 Overall performances of Women worker under the MGNREGS

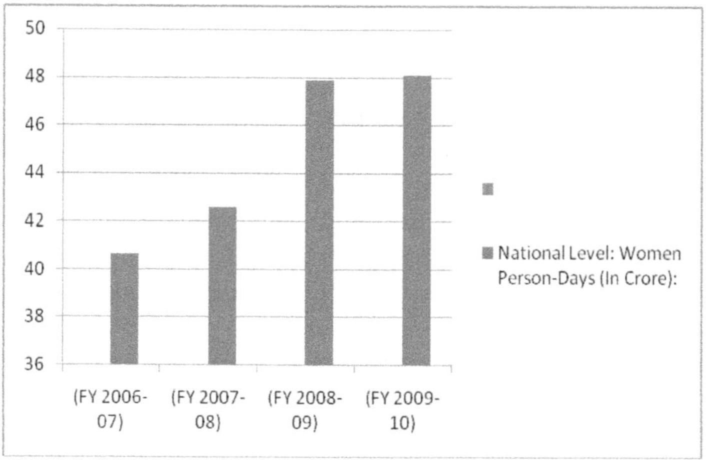

PERFORMANCES OF THE MGNREGS IN TAMIL NADU STATE

Table: 3

Performance Indicators	(FY 2006-07) 06 Districts	(FY 2007-08) 10 Districts	(FY 2008-09) 31 Districts	(FY 2009-10) 31 Districts
Employment Generated:				
Employment provided to household (lakh)	9.78849	13.54095	33.45648	51,94265
Person-Days (In Lakh):				
Total	**573.322**	**716.159**	**1203.5933**	**2226.54993**
SCs	344.853 (60.14)	430.629 (60.03)	725.3933 (60.26)	690.48232 (31.1)
STs	12.416 (2.18)	12.966 (1.82)	20.9269 (1.75)	30.0331 (1.3)
Others	216.053 (37.68)	272.564 (38.05)	457.2731 (37.99)	1506.03450 (67.6)

The above table 2.4 to examine that Employment generated under MGNREGS in Tamil Nadu in every financial year. The employment provide for 9.78849 lakh households only 6 back ward districts. Further, employment provide to household to increasing for every year, followed by during the financial year 2007- 2010, 13.54095 lakh, 33.45648 lakh, and 51.94265 lakh in 2009-10. The TNMGNREGS was cowered for entire state during the year 2008-09. 51,94,265 lakh employments was providing for households during the year of 2009-10.

PERSON DAYS

Distribution of the job card holders based on community like SCs, STs, and Others. The majority of the job card holders 60.14 percent belongs to SCs community in the year of 2006-07, and followed by 37.68 percent for Others community and 2.18 percent for STs was getting employment for during the year 2006-07. In the year 2006-07 total person days was 573.322 lakh for only 6 districts, further to increased for ever year followed by 716.159 lakh in 2007-08, and 1203.5933 lakh in 2008-09. 2226.54993 lakh person days of employment was generated during the financial year 2009-10. The participation level of others community was to increasing for ever year, followed by others participation was the year of 2007-10 38.05%, 37.99%, and 67.6 precent. The SCs and STs Participation level also decreased for every year. The level of SCs participation was during the year 2006-10, 60.14%, 60.03%, 60.26%, and 31.1 percent. The level of STs Participation was during the year 2006-10, 2.18%, 1.82%, 1.75%, and 1.3 percent only.

PERFORMANCE OF WOMEN UNDER THE MGNREGA IN TAMIL NADU

Table:4

S.no	Financial year	Women participation
1	(FY 2006-07)	469.793 (81.94%)
2	(FY 2007-08)	578.563 (80.78%)
3	(FY 2008-09)	958.8721 (80%)
4	FY 2009-10	1752.08644 (79%)

The table: 4 to examine that performance of women under the MGNREGS in Tamil Nadu. 81.94 percent of women were get employment in the year 2006-07, followed by level of women participation during the year 2007-10, 80.78 %, 80%, and 79 percent,. Women participation was around 80 percent the reason about more than wage. The majority of the 80.78 percent women were participated during the financial year 2007-08.

Chart: 2 Performance of women under the MGNREGA in Tamil Nadu

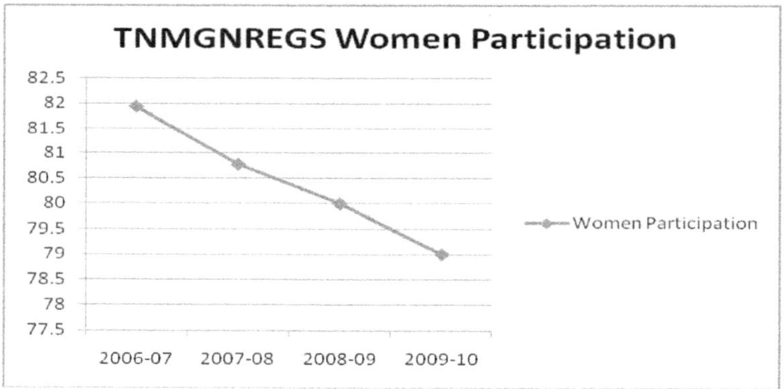

COUNGULSION

The MGNREGA has provided income earning opportunities for women and it helped them in taking care of children's education, enabled them to meet the day-to-day household expenses and facilitated them to save money. This programme also helped to avoid hunger, less dependence on male. The earning brings improved food security, treat illness. The government that directly touches lives of the poor and promotes inclusive growth of rural women. This scheme succeeded in providing wage employment to the unskilled workers in the rural areas, particularly to women, with least concern to promotion of social benefit. This scheme was reached poor and women through development of awareness. The economic condition of the women beneficiaries improved after joining MGNREGS.

REFERENCE:

1. Mahatma Gandhi National Rural employment Guarantee Act, Performance Review Committee June 1, 2011, Ministry of Rural Development, Government of India.

2. Performance of NREGS in kerala state a study, United Nations Development Programme (UNDP) New Delhi. December 2009.

3. Report of the Working Group on MGNREGA towards Formulation of the 12th Five Year Plan October 2011

4. Annual Report 2009-2010, Ministry of Rural Development, Government of India.

5. Discussion Paper: Rights-based Legal Guarantee as Development Police: The Mahatma Gandhi National Rural employment Guarantee Act, October 2010

6. National rural Employment guarantee Act 2005 (nrega), Report of the second year April 2006 – march 2007, Ministry of Rural Development, Government of India, New Delhi.

7. Mahatma Gandhi national rural Employment guarantee act 2005. Report to the people 2nd feb. 2006 – 2nd feb. 2010

8. MGNREGS Year Report 2007-2008

9. MGNREGS Year Report 2008-2009

10. MGNREGS Year Report 2009-2010

11. MGNREGS Year Report 2010-2011

12. WWW.NREGA.COM.

39 SELF- HELP GROUPS AS INSTRUMENT OF WOMEN EMPOWERMENT

Dr.V.Frank Rathnakumar, Mr. K.Iyappan

INTRODUCTION

Women are the most oppressed and neglected group in all sectors of society, especially in economic, social, political, education, health care, nutrition and legal. They represent 50 percent of the population but own just 30 percent of the wealth of the world. As women are oppressed in all spheres of life, they need to be empowered in all walks of life. Active participation in social, economic and political spheres would help in enhancing process of decision-making, empowerment and it will also give women the desired self respect and social dignity through empowerment. Though empowering poor people, especially women has become the stated goal of many development interventions, experience has shown that many of the poverty alleviation programmes through organized credit channels, have not achieved the required success. The self help group concept introduced as a means of empowering women in rural areas has gained wider acceptance. This paper aims to highlight the role of SHGs in promoting the welfare of women in Rural Areas.

EMPOWERMENT OF WOMEN

The term empowerment is frequently heard today, whether in the media or in the class room. It is clearly connected to the word "power". Simply speaking empowerment is deprived from the word 'empower' meaning to give or to acquire power or to increase power. Thus the word empowerment also implies a change in the equation or level of power. It can therefore be viewed as both a process as well as a result of social change. Srilata Batiwala,. a well known activist has defined women's empowerment as the "process by which women gain greater control over material and intellectual resources and the gender based discrimination against women in all institutions and structures of society" women empowerment is the process by which women negotiate a more equitable distribution of power, a greater space in the initial decision making process in the home, in the community and in economic and political life.

Empowerment is a long, complex process. Margaret (1949) described three levels to empowerment. The first is the awakening of individual consciousness; the second is development of collective consciousness, and the third and final, is at the level of translating collective skills and resource into political and legal action. Ultimately leading to women's empowerment. This is a process of social transformation, where women gain control of decision-making over issues that affect their lives, in order to have access to and control over resources and benefits. Thus, through empowerment, women become an important and active ingredient of social development. Empowerment means collective action by those affected to over come the obstacles of structural inequality which have previously put them in a disadvantaged group all over the world.

PROBLEMS FACED BY WOMEN EMPOWERMENT

Women empowerment can be described as the provision of adequate opportunities to women to develop their potentials and contribute to the development of the nation in particular and to the world in general. The disparities between women and men in terms of political, social, educational and economic achievements cannot be divorced from some problems which hinder parity between the two groups. These problems are:

a) Illiteracy

Cultures and sub-cultures in India give preference to male children as they are usually regarded as the heris or the pillars of the family. Female children are usually less privileged and consequently not given adequate opportunity to acquire education and formal training.

b) Sex Stereotype

During the period of socialization females are usually trained to believe that there are different roles for males and females as well as the superiority of males over the females. Generally, adults discourage competition between females and males and the two groups are thus exposed to different roles.

c) Religious beliefs

The leadership of different religions in India have different views as regards the position of women in wordily affairs. Some religious leaders and their adherents strongly believe that women should only be seen but not heard. Some view men as superior to women while few others see them as equals. The differences in beliefs adversely affect the way women are treated and the opportunities provided to them.

d) Discriminatory attitudes of males

Men have been in control of political, economic as well as social spheres of life for many years.

They have been able to utilize the opportunity to their advantage and this does not give women equal opportunities.

e) Low participation of women in politics

The level of women's participation in politics is still very low in India. The reason is may be related to their lack of rights and awareness in education and economic base, it has adverse and effects on women's struggle for emancipation.

f) Poor economic base

Most of women in India are poor. This situation is related to their low level of educational attainment. Poverty is reflected in almost all aspects of an average Indian women's life.

DIMENSIONS OF WOMEN'S EMPOWERMENT

The empowerment question needs to be addressed within the larger context of development we need to ask why empowerment? And while empowerment is not synonymous with development, the process of empowerment implies broader, systematic change in the way society is structured. And in that sense, empowerment is a necessary part and parcel of any genuine development effort that seeks to ultimately empower the disempowered. At the overall level women's empowerment aims at changing the balance of power between the sexes so as to create a more equitable distribution of power in society. However, when we examine this overall process of women's empowerment more closely we become aware of the economic, social, political and legal dimensions of the process. Each of these dimensions is interlinked to the other and have a bearing on each other. "Economic Empowerment" implies a better quality of material life through sustainable livelihood owned and managed by women. By "Social Empowerment" we mean a more equitable social status for women in society.

"Political Empowerment" is the provision of an effective legal structure which is supportive of women's empowerment. "Legal Empowerment" through struggle and movement based work are important preconditions for economic empowerment. Development workers at the grass roots level have debated for long on what kind of empowerment should take place first-economic, social or political. Women at the grass roots have been heard saying they must have food, a full stomach for the whole family and only then would they be able to discuss empowerment. Yet other development workers believe social and political empowerment through struggle and movement based work are important preconditions for economic empowerment

EMPOWERMENT OF WOMEN THROUGH SELF HELP GROUPS

Empowerment of women has emerged as an important issue in our country. In India, nearly half of the population consists of women. In India their work participation rate is less than half that of men. The role of women in the development of nation is very important nowadays. So women should be respected both in the society as well as in the family. To increase the status of women, they must be empowered in all aspects such as economically, socially, politically, and culturally. To empower women government has introduced such as DWCRA, TRYSEM, and SGSY but these programmes had not given as expected result to rural women folk. The emergence of SHGs as a limb of the women's movement for their development through empowerment. Women in the Indian context have less/no access to credit, SHGs gave them an opportunity to promote small savings and create credit of their own. Rural women do not have financial independence; they are the weaker section of society and have limited access to resources and employment opportunities. Only in 1980s the concept of credit for women came to India with the novel solution of group lending with joint liability. To give rural poor more access towards banking and credits National Bank for Agriculture and Rural Development (NABARD) was established in 1982. In 1992 NABARD introduced linking up of SHGs to develop a supplementary credit delivery system to reach the poor in a cost effective and sustainable manner. Over the last few years, "people's participation "and "Empowerment" have become the buzzwords in rural development and local planning. In this context, the self help group(SHG) has emerged as the most successful strategy in the process of participatory development and empowerment of women. Rural women are the marginalized groups of our society. Due to the presence of socio-economic constraints in the rural areas, women's potential for development remained far from fully utilized and they have been pushed further back into the social hierarchical system. Self Help Group is considered as a strategy evolved by the developing nations to empower women especially rural women to leap from the state of powerlessness to powerfulness. Empowerment is the expansion of freedom of choice and action. It means increasing one's authority and control over the resources and decisions that affect one's life. Access to productive resources, inclusion, participation and organization, accountability, local governance and organizational capacity and gender equality are the key elements of empowerment. SHG helps the women in uplifting their living conditions and also encompass the social, economic, educational level to improve their empowerment level. The components of empowerment of women are: a) Access to economic resources b) participation in economic decision-making c) Opportunities for self-development d) Participation in socio-political decision-making e) Scope for skill development and f) Impact on general welfare of the family and community.

CONCLUSION

Still women are affected by caste, class, divisions, feudal attitudes, patriarchal nature of the family and village social environment, ethnic and religious separation and the like. The introduction of SHGs playing a vital role in the empowerment of women. This is an important institution for improving the life of women on various social economic and political components. Therefore the empowerment of women through SHGs would lead to benefits not only to the individual and women's group but also for the family and community as a whole through collective action for development. They assume the role of decision maker in major and deciding aspects of the family and village community. The possible outcome of women's empowerment through group approach / SHGs at household level is self employment, sustainable livelihoods, improved health and education, enhanced social dignity and better status of women.

REFERENCES

1. Panigraphy R.L. and Dasarathi Bhuyan (2006) "Women Empowerment", Discovery Publishing House, New Delhi.
2. Geetha. B, Mangayarkarasu and Thara Bhai (2008) "Self Help Groups : A social movement", Social Welfare, Vol.54, No.11-12
3. Kamala. K, Aiyanna K.V and Chikkarangaswamy (2010) "SHGs as an Instrument for Women Empowerment", Southern Economist, Vol.48
4. "Pro-People Development Movement : A Case Study of SHGs in Kerala, Social Action Vol.61
5. www.The Counseller.com

40 TRIBAL DEVLOPMENT IN MANIPUR: BINDING IMPEDIMENTS

Sonkhogin Haokip

INTRODUCTION

Manipur is a plural society consisting of three major ethnic groups. The 'Meitei' (Manipur Hindus), 'Naga', and "Kuki-chin' (both tribal groups) with various migrant communities and the 'Pangal' (Manipur Muslims). Thus, social-cultural pluralism is the core of the social fabric of Manipur. The Meiteis were converted to Hinduism and accepted the caste system while the Nagas and Kuki-chin groups were converted into Christianity. The Muslim community while accepting Meitei language constitutes a distinct social and cultural group based on religious profession. Therefore, social pluralism has led to the perpetuation of the various groups as distinct entities (Gangumei Kabui, 2004). Though there was no traditional social disharmony among these groups, it has failed to evolve an integrated social formation in Manipur. With the coming of democracy in Manipur in the post independent period, social pluralism has been harmonized to some extent by the power sharing of the various cultural groups in a democracy. However, the problem of inter-ethnic conflicts and inter-societal hiatus continues as assertion of ethnic-identity become formidable. The process of ethnic 'identity formation in the North East region of India was based on the idea of large group formation. Attempts were made to bring several smaller groups together to project a unified identity. Ethnic consciousness leads to identity expansion by merging several groups and expand their identity. In this process of identity expansion, they also develop a belief in common origin as the Nagas and Mizos have done (Achary, 1990). This argument, however, may not hold valid in the case of Manipur where (as Rajesh Dev, 2004 argued), groups that had once identified with a particular ethnic name or group is reconstructing its identity independent of its parent body and legitimating the process through reification of alleged 'indignity'. For instance, 'Zalengrong', a conglomeration of the ethnic groups like the Rougmei, Langmei and Paomei, is asserting its own identity (ethnic) independent of the parent body i.e. the 'Naga'. Similarly, the Zome re-unification

Organization (ZRO), a conglomeration of the ethnic groups like the paite, simte, vaiphei, zou, etc. is asserting an identity independent of the parent 'Kuki' tribe.

Thus, continuing quest for 'independent ethnic identity' has reproduces images of otherness that is exclusionary, insular and ethnocentric. This has cascading effect in such a multi-ethnic region, where exclusive ethnic identities are being continually constructed thereby initiating ethnic contests between dominant and non-dominant ethnic groups. The contests is reflected in the form of 'dominant Meitei ethnic groups versus non-dominant Kuki and Naga ethnic groups' where the former submerges and excludes the latter from social, political and economic advantages. It (i.e. the contests) could also be seen to be taken place within the Kuki ethnic groups and Naga ethnic groups in the form of major-ethnic tribes versus minor ethnic tribes'. Replacement of colonial political structures by people-centric ones not only sharpened this inter-ethnic divides but also created new divides within ethnic groups as the flow of money from central governments contributed to the emergence of alternative and competing elites (partha S.Ghosh 2005). Thus, loyalty to group identities and the formidable assertion of ethnic identity eventually crystallized into "ethnic insurgencies" based on ethnic lines.

INSURGENCY

At present, there are about (thirty) 30 insurgent groups operating in Manipur some of which have an ideology whereas majority of them are allegedly purely extortionist groups that use the underground façade to their own advantage. Hill-based insurgent groups in Manipur are the offshoot of ethnic politics based on demographic domination and power politics, which have led to the process of ethnic domination of the majority over the minority (V.A.Shimray, 2004). This ethnic politics was based on false ideology. For instance, the Naga insurgent organization-NSCN-(IM) has been actively working towards the process of forcefully assimilating the smaller indigenous tribes of Manipur into Nagahood. Smaller tribes, which have been identifying under their indigenous tribes name, are lured into a false promise of greater power and assertion under the banner of Naga Nationalism. Smaller tribes, which were once considered Old-Kukis, such as anal, Maring, Kom, Purum, Chothe, Koirang, etc. have started identifying themselves as Nagas. In the process, they have lost their original identities. The Naga insurgent elements have coerced the smaller tribes into Nagahood in a bid to expand the Naga domain and the NSCN (IM) dealt with any exposition regarding the de-nagaization of the smaller tribes in a very violent manner. Ethnic conflicts in the hills of Manipur were a direct consequence of such hardened ethnic identities and exclusive claims. For example, the stiff oppositions offered by the Kukis to the Naga expansionism in the hills of Manipur had resulted into Kuki-Naga Ethnic conflicts in 1992.This paper dealt with the crisis of governability in the state of Manipur against the backdrop of the civil society that has been ignored and rendered completely irrelevant; the civil society that has suffered the outcome of the spillover of the counter-insurgency military operations in the state.

INTERFACE BETWEEN CIVIL SOCIETY AND GOVERNANCE IN MANIPUR

Both, state and militant violence have contributed equally to the shrinking of the democratic space and in silencing the voice of civil society in the state of Manipur. The basis for good governance is a well-functioning democratic political system that ensures representative and honest governments responsive to the needs of the people. This involves more than simply the holding of regular, free and fair elections. It also implies respect for human rights in general, and notably for basic civil liberties such as freedom of expression and of association, including a free and pluralistic media. These are fundamental conditions for the development of a vibrant civil society that reflects the full diversity of views and interests. The state and civil society are complementary not alternative to each other. The state performs certain indispensable functions and if those were subverted and under-mined, civil society would wither in the bud. On the other hand civil society cannot perform the crucial function of holding the state accountable and responsive unless it itself is democratized. To make the various institutions of governance accountable and responsive to the people and the society, space has to be created wherein the state, institutions of governance and the civil society work in partnership. A partnership between civil society and governance has brought to the surface, the various roles that civil society took on, in strengthening or weakening the institutions of governance (Neera Chandhoke, 1995).

A quick glance at the nature of civil society in Manipur would be helpful for our arguments here. Among the hill tribes of Manipur, Nagas are united on the overall issue of Naga identity and interest. The more than 50 years of insurgent violence and wide-scale killings of leaders of civil society organizations as well as political organizations has the resulting consequences of militarizing the entire Naga society to such an extent that today, civil society groups in the Naga society have been forced to work in close liaison with the militant organization. The hold of NSCN-(IM) over the entire Naga society in Manipur is so deep-rooted that no organizations (civil society or otherwise) can afford the luxury of going against the verdicts of NSCN (IM). Five sitting MLAs belonging to the Naga Ethnic community in Manipur have resigned from the Manipur State Assembly just ahead of the ninth Manipur Legislative Assembly. The resignations came in the wake of the campaign by the United Naga Council - which worked as per the "command from elsewhere" – against Naga candidates set up by any "political party", referring to political parties recognized by the Election Commission of India (ECI). The resignations of those MLAs could be treated as an open surrender by a good section of the political establishment in the hills, to "extra-political organizations".

The Kukis are dispersed in Senapati district (Saikul and Sadar Hills), Ukhrul, Chandel, Churachandpur and Tamenglong district. They are not so well organized and the recent threat from the Nagas (read NSCN-IM) is the only unifying force and motivation for their identity as a tribe. Kuki militant groups like KNA (Kuki National Army), KNF (Kuki National Front), UKLF (United Kuki Liberation Front), and KLA (Kuki Liberation Army) are operating in Kuki dominated areas of Manipur. They do not have any ideology, nor the capacity to defend the Kuki dominated areas and being fragmented, they can only perpetrate sporadic violence and thus escalate inter-ethnic as well as intra-ethnic conflicts in Manipur. Since political elites amongst the Kukis are competing to gained support of the militant groups, situation has arisen where there is a necessity to buy these militants and once blood is tasted by one group, other groups mushroomed in no time and money flows into their hands relatively easily. Virtually, there is no space for civil society to play its important role in holding the state accountable and responsive to the needs of the people especially when it is caught in the crossfire. The state has become so soft and civil society so weak. Civil society has been silenced at the barrel of the Gun. Everyone talks of the killing of innocent people by these groups or about the inter-group violence but violence is the only method through which they can communicate and that alone would give them legitimacy as insurgents to extract money from the politicians, bureaucrats, businesspersons and common people.

Therefore, governance in the hill areas of Manipur can be equated to "Laws of the Jungle" where "might is right" has become the principle means of governance. Misguided youths, who were recruited in large number in these militant organizations have became a potential threat not only to civil society but to civilization as well, since these groups stands on the margin of society, culture, and civilization. As Ajai Sahni and J.George have argued, the progressive 'withdrawal' of civil governance and the network of collusive arrangements with militant factions are compounded by the emergence of widespread patterns of illegal economic activity that become the mainstay and motive of all insurgencies after what may be called their early 'ideological' state. These include a thriving economy of extortion, smuggling, gunrunning, narcotics, and an oligopolistic control over government contracts. Indeed, the various 'ideological' factions and rivalries within militant movements in the state of Manipur are often thinly disguised 'turf wars' to retain or gain control over lucrative 'areas of influence', especially important routes of (illegal) cross border trade, including the drug trade. For instance, 'Moreh' a small Indo-Myanmar town in Chandel district Manipur, which is the main corridors for drug, and heroin smuggling, is a bone of contention for all the militant groups in the state. As far as the moreh entry point in Myanmar is concerned, the nearest point on the other side is Tamu, which is few k.m. away. The Moreh-Tamu trade is small in quantity and it is primarily a smuggling trade in Chinese, Korean, and Thai goods. However, the market in Imphal, the capital of Manipur thrives on this trade. Both Moreh and Tamu are predominantly inhabited by the Kuki-Chin groups). The growth of this underground terrorist economy, backed by the disruptive power of the militants, distorts and inhibits the processes and growth of legitimate economic and developmental activities. The civil society along with a wide variety of economic activities that were integral to the lives of the people of Manipur have been 'criminalized', forcing otherwise law abiding citizens into a collusive relationship with militants within their areas of influence (be it the Meitei militant group, the Nagas or the Kukis). Moreover, militant groups gradually usurp a wide range of governmental functions, including the (albeit conditional) perfection of life and property, and the provision of 'justice' to local communities. Militancy in Manipur can, in fact, fruitfully (though only partially) be examined as a conflict to defend or expand monopolistic control over critical functions – economic and administrative – against all 'intruders', including the government, with militant groups taking on the character of a 'primitive state' in a situation of widespread anarchy.

Government officials, especially of the engineering departments are on a routine basis, being taken into captivity by sundry organizations, all for huge ransoms. (Pradip Pahnjoubam, 2008) and there seems very little that the state can do either, for its adversaries seems to be everywhere having penetrated many of the government's own institutions. There seems very little that the militant organizations themselves are able to keep the semblance of an ideological struggle to the protracted turmoil in the land either because there is a constant mushrooming of new militant or else, semi-militant organizations. Sometimes these take the route of an organization splintering endlessly into numerous small factions, each of these units in the process acquiring an influence of its own through violent and intimidatory means. They also often come into brutal conflict with each other, taking a tragic toll of collateral damages from amongst the ordinary citizenry. Thus, Manipur with a population of 30,23,141 (2002 census) is perhaps, the state with the highest per capita "terrorist organization" not only in India but the whole world. (Of the 28 militant Organizations branded as "Terrorist" in India under POTA, ten are from the Northeast region out of which again six are from Manipur). Fratricidal fighting among these different insurgent groups has seriously eroded the civil society space; and as conflicts within the society increases, the state passed new emergency legislations. A number of "National Security Laws" are passed and operated upon in Manipur to curb insurgency. Such as (i) AFSPA (Armed Forces Special Powers Act), 1958, (2) The prevention of seditious meeting Act, 1911, (3) The Punjab Security of State Act, 1953, (4) Foreigners Protected Areas Order, 1958 (5) The Unlawful Activities (Prevention) Act, 1967, (6) The National Security Act, 1980, (7) the Code of Criminal Procedure (Manipur Armed) Act, 1983, and (8) The terrorist and Disruptive Activities (Prevention) Act, 1985.

However, with these comprehensive legal institutional and administrative arrangements to safeguard and protect "National Security" interest in Manipur over the year, the people are increasingly feeling insecure and being alienated from the authority. The impunity enjoyed by the Armed Forces under the various black laws requires no additional laws as they can get away with almost anything and everything they do. A large number of armed force personnel stationed in Manipur are routinely using the special power given to them under these laws. Hundreds of suspected militants as well as ordinary civilians have been reported to be arbitrarily arrested, tortured, extra-judicially executed, and involuntarily disappeared; while women are raped and sexually harassed. Manipur, which is under the veil of numerous black laws, is in the heart of a conflict situation that had raged the state for the past two decades and had claimed hundreds of lives. Rampant violation of basic human rights has been experienced over the years in both the hills and the valley of Manipur. The unarmed and innocent human beings have long been sandwiched from both ends of the armed groups – militant groups at one-end and security forces at the other. Civil society is suffering the outcome of the spillover of the counter – insurgency military operations. As the security of the state beefed up with the government constantly increasing the strength of the armed forces in Manipur, an immense increase in insecure constituencies has become a concern in the security radar screen for the Government of Manipur as well as the centre. All legal parameters of determining crime and punishment are being abused without any human consideration.

Added to the phenomenon of insurgency, numerous civil-society protests in the form of bandhs and strikes (partial or total) at the slightest provocations have become frequent phenomenon. The federation of industries in the N.E region has estimated, and published recently in a local newspaper, that one-day's strike causes the loss of Rs.50 crore due to disruption of economic activities. Such disruptions being frequent in Manipur, one can only imagine the extent of direct annual loss to the state economy and its negative impact on the economic environment.

CRISIS OF GOVERNANCE

Against this backdrop, governance has become a huge challenge for the state. The biggest impediments to good governance in the present state of affairs were the unresolved questions of insurgency and economic stagnancy moving in a vicious circle. The economic stagnancy that impedes employment and income growth serves as fertile ground for fortifying and sustaining insurgency (Atul Sharma, 2005). On the other hand, the growing militancy and the subsequent growth of the underground terrorist economy, backed by the disruptive power of the militants distorts and inhibits the processes of growth of legitimate economic and developmental activities. Throw into this mix the question of governability and we have the enduring challenge that the state of Manipur face today. Another complication is the half-hearted and unsystematic arrangement of the system of self-governance in the state. Although small population is in question, two systems of local government existed in Manipur and that too sometimes in contravention of the broad theoretical premise that dictated the criteria (Partha S.Ghosh, 2008). The two systems are Autonomous District Council under the Manipur Hill Areas District councils Act 1975, and the Panchayati Raj Institutions as per the 73rd Amendment of the Indian Constitution.

OTHER BINDING IMPEDIMENTS

1. Initial conditions:

The important initial conditions that continue to act as stumbling blocks are:

(i) Disruption of Traditional Trade Links: Partition led to disruption of the long existing transport and trade links that India's North East in general and Manipur in particular used to have. The alternative trade and transport routes that were developed in the post-partition have been much longer in distance and thus have involved hugely larger transport costs (Distance between Kolkata and Agartala is a little more than 300 km in pre-partition era while it is 1700 km in the post-partition period. To move a 9-ton truck from Guwahati to Calcutta, a distance of 1100 km today costs around Rs. 20,000. A Truck going from Chennai to Calcutta, a distance of 1600 km costs only Rs. 1600). This also reflects on the quality of road connecting INE with the rest of the country. As for railway links, some parts of INE are yet to have railheads while in the rest even the partial conversion of the meter gauge to broad gauge had taken years. (In the pre-partition days, boats laden with tea, coal and timber reached Kolkata from Dibrugarh in 8 days. But now from Kolkata to Guwahati it takes more than 25 days for lack of night navigation and customs formalities at various points).

    Partition further isolated an already isolated geo-politically sequestered region. It was left with over 4500 km of external frontier with Bhutan, China, Myanmar and Bangladesh but not more than a slender 22 km connection with Indian hinterland through the tenuous Siliguri corridor, the Gateway to INE. The very considerable market disruption, socio-economic distancing and retardation that resulted has not been adequately appreciated and compensated."

(ii) Population Influx: The influx of population that had begun since partition continues to remain at the root of social and political mobilizations leading to a prolonged disturbed situation in several parts of the region. This, in turn has vitiated its environment for investment and growth.

(iii) Unharnessed Resource Endowments: India's North East in general and Manipur in particular is a highly resource-endowed region. The region is endowed with mineral resources such as petroleum, natural gas, coal, limestone, water and forest resources, and fertile soil and so on. The region has a hydropower generation potential of 57, 000 MW or 60% of the country's 8400 MW (at 60% load factor) according to the chief managing director of the National Hydal Power Corporation (NHPC). There also exist oil and natural gas deposits in the region for further power generation. However, all these resources remain largely unutilized.

(iv) Enclave Economy: crude oil production and its refining as well as tea plantation and plywood industry are the few existing resource-based modern industries in the region. But both oil and tea industries, which have been there for more than one and a half century, have not induced any industrial growth based on their backward and forward linkages (for example, tea plantation requires a wide variety of inputs such as fertilizers, insecticides, chappals, umbrellas, small tools and so on. These backward linkages-based industries, despite their large market, did not come up in the region. Instead, the industry depends on supplies from outside the region).

Similarly, oil industry had been hesitant for long to develop refineries and petrochemical complexes which could have led to developing many downstream industries in the region. On the hand, the surpluses that accrue from these industries year after year are siphoned off to investment activities elsewhere. This has led to 'enclave economy' in which these few modern industries exist without having any linkage with the much larger segment of traditional activities. For reasons such as these, the resource-based extractive industries have come to be perceived as the symbol of exploitation.

(iv) Monopolistic Operations of Deeply Entrenched Trading Interests: India's North East in general and Manipur in particular is greatly dependent for the supply of its requirements on the rest of the country. Assam alone procures food items such as food grains, fish, edible oils etc. to the estimated amount of Rs. 3500 crore during the Eight Plan period. Such a vast requirement is available through a trade and distribution networks. But the trade network is organized on the basis of monopolistic competition. In many situations, traders collude for public advantage. Trade margin being high, the investment on commodity production is understandably not preferred. It is so because the risk factor is higher in a perennially disturbed environment as well as in a situation where adequate infrastructure is deficient, all leading to high transaction costs.

2. Infrastructure Deficiency

India's North East in general and Manipur in particular lacks the basic minimum physical, social and administrative infrastructure for unleashing growth dynamics in the region. Physical infrastructure such as power, communications, transports, irrigation and market access are grossly inadequate to generate a dynamic growth process. The High Level Commission (1997) constituted to examine 'Tackling Backlogs in Basic Minimum Services and Infrastructure Needs' for the North East estimated the requirement for infrastructure – power, roads, railways, irrigation, flood control and inland water way – at Rs. 93,619.01 crore in addition to the Ninth Plan requirement of Rs. 17,995.42 crore. In recent study, Assam was placed 15th among the major states in 2004 while all the six smaller states where at the bottom among the other small states of the country. Inadequate infrastructure particularly in the context of all hill states where market institutions, such as land market, have not developed which resulted in poor market incentives and thus low productivity and growth in different sectors of the economies of the region. As also obvious, poor infrastructure is not conducive to attracting private investment.

3. Distortion in Factor and Commodity Markets

In the north eastern states in general and Manipur in particular both commodity and factor markets are working to their disadvantage. To elaborate a little, with a low production base and heavy dependence on the rest of the country for their requirements, local demand generated within the region induces income and employment generation in the states with larger production base. Similarly due to inhospitable environment, savings arising in the region gets outlet into the more environment-friendly region. This explains the very low credit-deposit ratio in the north-eastern states. Such asymmetrical market integration – a large inflow of goods into and outflow of savings from the region – has impeded the pace of growth. At another level, the absence of land market particularly in the hill states acts as a serious impediment to investment. Labour market has also been hugely distorted by heavy population influx. With the supply side factor bring inhospitable, integrated product and credit market accompanied distorted labour market and non-existence of land market in the hill states of the north east have led to reverse flow of resources from the region to the more developed economies. The outcome of this process is low growth despite special dispensation by the Central Government.

4. Other Related Factors

Rising levels of unemployment is a disturbing factor leading the youth to nefarious activities like indulging in narcotics abuse and terrorism. In the absence of any healthy sustainable economic activity in the region, the expanding class of neo-literates (who have very limited employment avenues) may feel it immensely remunerative to join insurgency movements since they may be assured of material benefits. Insurgency should not be allowed to become an industry with great promise and fewer risks. There is also an absence of purposeful and vocational education. Another related problem is that of suspicion of outsiders, which has impeded economic development of the region. Certain examples of the negative fallout of this are: stopping of oil exploration and production by Naga Students' Federation, preventing railway extension in Khasi Hills, impeding development of immense hydro-electric resources because of lack inter-State consensus. This suspicion has discouraged external initiatives in the region. India's North East in general and Manipur in particular do not have large and enterprising indigenous business community. Business classes from other parts of the country are not likely to get encouragement or assurance of goodwill to start new ventures.

5. Distorted and ill-Conceived Development Perspectives

India's North East in general and Manipur in particular with only 0.5% of its territorial boundary with the rest of India and the remaining with the foreign countries is loosely fitted in the macro development perspective. This is because the development initiatives of the region are largely anchored on two perspectives. One is the security perspective rather than a well articulated development perspective, and the other is the perspective based on least interference in traditional institutions and practices. Incidentally, infrastructure like railways developed during the colonial period linked the areas associated with tea, oil, coal and plywood but not any of the traditional urban centres. Similarly the Stillwell Road that linked INE with Myanmar, constructed during the Second World War period was intended to serve as a defence supply line and not as any market linkage. A few examples would highlight the thrust on security consideration even in the post-independence period. Way back in the mid-fifties, with the finding of larger oil deposits, the Government of India (GoI) considered setting up an oil refinery. The Expert Committee constituted for selection of the site, did not find India's North East in general and Manipur in particular, suitable for setting up an oil refinery for strategic reasons. It is a different matter that eventually, in response to a prolonged agitation a toy oil refinery was set up in Guwahati while the main one, at least four times larger, was set up in Baruini in Bihar. Again the Armed Forces Special Powers Act (Assam, Nagaland and Manipur) against which Manipuris are currently agitating was enacted in 1958 when apart from Naga hostilities there was no other insurgency that warranted such a drastic measure. Another important initiative that the Government of India took gives an insight into its strategic obsession. Considering the interdependence of the seven North East economies, the establishment of North East Council (NEC) was a significant institutional innovation. But even this was designed mainly to sub serve a security interest than to promote an integrated development approach to the region. It is clear from the fact that NEC was placed under the administrative control of the Ministry of Home, GoI, and under the chairmanship of one of the Governors of the north-eastern states but not under any development ministries or the Planning Commission. On the other hand, major development projects were more in response to public agitation. There are numerous examples to show that many critical projects such as the first bridge over the Brahmaputra, conversion of railways into broad gauge, setting up of second oil refinery and the IIT were the product of ad hoc responses to public agitation. The point to note is that for far too long the GoI development initiatives were more the outcome of strategic/security consideration and ad hoc responses to public agitation than of anything following from a development perspective.

The other perspective on which the development initiatives are anchored especially in the hill states/regions is the least intervention in the traditional systems and institutions. The requirement of the 'inner line permit' for entry into most parts of the hill states and the ban on the land ownership by non-tribal are evidences of the attempt to preserve the traditional system and institutions. What perceptions and forces that shaped this perspective, or whether there exists any justifiability, are outside the theme of this paper. The point to highlight is that product and money markets are being integrated with the national and regional markets in the hilly regions as well. In this process the traditional system and institutions come under severe strain. To illustrate, varieties of industrial goods, say shampoo pouch, soap and detergent have entered the consumption basket even in the remotest part of these regions, but the traditional production system associated with low productivity and self-sufficiency can hardly sustain the changing consumption pattern requiring more and more cash transactions. On the other hand, even if marketable surplus is produced, farmers cannot get incentive prices for their disposable produce due to lack of easy and viable market access. Similarly, in the traditional system prevailing in large part of the hilly region, land market does not exist, land being owned by the community. The absence of land market is a serious hindrance to the flow of investment particularly from outside. This is also an impediment to the flow of formal credit particularly in the rural sector because land cannot serve as collateral and there does not exist any substitutable asset. Even the functioning of the labour market is constrained. In a traditional system, the concept of wage labour rarely exists. As a result, for development projects such as construction of roads and bridges, much greater reliance has to be placed on migrant labour even from across the border rather than on local labour. This has induced the inflow of migrant labour in large magnitude. Its impact is the outflow of labour income, which has been a source of conflict as witnessed in several parts of Manipur.

REFERNCES

1. Atul Sarma. 2005. "Why the North Eastern States Continue to Decelerate?", Spring, Vol.II, No. I

2. Chander Sekhar Panchani. 1987."Manipur: Religion, Culture and Society." Konark Publishers Pvt.Ltd. New Delhi.

3. Das, R.K. 1971. 'The Problems of Tribal Identity in Manipur." The Eastern Anthropologists, May-August, Vol.24 (2).

4. Das, Samir Kumar, 2003. "Ethnicity, State and Nation: Essays on Northeastern India." N.D. South Asian.

5. Das Rajat Kamti, 1998. 'The Need for More Dynamic Approach to Tribal Studies in North-East India." In Maniskumar Raha and Aloka Kumar Gupta (ed.), North East India: the Human Interference, New Delhi, Gyan Publishing House.

6. Devi, B.I., 1982. "Hill Tribes of Manipur: A Review of British Policies." Shillong: Journal of the Institute of Social Research, April, Vol.2.

7. Gangte, T.S.., 1984. "Search for New Identity among the Tribals of Manipur, Man and Life." July-Dec, Vol.103.

8. Haldipur, R.N., 1972. "Policy towards Administration of the Tribes of N.E. India."

9. Kshetri, R., 1993. "Study of District Councils in Manipur Hills." Imphal, Centre for Tribal Studies, Manipur University.

10. M. Romesh Singh.2000. "Tribal Development in the 21st Century: An Experience from Manipur." Mittal Publications: N.D.

11. Neera Chandhoke, 1995. "State and Civil Society: Exploration in Political Theory." Sage Publications: New Delhi

12. North-East Sun, Fortnightly, Jan. 16-31 (2007) Vol. XII, No. 12

13. Partha S. Ghosh, 2005. "Challenge of Governance and Globalisation: A Case Study of India's Northeast." Spring, Vol.II, No. I.

14. Prabhakra. M.S. 2004. "Is North East India Landlocked?" Economic and Political Weekly. Oct.16.

15. Rajesh Dev, 2004. "Human Rights, Relativism and Minorities in the North East India." Economic and Political Weekly, Oct. 23

16. Roy, A.K., 1990, Authority and Legitimacy: "A Study of the Thadou Kukis in Manipur." Renaissance Publishing House: New Delhi.

17. Sangma. M.S. 1995. "Hill Societies: A Study of the North East with special references to Garo Hills." Omsons Publications: New Delhi.

18. Sanjenbam, V.1998. Manipur Geography and Regional Development.

19. Sharma, H.H. 1984. "Some Economic Indicators of Development in Manipur at District level." Manipur Today, August.

20. Singh Romesh, M. 2006. "Tribal Development in 21st Century: An Experience from Manipur." A Mittal Publication: New Delhi.

21. Verma, M.M. 1996. "Tribal Development in India." Mittal Publications: New Delhi.

41 ASSOCIATION AND IDENTITY FORMATION AMONG BENGALI MIGRANT WOMEN IN BANGALORE

Ranita Paul, Dr. E. Arumuga Gandhi

MIGRATION

Migration is an area of study which permits multidisciplinary approach in social sciences, including as it does, social demography, sociology, social and cultural anthropology economics history geography and psychology. "According to M.S.A.Rao migration is such that he considers three major areas of migration studies .First, the nature of the process of migration why people move and how migration occurs where he mainly finds out that due to economic factors people have to move and sometimes it depends upon people's own decision. The second factor of what happens to the migrants at the place of destination? How do they adjust themselves to the new social and physical environment? The third factor of what changes happens to their lifestyle and their relation to other groups and situations?" The importance of Migration for developing countries cannot be overestimated. Migration is a major factor in economic development and manpower planning. Migration is a major factor in urbanization and social change. It is necessary to consider migration and settlement as inter-related aspects of social and cultural life of the people. Migration is a shift in the place of residence for some length of time. In some extent Migration is that which happens due to various reasons like jobs, marriage, virilocal, uxorilocal or neolocal and transfer migration. Even because most of the people in Bengal are migrating from Bengal in search of jobs and little more salary than what is being paid in their own states and mainly due to the infrastructure of education in west Bengal which is not good as compared to Bangalore.

ASSOCIATION

Association is an organized body of people who have an interest, activity, or purpose in common; a society or a mental connection or relation between thoughts, feelings, ideas, or sensations. Association is something where people have the same feeling same motives same interest where they mainly have form of a society or a club. There is a relationship between migration of people to Bangalore from Bengal and Association formed in Bangalore which is basically told in their profile.

BENGALI ASSOCIATION IN BANGALORE

The Bengali Association was founded and registered under The Societies Act on 16th September 1959. The present building of the Association near Ulsoor Lake was built in 1980 and has been expanded twice, once during 1995-96 and again in the year 2000. Tagore Cultural Centre under the aegis of The Bengali Association develops itself into an embodiment of our rich cultural heritage within the guiding principle of the Upanishad "Basudhaiba Kutumbakam". The Bengali Association has two definite directions of its activities and services. Primarily it is a social commitment, a home away from home, a link between varied communities, a mouthpiece to the local administration and a solace to the people in distress. On the other hand essentially it is a platform to propagate our rich cultural heritage, an arena to pursue integration of cultural diversity of our country, an institution to cultivate cultural passion. Activities of the Association is directed by its constitution of memorandum and bye-laws and governed by two statutory bodies. One is The Board of Trustees which is the custodian of immovable properties and looks after the allocation of funds. Other is the Executive Committee, responsible for all the activities and implementation of the Plans & Programmers. Both these bodies are elected in the Annual General Meeting.

To support the activities of the Association two wings were created with specific objectives. One is the Ladies Wing and other is Kristi - The Theatre Wing of the Association. A House Bulletin is published quarterly for information updates and private circulation. People who are coming to Bangalore due to various reasons want to have their own identification as Bengalis, even they want to follow their own rituals and cultural activities where they want to bring up that they didn't forget their own identification. To have an association is not bad because when any problem happened they can come together and can protest.

IDENTITY

Identification is something which every individual should have with them and it's very important when they are away from their home land. Even we can see that when Bengalis are away from their homeland and they met with other Bengali people they are usually very friendly and co-operative with each other.

CULTURAL BEREAVEMENT

Cultural bereavement as "the experience of the uprooted person - or group - resulting from loss of social structures, cultural values and self-identity: the person - or group - continues to live in the past, is visited by supernatural forces from the past while asleep or awake, suffers feelings of guilt over abandoning culture and homeland, feels pain if memories of the past begin to fade, but finds constant images of the past (including traumatic images) intruding into daily life, yearns to complete obligations to the dead, and feels stricken by anxieties, morbid thoughts, and anger that mar the ability to get on with daily life". The expression of such bereavement is influenced by many factors, among which are social, cultural and economic. The symptoms of cultural bereavement may be misdiagnosed due to problems with language, culture and the use of Western diagnostic criteria in non- Western peoples. Traditional healing and purification rituals as well as supportive psychotherapy, after the correct diagnosis was made, were essential in the treatment of this patient's syndrome.

CULTURAL IDENTITY

Culture is learned and passed through generations and includes the beliefs and value system of a society. Culture has been described as features that are shared and bind people together into a community. Identity is the totality of one's perception of self, or how we as individuals view ourselves as unique from others. Racial, cultural and ethnic identities form part of one's identity, and identity will change with development at a personal as well as at a social level along with migration and acculturation. Social identity can be thought of as the culturally defined personality characteristics, which are ascribed to social roles, such as the role of being a father, mother, friend, employer, employee, etc. Ethnicity is a source of social identity.

ACCULTURATION

Acculturation, a process that may be voluntary or forced, requires contact between culturally divergent groups of people and results in the assimilation of cultural values, customs, beliefs and language by a minority group within a majority community. During the acculturation process, both the immigrant and host cultures may change.

CULTURAL CONGRUITY

The importance of ethnic and cultural congruity, interaction patterns and cultural identity in the genesis and maintenance of mental distress in migrants. Cultural congruity may be thought of as the congruence or dissonance of an individual's culture, beliefs and expectations with the surrounding population. The surrounding population may be made up predominantly of people from the same or different cultural background compared to the migrant. This section discusses the methods of the study. The study aims to find out the identity formation among the migrant Bengalis in Bangalore. It is done by understanding their participation in the association activities. The term methodology in simple terms refers to a system of broad principles or rules from which specific methods or procedures may be derived to interpret or solve different problems within the scope of a particularly. This research is basically a quantitative study. In its simple term, quantitative research refers to the systematic empirical investigation of social phenomena via statistical, mathematical or computational techniques. Shank (Ospina 2004) defines research as "a form of systematic empirical inquiry into meaning."

NEED FOR THE STUDY

Bangalore is one of the largest cities in India. It attracted people because of its Information Technology (IT Boom) and employment opportunities. Studies and work becomes a major issue of the migrants to Bangalore. As the city is vast and dynamic in its culture it might be a problem to the migrants in the city because they come to a new place and there is always cultural disparities among the local people and even language becomes a big problem for the migrants and even the behavior of the local Bangalore people with the outsiders. The Bengali migrants are huge in number in Bangalore which is 11.5% of those who have migrated to Bangalore out of the total population of West Bengal from 2001 census. The increasing Bengali population in Bangalore, makes it becomes important to study their participation in their association activities and identity formation. Considering the importance of the study the following objectives are framed. They are:

OBJECTIVES

1. To develop the profile of Bengali Associations and their leaders in Bangalore
2. To understand the major activities of those associations
3. To study the involvement of members in the activities of the association
4. To examine to what extent these associations are functioning for the benefit of the migrant Bengalis and for their identity formation.
5. To understand the problems faced by the members in their association activities

SETTING OF THE STUDY

Study Area

Study area includes the different committees which are linked with the main association in Bangalore i.e., THE BANGALEE ASSOCIATION. The Bangalee Association has chosen as the study area for this research topic because in Bangalee Association we get different kinds of Bengalis coming from different parts of West Bengal and will be easy to know the reasons why they have joined the association after coming to Bangalore. Bangalore is very vast and to find all Bengalis who are in the association will be difficult so to find all the Bengalis this is the appropriate place.

Sources of Data

For the present study the researcher used both primary and secondary data. The present study depends on the primary data as no sufficient work is done selected field. As mentioned already Questionnaire was used to collect data from the 80 respondent's (members of the Bangalee association) in Bangalore. In addition to this the researcher also referred various articles, journals, books and secondary data is available on various forms or area of the study.

Selection of Respondents

For the present study, of the total numbers of 400 members in the selected association the researcher selected 80 members using Probability Sampling Method. Tippet's table was used to select the respondents and the sample size is 10% of the total members in the association.

Tool for the Data Collection

A questionnaire is prepared for the respondent to answers. The questionnaire includes questions that are relevant to the objectives. Questionnaire is being prepared for this study because this is the best way to collect the data and people will feel free and the respondents won't feel uncomfortable to answer. The questionnaire is basically based on those people or rather respondents who are from Bengali community and how they are forming their identification while they come to a different place where they cannot find their tradition, culture, language, way of behavior etc. now for all these things they need a place where they can have everything. Questions regarding their birth place or originating from which part of Bengal has been asked to know their day to day life. Social and cultural things such as the socio-cultural connectedness, a familiar way of life, whether active member or not, cultural difference from the native place, difficulty in the host place, impact of cultural activities, climate of Bangalore, surrounding, local language, has been asked to know the difference they have been facing and the adjustment they have done to overcome their problems.

SUMMARY OF THE STUDY

Age group in the association becomes one of the primary factor for joining the association because usually people wants to join when they want to do for their same culture and same group people which do not make them feel lonely in a foreign land where language, culture, way of behavior everything is different. So from the study it has been found that people who are between the age from 35-40 and 41-45 mainly people are there in the association and are very much active member of the association. People who come from Bengal to Bangalore mainly because of jobs or either they get married and then they migrate from that place and even sometimes it happens that they come after marriage and start doing their jobs. So from the research we found out that 32.5% are having their occupation as software engineer but they still are house wives also then after that it comes for teachers who are for 10% who are basically engaged in colleges as well as schools. Then we can see that about 20% are engaged as government employee and out of them some are retired and they basically does work in banks, LIC, BHEL, clerks etc. after that the last is the house wives who mainly comprises about 37.5% and they are mostly the highest in number because they mainly comes within the age group of 51-55 and even those who are in 60's they are there to organize the cultural programmes in the association and mainly they are very good in organizing the programmes and the people who are newly married they also join them. There they mainly does dancing and singing practice where they mainly engage them with these works and also they are house wives as well.

The male respondents who are also majority in software engineer and the survey gives the percentage of 52.5% and then comes the teacher which comprises of 25% and then the government employee are 22.5% which are mainly I.A.S, I.P.S and even the retired officers who settled over here because of Bangalore's climatic conditions. The government employee respondents are both presently working and some are retired and joined with the associations. In the past few decades, the world has seen major changes in the face of the family. Since 1975, the divorce rate has doubled resulting in the increase of single-parent households, remarriages and extended families. This is a discussion of the many definitions of "family" and how they demonstrate the changes that are occurring within the family. Family units take a variety of forms, all of which involve individuals living under one roof. The family form or structure does not indicate how healthy the family is or how they function. The family form is merely the physical makeup of the family members in relationship to each other without respect to roles and function.

From the research we found out that the respondents are having families which comprise member of four, less than 4 and more than 4. Here the families which are having more than 4 members are 47.5% but in this more than 4 means which comprise of people like parents their two children and their old parents. When people came from west Bengal they brought their parents also who was alone in their native place. Then next less than 4 are 45% means three members in the family whose members are basically staying in west Bengal only and it comprises of parents and their one children because usually Bengali parents prefer to have one child only rather than two or three. The proportion of ethnic minorities in Bengal has been increasing at least in part due to the migration of individuals from all over the world. Migration is a complex process, involving a heterogeneity of causes, experiences, cultural adjustment and stages, that influence the mental health of migrants. The stresses of the migration process itself combined with a lack of social support, a discrepancy between achievement and expectations, economic hardships, racial discrimination and harassment, and a lack of access to proper housing, medical care, and religious practice can lead to poor self-esteem, an inability to adjust, and poor physical and mental health. Social and cultural factors have been implicated in the etiology of mental illness in immigrants and refugees, and further study is needed to better understand the role of culture as pathogenic or pathos-protective.

Cultural bereavement, a paramount aspect of the migrant's experience, is influenced by, and mediated through, the interplay of the migration process, cultural identity and cultural congruity, along with biological and psychological factors. To appropriately guide diagnosis and treatment interventions, mental health practitioners must appreciate and recognize the socio-cultural factors that influence the manifestation of grief in people who have migrated. Cultural identity and congruity will affect the ability of the affected person to understand and work through the grieving process, and disturbances of identity and congruity are likely to lead to a pathologic, or complicated, bereavement. Rates of depression, phobias and schizophrenia are elevated in some migrant groups. The understanding of race, ethnicity, social isolation and a lack of social support, racism, unemployment and poverty, poor housing and a lack of access to appropriate medical care is important in explaining the increased rates of mental illness in ethnic minority groups. Additionally, cultural congruity and ethnic density, cultural identity, and biological and psychological factors are likely important influences in the development of mental illness in migrants. With further study, a better understanding of the complex interplay of these potential vulnerability factors may eventually lead to preventative measures and lessen the burden of mental illness in this growing population. The hypotheses of the study which was brought after the analysis by the researcher brings the result that there are no social rivalry among the members in the association as they are far away from their homeland and now the association is the main place where they come together to form such an environment. Here they feel less home sickness which depicts the fact that there is a formation of unity and solidarity among the members and proves right according to the question asked in the hypotheses that associations brings solidarity and unity. Then the main cause of coming together is to keep the culture and to celebrate every festival in a foreign land. The Association is very sensitive to inculcate aesthetic sense in the younger ones and also encourages learning the local language even by grown-ups. Experts in the Arts visit regularly to impart lessons in painting and music too. These classes are available to all interested persons at a nominal cost. Even all the cultural programmes like Durga Puja, Poila Boishakh, and Rabindranath Tagore's birthday where singing and dancing happens. Kannada language classes have now become a regular feature. These are the various timings of different classes that the association has facilitated for the Bengali people in Bangalore. The Timings for the various classes held are:

- Painting Class: Sunday from 9 a.m. to 1 p.m.
- Music Class: Sunday from 3 p.m. to 5 p.m.
- Kannada Class: Friday 7 p.m. to 9 p.m.

From the analysis the result is that about 85% responded yes of celebrating their cultural and religious activity thus the researcher proves the first hypotheses which asks about the socio cultural and religious activity in the association. Forming the identity of the Bengalis by following the culture, speaking in Bengali language and are helpful in each other's problems and happiness and the analysis brings that the rate co-operation is 60% which this proves the third hypotheses of the study that the Associations are active in identity formation of Bengali migrants and the last hypotheses is that problems faced by the member of the association regarding social rivalry and financial problem proves wrong that they have any kind of social rivalry because they have a very smooth relation among the members of the association and they stand by each other when any obstacles come on their way and the financial problem is not that much because they collect money among themselves and they get help from Trustees also because from the analysis the result came that 51% money comes from chandas and 48% money comes from trustees.

The association have highlighted the problems of the community and submit them to the right Authorities is one of their prime objectives e.g., implementation of Direct Train between Kolkata & Bangalore was initiated by the Association and became operative after they held a prolonged meeting with the then Railway Minister Ms.Mamata Banerjee and Member-Railway Board Sri Madhukar Reddy by the General Secretary of the Association Sri. A.L.Roy. Thus in the conclusion the researcher found out that the act of associating. An organized body of people who have an interest, activity, or purpose in common; a society. A mental connection or relation between thoughts, feelings, ideas, or sensations. A remembered or imagined feeling, emotion, idea, or sensation linked to a person, object, or idea. Thus the chemistry happens with various processes of combination, such as hydration, solvation, or complex-ion formation, depending on relatively weak chemical bonding. And the ecology of the association a large number of organisms in a specific geographic area constituting a community with one or two dominant species. Association basically forms a group of people having a common purpose or interest, a society or club the act of associating or the state of being associated friendship or companionship their association will not last a mental connection of ideas, feelings, or sensations association of revolution with bloodshed

CONCLUSION AND SUGGESTIONS

On the basis of the collected data of this research which proved this hypothesis (The association encourages the socio-cultural and religious activities of the members), the researcher suggesting: There should be cultural seminar once in a month for the Bengali migrants for uplifting their socio-cultural programmes like singing, dancing, painting etc. The seminar theme should be focused on socio-cultural identity of Bengali people. In this seminar valuable points must be based on Bengali norms, values and religious awareness which are related to historical background of Bengali. Bengali Association has different activities like collecting money for the cultural and religious festivals, for the betterment of these activities and has good role in bringing solidarity and unity among Bengali people in Bangalore; The researcher suggesting: The activities of Bengali Association in Bangalore may focus on following points:

1. In cultural activity Association may have focus on language, food, dress, Rabindra sangeet and religious festivals; all the above points should be clarified by invited scholars and specialists of West Bengal for the remembrance of Bengal unity and solidarity in the past.

2. In economic area Bengali Association in Bangalore may have donation box where the members can put some amount for helping the association activities from one hand; and from the other hand association can collect membership amount monthly. For example, If the association have 1000 members and they collect 100 rupees in a month its mean in each month association receive 1 lakh rupees. Based on these collected membership amounts they can have different kind of activities like publishing books, magazines, newspaper, conducting seminars and conferences on the basis of Bengali Identities for the achieving solidarity and unity.

The important issue is the rate of co-operation between all the new comers and the people who are already in Bangalore is little less so the researcher is suggesting that: For the better co-operation of new Bengali comers in Bangalore the Association may have one festival in Academic year in one of the Bangalore city universities. This festival should be based on multi socio-cultural activities and the role of Bengali Association in Identity formation, social solidarity and unity and supporting them in financial issues for providing some facilities for the Bengali students who are new to Bangalore.

REFERENCES:

1. "Bangalore, IT is life in Rush Hour." Saturday Extra. Bangalore, Karnataka: The Tribune, 01 13, 2007.
2. Bhugra.D. " Migration, Cultural Bereavement and Cultural Identity. London: Sage publication, 2003.
3. Bhugra.D. "migration,culture identity." economic politcal weekly, 2003.
4. Daniel. "Emigration, Immigration, and Diaspora Relations in India ." 2003: 269-282.
5. Gupta, Shamita Das. "Gender Roles and Cultural Continuity in the Asian Indian Immigrant Community in the U.S." Sage publishers, 2009: 253-274.
6. Khondker, Habibul Haque. "home,nation,world." ananda bazar patrika, 2004.
7. Williams, Gregory and. "english as a compulsory language." economic and political weekly, 2003.
8. Bangalore: Growth Opportunities in the Silicon Valley of India. (2008, 08 20). International Advisory . Bangalore.
9. Bhugra, D. (2001). Acculturation, Cultural Identity and Mental Health. London: Gaskell.
10. Chakrabarty, R. (2008). The Asiatic Society: 1784-2008, An Overview in Time Past and Time Present: Two Hundred and Twenty-five Years of the Asiatic Society' Kolkata: The Asiatic Society
11. Chattopadhyay, G. 1965. Awakening in Bengal in Early Nineteenth Century, Progressive Publishers, Calcutta.
12. Chaudhuri, R. 2000. Young India: A Bengal Eclogue: Or Meat-eating, Race, and Reform in a Colonial Poem, Interventions: International Journal of Postcolonial Studies, Routledge, Volume 2,

42 FINANCIAL INCLUSION FOR INCLUSIVE GROWTH – GENDER PERSPECTIVES

Dr.N.Lalitha

The strength of the Indian economy is evident from the remarkable transition to a high trajectory growth path which was achieved in recent years. The Tenth Plan Period (2002—3 to 2006-07) began modestly but then saw the economy accelerating steadily to achieve an average growth rate of 7.7 per cent, for the plan period as a whole which was the highest ever achieved in any plan period. In the last four years the growth ratae averaged 8.9 per cent making India one of the fastest growing economies in the world. The transition to high growth is an impressive achievement but it must not be forgotten that growth is not the only measure of development. The ultimate objective is to achieve broad based achievement in the living standards of all our people. Rapid growth is essential for the outcome because it provides the basis to expand the income and employment and provides the resources needed to finance the programmes for social uplift. However it is not by itself sufficient. It should be ensured that growth is widely spread so that its benefits in terms of income, employment are adequately shared by the poor and weaker sections of the society especially women, scheduled caste and scheduled tribes and Other backward sections and minorities. To realize this objective, growth must be inclusive in the broadest sense. It must occur notonly in cities but also in villages. It must encompass only women but also women. It must spread across all sections of the society. The rapid growth achieved during the past several years demonstrates that disadvantaged sections including women have benefited less than they should have. Gender imbalances and regional imbalances have emerged across and even within states. The lack of inclusiveness is borne by data on several dimensions of performance.

INCLUSIVE GROWTH AND GENDER INEQUALITY

Equality is the corner stone of every democratic society that aspires for social justice and human rights. The term 'gender equality' has been defined in multiple ways in the development literature and has been the subject of great debate. It often means women having the same opportunities in life as men, for instance equality of access to education and employment which does not necessarily lead to equality of outcomes. The United Nations Human Development Report (1995) refers to gender equality in terms of capabilities (education, health and nutrition) and opportunities (economic and decision making). Similarly World bank defines gender equality as equality of opportunity (including equality of rewards for work and equality in access to human capital and other productive resources that enable opportunity) and equality of voice (the ability to influence and contribute to the development process).

Three primary domains of equality between men and women emerge from both these framework:

- The capability domain refers to basic human abilities and measured through education, health and nutrition. It is the most fundamental of all three domains and is necessary for achieving equality in the other two domains
- the second domain refers primarily to equality in the opportunity to use and apply basic capabilities through access to economic assets (such as land and property) and resources (such as income and employment)
- The third domain namely the agency is the defining element of the concept of empowerment and refers to the ability to make choices and decisions that can alter outcomes. Gender equality in this domain can only result from equalizing the balance of power between men and women in the household and social institutions.

Gender inequality pervades in varying forms and degrees both in developed and developing societies. Women in general rural women in particular are deprived of basic economic opportunities and entitlements that are widely available to men. Large disparities are found between men and women in terms of facilities such as nutrition, health and education as well as access to employment and ownership of various means of production (Sen 2001). One such form of gender inequality is with regard to the access to banking services.

Objectives of the study: The objective of the present paper to investigate the gender inequalities in disbursement of bank credit, to find out the reasons for financial exclusion among women and to suggest measures to promote financial inclusion among women.

Methodology: The study is descriptive one based on both secondary as well as primary data. The secondary data on gender inequality in banking was collected from Basic statistical Returns, RBI. The primary data on financial inclusion at the grassroots was collected from the respondents from selected villages of Nagapattinam district of Tamil Nadu.

Extent of access to credit services: Lack of credit constraints economic opportunities available to women resulting in deepening their economic and social deprivation. The consequences are also found in increasing dependence of women on money lenders, who exploit the women with high rate of interest. The access to banking services for women can be examined using two indicators as of men below:

- Extent of credit supplied to women and
- Extent of deposits received from women.

Table 1 Percentage share of women in total credit Credit off take and deposits, India 1996 -2006.

Year	Credit to women-Percentage share		Deposit-Percentage share of women	
	share of women in No of a/cs	share of women in loan amount	share of women in No.of deposits	share of women in deposits amount
1996	6.4	5.7	22.9	20.6
1997	7.4	6.4	23.5	21.0
1998	9.0	7.9	24.1	21.0
1999	8.5	8.4	24.7	21.9
2000	9.0	9.1	25.8	22.2
2001	9.6	8.8	25.9	22.0
2002	11.8	11.8	25.5	21.8
2003	11.3	11.6	25.9	21.7
2004	15.8	15.9	25.3	21.4
2005	11.7	11.4	25.8	21.4
2006	11.7	12.0	24.7	21.1

Source : RBI Basic statistical Returns, 2006

Note : The figures, are worked out as percent of total credit to/deposits from individuals that is men and women taken together excluding credit/deposits of all institutional borrowers /depositors. There was a rise in the share of women in the total bank credit as well as total amount of deposits between 1996 and 2006. Inspite of the rise, the shares of women in total credit and deposits continued to be at disquietingly low levels. Notwithstanding the fact that women constituted about half of India's population (48.4%), only 12 % of the individual bank loan accounts belonged to women in 2006. The remaining 88 % of the individual bank accounts were held by men. In the case of deposits accounts, the share held by women was higher. In 2006, about 24.7% of the individual bank deposit accounts were in the name of women.(Table 1) The extent of disparity between men and women is also visible from certain other indicators of access to banking services. In 2006, number of bank deposits per 10,000 women was less than half the corresponding figure per men. For every 100 bank deposits in the name of men in the same year, there was only 35 bank deposits in the name of women (RBI, Basic Statistical Returns)

Table 2 Triennium average of percentage share of women in agricultural credit 1998 – 2006.

Period	Share in total number of a/c under direct agricultural credit	Share in total amount under direct Agricultural credit
1998 – 2000	6.5	7.0
2001 – 2003	6.8	7.4
2004 – 2006	5.9	6.3
Source : RBI, Basic Statistical Returns		

EXTENT OF ACCESS TO AGRICULTURAL CREDIT FOR WOMEN

Agricultural is the largest employer in India. Concepts such as 'feminization of Agriculture' 'feminization of Animal husbandry' are gaining ground. Agriculture has seen growing feminization of its workforces in recent years in India. In 2007, women formed about 40 percent of the agricultural workforce in India (NCW 2008). According to population census of India in 2001, women constituted about 33 percent of the total cultivators in India as compared to 20 percent in 1991. Despite their growing importance, in agriculture sector, women received on an average only 6 percent of the total direct agricultural credit during the period 2004 -2006. The remaining 94 per cent of direct agricultural credit was given to men who formed about 67 percent of the total cultivators. Considerable bearing on the fact that land is the crucial determinant for availing agricultural credit from formal institutions and land titles in the country as is well known are about entirely held by male members in the family

Table:3 Percentage share of women in total amount of bank deposits by regions in India

Regions	Share in deposit account		Share in deposit amount		Share- female population
	1996	2006	1996	2006	2001
Northern region	17.5	17.0	22.2	22.0	12.6
North-eastern	2.5	2.2	1.6	1.7	3.8
Eastern region	15.3	14.5	11.9	11.2	22.2

Regions	Share in deposit account		Share in deposit amount		Share- female population
	1996	2006	1996	2006	2001
Western region	16.1	17.7	23.6	23.4	14.3
Southern region	29.8	30.8	26.6	28.6	22.4
India	100.00	100.00	100.00	100.00	100.00

In terms of total amount of deposits mobilized from women, the share of southern and western regions were considerably higher than the share of north eastern, eastern and central regions in 2006 (Table 5.). The shares of eastern and central regions in the total amount of deposits from women (as well as the total number of deposit accounts) were significantly lower than the share of female population residing in these regions. More over there was stagnation, or even a fall in the shares of the north eastern, eastern and central regions with respect to the total amount of deposits mobilized between 1996 and 2006 from women. There was also a fall in the number of bank deposits per 10000/- women in the north eastern, eastern and central regions between 1996 and 2006. In the same period there was raise in the number of bank deposits per 10000 women in the southern and western regions.(Table)

Table:4 Number of bank deposits per 10000 female population by regions, India

Regions	1996	2006
Northern region	2837	2617
North-eastern	1280	1177
Eastern region	1335	1335
Central region	1491	1452
Western region	2173	2535
Southern region	2479	2922
India	1936	2043

Table:5 Table share of dalit and adivasi women in number of accounts

Year	Share of dalit and adivasi women in number of accounts	Share of dalit and adivasi women in amount of credit
1997	7.1	4.8
2001	3.9	1.9
2004	2.8	1.6
2006	2.2	1.3

Source: RBI, Survey of small borrowal Accounts, various rounds.

ACCESS TO BANKING SERVICES FOR WOMEN ACROSS SOCIO ECONOMIC GROUPS

The disparity in terms of access to banking services between women from various socio economic groups has also widened in the recent period. Between 1997 and 2006, the share of Dalit and Adiviasi women – socio economically one of the most backward sections of the population in the total bank credit (under small borrowal accounts) declined steadily. In 2006 dalit and adivasi women received only 1.3 percent of the total credit given under the Small borrowal accounts as compared to 4.8 percent in 1997. (Table) If we assume that a women not belonging to dalit or adivasi groups received Rs. 100/- as bank credit, an average dalit or adivasi women received Rs.9 /- in 2006. The corresponding figure for a dalit or adivasi women was higher at Rs. 35/- in 1997. The disparity was larger if we compared a dalit or adivasi women with a man not belonging to dalit or adivasi groups. In 2006, a dalit or adivasi women received only Re. 1/- as credit from banks for every Rs.100/- received by have male counterpart from non- dalit/adivasi groups.

CONCLUDING OBSERVATION

To conclude while there has been a general spread of the basic banking services in India over the years, women remain largely deprived of these services. Women contribute about one fifth of the individual savings mobilized through bank deposits. However, women receive only around one tenth the total individual credit from banks further increase in the spread of banking services to women has not been distributed fairly across various sections of women. The increase in spread of bank deposit has taken place primarily for urban women. Women from southern and western regions (comprising the historically vanguard states in bank in development) have seen a further expansion in their access to bank deposits, while the access to women from northeastern, eastern and central regions (comprising the historically the deprived states in banking development) has relatively narrowed down. Dalit and adivasi women belonging to socio economically backward groups have seen a fall in their share in total bank credit. In recent times. Micro finance has emerged as an important means of credit delivery from banks to the poor especially to poor women. The bank SHG linkage programme has been as unique way in India of involving public banks in the provisions of credit to SHGs. This programme was instrumental in financing about 22.3 lach SHGs between 1992 and 2006. Of these SHGs, over 90 percent have only women members. Not withstanding these affirmative efforts, micro finance still remains a minuscule part of total bank credit in India. For instance the total cumulative credit disbursed through bank SHG linkage programme right from its inception in 1992 to 2006 formed only 6 percent of the total agricultural credit disbursed in just one year 2005 – 06. The findings highlight the critical and urgent need for a more definite gender perspective in the policy of financial inclusion. Financial inclusion may be described as the delivery of banking and other financial services at affordable costs to the vast sections of the disadvantaged and low income group groups. To bring in 'the financially excluded' population within the formal financial system many policy initiatives have been taken such as making available a basic banking 'no frills' account either with 'nil' or very low minimum balances, issuing of General Credit cards to eligible beneficiaries without insistence on security, purpose or end use of credit, introduction of KCCs, ATMs allowing banks to utilize the services of NGOs, SHGs, MFIs and other civil Society Organizations as intermediaries in providing financial services, credit linking of SHGs, support to MFIs and introduction Banking correspondence scheme. Extent and causes of Financial Exclusion: In order to find out the extent of financial exclusion, survey was undertaken among the rural households of Vadakudi village in Nagur block of Nagapattinam district There were

OVER VIEW OF EFFORTS FOR FINANCIAL INCLUSION

Financial Inclusion includes meeting the small credit needs of the people, giving them access to the payment system and providing remittance facilities. This has led to some notable developments.

- No frill accounts: In November 2005 RBI asked banks to offer a basic banking "no frills" account with low or zero minimum balances and minimum charges to expand the out reach of such accounts to the low income groups. As on 31st March, 2009 there were 3.3 crore no-frill accounts.
- Easier credit facilities: Banks were asked to introduce a General Purpose credit Card (GCC) facility upto Rs. 25,000. The total number of GCC issued by banks as on March 2009 was 0.15 million.
- Simpler KYC Norms : In order to ensure that people belonging to low income groups, both in urban and rural areas, do not encounter difficulties in opening bank accounts, " Know Your Customer" (KYC) procedure for opening accounts
- Use of Information Technology: Banks have been urged to scale up IT initiatives for Financial inclusion speedily while ensuring that solutions are

Table:6 Nagapattinam District - Caste wise inclusion and exclusion of respondents

Caste	MEN			Women			TOTAL		
	FI	FE	Total	FI	FE	Total	FI	FE	Total
SC	22	58	80	12	80	92	34	138	172
	(27.50)	(72.50)	(100	(13.04)	(86.96)	(100)	(19.77)	(80.23)	(100)
ST	-	7	7	-	4	4	-	11	11
		(100)	(100)		(100)	100)		(100)	(100)
OBC	62	138	200	42	173	215	104	311	415
	(31.00)	(69.00)	(100)	(19.53)	(80.47)	(100)	(25.06)	(74,94)	(100)
Total	84	203	287	54	257	311	138	460	598
	29.27	(70.73)	(100)	(17.36)	(82.64)	(100)	(23.08)	(76.92)	(100)

Note: figures within parenthesis indicate column wise percentage

Occupation wise inclusion and exclusion of the respondents – Nagapattinam district

Occupation	MEN			Women			TOTAL		
	FI	FE	Total	FI	FE	Total	FI	FE	Total
Agricultural labour	26 (25.74	75 (74.26)	101 (100)	32 (15.53)	174 (84.47)	206 (100)	58 (18.89)	249 (81.11)	307 (100)
Marginal farmers	12 (21.05)	45 (78.95)	57 (100)	-	21 (100)	21 (100)	12 (15.38)	66 (84.62)	78 (100)
Small farmer	14 (36.84)	24 (63.16)	38 (100)	6 (33.33)	12 (66.67)	18 (100)	20 (35.71)	36 (64.29)	56 (100)
Big farmer	10 (83.33)	2 (16.67)	12 (100)	-	-	-	10 (83.33)	2 (16.67)	12 (100)
Non farm labour	22 (27.85)	57 (72.15)	79 (100)	16 (24.24)	50 (75.76)	66 (100)	38 (26.21)	107 (73.79)	145 (100)
Total	84 (29.27	203 (70.73)	287 (100)	54 (17.36)	257 (82.64)	311 (100)	138 (23.08)	460 (76.92)	598 (100)

Note: figures within parenthesis indicate column wise percentage

highly secure, amenable to audit, follow widely- accepted open standards to ensure eventual inter – operability among the different systems.

- Electronic Benefit Transfer (EBT) through Banks: To encourage banks to adopt information and communication Technology (ICT) solutions for enhancing their outreach, the RBI formulated a scheme to quicken the pace of adoption of the smart cart-based Electronic Benefit Transfer (EBT) mechanism by banks and rolled out the EBT system in the States that are ready to adopt the scheme. As per the scheme, the RBI would reimburse the banks a part of the cost of opening accounts with bio-metric access/ smart carts at the rate of Rs. 50 per account through which payment of social security benefits, National Rural Employment Act (NREGA) payments and payments under other government benefits would be routed to persons belonging to below poverty line (BPL) families. The scheme was implemented in Andhra Pradesh. So far, seven banks have been paid Rs.18 crore for smart cards issued by banks in Andhra Pradesh during July – December 2008. The process is at different stages of implantation in other states such as Karnataka and Uttarakhand and the scheme of partial reimbursement by Reserve Bank was extended by one year up to June 30,2010. Banks are advised to work in coordination with the respective government departments at the Central and State levels to ensure that at State benefits are delivered to individuals only through bank accounts within a specific timeframe.

- Business Correspondent Model (BC): The BC Model ensures a closer relationship between poor people and the organized financial system Reorganizing this, in 2006, RBI permitted banks to use the services of non – governmental organizations, micro finance institutions, retired bank employees, ex-servicemen, retired government employees, Section 25 companies, and other civil society organizations as Business Correspondents in providing financial and banking services. In addition , RBI has also permitted banks to appoint the following entities as BCs (i) Individual kirana/medical / fair price shop owners. (II) agents of Small Savings schemes of government of India/insurance Companies (III) individual public Call office (PCO) operators. (IV) Individuals who own Petrol Pumps (V) Retired teachers and (V) Authorized functionaries of well run Self Help Groups (SHGs) linked to banks.

- Bank Branch and ATM Expansion Liberalized: Reserve bank of India has totally freed the location of ATMs from prior authorization. Further, in the October 2009 RBI took another big step by freeing branch opening in towns and villages with a population below 49,999. After examining the recommendations of the Working Group constituted to review the Branch Authoriation Policy, RBI has permitted domestic scheduled commercial banks (other than Regional Rural Banks) to open branches in Tier 3 to Tier 6 centre (with population upto 49,999 as per Census 2001) without having the need to take permission from RBI The Domestic scheduled commercial banks (other than RRBs) are enjoined to ensure that at least one-third of such branch expansion happens in the under banked districts of under banked states.

- Project Financial Literacy: Financial literacy is a stepping – stone toward financial inclusion. Moreover, as financial markets are becoming increasingly complex with serious problems of information asymmetry, the need for financial literacy has become even more acute. The Reserve Bank of India has initiated a "Project Financial Literacy" with the objective of disseminating information regarding the central bank and general banking concepts to various target groups.
- Financial Literacy and Credit Counseling: RBI has advised the convener-bank of each State Level Bankers Committee (SLBC) to set up a financial literacy – cum – counseling centre in any one district on a pilot basis, and based on that experience, to extend the facility to other districts in due course. So far, 154 credit counseling centers have been set up in various states of the country. These centers are expected to provide free financial education to people in rural and urban areas on the various financial products and services, while maintaining an arm's length relationship with the parent bank.

Caste wise exclusion is found to be high among SC women (86.96%) as against 27.50 in the case of men. Among the STs cent per cent exclusion is found among both men and women.

Among all categories of occupation, women remain at a disadvantageous position with rate of financial exclusion. After tsunami, wage employment has declined. The NREGS provides only an average of 16 days employment, with the result the women had to rely on informal sources for household needs and education of their children. The factors responsible for financial exclusion are varied and thus no single factor could explain the phenomenon. Broadly they can be classified as supply side factors and demand side factors.

SUPPLY SIDE FACTORS FOR FINANCIAL EXCLUSION

The supply side factors usually arise from the structural operation of financial service providers. The principle barriers in the exclusion of financial services are physical access, high charges, penalties and condition attached to financial products which make them inappropriate or complicated and perceptions of the financial service institutions which are not liked by the low income people.

Other supply side factors barriers are

- inconvenience of the branch time
- inappropriateness of the products and services
- cumbersome procedures and documents
- collateral requirements
- language
- staff attitude
- high charges and penalties
- high transaction costs in availing bank credit
- risk perception of financial institutions about the poor

There are many reasons why formal financial institutions do not offer low income and poor women more access to financial services. The poor and low income people have latent demand but that cannot be satisfied by the financial products or terms and conditions and delivery practices offered by the financial institutions. Their requirements are practical, convenient, affordable, flexible, continuously available, reliable and safe financial services. The formal financial institutions often do not look through the eyes of their customers Demand side factors for financial exclusion The demand side factors mainly emanate from socio economic conditions of financial service users. They include mainly lack of awareness, assetlessness resulting difficulty in offering collateral required, low income and low productivity leading to weak and non viable demand, lower social status resulting in social exlusion and financial illiteracy barriers and information asymmetry. The most conspicuous demand side barriers are low income and assetlessness. Financial status of the women is always important in gaining access to financial services. Access to credit is frequently limited for women who do not have or cannot hold title to assets such as land and property or must seek male guarantees to borrow. Other factors affecting access to financial services to some extent are gender issues (access to credit for women limited), age factor (senior citizens and young are usually discriminated), legal hurdles (non availability of appropriate legal rights and documents) and psychological and cultural barriers resulting in self exclusion are also important in determining the easy physical access to financial services

In the rural areas the common reasons found for financial exclusion of women include the following:

- Non existence of bank branches in the area

- Physical distance of the bank from the people
- Fixed and limited timings of the banks
- Lack of awareness about the advantages of having a bank account and above all
- Low income of women that made it difficult to save especially in the case of Female headed households.

CONSEQUENCES TO FINANCIAL EXCLUSION

Losing opportunities to grow:

- In the absence of finance of, women who are not connected with formal financial system lack opportunities both for production and consumption purposes.
- Countries growth will be retarded : due to vast unutilized resources that is in the form of money in the hands of people who lack financial inclusive services.
- Business loss to the banks : banks will loose the business profit arising out of financial transaction of various sections of people
- Exclusion from main stream society: the marginalized sections who enable to access to credit facilities are social excluded
- Lack of opportunity to thrift and borrow: financially excluded people may loose chances to save a part of their livelihood earnings and it has to borrow from others
- Employment barriers: Now a days all salary and other financial benefits from various sources like government scholarship, any compensation, grant, relief etc, are paid through bank accounts.
- Loss due to theft : banks provide various schemes safety locker facility. It mitigates the risk due to theft.
- Other allied financial services: people who do not have bank accounts may not go to banks so they lack basic finance auxiliary services like demand draft insurance cover and emergency loans.

The various forms of financial inclusion based on the contributing factors are as follows:

- Access exclusion i.e restriction of access to both financial and physical resources emanating from the structural operation of financial system.
- Market exclusion: If the women do not have entitlement, market excludes some section of the people
- Condition exclusion: It occurs due to the terms and conditions attached to the financial products and services which make them inappropriate for the needs of women
- Price exclusion: Prices charged by the banks are not affordable
- Self Exclusion; People voluntarily decide not to opt for a financial product because of the fear of refusal to access by the service providers.

WAY FORWARD:

The opening of the accounts seem to be the sole criterion on which performance is measured. Once the account is opened it is deemed that the goals of the inclusion have been realized. The fact that the account should be operational and used by the account holder to save, borrow and remit money does not seem to matter. In the study area it was found that several women who opened accounts under the NREGS did not operate the accounts as the wages were paid in cash by the Panchayats and not credited into their accounts as per the provision of NREGS. Unless the account becomes operational, becomes a fulcrum of economic activity for the holder the objective of inclusion would stand unrealized. Financial awareness on opening and operating accounts must precede and accompany the inclusion initiative. SHGs and SHG Federation can play an important role in identifying the left out women and include them in the SHGs to access financial services across various regions. The decision of the government to waive loans creates a negative impact. For poor people instead of loan waiver, social investment is needed to cross poverty line. Funds are to be earmarked for capacity building, creation of common infrastructure

Establishment of Financial Counseling Centers

A systematic effort should be structured by establishing Financial Counseling Centers for providing financial services to the illiterate women in the rural areas

Involvement of Educational Sector for promotion of Financial Inclusion

Involving educational institutions particularly college students for financial inclusion drive would not only be cost effective but also would create wide public awareness

Partnership with dedicated NGOs

Partnering with trust worthy and reputed NGOs could certainly accelerate the process of financial inclusion in the rural areas. Specific financial and non – financial incentives have to be designed for the spirited involvement of such organizations.

Financial Inclusion as part of course curriculum in high schools

Financial inclusion should be imbibed into the course curriculum in higher secondary schools. The students would understand the importance of financial inclusion for inclusive growth in the economy which in turn them would motivate them to participate in the financial system.

Digitize the documentation process for opening bank accounts

One of the often stated reasons for slow pace of financial inclusion has been the hassles involved in opening of bank accounts and availing of loans from financial institutions due to the long process of documentation. To over come risk hurdle there is a need to Digitize the public records for dual purpose of easy accessibility and storage .

Strategy to revitalize the rural credit mechanism including the cooperatives

A need is felt to strategize the provision of national credit to the rural farmer house holds majority of the marginal farmer house holds are not covered by the formal finance .As such public sector banks and cooperative banks in the rural areas have to sensitize about the need for provision of timely and cheaper credit to the segments. Reserve bank of India in consultation with NABARD should come out with a comprehensive strategy of revitalizing the quiescent rural credit mechanism. I

Exclusive focus on the socially excluded and the poor

It is important to encompass the social excluded sections and women, tenant farmers oral lessees and share croppers, marginal farmers with small uneconomic land holding, agricultural laborers, rural artisans and people involved in making handicraft and also making weavers in handloom sector.

Procedural / documentation changes

It is inevitable and the part of the regulators to find out an easy way of procuring the documents for opening of bank accounts and availing loans. The present guidelines are more tedious and result in huge cost for the poor in accessing the banks for various kinds of financial services. Simplifying requirements, exemption from stamp duty for loans to small farmers and marginal farmers, saral documentation for agricultural loan need to be carried

Proactive role of Government

The state government should play an proactive role in facilitating financial inclusion. Issuing official identity documents for opening accounts, creating awareness and involving district and block level functionaries in the entire process, undertaking financial literacy drive are some of the ways in which the state and district administration can involve them.

Role of post offices

The post offices in the rural areas can provide their services in accelerating financial inclusion actively. In view of the post man's intimate knowledge of the local population and the enormous trust reposed, in him post offices can be of could use in the process of financial inclusion.

Effective use of Information Technology

The effective use of information technology will enable the banks to handle the increase in the volume of transaction of rural households, for processing, credit scoring, credit record and follow up. The use of information technology solutions for providing banking facilities at door step of villages holds the potential for scalability of the financial inclusion initiative.

Financial Inclusion as a Corporate Social Responsibility of all the Banks

It should be the endeavor of all the financial institutions to adopt financial inclusion as a corporate social responsibility and chalk out strategies in tune with the national policy on financial inclusion.

Awareness of availability of financial services

It is important to know whether the households studied are aware of the availability of various financial products and services. Awareness is an essential element of financial literacy. Lack of knowledge about the availability of financial services in terms of location and type of services is considered as one of the main barriers on the demand side for expanding financial exclusion particularly among the poor, illiterate and vulnerable segments of the society in rural areas. The process of financial inclusion begins with creating awareness about the availability of various financial products and services, terms and conditions in which they are available and the benefits that can be derived. Field data was collected on awareness of various financial products and services recognizing the significance of awareness in the promotion of financial inclusion, and presented in table.

43 INCLUSIVE GROWTH:- PEASANTRY-MODERNISATION

S.Gurusamy and B. Parthasarathi

PRELUDE:

Inclusive growth always indicates a growth where all segments of our population can be benefitted either socially, politically, above all economically. It needs certain exercise to recognize the input as well as output of the growth. Since we achieve independence, several plans, programs were introduced through various five year plans which categorically focused our agricultural sectors, industrial sectors and now tertiary sector to bring all segments of our population on boat of wealthy zones but it was unfortunate that certain segments vulnerable were missed that boat. These segments are basically uneducated, less empowered, unemployed or seasonal employed, affected by diseases like HIV/AIDS, racism and castes victims etc. Therefore they remain in lower strata of the society where they are witnessed various exploitation in every stage of their life. Poverty, malnutrition, untimely deaths etc is common for them. Now in the era of 21st century where we stand on global competition due to our liberation policy (1991) on commerce and trades and to promote more employment capacity, government of India has focused on modernization. Modernization mean more technological transmission from developed nations, industrialization etc. utilizing our natural resources i.e. land, mine, river, hills etc. Therefore, these resources are becoming scarce. Burgeoning population are one side, industrialization is another side put more pressure on land particularly on cultivable land whose extension is beyond human capacity. Therefore, it is a new challenge to the government to occupy this resource using various instruments and modalities. These instruments are nothing but policy, frequent change of policy, empowering local political leaders which not only pollute environment for cultivation but also create confusion among peasantry ulterior motive with easy encroachment of lands for modernization. To-days scenario is such that peasants not only losing their land ownership rights but also are rooted out from their originality. A humane notion of displacement must go beyond cash compensation, beyond even land for land and extend to compensate all opportunity-costs of uprooting from habitats, social, religious, cultural and material ways of life(see Fernandes,1989).Pupils demand is not restricted do the certain limits; it has enhanced beyond the capacity of nature. Now modernization has become such an essential requirement where cultivable lands are converted into fallow lands for the purpose of industrial developments which induce displacement of peasantry. Yesterday's land lords, today's pauperized and proletariats socially excluded and marginalized. Therefore, modernization may be a good plan for uplift and mainstreaming our people simultaneously, certain diversion of peasantry from main stream of society due to displacement from generation wise occupation, is a great challenge for government in this five year plan for **inclusive growth**.

Therefore, this paper reflects various issues of unrest peasants in changing global scenario and is also suggested land marks to main stream them in the valuable five year plan(2012-2017).Various studies are conducted in this issue as incorporated herein **Famine Commission report (1878)**stressed that the vast mass of cultivators in the N.W provinces and Oudh were already, however, classified legally as tenants, and they proposed unsuccessfully at the time that all unprotected tenants-at-will should be accorded occupancy status **Cf map(1879)** views the JAT's impatience of control extended to a reluctance to recognize the authority of even the village managers (lambardars) through whom he paid his revenue to the Government. Fission and dispersion thus deployed a clan in settlement groups over a wide area often intermixed with the villages of other clans or castes. The result was a patchwork quilt of local groupings (tapas) in each of which members of one clan had obtained dominance. **Woodward (1883)** expressed that the poor plot holder without tenant right, or the extremely poor area without significant production of cash crops, like Sholapur district in the Deccan, were at the bottom of the debtors league. **Marx (1879)** expressed his views that compartmentalize was the keynote of the economic and social structure, oriental despotism characterised its politics. Whether this arose as Marx believed primarily out of the need for a centralized bureaucratic authority to build and manage irrigation works upon which agriculture dependence or whether it represented simply the systematize of predatory military rule, is immaterial. But its consequences were the absorption by state taxation of the whole surplus produce of the soil beyond the bare subsistence needs of the cultivator. Hence private rent property in land and a stable all ordeal aristocracy based upon it never emerged **Dutt.(1906)** has strenuously kept alive the notion, first voiced by British administrators that Indian society suffered in consequences wanton derangement from arbitrary decisions as to what social group should be vested with the novel form of proprietary right in land **Marx(1920)**talks of the peasantry as the small holding peasants from vast mass, the members of which live in similar condition without entering into manifold relations with one another. The mode of production isolates them from one another instead of bringing them into mutual intercourse. Their isolation is increased due to bad communication; the small holding admits no division of labour in its cultivation, no application of science and therefore no diversity of developments, no variety of talent and no wealth of social relationship. **Lenin (1920)** talks of six different agrarian classes in terms of ownership of means of production and labour exploitation. To Lenin agriculture proletariat are wage labours who obtain their livelihood by working for hire in capitalist agricultural enterprises. The semi –proletariats peasants are those who obtain their livelihood partly as wage labour in agricultural and industrial capitalist enterprises and partly by working on their owner rented plots of land which provide only a part of the means of subsistence for their families. According to him, the small peasantry that is small tillers who hold either as owners or as tenants, small plots of lands which enable them to meet the requirements of their families and their farm without hiring outside labour. **Mukherjee Radhakamal(1926)** Expressed Down to the Second World War almost every school of historical interpretation, Marxist or non- Marxist, was read that whatever the novel degree of physical unity imposed the main effect of British rule on traditional Indian agrarian structure was one of dissolution **Manu(1932)** realized that the division of labour in the caste structure can be stabilized only if the numerical proportions among the castes were maintained If the proportions were to be disrupted and any one caste became too populous ,the commodity produced by that caste would be in oversupply, and the terms of trade would become unfavourable to it. **Mao (1933)** differentiated the peasantry in terms of ownership of means of production and exploitation on the basis of wage, labour, usury, rent and market forces. He talks of the five different agrarian classes in his selected works. Those are landlord's rich, middle peasants, poor peasants and workers. Maos characterization of peasants into various classes was not only undertaken by him from the point of view of economics class but more so to distinguish the real antagonism that sub serves between exploiters and the exploited. **Prestianni (1947,98-9)**expressed about the zone of intensive cultivation is composed of small or minute properties which are fragmented and dispersed and mostly derive from lease hold concessions; they belong to all classes of the population-the wealthy, professional persons, wage workers, artisans and peasants **Kroeber(1948)** define peasants as a part of societies with part cultures. They are definitely rural yet live in relation to market towns. They form a class segment of a larger population. They lack isolation the political economy, the self sufficiency of tribal population, but their local unit retain much of their old identity, integration and attachment to soil and cults **Mukherjee(1958)** views that the numerous historians have been the early British land-revenue settlements in Bengal and Madras as direct responses to Britain's new market requirements **Draisma(1958;Blaikie 1971)** views that the reduction in labour input with distance from the farmstead, associated with reduced gross and net yields. This general relationship is manifested spatially in patterns of land use on the farm associated with lower labour inputs at greater distances is a reduction in the amount of fertilizer applied to the land

Chayanov (1960) tried to look at it in great detail. In Chayanov's view, peasant motivations are different from those of the capitalist, they aim at securing for the needs of the family rather than to make profit **Pavlov (1964)** soviet historians have long since retreated from the notion of the unchanging East and the dogma of the absence of private property in land as the key to its history. The recognized development of an exchange economy and mercantile capitalism from at least the seventeenth century on wards. **Nehru (1961)** views that it was axiomatic that despite India's stormy history the village self- governing community continued. Its break-up began only under British rule **Murray(1965)** views the primary task of industrialization is to establish this balance by transforming the dualistic society into a well- integrated more equalitarian and economically homogeneous society based on higher level of technology and with much greater productive power.

MacIntyre(1965) has said that alienation is essentially a contrast concept that is before one can understand alienation one must be able to determine the nature of un-alienated life. **TeodarShanin(1966)** takes more or less a similar stand on peasant family farm. In his view, peasants consist of small agricultural producers who with the help of simple equipment and labour of their families produce mainly for their own consumption and for the fulfillment of obligations to the holders of political and economic power. **D. ThornerB.Kerblayet.al (1966)** expressed the views of Chayanov. According to chayanov the peasant economy could not be realistically evaluated and analyzed within the frame work of classical economic theories, for it did not follow the rules of the capitalist economy. Capitalist economy refers wage labour and profit neither was relevant to the peasant economy. Chayanov therefore concluded that the peasant economy is a non- capitalist form of production; it does not operate in terms of profit, wage or rent **A.V Chayanov (1966)** considered peasants production more efficient and competitive than capitalist production because peasants did not have to make profit. As such when capitalists go bankrupt, peasants survive and reproduce **Moore (1967)** discussed that the apparent political docility of the Indian Peasants in social origins of Dictatorship and democracy, lord and peasant in the making of the modern world. He explains that the politics as a self- contained activity and relegate rural India to the role of a dim shadowy backcloth to the political stage. **Althusser (1969)** also claims that the structure of dominance of the contradictions changes over time. So that in course of time a dominant contradiction may become non-dominant and the non-dominant contradiction may become dominant. The social structure of Bishalpur has faced severe onslaughts since the establishment of BSP.A good part of its cultivated land was acquired resulting in a section of the native moves out. Many of the natives and migrants took to industrial employment **Owen (1968) Sen**

(1971) views about the uses of transport services over bullock carts in transporting agricultural productions in India. They viewed that the spread of motorized transport in India, reducing transport costs to one-half or one-third; bullock carts still operate over a radius of 40 millimeters whereas previously the limit was 80

Hombergeret.al (1970) expressed each village was self –sufficing when the simple necessaries of life were manufactured by the village carpenter, potter and weaver who were supported by common contributions from village resources. The more prosperous men are with -drawing from the responsibilities of village life, the authority of the patil is disappearing and the village artisans are no longer supported .Trade is the great solvent which breaks up social organization. We really are nihilists, overthrowing the institutions of society and helpless to develop anything in their stead **Rothermund (1970)** views although after 1860 India began to produce on a significant scale for the world market, this was effected without the mode of peasant agricultural production undergoing any fundamental change: the essentially parasitic structure of ownership, credit and marketing on their view, simply skimmed cash crops off the surface of an immobilized agrarian society **Maddick (1970)** expressed Indian nationalists found it still harder to resist sentimentality and the Gandhian School shaped their soaring political ideals on the revival of a golden past in which panchayat raj and an autonomous village economy symbolized by the spinning wheel would re-emerge triumphant **Boudhayan (1970)**argued that the growth of commercial capitalism, especially during the Muslim period, would have led to the growth of Industrial capitalism in India had not this trend been interrupted by the British conquest and transformation of the country into a British colony. Recently that view has been challenged. **Schacht (1971)** in conceiving of this alienation in terms of a separation through surrender to another however Marx obscures its basic character and encounters problems of both over and under inclusiveness. It would seem more fruitful to drop all references to the meditation of an alien will in the explication of the concept of such alienation itself and to focus solely upon the relation of labour to the individual. **Finifter (1972)** appreciates one's activity is a self- creating force can impact a special significance to research that explores what is meant by the phrase alienation from work. If man is alienated it implies that his existence is in some way incomplete because he has lost the opportunity for self-creation.

Dungen(1972) expressed that the urban capitalists were more interested in rent receiving or in controlling the disposal of peasant-growth cash crops than in directly engaging in agriculture so that the introduction of legal private property rights in land tended to lengthen the chain of intermediaries above the actual cultivator and left the peasant petite culture intact. Compulsory alienation of land in satisfaction of debt was recognized by the British as a drastic innovation on traditional practice and official concern was being voiced at the extent of transfers under this head already by the 1850s.**Patnaik(1976)** had questioned the incorrect neo-classical and neo-populist way of classifying the peasantry since Indian Agriculture is characterised by high degree of concentration of both land and non- land resources with a minority of cultivators while the majority have command over disproportionately less share of resources. She further emphasized that the size of holding, to identify the class status. Because an acre of irrigated or high fertility land is obviously different from an acre of rain fed or barren land. She suggests her own criterion termed as labour exploitation criterion in terms of the use of outside labour relative to the use of family labour for categories the classes of peasantry which according to her serves as the most reliable single index. **Moore (1977)** tried to look at the class of peasantry in terms of super ordination and subordination. In his view a previous history of subordination to a landed upper class recognized and enforced in the laws sharp cultural distinctions and a considerable degree of de facto possession of land constitute the main distinguishing features of peasantry. These distinctions are blurred at edges **Godelier(1977)** says that in determining a social and economic formation we shall be able to produce a synthetic definition of the exact nature of the particular diversity and unity of economic and social relations which characterize a society during a specific epoch **Dasgupta(1977)**expressed the more successful forms of peasant agriculture appear to have emerged where owner-cultivator communities under Ryotwar or Bhaiachara forms obtained a novel security in their conditions of life. **Marx(1977;20-21)** visualizes a particular relationship between the economic structure and the non-economic structure of the society when he says" the totality of these relations of production constitutes the economic structure of the society, the real foundation, on which arises a legal and political superstructure and to which correspond definite forms of social consciousness. **Mill** views in his early school of development economists had believed that since all social strata above the peasant lived off disbursements of land revenue, the British had it in their power to shape society as they chose according to the type of land revenue system they adopted. **Romila** expressed the growth of feudalism and the decay of trade and manufacturing on land became almost the only source of income and the system of private property in land became more deeply entrenched.

Shiva Kumar (1978) differentiates the classes of peasantry in his study conducted in two villages in chengelpet district of Tamil Nadu in terms of two criteria that is ownership or non- ownership of means of production and the type of use of means of production are put to. Among these two, he took land as the critical variable to differentiate the classes of peasantry **Sen(1982)** stressed the need for alliance between peasants and workers as a precondition for successful revolution and attributed the failure of the three major communist led uprisings in India to the lack of support by the workers **David** suggested that in India during the nineteenth century, the rising classes of rich capitalist peasants had consolidated their power largely at the expense of the peasantry

Gurusamy (1991) views that the peasant organization are instrumental in the articulation of interests and exposure of the deprived conditions amongst peasantry largely known for illiteracy, ignorance and unawareness. The articulated interest is subsequently transformed in the form of pressure course of action for the redress of their grievances. In the process, there emerged conflict and confrontation between peasants and rulers in the State which ultimately brought the parties in conflict across table for negotiated settlement through consensus. **Guha(2007)**views that the displacement of peasants through the acquisition of land at any place in India cannot take place in a political vacuum. Because ,acquisition of land in the Indian states has to be a decision of the government and whenever the government takes agricultural land of the peasants for development projects, it tries to justify the decision at different levels and instituonalised for a by taking advantage of the democratic set up.

ISSUES:

Ours is agricultural based country where the majority of people live in the village and their livelihood depends upon agriculture and its productivity. Therefore, the pillar of economy now also stands on this sector. Immediate after independence, Government of India changed certain policy on this sector to have more access of product in international markets but it was unfortunate to get sound progressive response due to huge competition with developed nations. Within the country green revolution may be one of the land marks for product sufficiency but it was restricted to few states like Punjab, Haryana, Tamil Nadu and certain portion of West Bengal which was not sufficient to feed the vast population. The technological advancement, better quality of seeds, etc. are beyond the scope of peasants to equip themselves with requisite skilled in production of sufficient crops to compete with global markets. Therefore, the food crisis in the State, unemployment, poverty, drudgeries condition among peasants though remains a major unaddressed issues but government had no option other than to change this track to industrialization which provide employment to certain portion of our population those have that technical skill. Therefore, this modernization process is changing village status bringing into various industrial cultures where the peasants are motivated to leave the cultivation and move to industrial society for better livelihood thereby status. Government use this factor in such a manner today peasants are confused and take hasty decision to surrender their cultivable land to the government with ulterior motive to lead a better life in the contemporary society. This deal reflects genuine issues which involve many agencies to take appropriate decision to satisfy the peasants in achieving their ulterior desires. Therefore, it needs time to see various dimensions of the deal in which peasants lose their patience and take easy route for want of food and security. The new business, unknown place may have difficulty for their sustainability. Therefore, it is another dimension to accept violent path resulting in creation of Maoists, Naxalite and religious fundamentalists etc. in certain states of our country particularly eastern India like Assam, Manipur, **West Bengal, Bihar, Jharkhand, Orissa** and certain portion of Centre like Uttar Pradesh, Delhi etc. according to Vaswani et.al(1990) emphasized the necessity to identify the laws of the land that are to displace, compensate and rehabilitate people and to examine their contents in details. These displaced peasants often remained an undifferentiated and residual category who has to suffer the trauma of losing their homes and land for the greater interest of various kinds of development projects (see Mc. Cully (1996).The features of this **transitional** society in the era of modernization need to re- look for better policy formulation and promotional aspects to see our country as a global leader not only in quality of agricultural productivity but also in science and technology bringing together all segments of our population excluded, isolated from main stream of society because of socio-economic-politically disadvantaged by the end of this five year plan 2017.

OBJECTIVES:

- To examine the various issues of peasantry
- To discuss the effects of modernization on peasantry
- To analyses various scope in Xii plan in mainstreaming the peasant community
- To make findings and conclusion

METHODOLOGY:

This study is based on the secondary data collected through the articles published in related Journals, Newspaper, Books, websites etc. and also through focus group discussion supplemented by observation, experiences gained in various development programmes in rural areas. Based upon this, the inferences are drawn and logical conclusion is made. Certain useful suggestions are also presented based upon the findings and conclusions.

FINDINGS:

Marx righty mentioned about peasants' condition, they are like Gaani bags, vulnerable, worst to understand their good or bad. It is true now also. They are unchanged their attitudes now also. Therefore, they become soft targets by the capitalists, money launders, market brokers etc. We are witnessed pre-independence era when the condition of peasantry was such that our agricultural productivity was affected. There was a race of exploitation among rich, middle and poor peasants to fulfill the demands by British emperors which create a division in peasants' society; people were migrated to other profession for secure livelihoods etc. But it is unfortunate that the same traditions are still on after long years of our independence. The changes of govt. policies in agricultural sectors which confuse the peasants therefore, the results of the policy remain in the upper strata of the peasants' society or in the hands of political mortems. This political mortems have a good coordination with industrialists, capitalists, markets brokers, foreign investors and other vested interest groups to link up with peasantry which facilitate a better deals in gaining lands from peasants at nominal compensation. The commercial scenario in our country was restricted within states only. But after liberation policy (1991) of globalization changed the complete scenario which creates a tunnel for developed countries to transfer their used technology having less life expectancy. Ours is a populated country where un-education, unemployment, poverty is the main issue to-day .Therefore, this technological advancement becomes an essential to implement in agricultural sectors and industrial sectors to create more employment opportunities and livelihood resources. But this process of developments has another side where the unskilled peasants are rooted out from their occupation and migrated to other occupation, is a serious thought to-day. Technological advancement degrades the soils that affect the productivity. Various market players have penetrated into the agriculture sector in such a way in which land has come to market resulted in peasants are unrest. The escalating rate of fertilizers and pesticides has made a difficult task for peasants to control the production costs at the same time poor infrastructure for storing the products, govt. policies, middlemen interests etc. demerit their products and is scoring less profit out of their deals. Peasants are not only under pressure of debt but also mentally tortured by the market players in assuring their mental relief at the cost of their cultivable land. Therefore, it is a major issue for policy makers to be address on due course. Unable to accept the defeat, today peasants do not have any other option and they take the path for suicide, the recent statistics show suicide rates among peasants' different parts of our country like Maharashtra, Andhra Pradesh Orissa, west Bengal etc.

This inclusive growth plan is a right path to include these exhaustive peasants on both or socio-economic and political developments .The probable influence of the growth of manufacturing industry on the standard of general well-being is a different issue. In India, where industrial development must inevitable be far slower the most that can be hoped is that some part of the annual increase in population will find employment in Industry. In that case rural population, unless checked by other causes will grow more slowly, but it will continue to grow. The increased pressure on the land, which would have resulted from the same proportion of the rising generation assuming that it had lived-seeking employment in agriculture, will be somewhat mitigated; but the actual pressure, which exists at present to an appalling degree, will not be demolished.

Industrialization therefore, likes emigration, however, desirable in itself. Our country where population is a great issue and where the capitalism based on the exploitation of cheap labour particularly in agricultural sector, is a remote. Fresh waves of labourers do not sweep away the gains the modernization of industry makes possible a higher standard of life. Where and in what degree the possibility becomes a reality for the mass of ordinary people depends not merely on how much is produced, but on the terms in it is produced and on the manner in which it is used, therefore, it is a question not only of technology but of social organization and policy. It is question of circumstances and of the policy appropriate to them. Given large natural resources, a population mobile, adaptable and above all, small and the alternative to industrial employment offered by free land, the transition from the cottage to the factory may be swift and frictionless and the harassed peasants of yesterday undergo a painless sub limitation into the car-owning, cinema-haunting mechanic of to-day, no general diffusion of education, little accessible spare land and administrative services still in their infancy, the first effects of industrialization are likely if experience may be trusted, to be somewhat more speckled.

Therefore, the first space of industrial revolution affecting agricultural progress would the peasantry migrated to the industrial occupation is nothing but an exploitation in many regards like extended working hours, child labour, night work, not only for adults but children, a shocking accident roll, a new discipline of production which is resented as an interference with personal liberty, a deterioration of the environment which goes some- what to counter balance the rise in money wages. Therefore, it is pertinent to say that the condition of peasantry remain in the same place as it was during agricultural production, the bitter relation with land owners, market players, money launders etc. who push these vulnerable people in a well from where they are unable to come out with their ideas and experience. Therefore, the inclusiveness of these exclusive peasants are most important discussion today which not only show a clean way for economic development in the rural areas but also an indication of socio and political development for all segments of this population, a good sign today.

CONCLUSION:

This research is an attempt made to study various conditions of peasants today. This study is based on secondary data (letters, govt. reports, journals, news items etc. A careful reading of the literature revealed that there is a dearth of description and analysis on the ground realities of land laws which has a close relationship with the empowering institutions like land reforms act, panchayat, and various govt. rules function in the jurisdiction of State and Central power which make a big confusion among peasantry.

The displacement of peasantry through the acquisition of land at any place in India can- not takes place in a political vacuum. Because acquisition of land in the Indian states has to be a decision of the government and whenever the government takes agricultural land of the peasants for development projects, it tries to justify the decision at different levels and institutionalized for a by taking advantage of the democratic set up. Decentralized planning, the acquisition of agricultural land for large scale private industries though has a logical conclusion for development in Micro levels which in turn may help to pull up micro economy but still it is beyond expectation to success. As an example in west Bengal the land reform policy was a remarkable stone to distribute the lands to land less people for effective utilization of lands but it is ultimately a push factor for poor peasants in such a way that they become puppets of political leaders. These peasants have got the rights of habitats or cultivation without proper documentary evidence that makes another tunnel for easy encroachment of lands.

The establishment of industries through acquisition of agricultural land primarily caused dispossession and disempowerment of the peasantry who initially put up resistances against the decision of the government and it has a deeper political consequences besides land lessness. It is not only pauperized the peasantry but also dampened the spirit of success achieved through land reforms by the dispossession of Patta holders and bargadars. As an example Singur, west Bengal where 997 acres of land was acquired for the industries but no industry has been established which is an act of total failure of the panchayat leaders to establish the rights of the farmers on their land has further deteriorated their trust and faith upon the elected panchayats as well as government.

Any generalized macro level hypothesis regarding economic development should take into consideration the macro level realities of the field of its application. That land reform prepares the ground for industrialization may be true in some specific situations but industrialization without a down to earth policy of rehabilitation through the generation of employment and skill development could be a self-defeating endeavor.

SUGGESTIONS:

- Every case of land acquisition should be preceded by a socio-economic survey of the would be affected people in collaboration with the local gram panchayat before the preparation of the preliminary enquiry report by Land acquisition department. This survey should be specially aimed to make a socio-economic impact assessment of the concerned development project.
- There should be a correct method of calculating of monetary compensation of bargadars should be changed. The bargadars must be compensated by the following the same principles of compensation calculation as it is being done in case of the owner of the land.

- The bargadars may be given 75 percent of compensated money as per the position of land. The payment of land and bargadars should be made at a time.
- There should be arrangements to trace out the unrecorded bargadars for necessary compensation if genuine bargadars lose his rights for cultivation over barga lands due to land acquisition. In regards to cases of land acquisition where acquired land has remained unutilized by the In the LA act should immediately be made specific amendment
- Panchayat should be given priority for implementation of various poverty alleviation schemes. Here the project affected scheduled caste and scheduled tribes should be given priority
- Since it is very difficult to identify all the persons and families who derive some benefits in terms of acquired agricultural lands, it would be better to make an appropriate estimate of the said amount in monetary terms. For example, one can roughly calculate with the help of villagers the amount of straw eaten by the cattle through gazing in the agricultural fields during the post- harvest season
- Land acquisition Act should be amended to include the provision of the payment of collective compensation to the gram panchayat to be calculated in terms of market value.
- Like land acquisition, land reforms is basically a legal and administrative procedure. Though land reforms, the State govt. updates the various types of ownership rights according to the land and land reforms act,1955 and its further amendments in 1981 and 1986. The main objective of the act is to distribute land to landless by taking certain administrative steps.

REFERENCES:

- Ali, Ifzal. 2007. Pro-Poor to Inclusive Growth: Asian Prescriptions. *ERD Policy Brief*No. 48. May. Manila:
- Asian Development Bank (ADB).
- Ali,Ifzal and JuzhongZhuang. 2007. Inclusive Growth toward a Prosperous Asia: Policy Implications.
- *ERD Working Paper Series* No. 97. July. Manila: ADB.
- Ali, Ifzal and HyunHwa Son. 2007. Measuring Inclusive Growth. *Asian Development Review* Vol. 24,No. 1, pp. 11–31. Manila: ADB.

- ADB. 2007. *Toward a New Asian Development Bank in a New Asia: Report of the Eminent Persons Group.*Manila: ADB.
- Acharya, S.K. 1990. 'Ethnic Processes in North-Eastern India', in D. Pakem (ed.),*Nationality, Ethnicity and Cultural Identity in North-East India*, pp. 69–108. New Delhi:Omsons Publications.
- Areeparampil, M. 1996. *Tribals of Jharkhand: Victims of Development.* New Delhi: IndianSocial Institute.
- Baishya, P. 1991. 'Rural Industrialisation for Poverty Eradication in Assam', in R.K.
- Barbora, S.1998. *Plantation Systems and Labour Movements in North-East India.* Delhi:Department of Sociology, Delhi School of Economics (Unpublished M.Phil.Thesis).
- ———. 2002. 'Ethnic Politics and Land Use: Genesis of Conflicts in India's North-East',
- Chakravarti, T. 1991. 'The Riang Women of Rural Tripura:
- Das Gupta, M. 1991. *The Impact of Land Reforms on North East India.* New Delhi: Omsons.
- D'Souza, A. 1999.*North East India.* Jakhama: Kohima Region of the Society of Jesus
- (mimeo).
- Fernandes, W. 1990. *Women's Status in the Delhi Bastis: Urbanisation, Economic Forces andVoluntary Organisations.* New Delhi: Indian Social Institute (mimeo).
- ——— and G. Menon. 1987. *Tribal Women and Forest Economy: Deforestation, Exploitationand Status Change.* New Delhi: Indian Social Institute.
- Ferreira, F. and J. Gignoux. 2008. The measurement of inequality of opportunity. *World Bank Policy*
- *Research Working Paper* 4659. Washington DC: The World Bank.
- Grosse, M., K. Harttgen, and S. Klasen. 2008. Measuring Pro-Poor Growth in Non-Income Dimensions.
- Hansen, Stein. 2010. ADB's Contribution to Inclusive Growth in Energy and Transport. Consultant's report. ADB.
- *World Development Report*. Vol. 38, Issue 6. June.

- R.K. Samanta (ed.) *Rural Development in North-East India:*
- *Perspectives, Issues and Experiences, Rural Development in North-East India: Perspectives, Issuesand Experiences*, pp. 205–15. New Delhi: Uppal Publishing House.
- ———. A. 2001. *Traditional Systems of Forest Conservation in North East India: The Angami*
- *Tribe of Nagaland.* Guwahati: North-eastern Social Research Centre.

44 EMPOWERMENT OF DALITS: ISSUES AND CHALLENGES

S.Gurusamy and S.Rajangam (RGNSRF)

INTRODUCTION

Indian social structure is marked by inequalities due to caste, gender, religion and other social discriminization and deprivation seem to prevent and affect social relationships. There exists social hierarchy and those who are in lower categories their status is lowest. The dalits are victimized in view of the practice of social evils like untouchability, economic disparities, social segregation and alienation. The cumulative impact of all these practices have led to exclusion, marginalization of dalits in all walks of social life, particularly in rural communities. As a consequence of the political debate over the years the concept of "depressed classes" was systematically categorized in the 1931 census. This has ultimately led to evaluation of the term "Dalit in the Government of India Act of 1936, specifying certain castes in the term provinces of Assam, Bengal, Bihar, and Bombay. Central provinces are Madras, Orissa, Punjab and United Provinces. The depressed classes the aboriginal and hill tribes and other backward classes. The classification was given by a committee, under the chairmanship of OHS state in which B.R.Ambedcar and A.B.Thakkar were the members appointed by the former Bombay province. The committee submitted its report in the year (1930) (Shrikant, 1968:168-80) with the promulgation of the constitution of India, the Dalit were noticed under the constitution (Dalit) Order 1950 by the president in accordance with the constitution. After independence the concept of backward classes was expressed to include the harijans (ex) Dalit, who were socially, economically and educationally backward. Up to the fourth plan period, the term backward classes included the Dalits and tribes and other backward classes. However, by the beginning of the fifth plan period it was felt that these sectors confronted different social, political, economic and psychological problems. Hence it was felt that each sector needs a different set of handing. Consequently a separate plan was introduced for the tribals titled tribal sub plan (TSP) in the fifth plan.

By the beginning of the sixth plan, Special Component Plan (SCP) was considered for the SCs as specialized programme for these groups for Tribal Sub Plan (TSP) and for Dalit castes the Special Component Plan (SCP) were introduced. The addition there was a provision for Special Central Assistance (SCs) under the TCP and SCP. Similar steps were taken up for backward classes minorities and other disadvantages groups by allotting a certain proportion of the plan outlay for these sectoral groups. The Dalit cases in the country are placed in peculiar circumstances. They are not localized in a particular region of the country, by the dispersed all over the country. They do not stay away from the general population and have very close interaction with the people in the surrounding. Although they provide support services, yet their services may not be appreciated by the consumers of their services and conflict ridden situations may be created between the SCs and other groups. The source of dissatisfaction may be disproval of their services, all for self reliance of exhibition of independence by the SCs may not be tolerated, assertion for equity and social justice from the SCs may be straight or may get coloured with distortions. These prejudices and biases may still dominate the thinking of the people at large. The administrations may not be able to exhibit total freedom from these notions/ feelings. The rough estimate indicates that there are 3,000 castes in the country out of which 779 are Dalit. Moreover, even amongst these 779. Dalits there are further divisions. The SCs would broadly be bracketed under two broad heads: touchables and untouchables. These are considerable perceptual and actual differences amongst these groups. The touchable SCs may be acceptable to the other group in a locality. It is not known clearly as to how many of 779 SC communities are touchable castes and how many are the untouchable ones .But the problem of the untouchable communities get surmounted in various social settings. They have to struggle hard to initially find an acceptable place or dignified status amongst the so called other touchable SCs and then are expected to assert for rights with other communities.

The possible factors that have led to the realization and consequent attention on the development of SCs could be:

- Precise appreciation of the differentiated reality of Indian society and understanding of the inherent prejudices and biases against the development heads of the SCs by a sizable section of the enlighded group/ section of our society.

- Evolution of a significant number of leaders amongst the Dalits who could articulate the demands of the SCs in various levels.
- Due to reservation of seats in a parliament and assembly elections in our constitution, a number of SC members started contesting parliament and assembly elections and in turn constituted a lobby in these bodies.
- Participation of the members of the SCs by constants in election for political positions at local, state and national level and
- Assertion from these groups for appreciation of a holistic social reality than taking a fragmented view of our society. They seek support of existing constitutional pronouncements in emphasizing their view point.

NEED FOR THE STUDY

Dalit empowerment as well as the participation on the basis of equality in all sphere of society and economy are fundamental to the advancement or human right. Social justice and sustainable development are the ongoing discussion related to equality of Dalit with other community. The issues of Dalit are primarily development related. Although the major indicators of human development, like health, education and standard of living are positive for India the Dalit development index is still more frightening. The GOs and NGOs have undertaken several programmes for empowerment and welfare activities for Dalit development. Dalit are faced with a lot of problems such as social and inequality in economic status, political status in society. The soico-economic activities of the SHGs have generated enormous collection strength among Dalit. The majority of the village Dalits participation in decision making was not existent. Today Dalit have been elected to head panchayats. The first step in empowerment is to get groups of Dalit to analysis of their common problems and their collectively seek solution. The present study analyses the empowerment of Dalit with to reference to the role played by NGO in this regard in Palangarai panchayat in Tiruppur district.

OBJECTIVES OF THE STUDY

This paper is the outcome of empirical investigation carried out in a cluster of village in Tirupur district with reference to the following objectives:

1. To expose the social structure of the study area.
2. Highlight the nature of social discrimination between dalits and caste Hindu.

3. To examine the social inequalities and problems.
4. To suggest suitable measures to pursue the inclusive growth of dalits.

METHODOLOGY

The present study has undertaken in Anna Nagar in Tirupur which comes under Palangarai Panchayat in Tirupur District. The investigator has used simple random sampling techniques to select respondents for the study. Accordingly 50 respondents were selected out of 250 scheduled caste people in Anna Nagar. Survey Method as well as Descriptive study methods was used in this study. A structured interview schedule was the tool used in the present study for the purpose of collection of primary data from the selected head of households of Arunthathiyar community. Primary data were collected from selected respondents by means of personal Interview Schedule. Secondary data was collected from published sources like books, Journals, Reports and News-paper, etc., the primary data collected from the respondents are statistically processed and tabulated simple percentage is used to analyse the data in order to obtain result.

DATA ANALYSIS AND DISCUSSION

Sex

The distribution of respondents by sex of the total number of respondents interview in 62% of them male followed by female respondents. Majority of the Dalit respondents were males.

Age

It is observed from the table that 50% of the respondents are in the age group ranging between 30-40years followed by 20-30 (40%) and 40-50 (10%).

It is obvious that majority of the respondents were found to be in the age group of 30-40 years.

Educational

The educational levels of the respondents that 40% of the respondents were illiterate, 22% of the respondents were high school education upto middle school education 18% of the respondents were educated upto middle level. 16 per cent of the respondents were educated upto primary education and 4 per cent of the respondents educated Upto College. Majority of the respondents' education ranged from primary school education to collegiate education.

TYPE OF HOUSE

The type of house 36% of the respondents were having not pucca house. 28% of the respondents were having government colony house. 24% of the respondents were having semi-pucca house and 12% of the respondents were having kutcha houses. Majority of the respondents were living in not pucca houses.

LAND OWNERSHIP

The data divulges that 92% of the respondents did not posses land whereas only 8 per cent of them stated in the positive. Majority of the respondents did not have their own land.

The Role of NGOs in Educational Empowerment of Dalit

- NGO has engaged in education empowerment of Dalits in study area.
- Dalits benefited in supplementary education (80%), adult education (70%) tuition class (50%) and Vocational (30%).
- 80% of the respondents seek supplementary education imparted by NGO towards education empowerment.
- Supplementary education and adult education imparted by the NGO initiated the process of empowering the Dalit.

Factors Fostering the Empowerment of Dalit

- Improving standard of living and enabling the rural Dalit were the major role of NGO in empowerment of rural Dalit as reported by majority of Dalit respondents.
- LGP/ SHG/ EDP had the main role of NGO in the economic empowerment of Dalit.
- Leadership training and organizing committee reported to be lead in to political empowerment.
- Supplementary education of adult education imparted by the GOs/ NGOs in empowering the Dalit.
- Majority of the respondents faced the problem is that they are not allowed fully in attending income generating courses along with non Dalits.

FINDINGS

- Majority (62%) of the Dalit respondents were males.
- Majority (50%) of the respondents were found to be in the age group of 30-40 years.
- Majority (36%) of the respondents were living in pucca houses.
- Majority (92%) of the respondents did not have their own land.
- Majority (40%) of the respondents were illiterate.
- About 90 per cent of the Dalits experience physical exclusion and a similar percentage were subjected to social discrimination.
- Members of Dalit Community are unable to participate in village social life.
- The marginalized community is faced with problems like untouchability, unemployment, harassment in place of work.
- The programmes of empowerment are not fully reaching the Dalit Community.
- The process of empowerment remains incomplete in the study area.

SUGGESTIONS

- The inclusive growth model of planned and directed social change, economic growth with equitable and distributive social justice show the possible way for effective empowerment of dalits in contemporary society.
- Creating awareness among dalit is must about their rights.
- Provision of legal aid is facilitating the development of dalit people.
- Promote NGOs to work for development of the dalit people and to solve the problem.
- The National Commission for SC/ST should investigate rigorously and bring to book the culprits.
- The victims of human rights violations should be properly compensated.
- Social legislations enacted to protect the rights of marginalized should be implemented in its letter and spirit.

CONCLUSION

The study reveals the nature of empowerment of Dalits in the social exclusion and inclusion framework by way of improving their standard of living, providing leadership training supplementary education coupled with creation of awareness comprehensively. The NGO and GOs partnership definitely pave the way for Dalit empowerment on all walks of life in days to come the study concludes dalits are to go a long way in respect of their empowerment through education, employment and social participation. The empowerment of Dalit is affected by certain obstacles in effective empowerment of marginalized community. The dalits in general and dalit, women in particular are the worst affected segments in empowerment. The current problems may be eliminated only through collective social action for which the GOs/ NGOs, corporate sectors should involve and contribute towards effective empowerment of Dalits.

REFERENCES

- S.Gurusamy, Social Exclusion and Inclusion, A.P.H Publishing Corporation, New Delhi, 2011.
- K.C.Das, Dalit Empowerment Global vision Publishing house, Ansari Road, Daryaganj, New Delhi, 2010.
- David Byrne, Social Exclusion, Rawat Publication, New Delhi, 2009.
- Sing R.B. Scheduled Caste Welfare Myth or Reality A.P.H Publishing Corporation, New Delhi, 2003.
- Choudhury.R.C and Rajakutty.S. Ltd. Fifth Years of Rural Development in India, National Institute of Rural Development Hyderabad, India-1998.
- Fuller, C.J. (Ed) Caste Today, Oxford University press, Delhi 1996.
- Hilaria Soundari.M. Empowerment of Rural Dalit Women: A study of SHGs in Dindigul District. December 2003.
- Kameswar Counhary, Gandhijis vision of Empowerment of schedule caste Gandhimary, October – December 1999.
- Mathur, B.B. Women and Depressed caste publication in India, Chugh publication, Allahabad 1994.
- Ram Ahuja Social Problems in India Rawat Publication New Delhi – 2011.

45

INCLUSIVE GROWTH NEEDS OF TRANSGENDER IN TAMILNADU

S.Gurusamy and Mrinalini. S

INTRODUCTION

Transgender individuals disrupt the sex/gender binary in multiple ways. As gender is based on behavior and traits, a person who is one sex, for example, male, could learn how to be feminine and adopt the gender of the female sex. In addition, a person could combine both masculine and feminine traits and/or behaviors at the same time. Finally, a person might learn both masculinity and femininity and be able to switch back and forth between the two genders with ease. Transgender people feel that the gender, to which they were born, or assigned at birth, does not fit them. Transgender people include people born female who identify as male (female-to-male) and people born male who identify as female (male-to-female).

TYPES OF TRANSGENDERING

There are many different narrower categories of trans-gendering. Gender variance is a very broad category that includes a variety of people, some of whom display cross-gender behavior occasionally and others who do so full-time. Several different types of trans-gender behavior are discussed in this section.

TRANSSEXUALS

Transsexuals are individuals who decide to undergo either partial or complete sex re-assignment surgery. The process of changing from one sex to another is called *transitioning*. It is possible for a male to transition into a female (MTF) and for a female to transition into a male (FTM). To transition, transsexuals need to undergo a "real-life test" administered by medical professionals, in which they show that they are able to live full time in the opposite gender. This process takes years, and throughout, transsexuals undergo psychiatric and medical evaluation.

For transsexuals, there are different medical procedures that can be done in the process of transitioning. These procedures differ for MTFs and for FTMs.

MTF transsexuals undergo hormone therapy, which can include multiple hormones, such as estrogen and anti-androgens. Estrogen is a hormone that helps MTFs to develop breasts. In addition, MTFs may have their facial and body hair removed through processes such as electrolysis. Finally, multiple genital surgeries are done to construct a vagina.

FTM transsexuals also use hormone therapy, in this case, testosterone. They may undergo "top surgery," which involves the removal of breast tissue and reconstruction of the chest. They may also undergo "bottom surgery," in which a penis is constructed.

Both MTF transitioning and FTM transitioning may be done in whole or in part. For example, a person can undergo hormone therapy and not have any type of surgery done. There is a debate as to whether transsexuals are actually part of the transgender community or whether different needs exist in the transsexual community that does not need to be addressed in the transgender community at large. Because transsexuals change their sex to fit their gender identities, they are sometimes viewed as conforming to the sex/gender binary.

TRANSGENDERISTS

Transgenderists are individuals who live full time as the gender opposite their biological sex but have no desire to change their bodies through sex reassignment surgery. A person is considered to be a transgenderist if he or she has been living full time as the opposite gender for over 2 years.

GENDER QUEERS

Gender queer is a more recent term that is used by people who engage in a variety of gender-variant behaviors but do not agree with the term *transgender.* Gender queer individuals argue that because it has the root *Trans,* transgender implies that a person is moving from one gender to another. Some do view themselves as part of a transgender community, while others do not. Gender queers usually combine elements of both masculinity and femininity. In addition, gender queer individuals might have either male or female bodies.

ANDROGYNES

Androgynes are individuals who combine elements of masculinity and femininity. An androgyne can be either a male- or female-bodied individual who incorporates aspects of femininity and masculinity in her or his gender identity and presentation.

CROSS-DRESSERS

Cross-dressers are those who occasionally dress as the opposite sex, though they show no desire to change their sex or to adopt cross-gendered behavior for extended periods of time. A person may cross-dress from either sex into the opposite gender, though generally cross-dressers are thought to be men who dress as women. This is because female-to-male cross-dressing is thought to be more common and socially acceptable.

DRAG PERFORMERS

Drag performers can be either female- bodied or male-bodied individuals or those in transition; they perform on stage the gender opposite the sex they were born, in an exaggerated or campy fashion. A *drag king* is a person who was born with a female body and performs onstage in a hyper masculine style, while a *drag queen* is a person born with a male body and performs onstage as a hyper feminine woman.

OBJECTIVES

- To study the social structure of transgender community.
- To expose the socio-economic background and lifestyle of the transgender people.
- To know the process of transformation and
- To identify the problems faced by the transgender people.

METHODOLOGY

The data are collected from secondary sources i.e. from books, journals, articles etc and supplemented by specific case studies and focused group discussions covering transgender people in a settlement in Villupuram district, Tamil Nadu.

CASE STUDIES

Case 1: Name: Sabeena (Name changed) aged 34.

Sabeena is a 34 years old transgender from Kurumbankottai village in Koliyanoor, Villupuram district and now she is residing in Villupuram proper. Her first name was Nagarajan and at the age of 15 she changed her name as Sabeena. She is the third child of her parents. Her parents are working as agriculture labourers. She has one brother and three sisters. She has failed SSLC. In her childhood itself she used to cook food, cleaning utensils, putting kolam (rangoli) in front of the house and do other household activities. At the age of seven onwards she felt the girlish (effeminate) feelings and at the age of thirteen onwards she used to wear women attires. While she was studying in school for SSLC she fell in love with a boy. Meanwhile her parents got information that their son is behaving like a girl and used to visit the transgender people in Villupuram. Her parents got angry towards her and scolded her for this and advised her to behave like a boy and not to go to the house of transgender people. This infuriated her and decided to leave her parental home. Thus at the age of 15 she left her parental home and took asylum in Alamelupuram in Villupuram with other transgender people. There she was adopted by Radhamma as her daughter as per Jama-at rules. Thus at the age of 19 she underwent the emasculation surgery in Cadappa in Andrapradesh. The memories of her home, her parents and other family members haunted her during this period. The feelings of isolation felt in her very badly and the attitude of the public's hurt her very much. The youths were also tried to harass her physically many a times. During this period she faced the brutal type of sexual abuse from the side of police also. One day evening while she was walking through the road to her settlement (home) a man approached her and offered a seat in his motorbike and told her to drop her in her house. But that person cheated her and cunningly took her away and compelled her to drink liquor and to do sex with him. She refused his demands and ran away from that place to escape from his hands. On the way she met a police vehicle and they stopped in front of her to help, thinking that she is a female. When they found out that she is a transgender they also tried to beat her with their lathy and threatened to disfigure her. Somehow she managed to escape from that danger also. At that time a man was coming in a bicycle and he helped her to reach her house. At that time one of the neighbors in her settlement was working near her parental house. He identified her and told her parents about her sufferings and advised them to accept their child as a transgender. When they know about her sufferings one day her parents came to the transgender settlement in very secretly and convinced her to come back to home as their son. But she refused to go with them as their son. But her mother cried and compelled others to bring her back to home and to accept and take care of her child as transgender. Thus they started to coming and going publically in transgender settlement to see their child. In later she got married with a Muslim man named Rafeeq Bashah from Villupuram main, who is working as an auto driver. Now she is working as the President cum Director of Association for Community Empowerment. Before this she was working as an Outreach worker (Field Officer) in ARM Villupuram. She was the former member of the district transgender welfare board Villupuram.

Case 2: Name: Shalini (Name changed) aged 38.

Shalini is a 38 years old transgender from Pazhayachakkarapuram village in Gingi, Villupuram district and now she is residing in Gingi itself. Her first name was Murukan and at the age of 20 she changed her name as Shalini. She is the second child of her parents. . Her parents were working as agriculture labourers and her father has expired. She has one brother and one sister. She has passed Plus2 and DTP. Her brother is working in a company as supervisor. In her childhood itself she used to cook food, cleaning utensils, putting kolam (rangoli) in front of the house and do other household activities. At the age of seven onwards she felt the girlish (effeminate) feelings and at the age of thirteen onwards she used to wear women attires. Now she is living with her mom. From childhood onwards she used to visit Aravanis. Because her uncle (younger brother of her father) is a transgender. But at the age of 15 she went along with the aravanis. When the family members got information that their son is behaving like a girl, she faced physical and mental torture from family members. General people also used to tease. At that time felt very bad about this situation. While going for doing danda (sex work) during the night time police used to chase. Now she is working as a Field Officer (Outreach Worker) in Association for Community Empowerment in Gingi. Before this she was working as a field officer in TAI project in Villupuram. Before coming to join this work she was doing sex work. Now she stopped that work and changed her mind set, attitude and behavior towards sex work.

Case 3: Name: Maya (Name changed) aged 32.

Maya is a 32 years old transgender from Kandamanadi village in Ramanathapuram district and now she is residing in Janakipuram in Villupuram district. Her first name was Shanmugavel and at the age of 19 she changed her name as Maya. She is the fourth child of her parents. Her parents are working as agriculture labourers. She has one brother and two sisters. She has passed

SSLC. In her childhood itself she used to cook food, cleaning utensils, putting kolam (rangoli) in front of the house and do other household activities. At the age of seven onwards she felt the girlish (effeminate) feelings and at the age of thirteen onwards she used to wear women attires. While she was studying in school itself she used to visit aravanis in nearby places. Her parents got this information and advised her not to do like that. But she refused to obey her parents. This infuriated them and has given severe punishments to her. Due to this physical harassment and mental torture at the age of 17 she left her parental house and went to Mumbai with the help of other transgender people. There she was adopted by Mallika as her daughter as per Jama-at rules and regulations. At the age of 19 she underwent emasculation surgery in Hyderabad, Andrapradesh. Now she is living with her guru in Villupuram. Her family members didn't accept her as a transgender now itself also. In the earlier days she used to do sex work for livelihood earning. At that time she has faced brutal type of sexual violence and other forms of physical torture and mental harassments from the side police in Mumbai. Now she is the member of district transgender welfare board Villupuram. Before this she was working as a field officer (outreach worker) in ARM and (ACE) Association for Community Empowerment.

ANALYSIS

While I was doing the above case studies the inference drawn from them were very touching to the heart of mine.

FINDINGS

1. Most of the transgender people are leaving their homes due to the non-acceptance of their family members.
2. Many of the transgender people in the study area are involved in sex work and begging for their daily livelihood earning.
3. The transgender people are more vulnerable to HIV/AIDS infection due to the dangerous line of sex work.
4. The transgender people are facing extreme victimization from the mainstream of the society by denying the fundamental rights.
5. Many transgender people are facing extreme violence from police and local goondas or rowdies while they were engaging in their daily livelihood earning.

CONCLUSION

Transgender people in India have no safe space, not even in their families, where they are protected from prejudice and abuse. The prejudice is translated into violence, often of a brutal nature, in public spaces, police stations, prisons even in their homes. The discrimination based on their class and gender makes the transgender community one of the most disempowered groups in Indian society

SUGGESTIONS

1. Create awareness among the common people to accept, consider and treat transgender people as human beings.
2. The law and order system should not discriminate transgender.
3. The government should provide all civic facilities.
4. They need to be given better health care and support to the transgender people.
5. They need to be given ID card and organized under welfare board and also the civil supply system should reach them.
6. There must be certain percentage in education, employment and political participation.

REFERENCES

46 INCLUSIVE DIMENSIONS OF EXCLUDED WOMEN PRISONERS: REFLECTIONS FROM TAMILNADU

S.Gurusamy and G.Dharani (UGC-JRF)

INTRODUCTION:

The majority of women commit crimes for similar reasons, women are not naturally criminals. Most women are nurturing not violent. The term "discrimination against women" shall mean any distinction, exclusion or restriction made on the basis of sex which has the effect or purpose of impairing or nullifying the recognition, enjoyment or exercise by women, irrespective of their marital status, on a basis of equality of men and women, of human rights and fundamental freedoms in the political, economic, social, cultural, civil or other field. Women are driven to commit crime by factors such as being abused, low socioeconomic status, lack of health care, lack of parental guidance, being controlled by someone else, lack of education and many more factors.

As Beth Richie discussed in her women and crime book, many of those women were in previous abusive relationships. When a woman is abused she can only take it for so long before she breaks. So many women are oppressed that when they do get a chance to fight back, they fight with all of their might. In the film Thelma and Louise, they fought against a rapist, because Louise had been raped in Texas, and the man got away. Louise did not want to let another rapist walk the street. She was defending herself, Thelma, and in a sense making an example out of that man by showing society that men will not always be able to walk away from their victim. Some women do fight back, and they will fight to the death if necessary.

EMOTIONAL AND SOCIAL ISSUES

Prisoners and their families experience a tremendous sense of loss when incarceration occurs and that loss is compounded when children are involved. Couples are usually denied sexual intimacy and are unable to engage in the day to day interactions, experiences and sharing which sustain marital and other intimate, adult relationships. Loneliness and missing each other and a host of other feelings about the separation, justice system, criminal activity, and each partner's honesty and faithfulness are common. Guilt and a sense of relief that a troublesome relative has finally been sent away are also among the emotions experienced by prisoners' kin. A difficulty in adjusting to separation and loss has led to depression and other mental health problems among prisoners and their families (Daniel and Barrett, 1981; King 1993; Lanier, 1993). Incarcerated mothers cite separation from their children as one of the most difficult aspects of imprisonment (Baunach, 1985; Hairston, 1991b) and incarcerated fathers and mothers worry about what is happening to their children during their absence (Hairston, 1991; Hairston, 1995; Lanier, 1993; Martin, 2001). Parents believe their children are in safe living situations and are not being abused or neglected; nevertheless, they worry about their children's well being and about their guidance and supervision (Hairston, 1992, 1995). Some worries may be attributed to the fact that parents in prison have limited contact with their children and rely on relatives and friends for information about their children. Prisoners' children and families must also deal with feelings of same and social stigma. Imprisonment is not a reason for celebration or a reason to be proud. It is not the goal one seeks for oneself or one's children. Many family members do not tell even their closest friends about a relative's incarceration and go to great lengths to protect the prisoner's children from the consequences of revealing this family secret. Depending on the crime and the prevalence of imprisonment in the neighborhood in which they live, family members may not be the objects of social stigma or hostility in that neighborhood (Schneller, 1976). There is, nevertheless, a social stigma which families experience from other elements of society. The spouse, parent or child of a prisoner may not experience stigma directly until they reveal the incarcerated relative's status to a child's teacher or to a prospective landlord or until the family moves to a prison town (Fishman, 1990; Koenig, 1985).

WOMEN PRISONERS HAVE DIFFERENT NEEDS

The needs and concerns of women prisoners are different from those of men prisoners. Women prisoners are very often the sole or primary carer of young children and have other family responsibilities. They may be particularly vulnerable to abuse in prison. Women prisoners have different health needs, including those related to sexual and reproductive health. In some countries, women may be pregnant in prison and may give birth in prison. Women prisoners suffer from very high rates of mental illness. While problems such as overcrowding, poor hygiene and inadequate visiting facilities affect both men and women prisoners, there are many concerns that are specific to women or which affect women prisoners in a different or particularly harsh way. Particular groups of women, such as female juvenile prisoners, women with disabilities, women who are foreign nationals, and indigenous and other minority women, have further needs specific to them as women.

PRISONER-FAMILY COMMUNICATION

In most societies, women have primary responsibility for the family. Women prisoners are more likely than men prisoners to have been the sole or primary carer for young children and other family members, such as older relatives, prior to imprisonment. When a woman is sent to prison the consequences for her family are often very significant. Visits are crucial to a women maintaining family contact. Because there are far fewer women's prisons, women tend to be imprisoned further away from their homes and families. This makes it more difficult for people to visit women in prison and in general women prisoners receive fewer family visits than do male prisoners. Statistics from the USA show that "more than 60%of all women are incarcerated more than one hundred miles from their child's place of residence. The difficulty in maintaining contact causes both the woman and her family to suffer. It aggravates the damage to family ties caused by imprisonment and has a particularly harsh impact on young children. Research shows that lack of adequate contact with children and family members is a key source of anxiety for female prisoners. This dislocation of carer relationships also makes a woman's reintegration into society after prison more difficult. Prisoners who maintain family ties while in prison display fewer disciplinary problems and have better physical and mental health while in prison, and have been shown to be more likely to reintegrate successfully into the community upon release and less likely to re-offend.

Communication between prisoners and their families provides the most concrete and visible strategy that families and prisoners use to manage separation and maintain connections. Families visit their imprisoned relatives at the institutions where they are held, talk with them by phone, and exchange cards and letters as a means of staying connected. These contacts allow adults and parents and children to share family experiences and participate in family rituals, e.g., birthday celebrations, religious observances, etc. and help them to remain emotionally attached. They help assure incarcerated parents that their children have not forgotten them and children that their parents love and care about them. They allow prisoners to see themselves, and to function, in socially acceptable roles rather than as prison numbers and institutionalized dependents. Departments of corrections permit these type communications between prisoners and their kin and encourage the maintenance of family ties, in theory, as desirable correctional practices. In actuality, the support for prisoners' family relationships varies considerably from one jurisdiction to another and within jurisdictions from one facility to another. As a rule, prisons allow families and children to visit though prisoners in administrative segregation or super maximum prisons may be restricted to televise and other types of noncontact visits. Some jails allow only non contact visits and/or prohibit children from visiting. Six states permit prisoners to have private family visits on prison grounds with their spouses and children; a few allow non violent women prisoners with infants to reside in alternative community residences. Most prisons for women, and a few for men, provide parent education courses and a few offer other parenting supports including counseling, parent support groups, and special visiting areas and programs for parents and their children. (See Bates, 2001 and Jeffries, Menghraj, and Hairston, 2001 for descriptions of parenting programs).

The correctional policies and practices that govern contact between prisoners and their families often impede, rather than support, the maintenance of family ties. The security and safety rationale that dominates the prison environment is obvious in some policies. The primary intent of others, e.g. the rate structure for prisoner telephone systems, seems to be to subsidize prison budgets and generate profits and /or to exert social control, not only over prisoners, but over their kin as well. Rules frequently bear little relevance to correctional goals and are insensitive to prisoners' family structures, cultural differences and children's needs. Many rules appear to be arbitrary; others are inconsistently interpreted and applied by different staff members and with different visitors (Fishman, 1990; Jeffries, Menghraj, and Hairston, 2001). Policy obstacles to the maintenance of parent-child relationships include policies requiring children's custodial parents to escort them on visits, limiting children visitors to those for whom birth certificates listing the prisoner as the biological parent are produced and placement of prisoners in locations hundreds or thousands of miles from their homes.

For many families and friends of prisoners, the visit to a prison is a lesson in humility, intimidation and frustration and a highly charged and anxiety producing event (Fishman, 1990; Girshick, 1996). It is not unusual for visitors, the majority of whom are women and children, to endure many indignities. Among the problems noted in the Florida Legislature's report of prison visiting in that state were long waits sometimes in facilities without seating, toilets and water; the lack of nutritious food in visiting room vending machines and the absence of activities for children (Taylor, 1999). Body frisks and intrusive searches, rude treatment by staff, and hot, dirty and crowded visiting rooms are the norm in many prisons. Visitors may be denied entry to the prison for diverse reasons including constantly changing dress codes, no identification for children, and ion drug scanners that inaccurately signal that a visitor is carrying drugs.

POLICY DIRECTIONS AND STRATEGIES

The preservation and strengthening of prisoners' family ties and parent-child relationships will require vision and direction from the highest levels of public policy decision making and a fundamental shift in the prevailing system responses to prisoners' children and families. It is not reasonable to place the responsibility for the creation of family oriented prison environments and system-wide change on individual prison administrators and directors of corrections departments. In the face of escalating prison budgets and priorities focused on safety and security, few will make family matters and post release success major goals or priorities. Congressional bodies and state legislatures must take ownership of family related incarceration issues as a matter of national interest and make prisoners' family matters an integral part of the discussion on criminal justice and family policy. Sentencing policies, alternatives to corrections, prison locations and funding for family programs and services are legislative issues. It is equally important for legislators to exercise oversight over correctional policies and practices and to use the power of the law to remove obstacles to children's and families' well being. The correctional environment and what goes on in prison are not internal matters to be left to the discretion of prison administrators. They are instead public concerns with relevance to broad social welfare goals and of importance to different community constituencies. It is important for child welfare and correctional leaders and professional associations to develop principles and national standards covering parents in prison and their children and to adopt these standards as a part of the accreditation process for child welfare agencies and correctional institutions. When parents are in prison and their children are under the custody of the state, families and children experience unique problems and corrections and child welfare staffs are faced with unique challenges. Most states do not have child welfare policies or procedures to address parenting issues during incarceration and workers are left, more or less, to their own problem solving initiative and ingenuity. Child welfare-corrections system partnership models, family oriented policy directives and agency protocols are necessary components of serious efforts to meet the best interests of the child. Research on prisoners' family roles and relationships and family matters in the criminal justice system must be conducted and the findings incorporated in policy and program development and implementation. No federal agency or foundation has provided funding to launch a comprehensive program of research on families and the correctional system or identified this topic as a research priority. Most research studies have been one shot efforts with few ongoing programs of research covering any aspect of prisoner family functioning. Consequently, there are many unanswered questions and untested assumptions about the impact of parental criminality on children, the impact of parental attachments and responsibilities on adult recidivism, and other crucial areas. Knowledge of the impact of major human services and corrections policies, e.g., ASFA, community reentry legislation, and welfare reform, on prisoners' families is also limited and the true outcomes of policy directives and reforms for families and children must be inferred. Information about and understanding of program processes and outcomes must also be among the objectives of a knowledge development agenda. It is important to assess the current state of the field. These type assessments enable program designers and practitioners to build on the pioneering research and program efforts that have already been undertaken and on the day-to-day work and experiences of program providers, families and children. The Vera Institute of Justice review of programs serving fathers in prison and the community (Jeffries, Menghraj, and Hairston, 2001) and the University of Illinois study of programs serving children and families of prisoners (Bates, 2001) provide examples of these type reviews.

OBJECTIVES:

The following objective has been formulated for the present study

1. To understand circumstances leading to committing crime.
2. To analyze the problem faced by women prisoners inside the prison.
3. To study the nature of exclusion faced by women prisoners from family.
4. To suggest suitable measure to include women prisoners in the mainstream of the society.

METHODOLOGY:

This study is based on the secondary data collected through the articles published in related Journals, Newspaper, Books, websites etc., supplemented by specific case studies covering cross section of women prisoner logged in special prison for women in TamilNadu in Vellore, Trichy and Puzhal and also through focus group discussion supplemented by observation, experiences gained by authors in rural areas. Based upon this, the inferences are drawn and logical conclusion is made. Certain useful suggestions are also presented based upon the findings and conclusion.

MAJOR FINDINGS:

- Most of the women's those who are lodged in prisons were victims of circumstances and situation. Unorganized family and society are the major reasons for the development of women criminals.
- Majority of the crimes done by women are based on domestic violence, atrocities, harassments based on dowry and illegal activities.

- Most of the women committed crimes, not on the basis of any motivation or background; crimes are just because of violence against women. The women who are arrested and lodged in prison are facing more and more mental trauma. Mental trauma is mainly based on their family members, society and also about their future after their discharged period.
- Most of the women tolerate their bitter experiences up to the dead point and at one sparking point they want themselves to escape from all those violence, atrocities, and harassment. Therefore they involved in committing minor and major crimes. But because of their crime they were excluded from the family
- Almost all the women criminals thinking are based on their children, husband and other family members. They think that whether they accept us or not, without any family support what happen to my children etc.
- Most of the women are victims of exclusion from the family. They are highly neglected by the family members and they don't have any mental support from their family members, hence they are affected by mental trauma inside the prison.
- Majority of the women inside the prison are experiencing their punishment and they also face problems like mental trauma, psychological problems, loneliness, depression and so on.
- The special prison for women in Vellore, Trichy and Puzhal are having counseling centre and hospital. They give guidance and counseling for women criminals and they try to change their mind set of criminals.
- Most of the women criminals are almost realize their mistakes and crimes inside the prison and they want to live a peaceful life and they don't want to commit the crime once again in their life.
- Special prison for women are having rehabilitation centre like homes outside the prison for criminals particularly for women prisoners those who are not having family supports and or having problems in society and they really wants to rehabilitate themselves.

CONCLUSION

The ability and motivation to keep trying under the most difficult of circumstances that prisoners' families display and the sense of kinship and obligation that they have for a member who has been publicly sanctioned are solid strengths. These actions, and the nation's general interest in protecting children and strengthening families, provide sound reasons to promote and adopt policies which help prisoners maintain family ties and help families carry out their family obligations and responsibilities for their children. A social investment in prisoners' families and children will require the adoption of more positive views of prisoners' families and family relationships, better understanding of family needs and societal responses, and dedicated attention to changing the prevailing system responses. The Dislocation of carer relationships also makes a woman reintegration into society, prisoners who maintain family ties while in prison display fewer disciplinary problems and have better physical and mental health while in prison.

SUGGESTION

- The social structure and culture of our Indian society should transform and they should give equal rights and responsibilities to the women and girls.
- The women also should take care of themselves and avoid the things which are not suitable for their culture and tradition.
- Family and society should understand the feeling and emotions of women and avoid troubles to women.
- Family is considered as the primary group and the socialization process is starts from the family, but most of the crisis situations are arise from the family and women are the victims of those problems.
- Instead of punishing and excluded the women's from the family for their deviant behaviour, family members should forgive their deviant behaviour and give a chance to rectify their behaviour and rehabilitate their life.
- The prisons authorities should ensure cordial relationship among the prisoners inside the prison.
- The government should formulate policies and programmes to ensure proper reform, rehabilitation during conviction period and nit equation of women in society after their discharge.

REFERENCES:

- American Psychiatric Association. (1987). Diagnostic and statistical manual of mental disorders (3rd ed.). Washing- ton
- Bayse, D. J. (1989). How to keep your family alive while serving a prison sentence. Unpublished Manuscript.
- Bowker, Lee. 1977. Prisoner Subcultures. Lexington, Mass.: Lexington Books.

- Gupta, P. K., & Mueller, R. (1984). The correction of criminal thinking and behavior through the cognitive-moral approach. Correctional Options (Vol. 4). Canada: Govern- ment of Ontario publication, Ministry of Correctional Ser- vices. Hannon, G., Martin, D., & Martin, M. (1984). Incarceration in the family: Adjustment to change. Family Therapy, 11, 253- 260.
- Hans Toch, "Hyper-Masculinity and Prison Violence," in Masculinities and Violence, ed. Lee H. Bowker (Thousand Oaks, Calif.: Sage, 1998), 168-78.
- Reimer, Hans. 1937. "Socialization in the Prison Community," Pro- ceedings of the American Prison Association.
- Schneller, D. P. (1976). The prisoner's family: A study of the effects of imprisonment on the families of prisoners. San Francisco: R and E Research Associates.
- Swan, L. A. (1981). Families of black prisoners: Survival and progress. Boston: G. K. Hall & Co.
- www.journalseek.net
- www.nap.edu (National Academic Press-Books)
- www.oup.com (Oxford University Press-Articles)
- www.sagepub.in (Sage Publication-Articles)

47 EXCLUSION OF ELDERLY PERSONS: THE INCLUSIVE FRAMEWORK

S.Gurusamy and P. Dhanalakshmi,

INTRODUCTION:

Aging is an inevitable biological process in the life- a process marked by diminishing mental and physical abilities. Population ageing, a phenomenon involving a shift from high mortality/high fertility and consequently an increased proportion of older people in the total population, is a universal experience. Sudden spurt in the population of elderly in a country is bound to pose multiple challenges before the human society. Developing countries are going to face such a growth in a much quicker time as compared to the developed world which saw such a demographic transition gradually.

Ageing is a universal fact and no one can escape it. The human body is the most wonderful machine which nature has ever produced, but it also wears down with use and time. Ageing is a complex process involving biological, psychological, social and environmental components. "Ageing is a toilsome treadmill grinding to a tragic halt as years pass by. It is a life spanning process of growth and development running from infancy to old age through childhood, adulthood gets an end with the death of an individual by Mishra (1997)". Ageing is a process in human life and is inevitable unless one dies'. Each phase of life is a preparation of one, which follows it. The foundation laid on in our childhood determines to great extent the success or failure of our mature life, so also dies a behavior in mid-life, which decides the nature of our elderly life span. So if entire life is itself planned, old age is automatically planned.

The aged is a generally used in relation to young. It is really difficult to draw a diving line uniformly for all communities. Available research reflects that people grow old at different rates. One person may be physically old at 60 while another is 'young' at 70. It is really difficult old age. Aging is a universal phenomenon. One of the undesirable facts of human youth old age. Ageing refers to all age group and is not confined only to the elderly, but also extends to social and economic institutions; it is life long process through which all living beings go from birth to death.

WHO ARE THE AGED?

We often used the term "old"/Aged" willingly, there is no clear delineation which implies the aged as old. These us no widely accepted views regard it. The human life cycle according to Hindu belief is divided into four divisions. The last two divisions namely Vanaprastha and Sanyosa are considered the last stage i.e.old age. Owing to the physical features, one was look young at 53 or other may not. In the cultural aspect if one fulfill all responsibility or he/she has grand children considered as old. To remove inkling thoughts about it broadly the retirement is the marketing line. The United Nations defines senior citizens as these who are other 65 years old.

Old age is not an absolute concept. It is full of relativism. It is significantly related to time and space. According to WHO old age starts at the age of 65 years. Some people say that in India old age starts at 58 when a person retires from his government job but what about those who retire at the age of 60 or 62 in some of at the government job. Especially, the unskilled labour who do not retire till he is safe in his grave. Old age is usually regarded as synonyms with pensionable age or age at retirement.

So far as India is concerned, Indian census has adopted the 60 for classifying a person as old. The retirement age, also vary according to the appropriate governance. Thus the retirement age is taken as old age in India.

TYPES OF ELDERLY POPULATION

Taking chronological age of 60+ as an indicator of onset of old age, the followings have been categorized as;

a) Young-Old 60-69 years

b) Old-Old 70-84 years

c) Oldest-old 85 years and above

According to another grouping, old age is categorized as;

a) Octogenarians 80 years and above

b) Nonagenarians 90 years and also

c) Centenarians 100 years and above

The above categorization has come into vogue because our society is experiencing "first generation of the full timers' and we are now becoming a rectangular society in which all individuals, in absence of any mishap, are surviving to advanced ages. People of 60years and above, enter the territory of elderly so called "universe of geron"

WHAT IS SOCIAL EXCLUSION IN OLD AGE?

In the 1950s and 1960s, researchers such as Townsend and Wedderburn (1965) showed older people to be one of the largest groups living in poverty, with widowed and single older people being identified as especially vulnerable. Townsend (1981) widened the debate with the idea of older people being affected by forms of 'structured dependency'. This was produced by compulsory retirement, poverty and restricted social roles. It was developed through the 1990swith awareness of widening inequalities between pensioners dependent on welfare benefits and those with access to occupational pensions and savings.

Definitions of social exclusion typically draw together distributional dimensions of poverty (that is lack of material resources) and relational aspects (lack of social ties). This is reflected in the Government's definition of social exclusion representing 'a shorthand term for what can happen when people or areas suffer from a combination of linked problems such as unemployment, poor skills, low incomes, discrimination, poor housing, high crime, bad health and family breakdown'. Measures of social exclusion thus attempt to identify groups lacking in resources, as well as people whose lives are affected by, for example, discrimination, chronic sickness, geographical location, or cultural identification. The approach taken in the study undertaken here tends to follow this definition: lack of material resources is viewed as an important cause of nonparticipation, but the role of non-material factors will also be highlighted. Following the above, Burchardt et al. (1999) have sought to develop an operational definition of social exclusion, encompassing five distinct elements relating to an individual's participation in 'normal' activities. These are:

- consumption activity – the ability to consume up to a minimum level, the goods and services considered normal for society;
- savings activity – the accumulation of savings, pension entitlements or property ownership;
- Production activity – engagement in an economically or socially valued activity;.
- political activity – engagement in some collective effort to improve or protect the immediate or wider social and physical environment; and

- social activity – engagement in significant social interaction with family or friends and
- Identifying with a cultural group or community.

Scharf et al. (2002) have emphasized the spatial dimension to social exclusion, drawing on Perri 6's(1997) view that: '[Social exclusion] is a useful term in societies in which there is a growing polarization of access and opportunity, so that often small areas – a housing estate, an inner or outer urban area – are effectively cut off from life around them'. This idea is further developed by Madanipour et al. (1998) who refer to the multi-dimensionality of social exclusion and its impact on particular types of location. They suggest that: 'Social exclusion is defined as a multi-dimensional process, in which various forms of exclusion are combined: participation in decision making and political processes, access to employment and material resources, and integration into common cultural processes. When combined, they create acute forms of exclusion that find a spatial manifestation in particular neighbourhoods.' (p. 22)

CAUSES OF SOCIAL EXCLUSION

The next issue then becomes: what are the mechanisms/drivers that might result in older people not achieving one or more of the 'wants' or 'life chances' outlined in the previous section? In the case of older people we are suggesting that the conditions that might cause exclusion can be grouped under four headings: age-related characteristics; cumulative disadvantage; community characteristics, and age-based discrimination:

- **Age-related characteristics** refer to the way in which older people are disproportionately affected by certain kind of losses or restrictions relating to income, health or reduced social ties. Such changes might take place across all points of the life course but they are likely to feature more prominently in later life given retirement associated income changes, the impact of chronic disabling conditions, and increased needs among people adjusting to living alone.

- **Cumulative disadvantage** refers to the fact that birth cohorts may become more unequal over time. For example, limited educational and work opportunities at early points in the life course may in the long-term lead to reduced income in old age or limited awareness about how to access the full range of social and health services.

- **Community characteristics** highlight how older people, who may have strong attachments to their locality, May also be vulnerable to changes associated with population turnover, economic decline, and rising levels of crime and insecurity within neighbourhoods.

- **Age-based discrimination** refers to the impact of ageism within economic and social

Policies that contributes to various forms of social exclusion in old age. The debate around ageism has challenged the link with age as a form of dependency. It emphasizes instead various different forms of positive engagement that can be maintained throughout the latter half of the life course.

ISSUES

In Australia, the 'elderly' is generally a reference to people over the age of 65. Lots of over 65ers lead healthy and empowered lives, and many are involved in community volunteering. But for the elderly, health can be a big concern. Their bodies are more susceptible to illness, they may be physically frail, and many are on medications which are costly and ongoing.

An elderly person who is able to fund their own retirement is called a retiree. This means they had a job that paid them enough superannuation. Someone who is unable to fund their own retirement, and is paid welfare money by the government is called a pensioner. Pensioners may have difficulty affording medications or groceries on their allowance, especially if they are very sick, or have to pay rent.

Care for the elderly can take place in their homes. Groups such as Meals on Wheels deliver nutritious food for a small fee and home care programs clean houses for those elderly people who are unable to do it themselves. These services may be non-existent in rural areas.

If elderly people cannot take care of themselves, and their families are unwilling or unable to care for them, they have to find nursing homes. The conditions can be rough, especially if you do not have a lot of money to spend. Availability is also a big problem, since we have an aging population and nursing homes do not receive enough government funding.

Malnutrition:

The Dietitians Association of Australia says that 85 per cent of elderly Australians are "at risk" of malnutrition. This may be because they cannot afford nutritious food on their budgets, or because limited transport prevents them from accessing shopping centers. Cooking every day may also be too much of a physical or mental strain. There are common stories of elderly people living on cans of tinned spaghetti or spam because they cannot afford fresh food. Meals on Wheels provide one hot meal per day for $37.50 a week, but some pensioners cannot afford or access this service. Those who do make use of it still have two meals a day to make on their own.

PHYSICAL AND MENTAL HEALTH:

Physical health is an obvious a problem for the elderly, with the incidence of most diseases increasing with age. Heart disease is the most common problem for the elderly worldwide. Arthritis and osteoporosis are two conditions that affect physical structure and movement, while dementia and Alzheimer's disease affect memory and personality. In addition, lower immune systems mean that the elderly have a higher risk of catching infectious diseases.

Mental health is another big issue for the elderly, especially depression. Family, friends and health care providers often assume that depression is 'normal' for the elderly, so it frequently goes untreated. Elderly people are more likely to be depressed if they are suffering from health problems or poverty. Residents in nursing homes or other institutions are even more likely to develop depression or consider suicide, says the Department of Health and Aging, especially those who are lonely or isolated.

NURSING HOME

For elderly people who need full-time care, nursing homes are sometimes the only answer since full time home care is extremely pricy. Nursing homes in Australia are expensive and have long waiting lists, often so long that needy residents end up as long-term hospital patients until a nursing home can be found.

While there are many great nursing homes in Australia, more often than nor they are underfunded and under staffed. Poorly-run nursing homes can be responsible for instances of neglect or abuse. Over 270,000 elderly Australians suffer from bed-sores, a wound common when a patient is bed-bound and cannot move. Dehydration, unattended incontinence and frequent falls are common neglect issues in unsatisfactory nursing homes.

Abuse of elderly residents by staff is a sad reality in some nursing homes. Bullying or threatening residents is a common complaint. Using restraints or sedative medications on patients who don't require them is another tactic used to keep residents bed-bound and out of the way. The appropriateness of using restraints in nursing homes at all has also been questioned. Physical assault and sexual abuse are the most serious, and are hard for residents to report when the perpetrators are also their supervisors.

PERCEPTIONS OF THE AGED REGARDING THE CARE AND SUPPORT

Since the family is the most important social unit which is the major source of care and support to the aged persons, at least in India, it would be of interest to examine what the old age persons feel about the way they are treated by their family members. In this survey the aged respondents were asked: "How do you feel about the attitudes of your family members towards you now?" and the responses were categorized as follows: "Respectful", "Normal", and "Not Cordial". For this analysis, the old age respondents who were living alone and those living with spouse only were excluded. The results presented in Panel 1 of Table 3 indicate that only about 10% of the respondents reported that the treatment accorded to them was "Not cordial". It is very interesting and important to note that among the male aged respondents about 67% has expressed that the Treatment that they got was "respectful", while only 47% of the female aged respondents Expressed such a feeling. In contrast, only 9% of the male aged respondents felt that the Relationship with the other family members was "not cordial", as against 14% among the female aged respondents. These differentials again reflect the differentials in the role and status of males and females in the family as per the Indian culture. The senior most male member of the family as it has already been stated, is considered as the head of the household and will have the power of decision making about almost all family matters. The women, on the other hand, are generally restricted to the domestic sphere. Therefore, the younger members of the household often treat the male aged persons with more honor and respect and the female aged persons with more affection. Further, widowhood results in the loss of social status in the case of females, while in the case of males the transition will not make such marked difference in the status, power and authority they hold.

CHALLENGES OF ELDERLY IN MODERN INDIA

Indian societies are changing rapidly due to urbanization, the steep aspirations of the youth and the increased numbers of women workforce. All these factors have led to a decline in the number of joint families and an increase in the concept of nuclear families. The direct impact of this is that the care and support of the elderly in India is getting marginalized.

Let not the statistics that two thirds of the Indian population is under 30 years lead us to believe that we don't have a problem about our elders. The situation may not be as intense as it is in Japan but it is surely creeping in. In cities, when there is only one older living spouse, many problems stem from property ownership issues. The older people bear a lot of mental harassment to transfer the property to their children's name. On the one hand, property is the only security they have; signing it away will leave them extremely insecure. On the other hand, if they don't transfer the property, their day to day existence will be a living hell.

The last couple of decades have seen a great leap in life expectancy. The average age of human life has increased. This is being heralded as a marvel. This, however, means that that as people get older, unless they have had the discipline of following a healthy regimented life; they can be in for a long period of illness and suffering. The ill effects of chewing tobacco, smoking or alcoholism can catch up in old age.

Due to the lack of health awareness from of the previous generations, most elderly people have unhealthy habits that lead to medical problems like cardio vascular diseases, tuberculosis, asthma etc. In addition, there is a malaise of aging problems, the physical strength diminishes, mental recall and stability deteriorates; many have memory loss.

Geriatrics, a branch of medicine that deals with the diagnosis and treatment of illness among the elderly is getting more challenging as the incidences of impaired vision and hearing loss is increasing. A simple trip and small fall can lead to a fracture or breaking of the already fragile bones. Loss of memory and other associated diseases such as Alzheimer, Parkinson cause additional demands on the old age.

The biggest disquiet is the negligence from the younger generation. Lifestyles in modern India have driven the younger generation in a race of economics. The 57 million populations of elderly above the age of 60 years are learning to deal with loneliness, craving for companionship and a sympathetic ear to listen to their melancholy.

There is also the lack of a social security system where the government machinery pays for the food and medication of the old and needy. Acting as a Social Insurance system the Social Security of America keeps nearly 40% of the elderly beyond the ages of 65years, out of poverty. A western trend is for the affording elderly to hire an investment banker to look after their savings and to check into a well established home of the aged. In India, however, since the social grapevine and social scandal is such a deterrent, most older people prefer to live with their children and grand children, rather than live in an old age home, whether they are well tended for or not.

OBJECTIVES:

The following are the major objectives for the present study

1. To study the conditions of elderly persons in family and society,

2. To analysis the dimension of exclusion faced by elderly person.
3. To suggest some suitable inclusive measures for elderly persons.

METHODOLOGY:

The study was conducted in Ramapattinam, Devampadi in Pollachi North block. The primary data were collected from the respondents through focused group discussion and also through some case studies in the respective study area. Secondary data were also collected from journals, books, websites etc. Accordingly the findings and conclusion are drawn.

MAJOR FINDINGS:

- Majority of the respondents are not enjoying and leading a peaceful life with their family members and with the society
- Old age person are now living alone and separated from their own children house.(i.e.) they are thrown out from the house.
- Most of the old age people are above 70 years and they prepare food by themselves (i.e.) self cooking and staying in the corner of the house.
- Old age people need care and support from the family members, but they are in a position to provide care support to his own daughter-in-law.
- It is found that majority of the elders are suffering from the psychological conditions like frustration, health problems and mental illness, stress and tension, frustration and health problems.
- Old age people are not a sick person but they are physically weak. In old age, people are unable to work fast and quick, so they need the help of others to fulfill their needs.
- Old age care is very important for the family and also for the society, because they found almost in every society and in old age they were like a child and they become highly dependent.
- Family and society should take care of the elders and support them mentally and morally. If we support them with effective care means they feel very happy and lead their rest of their life peacefully.
- Government plans and policies are not properly reaching the senior citizens and they are not enjoying their old age peacefully.

- Old age people are highly excluded from the decision making process, many important family decisions are not consulted with the old age people and even they didn't include them in any special occasion etc.
- Old age people are excluded in the following dimensions: social, economic, decision making authority and so on.

SUGGESTIONS:

- Guidance and counseling should be given to the family members, neighbours and youngsters to protect the elders.
- Health care must be given to the old age people in the hospitals.
- GOs and NGOs should create plans and policies to take care of elders and they should look out whether their policies and programmes are reaching the elders and they are benefited out of it.
- The policy of old persons should be implemented at all levels of governance faithfully to ensure hardly happy and peaceful elderly life.

CONCLUSION:

We must diagnose the elder's problems and we have to take care of the elders in all the ways and dimensions. The family members and others forgot to give proper care and supports. The mind set should be changed and shaped fresh to safeguard the rights, feelings of the elderly person. It is the look out of the family members to take care of their own elders in the family and government also develop some plans and policies to include them as their family and societal members. Elderly is not regarded as any crime or offence, it is unavoidable physical condition, and so the family members do not separate the elders from the group and don't treat them as aliens. The GO'S and NGO'S should frame plans and policies for inclusive dimension.

REFERENCES:

- AGE, *Promoting active ageing and intergenerational solidarity through senior volunteering*, Position paper, Brussels, 2009.
- Aldremobilisering, *Hvorfor, hvordan, hvor lange og hvad sa? Et ojebliksbillede af de frivillige i Aldremobiliseringens frivillighedsprojekt, April 2005*, Frederiksberg, Aldremobilisering, 2004.
- Backer, G., Naegele G. et al, *Sozialpolitik und soziale Lage in Deutschland*, 2. Bande, 4. Auflage, Wiesbaden, VS Verlag fur Sozialwissenschaften, 2007.

- Caritas Italiana – Fondazione 'E. Zancan', *Ripartire dai poveri. Rapporto 2008 su poverta ed esclusione sociale in Italia* [A fresh start for poor people. 2008 Report on poverty and social exclusion in Italy], Il Mulino, Bologna, 2008.
- Clemens, W. and Naegele, G., 'Lebenslagen im Alter', in Kruse, A. and Martin, M. (eds.), *Enzyklopadie der Gerontologie. Alternsprozesse in multidisziplinarer Sicht*, Bern, Huber, 2004, pp. 387–402. Council of Europe, *Recommendation R (94) 9 of the Committee of Ministers to Member States concerning older people*, Strasbourg, 1994.
- Desai K.G (1985), "situation of the aged in India" journal of the anthropological society, vol.20, No.31, November, pp 201-209
- Erlinghagen, M., 'Informelle Arbeit in alternden Gesellschaften. Moglichkeiten und Grenzen des produktiven Alterns',in *Schmollers Jahrbuch*, Vol. 128, No. 2, 2008, pp. 237–259.
- European Commission, *Combating poverty and social exclusion. A statistical portrait of the European Union 2010*, Luxembourg, Publications Office of the European Union, 2010.
- Commission, *Joint report on social inclusion 2004*, Luxembourg, Publications Office of the European Union, 2004.
- Jayashree, active-work after retirement, social Welfare-oct.2000, vol.47. No.7. P(5-10)
- Kumar S.V.(2003) Journal of Ageing Soc policy, 2003; 15(2-3)
- Murali Desai et.al (2000). "Gerontology social work in India" some issues & perspectives, B.R.Publishing corporation (A Division of BRPC (INDIA) ltd), Delhi, pp.396-403.
- Om Raj Singh, "A Social Concern, Social Welfare, pct.2006, vol.51, No.7 pp(4-6)
- Prema Patill B, "psycho-Social problems of the retired, social welfare, Oct.2000, vol.47 No.7.PP(13-14)
- Rajan E.M, and Sarchandraraj T, problems of the aged in Pondicherry, social welfare, oct 2004,vol.51 No.7. PP(18)
- Ramaurti the psycho-social scenario of the elderly: Problems, priorities and perspectives, research & development vol.3, No.1 1996, pp3-9
- Wilson,G.(9940, "abuse of elderly men and women among clients of a community psychogereiatric service", british Journal of Social work, 42, 681-700
- World bank (1994), Averting the old age crisis, Washington, D.C, world bank

- www.delhigov.nic.in,25/06/03.
- www.seniorindia.com4/7/2003
- www.socialjustice.nic.in;accessdate5/07/03

www.ingramcontent.com/pod-product-compliance
Lightning Source LLC
Chambersburg PA
CBHW080933240926
51849CB00003BA/441
9788180941603